Rescuing Nicholas: The Secret Mission to Save the Tsar

MARTIN HUTSON'S STORY AS TOLD
BY HIS FAMILY 100 YEARS LATER

FOR
MARTIN, GEORGE & CORINNE

RESCUING NICHOLAS | DISCLAIMER

Published in the United States by Cannon & Caius LLC, Florida.

Printed in the United States by Amazon.

Education Edition.

Rescuing Nicholas: The Secret Mission to Save the Tsar is a non-fiction work based on historial research.

Endnotes and citations provide additional detailed background information on subject matter used in this book. Quotations cited are done so under the Fair Use Act. Ownership of those quotations, which are noted at the end of this book, are the sole property of those cited authors. Common phrases used regularly in public forums have not been cited and are assumed known and not equitably attributable to one source.

We gratefully acknowledge the work of those authors we cite for the updated historical record of an event that happened 100 years ago and the effort to educate a new generation of Americans on what the AEF Siberia mission meant to the USA.

ISBN-13: 978-0-9989115-3-3

About the Book Cover

The cover for *Rescuing Nicholas:*
The Secret Mission to Save the Tsar
was designed by Jeff Brostoff of Brands On Fire.

Also by Ben Everidge:

HOYA: THE WATCHMEN WAKETH

Rescuing Nicholas | Contents

Definitions From Merriam-Webster:

re · dact
verb \ri-ˈdakt\

Definition of *REDACT*
transitive verb

1: to put in writing:

2: to select or adapt (as by obscuring or removing sensitive information) for publication or release; *broadly*:

3: to obscure or remove (text) from a document prior to publication or release.

lore
noun \ˈlȯr\

1 *archaic*: something that is taught:

2: something that is learned: knowledge gained through study or experience

AUTHOR'S NOTE | YEKATERINBURG

There have been two popular principal spellings for the Russian village of Yekaterinburg, which you will see extensively mentioned in this book. Many historical documents and quotes cited in *Rescuing Nicholas* will occasionally use the spelling, Ekaterinburg, or some other variation of that spelling.

Where used today, more contemporaneously, the village's name will be spelled as Yekaterinburg. Where quoted or cited, the village's name will be spelled as applied by the source.

As for these sources, they are cited in detail in *Rescuing Nicholas* as End Notes and are outlined appropriately toward the end of this book. Without these pioneering sources, the Romanov mystery would be even more perplexing - and even more uncertain.

Thank you to all who came before seeking to unveil this remarkable saga. And good luck to those who might want to follow where the new leads in this book might take you!

Prologue | Verifying History

It was, and still is, a grand political tale. Riveting for its human drama and tragedy. Unending in its ability to feed the insatiable appetite of a world which wants to know more about what really happened in this political thriller that is at times more murder-mystery than historically-inspired biography.

It was then, and even now is, a century later, an Academy Award-worthy performance, literally. Except, the facts twisting around Tsar Nicholas II and the Romanov family fate keep getting in the way of the final curtain to this epic story, despite DNA evidence that is often cited as being conclusive.

This book, *Rescuing Nicholas,* has a very simple objective: take an astonishing story that has been historically *redacted* over time and academically, journalistically, and politically test its accuracy based on previously undisclosed eyewitness testimony that has been protected through several generations of one family.

Was this incredible episode simply *lore,* or did it really happen as told to family? Did time past whittle away at the remembered detail or is the record of what might have happened in the months following the end of World War I essentially still intact ten decades later?

For the most skeptical reader, the initial chapters in this book might be viewed as a potentially fictional story - an adventure based on a globally historic event that may or may not necessarily bring forward our knowledge of circumstances surrounding the disappearance of Tsar Nicholas II and his family 100 years ago in the quaint village of Yekaterinburg, Russia.

For a more considered reader, *Rescuing Nicholas* represents an unexpected giant leap forward in the Romanov saga when it comes to knowing what really happened in those fateful closing months of "the war to end all wars." An eyewitness account has finally come to light.

The central character in this story is the man our accomplice came to call simply, Nicholas.

Re-told and potentially modified a little each time it has been recounted, it is up to context and relevance, which will be provided in the chapters following the eyewitness' account, to determine whether the tale is just that - a tale - an embellishment - or an eyewitness account of a monumental event the world assumed had long passed with credible first-hand testimony to verify the rumored, and we hope, now revised and un-redacted record.

Not surprisingly, there is today great confusion on just what is the real Romanov story, as we now know it. That was intentional, we believe, an effective and necessary cloak that was draped over this historical event by richly talented Allied Intelligence agents in an effort to ensure the very success of perhaps one of the most daring political rescue missions in American, British, and of course, Russian history.

Toward that end, there is a methodology to this book that is worth noting which is designed to take us beyond just the testimony as provided by former U.S. Army eyewitness soldier Martin Hutson. A great deal of literature has been generated on the topic of the Tsar's reported murder that has been substantially updated in recent years as archives in the now former post-Lenin Soviet Union have opened after years of repressive secrecy. These records have been made available to researchers by succeeding Russian governments and offer a wealth of insight into what might really have happened on that notorious July morning.

Rescuing Nicholas takes a close inventory on this emerging research and strives to put these findings or arguments into context so that Martin's story can better be tested. *Rescuing Nicholas* reports extensively on the literature in the marketplace of late on the Tsar's fate - from those who say he was dead long ago, the victim of the Bolshevik Revolution, to those who allege he survived and lived out a long and quiet life in exile, to those who do not know what to make of history to date.

With context better understood, at least from an historical literature perspective, *Rescuing Nicholas* then seeks to provide new research through recorded first-hand testimony to advance our common knowledge of the events surrounding July 17, 1918.

It is our goal in each chapter, to either substantially improve our understanding of these events that transpired or to significantly clarify events so that we can better present the record on the Tsar's mystery and Martin's account. This research comes in the form of additional searches of the printed evidence, audio archives revealed for the first time which yield new clues to the mystery, and interviews asking those knowledgeable nearly 100 years later, "what if?"

Journalism's Core Principles

At the very foundation of our research is a dedication to being thorough and accurate, at least as much as history will permit.

The Pew Research Center for Journalism & Media says there are nine core principles of journalism which prides itself as an industry on being thorough and accurate, as well, a standard we hope to meet here without any pretense that we are trained journalists ourselves. If anything, you might say we are citizen scribes but you cannot contend for this exercise that we are journalism experts. Nevertheless, we, like journalists, are committed to finding the truth and the truth does matter, to every citizen of the world, we hope.

Pew notes the following concepts, which we re-present here again, by which you might judge the accuracy of Martin Hutson's account recorded several decades ago:

- *Journalism's first obligation is to the truth.* Pew says that one must have reliable, accurate facts to put in any meaningful context and then one must be able to assemble and verify the facts as they find them, subject, of course, to further investigation. These facts and their sources "should be as transparent as possible about sources and methods so audiences can make their own assessment of the information."

- *Journalism's first loyalty is to it citizens.* Journalists, Pew notes, must be able to maintain an allegiance to its citizens first and foremost as well as to the larger public interest above all.

- *Journalism relies upon the principle of verification.* Verification demands, Pew observes, "a consistent method of testing information – a transparent approach to evidence – precisely so that personal and cultural biases would not undermine the accuracy of their work." Verification also seeks out "multiple witnesses, disclosing as much as possible about sources, or asking various sides for comment, all signal such standards."

- *Journalism maintains an independence from those it covers.* Independence is the cornerstone of reliability, intellectual fairness and an ability to inform is valued over any perceived or real devotion to a certain group or desired outcome, Pew says.

- *Journalism must serve as a watchdog for freedom.* And more importantly, Pew rightfully posits that it should be free of intent for commercial gain or frivolous use.

- *Pew also says that journalism must provide a forum for criticism, debate and compromise.* "This discussion serves society best," Pew writes, "when it is informed by facts rather than prejudice and supposition. It also should strive to fairly represent the varied viewpoints and interests in society, and to place them in context rather than highlight only the conflicting fringes of debate. Accuracy and truthfulness require that as framers of the public discussion we not neglect the points of common ground where problem solving occurs."

- *Journalism must strive to make the significant interesting and relevant.* "The effectiveness of a piece of journalism is measured both by how much a work engages its audience and enlightens it," Pew argues. We agree that journalism can be interesting and relevant but we also note, quite obviously, that journalism cannot be made interesting at the expense of the relevant or accurate.

- *Journalism, Pew continues, must keep the news comprehensive and proportional.* Do not leave important things out of the story, Pew says; and, finally, Pew concludes,

- *Journalism must allow for the exercise of personal conscious.* Journalists, Pew reminds us, should have a moral compass from which to guide their work and a forum in which to express their perspectives. Our moral compass, we hope you will find, is to tell Martin's tale as precisely as we might consistent with what Martin Hutson understood history to be at that time and consistent with the cogent roadmap Pew has provided amateur historians like ourselves.

Reinforced with Academic Rigor

To raise the bar even higher than journalism itself has set, as described by the Pew Research Center above, we add to this methodology relevant academic rigor as well.

It is our intention to use at least three sources to here again validate the potential of Martin's story. It is also our intent to seek and include the dissenting voices of reputable authors who believe that the Tsar and his family were indeed murdered on that July night in Yekaterinburg long, long ago. We will endeavor to use at least three sources of dissention, wherever possible, too.

In order to promote greater transparency and more academic research to come once this material has been revealed, we have established an integrated web site (designed to grow) at: www.CannonAndCaius.com/Nicholas so that others can share their information so that future researchers will have a place from which to non-commercially advance the mystery themselves as new data undoubtedly will become available. For example, there were eight other men on the rescue mission in 1919 with Martin. Maybe, hopefully, one of their families will know something that can be added to the story later, too.

Through all of these voices, and with their varying perspectives, we hope that the truth about the Romanovs can and will emerge with a higher degree of certainly than has been exhibited thus far, using the foundation of Martin's story as a continuing point in the evolving revolutionary saga. For our part, we picked up where the author Shay McNeal left off in her intriguing, and we think, well-researched book, *The Secret Plot to Save the Tsar.*

No doubt, this methodology - these questions - will generate yet more questions, which we will ask with each chapter, where and when appropriate. At the end of the book, in a chapter we call, *From the Bones of a Tsar,* we will try to answer these questions in as logical and as objective a manner as we can with as much evidence as we can present in return, leaving the final analysis to you: Is it, was it, true?

In the meantime, for the first time we believe, a detailed and recorded eyewitness account of the Tsar's rescue is being told through *Rescuing Nicholas.* You will find a transcript of Martin's testimony in Appendix A of this book. There you will read for yourself an eyewitness account from a young soldier who spent an extraordinary two weeks with a very much alive, he says, Tsar Nicholas II as he and two other members of his family escaped revolutionary Russia through Siberia, with the help of an American President, a railroad executive, a hand-full of dedicated and daring spies, and a few surprising political leaders, including, we believe, a cousin King.

The later chapters of *Rescuing Nicholas* will be left for you to decipher. Were startling recorded statements by Martin Hutson real or just wishful thinking of a generation now long since gone? Or, is the evidence presented here, convincing? Does this story move past stories that many pretenders have told before?

Rest assured. Martin Hutson and his family were real people living in real time. George, Martin and Corinne were not fictional characters in a novel. They were very deeply loved members of our family - our parents, our grandparents, our aunt and uncles. Quintessential Americans to the core.

This story, Martin's story, as told through our family some 100 years later, is dedicated to them, and all of those they touched through this family lore, with the hope that history does care. That history does matter. That the search for yet more truth about the Romanov mystery will continue until we can all answer the question about his fate with clarity and sound, unbending evidence.

Part I: Remembering the Mystery

1 | An Enduring Saga

For on this cold, bitter evening, very far from home, Martin was focused on following instructions like those his own father had taught him to follow years before. Martin was focused solely on safely escorting out of the country the last Tsar of Russia, his wife Alexandra, their young daughter, and treasures of an empire about to be lost to history.

- *Rescuing Nicholas*

It was an extraordinary secret to keep from Congress. It would appear that the 28th president of the United States had just ordered arguably one of the most riveting rescue missions in world history. But he did not want anyone on "the Hill" to know otherwise.

In fact, Thomas Woodrow Wilson went to great lengths to keep this mission secret from many members of his own cabinet and the other relevant Constitutionally-mandated body of American government that he mistrusted. Congress.

In another era, subterfuge of this political intensity might have generated impeachment from within the Capitol dome, not the celebration of victory one would expect from a mission of this grandeur.

It was the Wilson mystique. It was vintage Woodrow Wilson. It was because of "the War," the President might have reasoned.

The rescue mission President Wilson had authorized was for "Cousin Nicky," the last Tsar of Russia. The Tsars had ruled Russia for over 400 years, but Nicholas was now the last. He had abdicated months earlier as the Russian Revolution, a civil war really, had fully blossomed. Nicholas' predicament was of great concern to other world leaders. Nicky was second cousin to the King of England, George V.

Nicholas was also first cousin to yet another world leader, Kaiser Wilhelm II of Germany. Together, they were the grandchildren of England's legendary Queen Victoria. And, the three cousins were engaged in a war amongst themselves that was better known as World War I. Nevertheless, Wilhelm II and George V were asking themselves, how could they help Cousin Nicky? *If,* they could save Nicky?

The Hutsons, on the other hand, were brothers, not cousins. The brothers were young men from the coal mine region of Tennessee. Their father, a murdered lumberman from the old school, had taught them to love their country and do as they were told. In those days, you did not question authority. You did as you were instructed. Everybody did. These boys just did it a little better than the best.

The brothers had honed their survival skills as young boys playing in the backwoods near their home. They played at surviving with their play rifles day in and day out until one day, as young men, their country would call them - accept them - into service. President Wilson had a mission both brothers would play a role in achieving, with honor. One brother would even earn the Distinguished Service Cross and a Purple Heart, not to mention a lifetime of uncomplaining debilitating physical challenge thanks to lethal gases he inhaled while on the European continent.

At a few days older than a believed 18 years of age, after begging his local recruiter to let him sign up early to fight on the Mexican border, Martin was asking himself how in the world did he end up here? Half a world away, riding a train in bitter cold escorting a man in a box - alive, no less?

He had stood on the steps of a train depot only days before and spied death all around him. The pictures he took and gathered from others would last a lifetime. The images in his memory were even more traumatic. He knew people wanted this man dead, desperately. He now carried a sword from the scene of the massacre between troops loyal to his new friend and troops committed to his ouster. The sword was not so much a souvenir from his newfound friend, but a reality check of what he had witnessed.

Thousands of miles away, his older brother, George, was distinguishing himself in the Black Forest of Germany under the command of a very famous American General known as *Black Jack.* He and a number of his fellow infantrymen would earn some of the highest medals the United States would award its bravest soldiers that war.

Half a century later, their older sister, Corinne, would tell and re-tell their stories to younger generations of family members. These stories became family lore. She would always recall harassing her younger brothers for playing such dangerous survival games in the back woods of their home. But she also knew now that their expert skills kept them both alive and it was something she was encouraging her grandsons to learn themselves.

Had Corinne Hutson Miller's own husband, John, been a newspaper reporter rather than a newspaper pressman for *The Columbus Dispatch*, the brothers' astonishing stories would most likely have been publicly told decades before. Of course, there had been a stray story printed here and there in other newspapers. But no one had connected all of the dots.

As the old cliché posits, this is now and that was then.

Martin and his own fellow soldiers had come into country expecting to rescue American Red Cross nurses. For crying out loud, Martin thought he would be going to Mexico, not Russia. They were soldiers in the American Expeditionary Forces Siberia.

Their train bore the now internationally known symbol of the Red Cross with giant painted letters below so that they could not be missed – "AMERIKANSKI." It was the supplemental orders to kill everyone in the event of capture that confused Martin greatly.

The windows were blacked out on the regal, dark blue train consisting of a line of cars and an engine with a tenderbox. And even though the camouflaged train of well-appointed carriages with Imperial icons strategically and ornamentally placed throughout raced through the isolated countryside, past village after village, some in Russia and some in China, on winding tracks far from any obvious threats, tension ran frighteningly high.

They had already unexpectedly encountered a man named, Chang, near the border where they planned to escape. The Chinese General had tried to stop the party, burned some of their cars made of wood, but upon seeing the American soldiers traveling with a Japanese General, decided to let the passengers pass. This was not a fight that needed further fighting today, at least.

Martin and his comrades had no idea Chiang Kai-shek was inside an area where he did not belong and was thus in no mood to mix it up with someone other than the enemy he knew. It meant on this night, especially considering orders, everyone would live.

The gentleman in the center "car" was friendly enough. His young daughter was even friendlier and more gregarious. She liked to play games and was quite bright. Martin enjoyed the opportunity to share the lighthearted moments when they presented themselves but even these moments were becoming far fewer. He liked everything but the tea he had to drink with the gentleman's wife and friend, a personal aide of some type he surmised.

Bad enough a newly inducted soldier from Tennessee would have to experience what he had these past weeks, but sadder still that a young, delightful girl not much different than his own age, it would appear, would endure even greater trauma. Still, she smiled and laughed, despite the uncertainties ahead, or the experiences earned. Being a war refugee, for all practical purposes, was hell experienced several times over, he thought.

It was far too early in their mission for any of the American soldiers to realize they were first-hand witnesses to the first great mystery of the 20th century, particularly, young Martin. Right now, Martin was freezing. He was exposed to the rushing night air. He had never been this cold in Tennessee. This was not the Mexico he thought he would encounter. And, of course, he wondered how his charge was faring himself. The officer, as he appeared to be, albeit now dressed in civilian clothes, was better dressed for the extreme temperatures. The heavy beard had to help, too.

It was clear to Martin that the middle-aged man in front of him was lost in thought. He knew that Allied British elite forces, aided many speculate by the Germans, had supposedly taken his only son and three older daughters out of the country already and he was reasonably certain they were safe. At least that is what the gentleman would tell Martin. He also had reason to believe his wife and younger daughter would gain freedom soon as well. They were in the car just ahead with a French-speaking woman. Surely that meant freedom for them, too? Did it not?

After all, that was the deal he had struck with the Japanese, the Canadians, the British, the Czechs, and the Americans - allies, all of whom had high-ranking officers riding on the train this night with him, that was numbered to symbolize an American president in a rather ironic way. There was even American and British Consul Generals aboard. Surely, he could count on them to keep their word? After all, at least the Colonel and one of the Consul Generals worked for his cousin, the King.

Not to mention, the young soldier suffering the elements with him gave the gentleman some degree of added comfort. Doubtful any rouge troops could now get near him before being shot. It was good to have a capably armed bodyguard nearby, even if he was only armed with a .45 and an often-frozen rifle that would have exploded had it been fired. The extreme cold in Siberia was nothing to take for granted.

As the train approached the Chinese border with his young daughter safe in the car ahead, the former officer was indeed growing in confidence all of them would soon be safe, in British hands again if all went according to plan.

It had already been a long and stressful journey. The passenger had shared a few stories with young Martin, but, just a few. And, very brief when he did share, but chock-full of entertaining, controversial detail.

Fast Forward

The bones would later yield a story that history could not accept. It was and still is a story that Martin did not experience and certainly did not remember in that way.

The father would be found, or so the experts would claim. Of course, like all good mysteries, an argument would subsequently be made that the bones of the father were in fact from a man measurably larger than he. Another relative perhaps? A loyal friend? A stand-in who had not expected to die for volunteering his shadow role? A convenient genetic relation for more modern history and science?

A daughter and son would also turn up missing, at least for a suspicious while. But the other sisters and a few trusted aides would be reported in the grave deep in the forest - the doctor, a maid, and a cook, too.

Forensic scientists would disagree about this as well. DNA would apparently not prove inarguably conclusive, especially on one daughter and the man himself. And questions would, quite naturally, yield even more questions.

Reliable answers would be rare. A key forensic pathologist who dissented would conveniently die too young himself. Logic, it would seem, would not exist. Books would speculate endlessly. Related film, award-winning related film, would prove to be blockbuster hits in commercial theaters.

Rumors would say the man's son would live out his years in Ireland.

The bearded man, the distinguished father with the accent that Martin would later say, would make an Oxford professor envious; himself would be whispered to have been photographed in White Russian émigré village near Collon, north of Dublin. His wife and daughters would be said to have lived nearby as well. The youngest daughter would even be rumored to have lived a pedestrian but eccentric life in Virginia, although later DNA testing would theoretically, at least, dispel that myth, too.

And yet history convincingly told the story they were all dead, executed by troops loyal to the new revolutionary government. Burned beyond recognition or identification in another age when nuclear and mitochondrial DNA did not exist as a forensic tool and the 24-hour news cycle with exploding social media could not explore the inaccuracies of the event in a timely fashion.

History, it seemed, wanted the Romanov family dead. History, it seemed, *needed* the Romanov family dead. What makes this murder-mystery-disappearance so fascinating and perplexing, however, is what was not done when all of this drama become public many days and weeks later. There would be no credible or obvious investigation by British authorities into what happened to the murder victims.

Astonishingly, one victim, the Empress Alexandra, was the treasured and popular granddaughter of a most legendary and highly influential Queen of England. Still five others were that same storied Queen's great-grandchildren. Did these famous and connected murder victims not merit more attention, or angst in the United Kingdom at the time of their supposed murder?

Even more intriguing to the ongoing controversy over the Romanov fate are recent disclosures that present Russian President Vladimir Putin, himself a purported former spy in the notorious Soviet KGB, would like to see the Russian royal family reinstated and the Tsars brought back to a more formal role in his legendary nation.

History tees up many surprises; it would appear.

But what if Tsar Nicholas II and his wife, the Empress Alexandra, were not in fact buried in that grave outside of Yekaterinburg in the early days of the Russian Revolution? What if the 1.5 percent DNA uncertainty was in fact, fact? What if 1.5 percent meant that DNA evidence could actually be in error?

Is it possible?

What if the DNA tests conducted under the post-Soviet-era president Boris Yeltsin were forged and the Tsar's body was not actually the Tsar's body as history has been told? Or what if the Tsar had lived out his life in exile and his bones were eventually returned to make it look like they had been in the grave all along?

Was a cover-up of this magnitude actually feasible?

What if the fabled Anastasia, the youngest daughter of the Tsar and the Tsarina, actually did indeed make her way to the United States as legend has it and settled into an eventual quiet life as the Grand Duchess, as her maternal grandmother, the Empress Dowager once appeared to believe? Could the DNA evidence have been wrong yet again?

And, if so, how?

What if her youngest brother, the crown prince of the now-overthrown Tsarist Russian Empire, escaped into the life of a typical Irish citizen? What if he had lived despite his hemophilia? There was an abdication. Who, then, might be the rightful heir to a 400-year-old dynasty? Is there one, can there be one, 100 years later?

Does the earlier induced abdication still matter?

What if members of the family did escape? Perhaps Nicholas himself?

Could it be that the Romanovs escaped with the help of the Bolshevik Russians who wanted at almost all costs to get the former Tsar out their homeland? Surely, the Americans and the British would have needed the help of the Bolsheviks to pull this rescue mission off under the political and military circumstances of the times?

What if the Tsar's relative, the King of England, George V, Nicholas' second cousin but his wife's first cousin, had indeed given his two cousins political sanctuary after all? What if his first cousin, the German Kaiser, Wilhelm II, cooperated with his British enemy so that Nicky could live, even though he might have appeared to die?

Could global politics of war and peace have been so ironical, so manipulating?

What if Woodrow Wilson had engineered the most successful rescue in world history with few people knowing what happened? Could Congress have been snookered like that? Are the president's commanding generals to be exonerated now for their actual success, as opposed to reported failures at the time?

What if the King and the President were heroes in this story, unlike history have portrayed them so far?

What if Martin Hutson had witnessed a history much different from that that was eventually recorded? What if Tsar Nicholas II and his wife Alexandria and at least one of their children cheated death and escaped Lenin's troops, thanks to his own loyal guard?

What if the westernized villain, Vladimir Lenin, actually helped the Tsar and his family escape - did not kill them as common knowledge now alleges? Was Lenin, at least in this case, more humane and practical than we have been led to believe?

What if conclusive DNA results, obtained nearly a century later, were not conclusive at all? What if the DNA results were engineered to appear conclusive?

What if it was not the Romanovs, after all? What if history did not tell us the truth?

Would history care?

These are all thought-provoking questions. But on this night, as the Chinese border loomed and the tome from Yekaterinburg fell far behind, U.S. Army Private First Class Martin Van Buren Hutson would not care about history, or rumors, or what-ifs, or why his "guest" was riding in great secrecy in a box on his own train.

For on this cold, bitter evening, very far from home, Martin was focused on following instructions like those his own late father had taught him to follow years before. Martin was focused solely on safely escorting out of the country the last Tsar of Russia, his wife Alexandra, their young daughter, and treasures of an empire about to be lost to history.

Recommended reading:

- Robert K. Massey, *Nicholas and Alexandra,* London, England: Gollancz, 1968, ISBN-10: 9780679645610.
- Peter Kurth, *Tsar: The Lost World of Nicholas and Alexandra,* Madison Press Book produced for Little, Brown and Company, Toronto, Ontario, Canada, 1995, ISBN: 0-316-50787-3.

2 | Martin's Story

"Nicholas was not killed in Siberia – three other people were killed, and their bodies chopped up with broad axes, dumped in a lime pit, poured crude oil on them and burned 'em, which was a very, very good camouflage to throw the Red Army off. That was done by the Tsar's own home guards before they fled."

- Martin V. Hutson audio recording, 1971

Martin recorded this startling statement some 20 years before history would report that Russian and American researchers had in fact located the Romanov family's bodies in a lime pit not far from the farmhouse in which the Tsar and his family were reported assassinated by Bolshevik soldiers on July 17, 1918.

Hutson's encounter with the Tsar would take place, according to the recording, some sixteen months (more than a year-and-a-quarter) after the Russian ruler's reported assassination. Controversy over the bones' authenticity continues, 100-years later, with reports as of this writing that post-Soviet Russia has agreed to further test the remains of Romanov children thanks to the continued refusal by Russian Orthodox Church officials to recognize the bodies the modern-day government wishes to rebury in St. Petersburg with the other reported Romanovs.

How could it be? Is it possible that the Tsar and his party were able to escape Russia alive? Is it possible that history is wrong? Why was Martin chosen for this mission in the first place?

Why would the United States government want to keep such a story secret for all of these years – all these decades – all this century - if in fact, the American government had known this evacuation had taken place? Why would Russian officials not clear up the record, especially after the fall of the Soviet Union?

Sitting at a microphone half a century later, now much older, grayer and with family at his side, an aging and dying Martin Hutson clears his throat, takes a drink of water and tells all who are listening, "this is an episode in my life."

Martin's story begins in his home state of Tennessee where as an 18-year-old, he determined that he should enlist in the Army, like his older brother George did earlier, to fight for their homeland in its hour of need. World War I had ended, but America still needed men on its former battlefronts. Martin did not want to miss out.

The Army recruiting office in Martin's hometown of Knoxville tells the deeply disappointed young man that he is too young to enlist.

The recruiting officer knew Martin and knew Martin's family. He told me, "Martin, you can't go, you're too young."

A week later, however, Martin is told by the recruiter that if he will come down to the post office, and if his mother will sign his enlistment papers, the Army will send him to the Mexican border where soldiers are badly needed. His physical is scheduled for 7 a.m.

"I went down the next morning to the recruiting office at 7 a.m.," Martin says. It was quite the unexpected reversal of fortune for young Martin.

The enlistment date was August 20, 1919. Martin's Enlistment Record notes that this is his first service in the Army and states that his marksmanship, gunner qualification or rating is, "Machine Gun, Sharpshooter, Pistol, S.S.," but also notes that he does not have mounted horsemanship skills.

Arriving shortly after enlistment at Fort Oglethorpe, Georgia, Martin encounters a First Sergeant who "calls for a Martin Hutson" and then instructs him to go to the Quartermaster's office and draw Arctic clothing.

Now Private Martin Hutson, Martin silently questions why he needs Arctic clothing when he is going to Mexico, where he understands that it is hot, not cold. Certainly warm, not arctic, at least.

"I went to the Quartermaster's office and he laughed at me. I went back to my barracks."

The Sergeant came back and asked him why he was not ready and Martin shared that the Quartermaster did not outfit him.

"The Sergeant took me to the Quartermaster, told him to outfit me with arctic clothing right now," Martin says.

By Train to California

As 10:00 a.m. approached that same morning, Martin has with him two barracks bags. The newly-minted Private First Class is being sent to the Chattanooga Depot, where Martin will catch a train and travel all day, all night, and all the next day to his next destination: a tugboat in the San Francisco Bay near Fort McDowell, off of Angel Island, California.

Fort McDowell, which was situated on a little one-square-mile island in the middle of San Francisco Bay, is under the command of Major General William Sidney Graves. To his north, General Graves would have almost been able to see California's Napa and Sonoma wine counties from the little island that got its name in 1775 by the Spanish explorer, Juan de Ayala. To the South, the City of San Jose was within sight as was the new military prison at Alcatraz. The little island had, as you might say today, "curb appeal."

Martin becomes friends with a group of other soldiers he meets who sit around the barracks with him for another three-to-four days, awaiting orders.

"I was assigned a bed," Martin remembers. "The next morning they told us where to go and eat breakfast. We were in a large dining room. We ate breakfast, the other men who came with me on the train."

The orders eventually come and Martin is loaded back on a tugboat and sent back to San Francisco where he is placed aboard the United States Army Transport (USAT) *Great Northern*. "At dark, we took off for sea," says Martin. The transport boat has 1,800 men on board, the majority of whom Martin reports got seasick during the voyage across the Pacific Ocean.

The *Great Northern* had been first delivered into military service in April 1915, some four years before Martin would ride her across the Pacific Ocean. The *Great Northern* was designed to be a passenger ship built in the storied Philadelphia shipyards. She was 509-feet-six-inches long, drafted 21-feet and could race up to a top speed of 26 miles per hour, or 43 kilometers per hour for metric fans. Her 63-foot one-inch beam gave her a smooth and deep ride, it was reported. Before seeing Pacific service, the *Great Northern* made 18 transatlantic trips for the United States Navy transporting American Expeditionary Force troops, including the famed Doughboys, across the Atlantic Ocean to battle zones in Europe where they, too, would serve under Black Jack Pershing.

The Navy decommissioned the *Great Northern* in New York City on the 15th of August 1919. But the Army put her right back into service sending her to duty in the Pacific Ocean where she made two long trips from Honolulu to Vladivostok,

Russia to pick up approximately 3,000 American troops returning from the war in Russia. She would return to San Francisco in the summer of 1920. The *Great Northern* would see service in World War II and then decommissioning in 1948 when she was unceremoniously sold for scrap metal.

If these dates for the *Great Northern's* service are true, then Martin was one of the first, if not the actual first, troops to take passage across the Pacific Ocean as an Army transport as opposed to a Navy transport instead.

The dining room onboard the *Great Northern,* according to Martin, was a large, elaborate room, with cafeteria-style tables, which hung from ceilings by chains. It takes Martin and his fellow passengers two hours in line to get their food each meal.

"At dinner time, I went down. There was a tremendous crowd," Martin remembers. One thousand eight hundred men. "I guess I was two hours getting my food."

Martin explains how he figures out a process that cuts down on his daily wait time. He gathers food up near the cafeteria door from men who are too sick from the crossing to eat. Martin then puts it in his knapsack and waits to eat his morsels when he is hungry.

Seven days and nights later, the *Great Northern,* with Private Hutson on board, arrives in Honolulu, Hawaii. Martin is granted shore leave with only a nickel in his pocket. He had heard of pineapples before but wanted to see what one tasted like for himself, so he uses his nickel to buy a pineapple and a sack full of chocolate, given to him by a friendly woman he runs across.

"The lady had seen me looking through the window," Martin appreciates. "I asked for a nickel's worth of chocolate and she gave me a sack-full."

Destination Vladivostok

Fourteen more days at sea and young Martin Hutson is ready to stand on dry ground. He and his fellow soldiers finally arrive in Vladivostok, Russia, where the ground is solid all right - frozen by a chill of some 60 degrees below zero. Vladivostok, he noted was not Tennessee, and clearly, it was not Mexico.

Martin's arrival date in Siberia is noted on his Enlistment Record as being October 4, 1919.

Vladivostok in the second decade of the early 1900s was a bustling town having been founded in the 1860s as a military outpost. Its first street, interestingly enough, was called, *Amerikanskaya Street,* and it was from Vladivostok that the Trans-Siberian Railroad began in 1891. Its streets by the time of Martin's visit had trams operating, transporting people of diverse and multiple nationalities to all forms of engaging locations. In fact, Vladivostok was becoming quite the cultural hub of the Asian continent, it is noted.

By New Year's Eve 1917, American, British, and Japanese naval forces were operating in the port city, which was now reacting to the Russian Revolution.

Martin stays in a building near a hanger on a large hill just outside Vladivostok with a winding road but no dirigible balloon inside as should be.

"They gave us canvas cots - 1,800 of us sleep in this building and there was still plenty of room left." PFC Hutson stays three days and three nights.

On the third night, a corporal comes and picks up Martin and seven other men. He instructs them to follow him. Martin and his fellow soldiers dutifully follow the corporal for three miles through the woods where they eventually come to a church.

At the church, Martin discovers that Company H, 31st Infantry is bedded down asleep on cots following their meal. The company's cook, who had 27 years of experience in the Army, made the young soldiers corned beef hash and offered them "a whole pan" of pumpkin pies he had baked.

Known affectionately as *The Polar Bears*, the 31st Infantry was created in August 1916 at Fort William McKinley in the Philippine Islands as part of the National Defense Act expansion strongly recommended and supported by President Woodrow Wilson. *The Polar Bears* were assembled for the Russia campaign in response to America being perceived by its military and political leaders as not having been prepared troop training-wise for its battles in Mexico against the legendary bandit, Pancho Villa. Infantry troops are called upon to engage, fight and kill their enemy in close quarters, generally with pistols, rifles, and machine guns, or in hand-to-hand combat with knives and bayonets.

Martin's first night in the field was cold and fitful.

"I took all of my clothes out of my bed and put it under my pup tent. I should have put half of it on top of me. I slept cold that night. 60 degrees below zero is a little cold," Martin says.

"We drilled six weeks at close quarters."

One day, Captain Roberson, asked Private Hutson to come to Captain Rogers' office. There Martin met Kashiba, a natural-born Russian. Kashiba is instructed to make Martin ready within a week's time and deliver him to General Graves.

Kashiba and Martin train together. When the week passes and Martin is deemed ready for action, Kashiba and Martin are loaded on a wagon and taken down to the train station in Vladivostok.

"Kashiba, is this man ready?" queries the Captain. "Yes, captain," said Kashiba, "but I cannot take this man. This man is just a boy. This boy can't even shoot a gun."

Responds the Captain to Kashiba, "Orders come from Major General Graves. You have got to deliver this man alive."

That night they took Martin and eight men (Martin had trained with seven) down to the station in Vladivostok on a large steel Pullman car, with a large red cross in the center of car with the word, "Amerikanski" written across the exterior panels.

"We wore wrap leggings with shoes that you could see from top to bottom," Martin remembers.

"Our officer," Martin said, "made us exchange them for moccasins that we were instructed to make certain was the right size. They needed to be good for arctic conditions."

"Clearly," Martin laughed.

"The streets of Vladivostok were made of cobblestones." They had one pair of moccasins and they didn't fit any of the young soldiers, "so we put on all the socks we had. I put on 17 pairs of socks. Two pairs came up to my knees!"

At 11 o'clock, Martin says that their train started out for Irkutsk, "but I did not know at the time that it was Irkutsk. We went through the Manchurian desert, which was as flat as far as you could see. All around there were these great stacks of wheat," Martin said.

"Along this Manchurian railroad, there were little towns with only 11 houses or less. We would ask for the name of the towns we were in but they would not tell us where the Red Army was."

Captain Cross of the Red Cross was in charge of the Red Cross train that was a supply train. Captain Cross confirmed to young Martin and his soldiers that the team was going to Irkutsk.

A center of trade then both on land and by water, Irkutsk is located in the Southeastern corner of Siberia at the Angara and Lena River Basins. Descriptions of the Angara River say that it is more than 1,100 miles long originating at Lake Baikal where it drains into the headwater of the Yenisei River.

The Yenisei River, it is also said, with an average depth of 45-feet, meanders itself along a northerly and then westerly path through Siberia flowing eventually into the Arctic Ocean. The Lena River, the eastern-most river of the two, at more than 2,700 miles long, is a very large river that lies entirely within Russian territorial boundaries and it flows northeasterly into the Arctic Ocean as well.

Nearby Lake Baikal is a 200-mile-long freshwater lake, the largest, deepest, cleanest, and perhaps oldest of its kind in the world. Various descriptions of Lake Baikal claim that it is an extraordinary lake.

Despite some objections from the team that the Red Army was in Irkutsk, the group went through 49 tunnels in one mile at Lake Baikal.

"We proceeded on to Irkutsk," recalls Martin, "and when we got within about a mile of Irkutsk we could hear gunfire. The Lieutenant said that we might be going into a hornet's nest."

The Red Army was on the east bank of the river. The White Army was on the west bank.

"The Lieutenant told me to get my rifle and come with me. I put a .45 automatic in my coat," said Martin, still nervous all these years later when he recalls the moment.

Meeting A Ghost

"He took me five tracks over and there sat another steel Pullman car with the words 'Amerikanski' written on its sides too. He gave me orders that nobody was to leave or enter and shoot to kill if necessary." Martin remembered as if it was instructions ordered yesterday.

"I stayed there for several hours and the door opened," Martin said. "Out stepped, I took it to be an English or Canadian captain, down on the first step of the car. I challenged him to go back in. He said that he came out to get a breath of fresh air. I told him to go back in.

"My orders are my orders," Martin explained. About that time, Martin says a bullet hit the step "the Captain" was standing on, "and I did not have to tell him to get back inside."

Martin says he guarded this car for three days and three nights.

"At night and during the day, on the second day and night, they began to fire from the east bank and the west bank under the car. I backed my legs behind the steel wheels," Martin recalls.

"Many people were hit, but I wasn't."

The troops on the west bank, the White Army, eventually fled.

"Three men were coming running down between the trains. They had their rifle with big bayonets. I made my mind up that nobody was going to get me with a bayonet," said Martin.

"I cocked my .45 automatic, put my back against the car, when they got within six-to-eight feet from me they pointed their bayonets at me. I figured I could get three," Martin boasted.

"The Lieutenant hollered, 'stay perfectly still, I am coming.' He spoke to the three men. They dropped their guns and went on down the tracks," Martin said.

"They relieved me from this car and took me back to my car. The next morning the Lieutenant sent for me. 'Private Hutson, I have a job for you. Do not mention it to anyone. If you do, you will face a court martial. Put your rifle away. Put your pistol away.'"

Martin says the Lieutenant took him back "to the car I left before." Martin says, "There was a Japanese General, an English Colonel, an Italian Colonel, a Czech Colonel, and my Lieutenant."

Amazingly, Martin says the Lieutenant "ordered all of them to leave the train. They offered no resistance" and, he says, "gave no argument. They left."

Martin said that "All this time I was watching them." Martin thought it was strange that an American Lieutenant was ordering a General and three Colonels what to do, even if the officers came from another country, they were still ranking members of the Allied Forces.

"When I turned around there was a man sitting in the center of the train wearing civilian clothes," Martin remembers. "I think he weighed about 150 pounds, but, I never saw him stand up. The Lieutenant said to me, 'Your job is to talk to him every day for two hours. I will come and get you.'"

Martin said, "This man asked me my name and I could have dropped to the floor. I had never heard a man speak perfect English like that before. He could have been an Oxford professor. His English was clear as a bell. He had no accent at all," Martin said.

"For seven days I went to this train at 2 o'clock and stayed and talked to him for two hours. On the seventh day, he said that we were going to move to a small town. 'I want you to pick up any newspaper you can, bring them back, and I will read them to you,'" says Martin of his instruction from the well-spoken gentleman.

Martin said that his orders were to teach the former Russian monarch a Southern accent so that he might better blend into his new life in obscurity.

"The next day, he asked if I had found any Chinese newspapers?" says Martin. "I did not know you could read Chinese," Martin says he responded. "'I can read and write any language in the civilized world,'" the gentlemen said back to Martin.

"He read to me for the next few days," Martin said.

"One day, the Lieutenant took me over and told me he was going to come after me at 2 pm but would ask me to go to the other car and have tea with three ladies," Martin says. "I told the Lieutenant I do not like tea.

"The next day, I went down to the car and a French lady came to the door. I went in. They had a table there with three chairs. At one end of the table sat a woman about 50. At the other end was another young lady, probably in her 30s. Across from me sat the French lady in her 40s," remembers Martin.

"She," the French lady Martin says, "served the tea and did most of the talking. Except for the lady on my left, the older lady sat stiff in her chair and spoke fairly good English. The young lady spoke some English. The French lady spoke perfect English."

"So," says Martin, "I had two jobs to do: Drink tea and talk. All this time we were stopping in small towns for about 40 minutes and then we would move out."

The next morning, Martin says they passed through Manchuria City.

"The Lieutenant said that we could go into town in groups of two for Vodka. I did not care for Vodka," Martin says.

"A young lady come out and spoke very good English and asked if we all were going to Vladivostok? I said, yes ma'am." Martin says the women then said, "'Can you take me with you?' I said I am afraid not. She pulled her dress back where a bayonet had pierced her shoulder blades. She said, 'if you leave me I will not survive.'"

The Episode Continues

Martin said that after the encounter with the lady, they went back to the station and started out for Chita. "When we got to Chita we made a very brief stop because there were a lot of Red Army there." Martin said that you could tell Red Army because they wore a small red ribbon on their lapels. White Army, he said, wore a small white ribbon on their lapels.

The city of Chita was nestled against the Trans-Siberian Railway, about 560-miles east of Irkutsk. The Japanese had occupied Chita since 1918 and strongly controlled the surrounding area, militarily, up until that time. The Japanese would lose control of Chita the following year.

Nicholas had history in Chita. He had crushed an independence rebellion there a decade before, led by the city's then leaders who wanted their own republic free of Imperial Russia.

"A few miles down the line after we set out we were attacked by a small group of Chinese bandits, who set our wood cars on fire. It was late and getting dark. I saw all of these people come off our train who I did not know was even on our train," recalls Martin.

"When they all got cleared out we cleaned up what mess we had, and sat out for Harbin," Martin says. "They got desperately mad at us because we did not take what they wanted."

Located in Northeast China, Harbin was a fishing village in 1919 hosting a very significant population center for Russia refugees. It was also a hub city for the Chinese Eastern Railway, providing a more direct route between Chita to the west and Vladivostok to the east. In fact, Russia used the city, which dates back unofficially to the Stone Age, extensively for its military operations during the Russo-Japanese War of 1904-1905.

Martin remembers, "Before we got to Harbin, I was guarding the outside door of my car. This man came down and said I had been good to him. He showed me more diamonds and rubies than I had ever seen before. The rubies were as big as the end of your thumb.

"He asked if I wanted to buy some. I told him I had no money. I never told anybody that he had them because that would have been the end of him," Martin reminisces.

Martin's group then pulled into Harbin. "A contingent of English soldiers, the Consul General of England, and the Consul General of the United States came in to the car and sat down," he says. "We served them coffee ...

"Our Consul General raised his foot and put it on top of a big box and the Lieutenant jumped up and said, Sir, remove your foot from that box - that is his Imperial Highness! I beg your pardon and moved his foot," an incredulous Martin remembers.

A short period of time passes, and Martin says, "He brought three boxes to a wagon and left.

"So, I figured we had been through a hot time and we could go home. But no, our orders were we were to go back on the same train to Siberia," Martin said, nervously even this day all these years later.

Relief Short-Lived

"We got an engineer to drive the train back to Vladivostok. He said that he was not going."

Martin's superior instructed him, "Private Hutson take your .45 and tell him to get into the engine."

Martin says the engineer, "He begged me with tears in his eyes to let him go." He said that he had done nothing to me, Martin says. "He had a young wife and children. The Red Army was down the road and would kill him. I told him the Lieutenant gave me no choice."

Back into Siberia, about 90-miles, Martin says, a terrible battle was going on to their left in the town, so they turned out their lights on the train and went down between the boxcars where fighting occurred all night.

"People were hollering and screaming," Martin said. "About daylight, they rode out on very small horses, Martin recalls. "Cossacks. Semenov.

"We proceeded on down about 50-miles and they blocked us," Martin said. "I was on guard. Five men approached me and said that if you will take these three men to Vladivostok, you can go safely. If you don't take them, you have gone as far as you are going to go."

Martin said, "Those trains over there had compartments. I took them down and put them in to my compartment."

A 14-year-old spoke very good English, according to Martin. Martin said the boy told him that he had learned English because war broke out. "I told him to get three men he wanted, two elderly men and a young boy. They did not talk or move.

"We pulled into Vladivostok the next day," Martin said. "When those three men stepped off the train all hell broke loose. I stayed on the train. About an hour, an hour-and-a-half, I went out there were dead bodies all over the depot and the railroad yards, with red ribbons and white ribbons both," Martin said.

In telling his story, Martin says at this point that he wanted to "backtrack a bit" on his testimony.

"In Manchuria City, the Red Army arrested this general, by the name of Admiral Kolchak. This boy told me. They arrested him."

Aleksandr Kolchak was a highly controversial naval admiral who had sworn allegiance to the Russian Provisional Government in the hours after the Russian Revolution. He became close to allied forces, including the British, and was eventually elevated to Supreme Commander. Lenin had him arrested in early January 1920 and executed the next month.

"My sergeant spoke very fluent Russian," Martin claims. "The Lieutenant got us together and said that we needed to make a decision we fight or run. We took a vote but voted to fight. We only had one box of ammunition and 120 rounds in our bandoliers each. We gave them until 12 o'clock to give us our man back," Martin said.

"Around 11:30 they moved up four 75mm cannons broadside on our car." Martin says his Lieutenant said, "'We don't stand a chance on this plan. When I give a signal, open the door and run in every direction you can. We stand a chance.'"

At 11:50 a Japanese regimen showed up and drove them off, Martin said.

"We had a Japanese General on board."

General Graves, Martin said, "did not come help us. Said every man to himself. He had problems of his own."

Back-stepping in his story another time at this point, Martin said that for Christmas dinner in 1919, "I had one big loaf of black bread. Had to take a bayonet to cut it but it was good."

"I withdrew from Siberia in February 1920 on the *U.S. Transport Crook* to Manila," where Martin reports they were all loaded into trucks and taken to Camp McKinley. At Camp McKinley they were each assigned quarters and started an eight-hour drill.

"The hospital was full with full tents," Martin said.

"I recall one other instance," Martin said at this point. "One of my own men in Irkutsk tried to kill me, but missed," said Martin.

"I came back to the United States, Camp Bliss, Washington, 3rd Tank Company, Martin explained. "I was discharged honorably."

In 1932, Martin said he picked up the *Louisville Courier-Journal,* and there was the story by the American Consul General Harbin explaining how he had met Special Evacuation Train #28 and how it carried the Tsar and his family out of Russia. The Consul General recalled how he put his foot on the box the Tsar was riding in and he was still alive.

"My story is this," said Martin. "They picked me in Knoxville in Tennessee as an 18-year-old boy. They did not want the Tsar to recognize me. I wrote this story once before but the State Department did not want me to publish the story. Would not let me reach the Consul General under any circumstances.

"I think I was used as a tool but they did not want me back alive because they were afraid I might go to thinking and put the puzzle together," Martin said.

"Nicholas was not killed in Siberia," Martin concludes.

"Three other people were killed and their bodies chopped up with broad axes, dumped in a lime pit, poured crude oil on them and burned 'em, which was a very, very good camouflage to throw the Red Army off," Martin said. "That was done by the Tsar's own home guards before they fled."

Martin ended his Army career according to his Discharge Record signed by a Major from the 7th Infantry on August 19, 1922, at Camp Lewis, Washington. The Discharge lists his Army identification as "6319564." His occupation is listed as a Clerk, his enlistment age was noted as being 18 years of age.

The Army also recorded that Martin had grey eyes, brown hair, fair complexion, and was five-feet-seven-inches tall.

His discharge was noted as "Honorable." Martin's Enlistment Record noted of his character that he was, "Excellent," serving in A.E.F. Siberia from October 4, 1919 to February 15, 1920, Philippine Islands from February 24, 1920 to October 15, 1921."

It also said that Martin's service was "Honest and Faithful."

Questioning What We Know

Martin's story represents perhaps one of the only first-person accounts historians have been able to find to date in the Romanov mystery that definitively says that the Tsar was alive, some sixteen months after his reported murder.

In doing so, Martin's story also begs the following questions at least:

- Why was Martin chosen for this special mission?
- Why did Martin originally think that he was going to Mexico? Was there a Mexico mission in the works, and if so, why?
- Who planned the rescue mission in Siberia and how did they pull it off?
- Did the Bolsheviks allow the "late" Tsar to be rescued?
- Were the Germans complicit in the Romanov escape, too?
- Was the American Red Cross normally used as a spy agency of its federal government?
- Is there any evidence of Captain Cross of the Red Cross in any archived records, anywhere?
- Do U.S. Army personnel records corroborate the existence of a Captain Roberson, a Lt. Humphries, and a Kashiba, in theater at the time of Martin's service?
- Which Romanov daughter was aboard Evacuation Train #28?
- Who was the Japanese General onboard the evacuation train when it was attacked by Chinese bandits?
- Moreover, can we find out who the British Consul General was on board the train as well as the names of

the other allied officers who were sitting in alleged Russian monarch's car?

- Do historical records support Chang's potential encounter with the American troops?

- Who were the seven other soldiers on Martin's mission and is there a record of their activities? Or was there eight, Martin says both at various times in his account?

- Is there any evidence of a Special Evacuation Train #28 in the U.S. National Archives, or elsewhere, today? What do official records reflect?

- Who was the French-speaking woman traveling with the Empress?

- When "all hell broke loose" was it over the Tsarevich Alexei? Although unnamed by Martin, was the Crown Prince onboard the train, as well?

- Is there any evidence of a significant gun battle in Vladivostok around the time of the 14-year-old's appearance?

- Who tried to kill Martin, and why?

- Was Martin truly 18-years-old at the time of his enlistment?

- Why was Martin's story not revealed before now?
- Who were the three killed in Nicholas' place, if in fact Nicholas' murder was staged?

- Which British troops were given custody of the former Tsar if he was transferred to them in a burial box, alive?
- Did the United States Department of State know all of these details all along?
- Moreover, if Nicholas lived, where did the former Tsar go after leaving Russia?
- And why have these details remained secret for a century now?

There are certainly a lot of questions that need answering.

In the meantime, you should know that Martin Hutson would die from cancer two months after he recorded this "episode in my life."

Martin never sought, or did, materially benefit from his time with Nicholas in Siberia in late 1919, at least according to evidence found to date.

A word-for-word copy of his account can be found in Appendix A of this book. The actual recordings from Martin in 1971 are now available for you to listen to at: www.CannonAndCaius.com/nicholas.

Recommended reading:

- Greg King and Penny Wilson, *The Fate of the Romanovs,* John Wiley & Sons, Inc., Hobokon, NJ, 2003, ISBN: 0-471-20768-3.

- State Hermitage Museum, *Nicholas and Alexandra: The Last Imperial Family of Tsarist Russia,* Harry N. Abrams, Inc., Publishers, Mark Sutcliffe, Managing Editor, New York, NY, 1998, ISBN: 0-8109-3687-9.

3 | Whispers & Theories

"Our Consul General raised up his foot and put it on top of a big box. The Army officer jumped and said, Sir, remove your foot from that box, that is his Imperial Highness. And he begged' your pardon.' Removed his foot."

- *Incident aboard a former Imperial train some 16 months after the reported assassination of the Tsar and his family in July 1918, as recounted by Martin V. Hutson*

History now tells us that Nicholas II of Russia, his wife and five children, his personal physician, and two servants – eleven people - were all killed on July 17, 1918, by Bolshevik soldiers in the basement of the Ipatiev house at Yekaterinburg.

History now tells us that the Tsar's party was found some 74 years later in an unmarked grave in the Koptyaki woods, by a group of "amateur sleuths," at least one of whom had copious ties to the famed former Soviet spy agency, the KGB.

History would eventually share with us that the grave of the Romanovs had been found by these same amateur sleuths in 1976, twelve years before the rest of the world would learn of their alleged fate. Five years after Martin Hutson's passing. The crime scene had been admittedly tampered with on numerous occasions according to published accounts in an excellent book published in Canada by Peter Kurth called, *Tsar: The Lost World of Nicholas & Alexandra.*

History would tell us that subsequent DNA tests would ultimately determine with 98.5% certainty that the bones found were indeed those of the royal family. Even "a computerized juxtaposition of his [The Tsar] skull with his [The Tsar] face was purported to show an exact match."

American forensic scientists would dispute this conclusion.

History even told us at one point that one of the daughters - one the grand duchesses - was missing from the grave near Sverdlovsk, the new name of the old city, Yekaterinburg. Was it Marie? Or, the fabled Anastasia?

Equally astonishing was news that Tsar Nicholas' son, Alexei, was missing, too. The great Romanov mystery was made even more intriguing in the confusion.

History tells us that the American forensic scientists who were called in by the post-Soviet government in the Ural province to examine the find said that the missing girl was Anastasia.

Dr. William Maples from the University of Florida's Human Identification Laboratory concluded that "all the skeletons appear to be too tall to be Anastasia" and he also observed that all three other daughters' bones showed "completed growth." Anastasia had just celebrated her 17th birthday.

History would tell us years later the two missing bodies were found some 70 meters away from the original grave. They had been buried separately, it would appear, or least we were now being told. Nothing in previous testimony from the time of the "murder" to the time of the discovery had ever previously indicated that there were two burial sites.

History tells us that eighteen witnesses from the city of Perm testified that the Empress Alexandra and all of her daughters had been seen alive in September 1918 – two months after their alleged murder at the Ipatiev House.

History tells us that there were other Romanov sightings as well in the months following the "assassination." The Swedish Red Cross Siberia mission chief stated, "… I traveled in a private railway car. At some place, the name of which escapes my memory, the train stopped and was searched for the Grand Duchess Anastasia, daughter of Tsar Nicholas II. The Grand Duchess, however, was not aboard the train. Nobody knew where she had gone." If she had died months earlier, why were the authorities from that era still looking for her on passing trains?

Another report recounted by the outstanding historian, Robert K. Massey, who also wrote the wonderful *Nicholas and Alexandra,* cites a British high commissioner dispatch to Foreign Secretary Arthur Balfour, stating that "On July 17,' he wrote, 'a train with the blinds down left Ekaterinburg for an unknown destination and it is believed that the surviving members of the Imperial family were in it.... It is the general opinion in Ekaterinburg that the Empress, her son and daughters were not murdered."

Now, history as recorded by an eyewitness, says that the Tsar and at least two members of his family were alive in late 1919, more than a year after their reported assassination, in the company of American and Allied soldiers, some of who were officers and high-ranking diplomatic officials. Based on conversation with the Tsar, it is claimed, the Tsar also said that the other members of his family had escaped, too.

History has given the world very conflicting accounts of what exactly happened to Nicholas II and his family, despite nearly a century of investigation and intrigue.

Why, then, was history so confused?

The Persisting Romanov Mystery

The Romanov mystery has generated many twists and turns over the past century with rumored sightings of family members long after their reported deaths, to fanciful stories of their remarkable escape through competing portals peppering Asia and Europe, to Martin's own mention of the news story in the Louisville *Courier-Journal* by the American Consul General of Harbin stating that he had the former Russian leader onboard his "special" train.

Four very distinctive accounts, worth examining in great detail, stand out, and can help put Martin's story into better context: Gray's Alexei survives; McNeal's discovers; Harris' ashes; and, Occleshaw's shadow dancing.

We start with the outsider accounts provided by Michael Gray and Shay McNeal.

Alexei Survives?

In his 1998 book, *Blood Relative,* author Michael Gray - not his real name - claims his father is the surviving Romanov son, Tsarevich Alexei, known since the 1917 Russian Revolution in his parts as Nikolai Chebotarev.

Gray contends that he was raised by surrogate parents but came to realize his birth father's true identity at a much later age, when he himself had a son to raise. Gray believes Alexei escaped Russia and death through Siberia passing through Constantinople, Yugoslavia, and circuitously, New York, finally settling in Ireland where he eventually dies on January 2, 1987, five years before any bones of the Romanov family would be formally discovered.

Chebotarev, according to Gray, is buried in Holt Churchyard, Norfolk, England, under a tombstone that reads with the proper Russian spelling of his adopted name: Nicholas Tchebotareff.

Chebotarev's home is reported to be in and around Collon, Ireland, a picturesque and unassuming little town far off the beaten path northwest of Dublin.

Nikolai, Gray observes, spoke fluent English and French, consistent with having been expertly tutored in English and French by Charles Sydney Gibbes and Pierre Gilliard. Gibbes and Gilliard are well-established and historically documented tutors for the royal family.

What makes Gray's story so intriguing, whether true or not, is the list of names of prominent friends and loyal supporters of Tsar Nicholas II and his family have with Russia and Ireland in common, according to Gray's story. For example, Gray provides compelling vignettes such as the following:

- A late middle-aged man matching the description of Tsar Nicholas II, or his first cousin King George V of England, appears in Collon in 1948, causing quite a stir in the community who believes royalty is visiting. The gracefully greying bearded gentleman's name is, Gray writes, Nikolai Alexandrovich.

- Lydia, a sister of Chebotarev is pictured on occasion in small groups possessing a right ring finger scar that is remarkably similar to one that was suffered by the Grand Duchess Maria in a train door accident in 1910.

- Alix Hill, the determined daughter of Alexander Hill and Olga von Berg, a Red Cross Nurse during World War I who served in and around Siberia, a constant companion in Gray's story. Alix's father was cousin to famed British agents George Hill and Freddie Hill and of Dame

Elizabeth Hill, whose mother, Gray says, was in love with Paul Stepanov, one of the notorious Gregory Rasputin's murderers. Both Grandfathers were reported by Gray and other authors in various sources to be friends of Tsar Nicholas II.

- Freddie Hill was the described sidekick to Robert Bruce Lockhart, the top British diplomat in Russia in 1918, according to published reports.

- George Hill, Gray notes, admitted to being an agent in the British Secret Intelligence Service.

- Maureen Hill is said to have been told personally by Nikolai Chebotarev that, "I am also Alexei."

- Colonel Joe Boyle was a Lieutenant Colonel in the Canadian militia and a close friend of King George V and the British Royal family. Boyle, who appears at various times in the Tsarist murders literature in recent years was awarded his country's Distinguished Service Order for services he rendered in actual combat during World War I. Boyle was such a royal insider that he was an overnight guest of King George V at Buckingham Palace on more than one occasion.

- Dame Elizabeth Hill was a cousin of George Hill, and cousin of Joe Boyle's deputy, George Hill. George Hill was reported to be Colonel Boyles's deputy and was reputed in Gray's book and elsewhere to be one of the most active British agents in Russia during the Russian Revolution and Tsar's abdication period.

- Count Peter Apraxine, who was an influential secretary to the Tsarina, Alexandra.

- Nikolai Couriss, a close childhood friend of Grigori Chebotarev in Tsarkow Selo, the Tsar's winter home. Couriss' father was a Colonel in the Life Guards during the Russian Revolution, and fought in the White Russian Volunteer Army, which sought to preserve the Tsar's Imperial rule as we have seen in the previous chapter of this book.

- Mrs. Preston was a friend of Sana Couriss, cousin of Prince Pail Lieven and a friend of Sana Couriss. She was also surprisingly the wife of the British Consul in Yekaterinburg when the Imperial family disappeared. The British Consul, as you will soon see, appears to have played a major role in rescuing Nicholas.

- Allison "Zonny" Fox was first cousin of British Prime Minister Neville Chamberlain, and was credited with bringing Nicholai Couriss to Ireland, setting him up in business or employing him with a chicken farm.

- General Peter Krasnov was the commanding officer of White Russian troops against the Red Russian Bolsheviks, and is credited with organizing White Russian nursing services in southern Russia. He was said to have been pro-German and an eventual General in the Cossack Division of Hitler's feared SS. The Tsarina was of German ancestry, history notes.

- Count Grabbe was commander of the Tsar's bodyguard, the Cossack Konvoy, and ended up being described as a close friend of Nikolai Chebotarev. The Cossack's, of course, were noticed by Martin in his account of Nicholas' evacuation from Siberia.

- Colonel Michael Zmeova, began his service in World War I in Harbin in Northern China, where after the Russian Revolution he had been put in charge of transportation for the White Russian government on the Trans-Siberian railroad. Iya Zmeova's mother was Lydia Zmeova and Iya was reported by Gray to have been a niece of Chebotarev's. Harbin was a significant city on Martin Hutson's adventure and the place where Martin contends the Americans handed the Romanovs over to the British in burial boxes.

- Prince Paul Lieven, also a close friend of Chebotarev was a qualified engineer Gray reports worked on the Omsk-Tomsk section of the Trans-Siberian railway. This section of the railway served numerous purposes for allied missions both during and immediately after World War I, including as Martin has noted, his own AEF Siberia mission.

The railroads in Russia certainly do factor very prominently into many of the rescue whispers about the Romanovs, including Martin's story, as you have already seen and will learn more about later in this book.

According to Anthony Summers and Tom Mangold in their sensational book, *The File on the Tsar*, the two note that "it was on the Omsk section of the line that an attempt had been made to rescue the Tsar in 1918." Shay McNeal's research, you will learn shortly, credibly documented a number of plots to save the Tsar and his family.

Prince Paul Lieven had been, according to his eldest son in an account by Gray, the chief engineer on the Omsk-Tomsk sector of the Trans-Siberian railway at the time of the Revolution. A related role, such as this, was common for allied intelligence in the years leading up to 1920.

"That, writes Gray, "was the sector where the mysterious Yakovlev, who had been sent by the Central Committee in Moscow to move the Imperial family from Tobolsk to Ekaterinburg, staged what looked suspiciously like a rescue attempt with the object of taking the Tsar, Tsarina, and Grand Duchess Maria east to Japan." This route, you will remember from Martin's story in Chapter 2, is remarkably similar.

At an even higher level, Britain's King George V was almost certainly involved in these rescue missions, based on Gray's research, as well as that of others such as McNeal, and now Martin. Boyle stayed with the King on occasion and was even honored by the King, says Gray and history. It had been a failed attempt to rescue the Tsar by fast motor boat on the Ob River and Kara Sea, for example, in this reported case.

The Imperial tutor, Charles Sydney Gibbs it is written in Gray's book, even confided to Alix Hill that "he knew for certain that the Tsarevich and other members of the Imperial family had survived."

According to Gray's account, Gray rightly believed that the Bolsheviks needed "material" to bargain with, as they dealt with the Allies during World War I immediately in the days following the Tsar's abdication. Gray reaffirms that in the great game of peace and war the Romanovs were fair tradable goods.

Gray notes, too, that there was and still is sufficient evidence of significant diplomatic activity surrounding the Tsar's situation. Allied interests are reported to have made it crystal clear to the German government how important this matter was, forcing the Germans to at least make it look like they, too, had a real interest in the fate of the former imperial family. Uncertain as to the outcome of the war, Gray observes and argues, Vladimir Lenin could not afford to take chances with German monarchist sensibilities. Seen in this light, then, the choice of July 1918 as an appropriate or opportune time to liquidate the former ruler and his family makes no sense at all, Gray surmizes.

Summers and Mangold in their book further described a Bolshevik proposal "for the exchange of two Communist activists" who were in German custody – Karl Liebknecht, the German Spartacist leader, and Leo Jogiches, a Polish Marxist and friend of Rosa Luxemburg. Gray says that for his family - for the Imperial family – this proposal was "'the strongest possible diplomatic evidence that the imperial family were still alive.'"

Second, Gray also notes that, "it is entirely plausible that some sort of international action at the royal level had been concerted to obtain the release of the Romanovs. Queen Victoria had been the 'grandmother of Europe.' Numbering the Tsarina, the Kaiser, King George V, his sister Princess Victoria, Grand Duke Ernst of Hesse, and Queen Marie of Romania among her many grandchildren. These grandchildren were understandably concerned for the fate of their Romanov relatives, cousins they had grown up with, holidayed with, been godparents to, care for and even, in some case, loved."

What makes this observation so interesting is that same royal relatives were notably silent about the fate of the Imperial Romanov family in the immediate aftermath of the alleged July 1918 assassination.

Gray contends that there may have been a royal secret pact he referred to as "The Trust of Kings." The Trust of Kings essentially asserted, Gray says, that the other relatives would need to intervene and rescue "Cousin Nicky," lest something similar happen to them and then need rescuing too by the other "Kings." Gray implies here that King George V might have been motivated to rescue his first cousin, with the American president's help, because of the so-called Trust of Kings. Evidence on this Trust, however, is still questionably slim despite some great research on the topic to date.

"If the Bolsheviks were to stand a chance of defeating the anti-revolutionary 'White' forces," Gray concludes, then they "needed peace with Germany; and the Romanovs were prime bargaining counters in their pursuit of this end. "

This observation makes perfect sense.

The German Chancellor, Gray further alleges in his book, was therefore involved in trying to find out what happened to the Romanov women in particular following the reported assassination in 1917. There is ample evidence in the files in Germany post-World War I to support this conclusion, he and others note. And, logically, as Gray argues, the "Bolsheviks were bound to be in the business of trading Romanovs for whatever their royal relatives were willing to offer."

"Logical it may have been," argues Gray in agreeable fashion, "but was it what actually happened?" He asks:

> *Any evidence of the operation of something as nebulous as the Trust of the Kings would inevitably be scant. The royal families and their agents were well practiced in the arts of concealment; and, since they operated outside official governmental channels and beyond any legal constrict, they had the means to obliterate all trace of what they had done. They would be aided in this, moreover, by the sheer chaos that was Russia in 1918. Nothing provided a better smokescreen than disorder.*

And, so it proved itself out Gray notes. He says in his research, "a lead turned up in the unlikeliest of places: the Public Record Office of Northern Ireland - not somewhere you would expect to find material relating to Russia in 1918. Yet there it was. Locked away in the papers of a Canadian militia Colonel were clues to the shadowy operations of the Trust of Kings." Gray is talking about the notes of Colonel Joe Boyle.

Gray then relates that Dr. Una Kroll, George Hill's daughter he notes, "told me how her father and mother, then Evelyn Pediani, had spirited the Romanian crown jewels, £25 million in gold and the state archives - which, somewhat ironically, had been stored with the Tsar's government for safe keeping - out of Bolshevik Russia, her mother literally sitting on them in the railway carriage while her father rode shotgun."

Joe Boyle, he writes, was a Chicago fireman and alleged lover to Queen Marie of Romania, and also led efforts to rescue the Romanovs. Gray says, "Queen Marie was uniquely placed to operate on behalf of the Trust of the Kings in the matter of the Romanovs. She was cousin to King George V, the Tsarina, and the German Kaiser, Wilhelm. Romania shared a border with Russia, he says. The Black Sea was power. Even Vladimir Lenin had asked to see Boyle.

In August 1918, Sir Charles Eliot, the British High Commissioner in Siberia, as reported on earlier, had taken up his post in September and, as Gray, discusses, "Had reliable sources" who dismissed, too, the idea that Romanovs were murdered in Yekaterinburg as reported. Gray reports that Sir Charles contended that "the imperial family had been disguised before their removal and that the murder stories were clumsy falsifications. Eliot wrote, Gray says that "'It is supposed the victims were five, namely the Tsar, Dr. Botkin, the Empress' maid and two lackeys. It is the general opinion in Ekaterinburg that the Empress, her son and four daughters were not murdered but dispatched on 17 July to north or west," he says. For consistency's sake, remember that Martin Hutson said that three people had been killed in the Tsar's stead, not the five Eliot wrote about.

In 1932, Gray writes that George Hill published a book entitled, *Go Spy the Land.* In the book, Hill reports himself that Tsar Nicholas had escaped Russian death and been sheltered by supportive peasants or White Russians. Another British agent, Gray says, said to a French envoy, that "even if the Tsar and the imperial family are alive, it is necessary to say that they are dead!" That reputed spy was also a *Times of London* correspondent, according to Gray. Remember, too, that 1932 is when Martin Hutson says that he saw the news article on the American Consul General, Ernest Harris, claiming to have taken the Tsar's ashes out of Siberia aboard and American Red Cross train.

The point is, as Michael Gray finally states, "Whatever actually happened, there was no shortage of operatives on the ground - or of varying, even conflicting, motives and agendas." Obviously!

As you will see later in this book, the team required to pull off any rescue of the Tsar or members of his family would have to be evident and capable. We believe, as you will discover, that they were.

Succinctly said, Gray concludes his section on the planned rescues with this:

> *The charmed circle of royal cousinhood had centuries of experience of cover-up, far more than any twentieth-century secret service. Covert operations are part of the ivy that grows round those intertwined royal family trees. Artificially created history is second nature to them. Removing Nikolai II and his family from Russia to lives of obscurity as commoners living*

separately from one another was something the royal club would know exactly what to do.

Some attempts at rescue may have been aborted; some may have been deliberate decoy operations. As the story unfolded, it was not the paucity of such attempts, but on the contrary their multiplicity, which impressed. And all of them were connected one way or another, with royalty.

Gray believes that the Tsarvich Alexei, his father he says, eventually left Russia on board the same ship as the Dowager Empress, Tsar Nicholas II's mother and the Tsarevich's paternal grandmother. She found a cabin for Alexei, Gray says, aboard the British Warship *Marlborough,* which would dock on April 11, 1920 in Constantinople. Constantinople was chosen, Gray says because Nikolai Couriss, was manager of the American Red Cross warehouse in Constantinople.

A number Gray's story elements are present in Martin's story as well, as you have already witnessed and will more so later in this book:

- Starting with the last point first, the American Red Cross clearly played a major intelligence role in at least Gray's and Hutson's rescue attempts.

- Second, the principal intelligence operatives working on behalf of King George V will also be found around the AEF Siberia mission to Irkutsk, namely Colonel Boyle. The number of operatives on the ground around Yekaterinburg in July 1918 was, as Gray observed, plentiful.

- Third, the British Consul General, we believe, did indeed play a leading role in spiriting the former

Tsar out of the Ipatiev House when the alleged murder would have had to have been staged. Martin attested to this as you will see.

- Fourth, George Hill's book mentions that the Tsar was held by friendlies until his rescue. This is consistent with Martin's understanding that the Tsar and his family were held in a safe house around Archanglesk or Omansk. Shay McNeal has a lot to say from her research on that subject, which follows.

But there are some notable differences to outline, too:

- Gray places the alleged Alexei escape route through Constantanople east to Japan via Siberia. A Romanov evacuation would not likely after taken this circuitous route, nor would it have need to. If Alexei had left through Constantanople with his grandmother then he would not have needed to double back toward Japan or Vladivostok. The Japan route, however, is consistent with Martin's story, but it began in Irkutsk, not Constantanople.

- Joe Boyle had Chicago connections as Gray notes and mentions that once in the United States on his way to Ireland, Alexei went through New York City. As you will learn later in this account, Martin understood from his superiors that Nicholas was to leave Russia via Vladivostok to San Francisco with a path to England via Chicago and New York by train. The Gray and Hutson accounts would be consistent on the later part of this suggested escape route.

McNeal Discovers

Shay McNeal, in her 2001 book, *The Secret Plot to Save the Tsar*, takes the rescue plots even deeper uncovering evidence "that there were several complex operations mounted in 1918 to save the Romanovs and that perhaps one may have succeeded, at least in part," she writes.

McNeal's book is most interesting for its excellent analysis of newly discovered files at the time revealing just how extensive the network of intelligence operative was working behind the scenes with U.S., British, Canadian, French, Italian, Czechoslovakian, and Japanese agents to liberate the Imperial family and safely deliver them from the Bolshevik captors. Remember that these are the same parties that Martin says were evident on his own rescue mission.

McNeal argues that one possible rescue attempt involved the German high command itself, while another was conducted by a lone British Secret Service agent named, Charles James Fox, who had successfully infiltrated the Ipatiev House guard unit.

Writes McNeal:

> *However, with the aid of new forensic evidence and heretofore undiscovered and understudied source material, it is possible to prove that the traditional account of the months leading up to the night, as well as during the night of 16/17 July 1918 itself, simply cannot have occurred as described."*

McNeal argues that after reviewing the evidence over a five-year period of full-time research, further evidence revealed itself that differed vastly from the official story of the last days of the Romanovs. "Not only was the traditional history shown to be fraught with discrepancies," McNeal says, "but it also became apparent, by the compilation of facts gleaned from disparate sources, that there were at least three and possibly four serious plans for the withdrawal of the Tsar and his family from Russia after the February Revolution in 1917. The Allies worked clandestinely, co-operating with one another at the highest level, even flirting with Bolshevik complicity, to come up with plans to pluck the Romanovs from the Bolshevik's grasp."

McNeal says her book demonstrates, "that what history has told us of these events is very far from the full story, and that some 'authors' of that history may have had ulterior and hitherto unsuspected motives." It would appear that McNeal made the point with her research. Since, as she points out, five of the seven Romanovs were laid to rest on 17 July 1998 - the 80th anniversary of the reported Romanov murders, the question begs itself: Who did they actually bury?

Helen Rappaport, a very well regarded Russian historian, has concluded in her work that the Romanovs' lives ended on July 17, 1918 at the hands of Bolshevik Revolutionaries at the Ipatiev House in Yekaterinburg, and further argues Rappaport, that is (or should be) the end of the story.

But questions through McNeal and others have been raised about how the Romanov bones first made their appearance in Russia in the first place from irregularities at the so-called Romanov gravesite to "the questionable provenance of the putative Romanov samples did not find their way into the press conference or the news stories."

Conclusive DNA analysis does not appear to McNeal or us to have been so conclusive after all. Vital facts have been obscured - redacted - it would appear. Writes McNeal, supportingly:

> *The issue at the heart of the entire controversy is that both the FSS (British Home Office's Forensic Science Service, which had been responsible for Prince Philip's DNA testing) and the AFDIL have consistently refused to release the full case file to the members of the Russian Expert Commission Abroad (RECA), so that the Commission, which has served as a watchdog committee, can release the full case for independent peer review and the legal procedure of discovery by a truly independent body.*

Prince Philips' DNA, was used by official parties to validate and relate to those of Tsar Nicholas II. AFDIL is the United States Armed Forces DNA Identification Laboratory at Dover Air Force Base in Delaware.

McNeal says that another problem, "is the simple fact that, despite widespread media acceptance, experts agree that DNA evidence alone cannot at present (nor will it in the foreseeable future) be the sole factor in identifying an individual. Unlike an actual fingerprint, which is considered unique to the individual, the DNA profile, because it uses a miniscule fraction of the total DNA 'signature', is definitely not unique."

"Concerning the alleged Romanov remains in particular," McNeal argues, "Dr. Shields (Dr. William Shields, State University of New York, noted genetics expert with extensive experience reviewing forensic DNA analysis and is an official consultant to the National Alliance of Families of POWs and MIAs on the forensic use of mitrochondrial DNA [mtDNA]) emphasized that the demonstrated mtDNA match with Prince Philip cannot be accepted as proof of the identity of the Empress Alexandra and her children:

> *Even if a mtDNA sequence matches that of Prince Philip, it doesn't mean that the person is his relative. For unrelated individuals can and do match at their mtDNA sequences. So one needs to know the frequency of matching Prince Philip's sequence with the general population before one can determine what it means that a particular mitochondrial sequence matches his, and how much weight to give it in terms of making a positive identification.*

Thus, McNeal says, "In the overall scheme of a forensic analysis, DNA should be considered as one element - one compelling element, but nevertheless only one - in the forensic fabric. Before jumping on the DNA bandwagon, Dr. Shields pointed out that we should indeed review the very curious manner in which the samples of the 'Romanov' bones literally surfaced. The trust is, the entire circumstances surrounding the collection of the Romanov bones appear strange and their subsequent DNA analysis is open to further examination."

As we have briefly encountered earlier, the Romanov bones were first discovered by Geli Ryabov, a mystery writer and filmmaker and Alexander Avdonin, a geologist, in late May 1979. Ryabov and Avdonin, we are told, were accompanied on the initial find by their wives and a couple of friends, but curiously there was, or appears to have been, no film related to the event, even though one of the two mystery sleuths was a filmmaker by profession. Even more, troubling, as McNeal points out, the four intrepid and budding archeologists reportedly took three skulls out of the grave after examining the bones, then reburied them and conveniently announced their discovery some ten years later.

Ten years?

By the then, it was clear to those who eventually examined the discovery site that it had been thoroughly compromised. Moreover, surprisingly, bones were found at this site which was allegedly searched by investigators in 1918 and 1919, who found nothing of this magnitude in their own investigations.

As evidence of her incredulity, McNeal discusses the findings of John O'Conor, an attorney by profession who examined the Sokolov investigation in detail and published his own observations in a book, *The Sokolov Investigation*.

McNeal notes that it was O'Conor who was the first to raise the "incoherence and absurdity of many of Sokolov's conclusions, including the theory that the family's remains were burned." O'Conor, McNeal says, "suggested that the family, or at least the Tsarina and the daughters may have been secretly removed to Perm, not far from Ekaterinburg, before the night of 17 July 1918."

Years later, in 1970, McNeal points out that a New York reporter named Guy Richards followed up O'Conor's book with a book of his own entitled, *The Hunt for the Czar*, a book that for the first time mentioned the existence of an intriguing work published in July 1920, in San Francisco, entitled, *Rescuing the Czar*.

This later book, *Rescuing the Czar*, details a rescue of the Romanov family that McNeal says, interestingly, was withdrawn from circulation less than a year after its publication, "shortly after one of its translators had met the former head of the United States Secret Service." McNeal adds that Richard's book, "further shook the underpinnings of the traditional account that all seven members of the Imperial family had died in July 1918 and the foundation cracked again when Anthony Summers and Tom Mangold, two BBC journalists, published *The File on the Tsar* in 1976, arguing that the assertion by Sokolov and the Bolsheviks that the family had been burned was a fabrication."

Asserts McNeal:

> *At a minimum, they showed that Sokolov's and the Bolsheviks' characterisations of the events were fundamentally flawed. What seems more likely is that Sokolov had in fact been an unwitting participant in a closely held but elaborate cover-up.*
>
> *In 1989 the official story was questioned once again. Mark Crocker, who wrote a biography of Richard Meinertzhagen, a former British intelligence operative, cited an entry in Meinertzhagen's diary in the Rhodes House Library at Oxford University, alluding to the escape of a daughter of the Imperial family.*

In 1991, the Romanov gravesite is opened yet again for what appears to have been the last time. Dr. Maples of Florida is called in to assist the Russians because the Russians, at this time in history, do not have money to conduct the very expensive DNA analysis that would be required by a discovery of this magnitude. Maples concludes that Alexei and Anastasia are missing, however, and also finds an insufficient number of bone fragments to make up the eleven corpses that should be present in the mass grave.

Michael Occleshaw, a British writer then readying a book in 1993, *The Romanov Conspiracies*, argues at the time his belief that a daughter had survived the Yekaterinburg debacle and was under the watchful eye of the British until she died in 1926 at the alleged age of twenty-eight. McNeal notes this development, too, which means that if true, either Tatiana, who was born in 1898 or Maria, who was born in 1899 would have been the daughter in question.

Clearly, as McNeal says, there were another number of failures present on the evidence related to the discovery and identification of the Romanov bodies. For example:

- Radioactive isotopes, which are present in all people born after atomic testing began in the 1940s, was not conducted.

- Testing for the Hemophilia gene in the Tsarina and her daughters, which one would assume would exist given Alexei's condition, was not conducted either.

- The chain of custody for the Romanov bones, the burial site, and the DNA had obviously been interrupted.

- Nicholas was attacked at age 23 by a potential assassin in Japan and was severely wounded on his head by a sword that left a two-and-one-half-inch gash, as it has been described, yet the skull found in Yekaterinburg, experts have pointed out, do not show such injury and should, they argue.

"The discovery, transportation and storage of the remains have never been convincingly documented and recorded," argues McNeal. Dr. Shields, she points out, "feels that the lack of documentation raises speculations concerning the provenance of the bones."

McNeal continues on this point:

He [Dr. Shields] suggested that: 'It would be easy to get samples from bones of either Nicholas or Alexandra's maternal relatives and use them to salt the gravesite in Ekaterinburg'. Dr.

Shields raises the possibility that Prince Michael, the Tsar's younger brother, who was supposedly taken away and shot outside of Perm, not too far from Ekaterinburg and whose burial site is not known in the West and remains reportedly unknown in Russia, could have been used if someone had indeed known the location of his bones. Michael's bones could produce exactly the same result as the bones of Nicholas himself.

McNeal's position is that "an objective court of law would never have arrived at the same conclusion as that of the official Russian Governmental Commission. In all likelihood, McNeal argues, the case would have been thrown out prior to reaching the courts because of unreliable evidence.

Until, she says, an independent commission has reviewed the raw data, the DNA evidence cannot be considered historically conclusive.

By late 1917, McNeal writes that the situation "no longer seemed as simple as it had in late 1916 and early 1917 when it was believed that Russia, under the new leadership of the Provisional Government, was on its way to democracy and a full resumption of the war against Germany and Austria. It had originally been thought that the Tsar and Tsarina could, of thought prudent, perhaps be reintroduced as constitutional monarchs or, if not, it was envisaged that they could leave quietly for England."

McNeal's position on this potential is solid, as stipulated in the following passages from her book:

Nicholas had been a loyal ally to London in the war against Germany. Tsar and Tsarina were both first cousins of King George V. The King's mother, Queen Alexandra, was the sister of Nicholas' mother, the Dowager Empress Marie, making Queen Alexandra the Tsar's aunt. The King's father,

Edward VII, was the brother of the Tsarina's mother, Alice of Hesse, making Edward the Tsarina's uncle. Also, Edward VII's sister, Victoria, had married Frederick III of Prussia, making the Tsarina's mother Alice, aunt to their son, Kaiser Wilhelm. And finally the Tsar's mother, Marie, was sister to the Queen Mother Alexandra, the Kaiser's aunt. The inter-webbing of European and Russian royalty was extensive and such intimate interconnections were not ties that England or Germany wished to be scrutinized as their nations clashed.

Prime Minister David Lloyd George concerned about King George V providing safe haven to Wilhelm cousin, Nicholas. Lot of anti-monarchy feelings in Europe and Great Britain even in those years.

On 22 March 1917, the Imperial War Cabinet met to consider a request by Pail Milikuov, the Russian Provisional Government's first Foreign Minister, to Sir George Buchanan how the British would take the Tsar and his family out of Russia into exile Britain. Decision was taken to offer Tsar asylum in Britain after the war ended. Telegram sent to Provisional Government confirming. So much of concern, that George V changed the family last name from very German sounding Sace-Coburg-Gotha to very English Windsor.

Thus, in one of the main points to her intriguing research and argument that there was a secret plot to save the Tsar, McNeal writes:

Yet despite all the potential political fallout, a small but extraordinary group of politicians, invisible diplomats, intelligence operatives, an industrialist, and several members of British, European and Japanese royalty did, in fact, formulate plans for the safe removal of the Tsar and his family. These parties in interest helped to contribute to the confusion and obfuscation surrounding the Romanov's demise. Ultimately, these same parties were successful in planting their own versions of the events of the night of 17 July 1918 – in the shadow of the Great War while the world looked the other way.

McNeal notes that George V, at least three times, had extended his protection to sovereigns who were more distantly related to him than Nicholas and Alexandra. "For example, he agreed to a secret Allied plan to rescue the Romanian royal family when it was threatened with capture by the victorious Germans in the winter of 1917. The King's personal protection even extended to monarchs who had been his enemies during the war as was the case with Emperor Charles of Austria-Hungary. And, in 1918, he helped rescue the Dowager Empress Marie from Crimea. She believed then that Tsar was still alive and refused to go with first rescue group from the *HMS Tribune* on 21 November 1918.

Like Woodrow Wilson, King George V was not known for consulting his government before acting. He did so again, McNeal observes, when another first cousin, Prince Andrew of Greece needed rescuing from Greek Revolutionaries when David Lloyd George was Prime Minister, points out McNeal. McNeal says, there are other clues evident that George did take steps to rescue the family after their exile and even continued to do so once the Bolsheviks seized power.

Thus, for their individual reasons, various top-level members of the Allies were rapidly coming to the conclusion that the safety of the Imperial family had to be taken into their hands. Since the King of England and the German Kaiser were both involved in a war and closely related to the Russian Imperial family there was a need for secret action of they were not to be accused of putting family ties before loyalty to their countries.

In America, Crane had ties both to Russia and their family, and favoured their protection. Japan's Emperor had several compelling reasons, from political to personal, for protecting the Tsar. France's interests were pressing - their Russian loans were a significant part of their debt and over fifty per cent of French households at the time held Tsarist bonds. But for any of the Allies or Japan to offer support overtly would have been tantamount to committing political suicide. The propaganda that had been mounted so effectively against Nicholas and his family had made any public support of the Tsar all but impossible. The political situation required careful, calculated maneuvores if the Romanovs were to be snatched from the Siberian exile. And the only conceivable method of doing this would require the involvement of what the intelligence community regarded as the "hidden hands."

McNeal presents other compelling evidence in her book that "a few people at the highest levels of the Allied governments decided that the Tsar should be freed and that he and his family should take up residence in northern Russia to await the outcome of the war. Then the option would be available, at the appropriate time, to consider a reinstallation of the monarchy, perhaps in the form of a constitutional monarchy, with, if acceptable, Nicholas as its head."

This argument by McNeal as she offers it, "is further supported by a piece of correspondence forwarded later, in December 1918, by Charles Crane's friend and another of Crane's nominees, American Ambassador to China, Paul Reinsch, to the State Department. Reinsch was responding to a request that had apparently been sent by the State Department regarding the political atmosphere and the possibility of a restoration of the monarchy in parts of Russia:

> *Report on monarchical reaction in Transbaikal, Siberia and Ural district. Resume of reports upon this subject from all consular officers under my direction ...Ekaterinburg district. 80% of the inhabitants would not oppose monarchy ...Dheliabins district. General consensus of opinion there is a strong reaction in favour of monarchy, especially among peasants who are tired of disorder .... and goes on, "Liberal leaders who were keen on revolution two years ago are no longer enthusiastic in that direction and in contact with Bolsheviks is making them behave like persons awakening from a nightmare.*

Even our erstwhile Consul General Harris, whom Martin Hutson had attempted to contact again in the early 1930s through the State Department after sitting with him on Special Evacuation Train #28 in Harbin, makes an appearance in McNeal's research as well:

> *Ernest Harris, who had been the American consul in Irkutsk in Siberia, conducted this remarkable assessment for Reinsch. Harris concluded by saying that it could be six months to two years before a monarchy of some description could take hold in Russia but he was unwilling to speculate on how long one would last. One of the more noticeable aspects of this report is that it was filed from Omsk, where Harris was in the company of Supreme Ruler Admiral Alexander Kolchak, the man under whom the Romanov investigation had just fallen.*

"Days after this interesting communication," writes McNeal, "another series of intriguing telegrams mentioning, 'Urgent ... verify family seven times' had been forwarded from America to London and Paris on 29 and 30 December." McNeal says there are even more curious because President and Mrs. Wilson having dinner with King George and Queen Mary at very same time.

Archives of the Hudson Bay Company in Winnipeg, Canada, show conclusive evidence, McNeal says, that a "residence was being built for Tsar and that the Allies were planning a rescue attempt." According to McNeal, the Hudson Bay Company, it appears, was the purchasing agent for Russia, France and Romania and was assembling the residence in Arckangelsk but planned it to be constructed and erected in Murmansk by end of November 1917 as safe house for Tsar and family. The house, McNeal finds during her research, was paid for by the British Admirality. To support her observation, McNeal points to an October 1918 telegram relayed from the British Admirality in Arckangelsk saying the following:

> *Following received from Mr. Browd on behalf of the Murmansk Scientific Industrial Society the offer of a building to be erected on the Dvid Company's land near the British Consulate Murmansk formerly intended for the late Tsar and now offered for occupation by General Poole or Admiral Kemp. Buildings complete with heating light utensils etc. and now in charge of Kambolin Engineer erecting them …*

McNeal says that the knowledge of the activities in Russia to save the Tsar was confined to a tight group of men. "The plan," McNeal says, "for indirect, covert financing of anti-Bolshevik armies in southern Russia was very sensitive, since it was essentially illegal and would be a political disaster if it became know that Wilson and Lansing left some of their closest aides at the State Department out of the loop."

"On 21 December [1917]," McNeal writes, that "a telegram was received from Colonel House confirming Wilson's willingness to have the money transferred via France and England." McNeal says that as David Fogelsong points out in his, *America's Secret War Against Bolshevism,* "the reason Wilson structured the United States support as he did was to pass 'money through America's allies to get around legislative restrictions on presidential authority.'"

McNeal continues:

> *Soon afterwards, Lord Cecil, accompanied by Lord Alfred Milner, another member of the Russia Committee, went to the Quai d'Orsay in Paris, where they decided that the French would finance the Ukraine and the British would find money for the other regions, with the understanding that the United States would provide additional financial assistance. The French government had authorized a 100-million-franc endowment to General Alexeev to lead the effort against the Bolsheviks. Shortly thereafter American Consul DeWitt Poole travelled to Rostov under the guise of assessing the 'commercial situation', while his real objective was to meet Kaledin and assess the military situation. He likewise felt the US should support the Kaledin contingent. Kiev and Rostov were centres of activity Crane, Mesaryk and DeWitt Poole had all visited.*
>
> *Dark clouds continued to gather on the horizon. Phillips, Crosby, Page and House, who had all initially opposed the financing of the two-track policy, now appeared to support it. Phillips noted on the day after Christmas [1917]: Our policy in Russia seems at last to be clearly defined. We have secretly telegraphed Crosby to inform the British and French governments that this Government is willing to*

> *advance sufficient credit to those governments so that they may send whatever cash may seem necessary to the leaders in Southern Russia opposing the Bolshevik regime. It is not considered wise for all the Allied governments to step into the boat at once and the United States is keeping completely in the background so that should the southern Russia developments fail, one of the Allies at least would not be in bad.*
>
> *Obviously, there was some fear that all would not go well, and it appears that the United States would have the high moral ground in the event of any disastrous outcome. When the pieces all came together in the summer of 1918, it was apparent that this is in fact what happened. For historically, the United States escaped the harsh criticism that both the French and the English received for the fiasco.*
>
> *The man who tipped the scale and won the battle in favour of supporting Kaledin and the other White Russian leaders was Charles Crane, friend of the nobility and Provisional Government leaders, who had influenced Wilson during their December [1917] meetings. Again, Foglesong sums up the United States posture: 'Hence, the United States planned to "maintain a neutral and expectant attitude" in public while privately working with the British and French along a different line.'*

The McNeal string of evidence takes on an even more intriguing aspect when she further notes that the Second Secretary to the Russian Ambassador and son-in-law of none other than William G. McAdoo, President Wilson's son-in-law, was Boris Bakmetieff. Bakmetieff, McNeal notes, would have been the ideal candidate to handle covert financial transactions with Lenin.

McNeal contends that the Allies had a secret banking scheme that among other things paid Lenin to release the Romanovs and alleges that at least one attempt to do so did occur prior to July 17, 1918.

"Lenin's strategy," McNeal says, "seems to have been to persuade the Germans not to occupy the Soviet heartland and to relax the burden of the 300 million gold rouble indemnity imposed by the Treaty of Brest-Litovsk the previous March." In return for Lenin delivering the Romanovs into their hands McNeal says, "he was at the same time leading the Allies to think he was also co-operating with them following the £500,000 paid to him the previous February, ostensibly to buy out pro-German stockholders in banks he already nationalised." McNeal notes that Leon Trotsky wanted Nicholas Romanov returned to Moscow for a "show trial." There were, McNeal noted, deep divisions in the Communist Central Committee in Yekaterinburg over just what would the fate be of the Romanov family. In either case, McNeal makes the argument, in essence, and we agree, it was not likely that the Committee would have acted on the Romanov's fate without Vladimir Lenin's prior knowledge, least they pay a price with their own lives.

The first attempt to rescue the Tsar, according to McNeal, was in Tobolsk, "through the Brotherhood of St. John of Tobolsk," she says. The Brotherhood's symbol was a reverse swastika, a good luck symbol with origins in Tibet that McNeal notes was also found by White Russian investigators in the Ipatiev House after the presumed deaths of the Romanovs. The plan, McNeal says, was to grab the former Tsar and spirit him away from his captors in a fast motorboat through the Kara Sea. This plan, she says, called for, "a British boat to berth nearby and take the family downriver in one of his cargo boats.

Other intrigue was afoot, too, McNeal writes. For example, "A telegram, sent from Washington by the Third Under-Secretary of State, Breckingridge Long, to a close associate of President Wilson's, Gavin McNab, in San Francisco, queried the readiness of Californian Jerome Baker Landfield to serve in the State Department." Landfield had a particular expertise in things Russian according to Long, who Colonel House said, "ran his own State Department and was known only by Wilson himself." Franklin Delano Roosevelt would use him later in World War II to evacuate important refugees according to his memoir, McNeal says.

Long, McNeal also says, "was a known courier between Colonel House, Sir William Wiseman, head of British Intelligence in North America, and the British Foreign Secretary, Arthur Balfour, for Wilson in 1918. "Long's relationship with Balfour had become so close that Balfour generally resided in the Under-Secretary's home while he was visiting the United States. From Long's correspondence, it is evident that he enjoyed the deepest confidence on matters of great magnitude from Wilson, House and Balfour."

According to McNeal, Karl Radek, an Austrian citizen traveling with Lenin and member of the Foreign Office alerts the Yekaterinburg Central Committee to another possible rescue attempt involving the U.S. Transport *Thomas,* who had previously taken AEF Commander Major General Graves to Siberia, saying that the ship was scheduled to arrive in mid-July in Vladivostok with 14,000 rifles aboard for the Russian Whites and, "as well, doubtless as embarking the Romanov family ..."

The most stunning news in this account is the fact that it appears to have hardly been a state secret as to what the United States government and military was planning to do. Was there a mole in the US operation? Or, was the United States just that bad at keeping secrets secret? In either case, McNeal notes mention that there existed a US-Allied/Czechoslovakian plot to save the Tsar with the US Transport *Thomas* involved. The supposed route would take the *Thomas* from San Francisco to Vladivostok in Siberia to Nagaski, Japan on to Manila in the Philippines, then to Honolulu, Hawaii through Guam Island, ending in San Francisco. Remember here again that Martin attests in his statement that a Czech officer was aboard Evacuation Train #28 as well.

"And in the United States," McNeal writes," Masaryk was preparing to speak officially to President Wilson, in a meeting that was being arranged by Charles Crane - for public consumption. This confluence of events suggests that the Czechs, under the guidance of Thomas Masaryk, certainly appear to have been more closely involved with the attempted overthrow of the Bolsheviks and the extraction of the family than conventional history would have us believe."

Says, McNeal, "The new evidence suggests that there was in actuality a strategy to have the Czechs, Savinkov's forces and Alexeev from the south, the Japanese from the east, as well as the British, who had entered northern Russia under the command of General Poole, all converge in an effort to overthrow the Bolsheviks in the spring and summer of 1918. The code names for the British operations were 'Syren' and 'Elope.'" McNeal asks, "with whom did the British think they would be eloping? The Imperial Family remains the only likely candidate and all the new evidence unequivocally points to that conclusion."

"The evidence we have seen thus far," McNeal says, "suggests that British, American, Czech and French secret agents worked in unison to overthrow the Bolsheviks as well as rescue the family. To do so would require both the military and the diplomatic branches of the various governments to act in concert."

As McNeal and others will no doubt tell you, current history wants you to believe that with the Czechs approaching Yekaterinburg, the Bolsheviks panicked and killed the Tsar and his family without knowledge of Lenin and others in Moscow. But, as we all agree, "the intense activities that occurred in Russia, England, America and Japan in May 1918 were not coincidental - these were desperate times and the dangerous environment in which the Romanovs were confined was growing more threatening by the day. McNeal observes that Prince Arthur's visit to the United States and Japan at the behest of King George V becomes more understandable when we accept that the political situation was spiraling out of control. Talks of an escape plan which would remove the family to Northern Russia were taking shape," McNeal says.

Another rescue mission profiled by McNeal operated out of Murmansk "under the guise" of "a commercial trade mission." According to McNeal, Henry Armitstead, Leslie Urquhart and Sir Francis Lindley participated in June 1918 plan which was delayed because the Tsarevich Alexei became ill, unseasonable cold weather in northern Russia had set in, and other events McNeal says were beyond their control. Admiral Hall, known as "Bubbles," Director of Naval Intelligence, McNeal notes, was also involved in efforts to save the Romanov family through the use of his naval operations staff and one of the Grand Dukes. Communicating through letters in French with the Tsar who had been warned that a rescue mission was in the works, Tsar Nicholas II was so aware of the rescue attempt that he even reportedly worried about what containers would be included with valuables.

This information will be important in understanding events presented later in this chapter pertaining to an alleged evacuation route through Tibet. Nonetheless, we know from history and McNeal's accounts that numerous counter revolutionary revolts were being putting down in and around Yekaterinburg as late as the 25th of June 1918.

Yet more intrigue from McNeal's account:

> *On 28 May 1918, just one month before the second Murmansk rescue attempt, the Director of Military Intelligence wired Brigadier-General Poole in Murmansk regarding Reilly, who had already been in Russia for at least two months posing as a Bolshevik: 'The following two officers are engaged on special secret service and should not be mentioned in official correspondence or to other officers unless absolutely unavoidable, Lieutenants Mitchelson and Reilly.'*
>
> *In Moscow, just two weeks after the family vanished, it was revealed that Robert Bruce Lockhart of England, Consul General Grenard of France and Consul General DeWitt Poole of America, as well as the American secret agent Xenophon Kalamatiano, had all been involved in a plan to overthrow the Bolsheviks.*

Reilly allegedly, according to McNeal, arranged for a large sum of money to be paid to Russian Orthodox Church, supposedly because they represented "a rampart" against Bolshevikism. Would this payment, in some way relate decades later to the Church's refusal to recognize the Romanov bones as being Romanov by name when buried 80 years later? Did the church know something that history did not yet want to acknowledge?

Whatever the fate of the Romanovs, McNeal wryly says, "it is safe to assume that the Church would have made it best efforts to assist the former head of the Church, as in the eyes of the Church the Tsar was God's representative on earth." McNeals points out that in Tobolsk, for example, the Church had been involved in passing messages to the family, "and now the actions of Reilly, who ostensibly was taking money to the Church for propaganda purposes, might have been actions that were instead involved in taking money to the Church to assist in hiding the family for a time before they were to be moved or restored."

What is surprising to the research by McNeal and others like us is that there is very little first-hand accounts, especially in testimonial writing, as to what happened. Even though there was a small number of folks involved in at least the planning of the Tsar's rescue (whether it really succeeded or not), enough people and "loose lips" existed that one would believe there would be more accounts of the Tsar's true story.

To this point, McNeal says, "The collection of Anthony Summers contains an interview with the daughter of British Major William Peer Groves in which she maintains her father told her that the family had escaped from the cellar with the aid of British Secret Agents and loyal guards and had been taken to Japan and Canada." McNeal says that this account, "is very nearly the scenario outlined in *Rescuing the Csar*. It is also very similar to the version of events that Martin Hutson recounts.

McNeal says that in 1919, "Peer Groves was assigned to British intelligence in Odessa at the same time that Reilly and another intelligence officer, Captain George Hill, were posted there. His duty was to escort member of royalty out of Russia." McNeal says that Peer Groves "is said to have been the person who took a token from the Tsar to the Empress Dowager in April 1919 to confirm to her that the Tsar and his family and her youngest son was still alive.

McNeal contends research shows that, reports that Nicholas had been killed began circulating in June 1918 a month before he was supposedly murdered. Lenin, she says, clearly took steps to ensure that nothing of the sort had happened to the former Tsar. In fact, McNeal says that it has "often been claimed that the rumours of Nicholas's death were a Communist plot to test public reaction to his demise in order to assess the danger that might arise when their alleged plan to murder the Romanovs became known. It is an argument that does not stand examination and makes convincing arguments as to why," McNeal concludes.

Interestingly, McNeal details three witnesses who saw and reported to White Russian investigators direct telegraph exchanges between Lenin and Berzin in Ekaterinburg in which Lenin ordered Berzin "'to take under his protection the entire Imperial family and not to allow any violence towards them whatsoever. McNeal says the testimony was that if there was any such violence, Berzin would answer to Lenin for it with his own life.'"

McNeal concludes that Lenin, "clearly places great importance on protecting the lives of the former Tsar and his family, "which as McNeal points out, "attests to the critical nature of them as negotiation devices with the Allies, and one would suspect, the Germans." Lenin, she notes, replaced the original Yekaterinburg guard under the brutal Avdeyev on 4 July 1918 with "Yakov Yurovsky, a medic with photographic training." Yurovsky's new detachment of guards is described by McNeal and witnesses she cites as "hand-picked me who were utterly loyal and disciplined." McNeal says that the record on Avdeyev "mark him as the ideal man to humiliate and slaughter the family, if that was what Moscow wanted." The family disappears very shortly thereafter, McNeal says, and "former Russian monarchists would tell one of Germany's top diplomats that rumors of the death of the Tsar would be circulated between 16th July and 20th July and the news should not alarm the Germans. It would be false information. But, 'it would be necessary for certain reasons, namely the tsar's rescue.'"

At the time, McNeal finds that Henry Palmer, the American consul in Yekaterinburg was negotiating with the Boslsheviks and was in close communication with Sir Thomas Preston, the British consul in Yekaterinburg. Sir Thomas, McNeal says, telegraphs the American consulate in Moscow that "'gold' and platinum' being removed." McNeal thinks they might have been code words for Tsar and Tsarina. "What is significant about Consul Preston's telegram," McNeal says, is that it suggests the Allies could now have been trying to bid against the Germans for the Imperial family."

Another interesting passage by McNeal: on the 7th of July: "'If Matveyev's train not yet dispatched, detain it, if dispatched take all measures to detain it en route so that it will not in any case reach place indicated by us. In event risk at new place of holding, return train to Perm. Await coded telegram.'" McNeals says that Matveyev had been an Ensign in the Tsar's Lifeguards at Tsarskoye Selo and was now head of the 'Special Purpose Detachment' after Yakovlev had left. Moreover, McNeal notes that he had accompanied Yakovlev, which links him to the possible attempt to remove the Romanovs to the safety of 'Moscow or wherever.' McNeal further notes that after his service with Yakovlev he was based at Perm and was in charge of a train that appears to have been destined to take the family to safety – of it could be arranged."

At about the same time, McNeal says that "In America the diary of Will Starling, a United States Secret Service agent, assigned to the White House, who had become a friend of Charles Crane as well as President Wilson, recorded that on the night of 25 July the President cancelled a trip due to the 'Russian situation.' This was an unprecedented step by Wilson. Even with battles raging on the Marne, he had always continued to meet his scheduled commitments. What other news could there have been from Russia to cause the President to take a step that he had never took at any other time?"

Rescuing the Czar, McNeal says, "does allude to the fact that family was taken out of the Ipatiev House through a cistern, by an English intelligence agent, after an independent agreement had been reached between King George V and Kaiser Wilhelm." Martin attests to this scenario as well based on the conversations Martin says he had with Nicholas on the train from Irkutsk to Harbin.

The agent, says McNeal, is "Charles James Fox," who according to McNeal, "purportedly committed to his diary that he and the family remained inside a tunnel leading from the Ipatiev House to the nearby British consulate for a number of days before surfacing in the consulate. He maintained that he had infiltrated the guard when the new guard had been installed and had been aided in doing so by Bolshevik officials."

Asks, McNeal: "Was Wilson on 25 July anxiously awaiting confirmation of a successful mission that had begun on the night of 17 July - a confirmation that must be for his eyes only? And where the Romanovs finally in the hands of the Allies, where they would begin a journey to another life? Or is the traditional story of their death by a firing squad, comprised of eleven men on the night of 17 July, the answer to one of the great mysteries of the twentieth century?"

So this begs the question: were King George V and Kaiser Wilhelm II as callous as they were both made out to be regarding their first cousins the Tsar and Tsarina of Russia? It appears that McNeal makes the case they were not the callous, uncaring, ambivalent relatives that have been accused by historians for being when it came to the Tsar's request for asylum. Findings is McNeal's book demonstrate, as she says, that, "on the contrary, there was a small, multinational cadre of powerful politicians, diplomats, intelligence operatives, religious leaders and several members of European royalty who worked at the highest level to attempt the safe removal of the Imperial family."

This is a position that Martin supported.

McNeal provides an excellent detailed analysis that indicates the existence of "a two-track policy in 1918 Russia: publicly deal with the Russian banking system through the British and French to support White Russian military activities in southern Russia; and, privately overthrow the Bolsheviks by the Whites and the Czechs in the summer of 1918, and rescue the Romanovs."

"The hidden agenda to save the Romanovs," points out McNeal, "was extremely complicated and faced numerous obstacles. However, its ultimate success may have been announced by the anomalous telegrams issued by the United States State Department and forwarded to London and Paris at the very time President Wilson and King George were meeting. On 30 December 1918, just five months after the family had vanished, a coded telegram containing the words 'Urgent ... verify ... family seven times' was issued from the American embassy in London in response to a telegram received the preceding day from the United States Department of State, which had used, in code, the term 'family' also seven times."

The Romanov's initial death, McNeal notes, was announced on the 18th of July by Yakov Sverdlov, Chairman of the All-Russian Central Executive Committee of the Soviets. Sverdlov said that the execution was carried out on the 16th of July. The announcement also said that the Tsar's wife and son were not killed and were sent to a safe place.

Later, on October 5th, Sir Charles Eliot, the British High Commissioner in Siberia, sends his report from Yekaterinburg to Arthur Balfour, the British Foreign Secretary, reporting that: On July 17 a train with the blinds down left Ekaterinburg for an unknown destination and it is believed that the surviving members of the Imperial Family were in it." Thought to have gone North or West.

In an irony that could only have happened to the Romanovs, McNeal remembers that, "Several hundred years earlier, Ivan Sussanin had saved Nicholas's ancestor (the first Romanov) from the Poles by hiding him in the Ipatievsky Monastery in Kostroma and pronouncing him dead, only to have him reappear when the threats to his life had abated." Other descendants of Sussanin, McNeal said, "had not only kept Alexander II from assassination but also attended Nicholas's and Alexandra's wedding. Parfen Dominin who insisted to investigators later that the Tsar lived, was rumored to have been a Sussanin descendant."

By the 25th of July 1918, Yekaterinburg falls to the White Russian and Czech forces. According to McNeal, one of the senior guards at the Ipatiev House, Ivan Starkov, reports to White Russian investigators, "that the Imperial family has been taken away and not shot in the basement." Another guard, McNeal says, Alexander Varakushev, "claims the Tsar and his wife and family were still alive."

Summers and Mangold, according to McNeal, reported these accounts as well in their documentary. The story of the Tsar's death, McNeal also says in chapter 11 of her book, was being distributed by State Department intelligence operative Carl Ackerman, a reporter for *The New York Times* and *Saturday Evening Pos*t. Ackerman, according to McNeal, told the story of Parfen Domnin, the Tsar's personal servant, which nobody can figure out how he got from Slaughter. He reported:

> *The Bolsheviks needed the family to die since the feeling among the majority of their rank and file was that if the Tsar were alive he would represent a rallying point for all*

monarchists and that would further hinder he takeover of Russia by the Communist party. If the Whites and Allies could prove the family died it would help in demonstrating the true violent and bloodthirsty character of the Bolsheviks – that would soon be exposed in any case by the Red Terror.

McNeal's book is also very interesting and enlightening because of the various other players who were reported by McNeal to be hidden hands – or better said, Allied spies. They include:

- The Czechoslovakia General was Gaida who told Commandant Joseph Lasies, a former member of the French National Assembly and French Military Mission stationed in Ekaterinburg, on train journey from Glazov to Perm, that "the Imperial family had not been murdered." In his book, *La Trage'die Sibe'rienne,* Lasies puts forth a convincing case that no murders occurred in Ekaterinburg. Lasies also says he met a Japanese officer who felt he knew the real story about Ekaterinburg.

- Charles Crane, an American a multimillionaire industrialist who owned Crane Plumbing in Chicago and was found by McNeal to be an expert on Russian policy who was also known to be advising President Wilson. So much so, Crane, McNeal notes, funded a Russian studies department at the University of Chicago, and it was he who were have seen earlier, helped engineer President Wilson's re-election in 1916. McNeal reports that Crane is also said to be close to the inner circle of Tsar Nicholas II and Tsarina Alexandra's court. Crane reportedly persuaded Westinghouse Corporation to donate considerable funds to the Tsarina's hospital for the sick and wounded. McNeal finds that Crane attended meetings with Prince George Lvov in Kiev, the first leader of the Provisional Government, and one, she says, who would ask England to grant the Romanovs asylum. Crane was found by McNeal research to have been in Russia in 1917. McNeal says Crane, like Wilson, was known to subscribe to the concept of self-determination for nations and is described by the president of Czechoslovakia as being a "Wilson fixer".

- Canadian Colonel Joseph Boyle rescued the Romanian royal family for King George V in an account shared by McNeal and was reportedly sent to rescue Dowager Empress in Crimea. The Dowager Empress, McNeal says, left in 1919 aboard the *HMS Marlborough* to Malta, a British base. "The Marchioness of Milford Haven, one of the Tsarina's sisters," says McNeal, "wrote that the Dowager Empress had told her that the family was hidden in the far north of Russia, which could only be reached in summer." Could Boyle have been the Canadian Colonel aboard Martin's Evacuation Train #28?

- Boris Savinkov is a Kerensky aide McNeals says figured in to attempts to save the Imperial family.

- Richard Crane is the son of Charles Crane and was Secretary to U.S. Secretary of State Lansing.

- Thomas Masaryk is the eventual president of Czechoslovakia and is married to Crane's daughter. He was a close friend of Charles Crane who visited Kiev in the summer of 1917 and is credited by McNeal and others for successfully negotiating the release of Czech prisoners with White Russian General Alexis Kaledin.

- William G. McAdoo, Wilson's son-in-law who is former head of the United States Secret Service and now head of the American Red Cross in Siberia makes an appearance in McNeal's accounts, too. His daughter is also said to be conveniently married to the Second Secretary to the Ambassador of the Russian Provisional Government.

- Colonel House. Wilson's de-facto Secretary of State, makes an appearance in McNeal's account as well.

- William Wiseman, is close to Colonel House and is head of British Intelligence in the United States.

- British Intelligence Agent Sidney Reilly, is known as the "Ace of Spies." He is, according to McNeal the agent of record for a shipment of 1.2 million rifles for the Russian government to be manufactured by the Remington Arms Company. Sir Winston Churchill's secretary later confirms this in a book and says that Reilly is a right-hand man, according to McNeal.

- The Hudson Bay Company is documented by McNeal as constructing a safe house in late 1917 for the Tsar and his family. Henry Armitstead was in charge of assembling the house in Murmansk, according to McNeal.

- General Frederick Poole was the British commander in Northern Russia.

- Sir Francis Lindley was the British Charge d'Affaires.

- Raymond Robins of the American Red Cross is documented in McNeal's research demonstrating that he, too, was a spy working for the American Red Cross at the same time.

- Breckingridge Long, Third Under-Secretary of State, who essentially ran Woodrow Wilson's State Department.

- Gavin McNab of San Francisco, appears too in McNeal's account, as being the close associate of President Wilson we know who ran the Western U.S. campaign for Wilson's re-election in 1916. McNab was a National Committeeman for Democrats and is credited by McNeal for escorting Romania's Prince through San Francisco in 1919 after his rescue by Joseph Boyle. In a familiar sounding pattern, McNab had hosted Prince Arthur as his guest in San Francisco while on his way to Japan with a special message for the Emperor from King George V.

- William Rutlidge McGarry is reported by McNeal to have believed to his dying day that the Romanovs were rescued as alleged. McNeal reports that he two letters called the "My Dear Fox" letters supposedly written to the mysterious James Charles Fox thanking him for his participation in the release of the Romanov family and further maintaining their "state secret." McNeal says that copies of these letters currently reside with Barbara Finlayson, McGarry's granddaughter.

- Jerome Barker Landfield, the Russia expert, who graduated from Cornell University a university St. Petersburg, Russia, knew Siberia very well; was fluent in Russian; and knew Professor Ipatiev, whom the Ipatiev house was owned by before its destruction by Russia in the late 1970s. He was reportedly married to Princess Louba Lobanoff-Rostovsky, a lady-in-waiting to the Tsarina, according to McNeal. Landfield was linked by marriage to the courts of the Tsar and King George V, McNeal says.

- Prince Arthur of Connaught was a close confidant to King George V and was also the King's cousin and a grandson himself of Queen Victoria. McNeal notes that he was therefore first cousin to the Tsarina as well. According to McNeal, Prince Arthur works closely with Landfield and was a trusted emissary to Wilson via the King. McNeal believes he was the conduit between King George V, President Wilson and the Emperor of Japan on how best to rescue the family through reported trips to New York and Tokyo McNeal documents.

- Ralph H. Van Deman is reported by McNeal to be in the area around the time of the Tsar's assassination and the Czech uprisings; was often called the "Father of US Intelligence"; and writes in his book, *Memoirs, The Final Memoranda,* edited by Ralph E. Weber, about a "special mission," McNeal says.

- Charles James Fox is the British secret agent who McNeal says is reported to have rescued the Tsar and his family through a cistern at the Ipatiev House after pretending to be a Bolshevik guard.

- Captain Digby-Jones was an engineer with the British Royal Engineers who arrives from Arckangelsk on the 16th of July and stays at the British consulate across from the Ipatiev House around the time of Tsar's reported murder. He is said by NcNeal to have been considered to be with British intelligence.

- Captain Homer Slaughter of American Military Intelligence files a report McNeal says on the 17th of July events and is known to have been liaison to Czech forces. Graves it is believed by McNeal and documents to have been the officials who sent the "family seven times" dispatch at the time of King George's and President Wilson's meeting in London in 1918.

- Major Guinet of France was an intelligence officer McNeal found was operating around Ekaterinburg at the time of Tsar's disappearance.

- White Russian General Tcherep Spiridovitch is reported by McNeal to have contacted William McAddo about their "state secret".

Needless to say, there were a lot of hidden hands in McNeal's account of the secret plot to save the Tsar. And, in Martin's account, too. Each is fascinating in their own right and worthy of the plot unfolding here in Martin's story as well. In the meantime, McNeal's plot, and this version of the story, thickens:

> *In May 1919, Lasies encountered Robert Wilton, a correspondent for The Times, on a platform at the Ekaterinburg train station. Wilton, who was also on the payroll of the British Foreign Office, had developed what local British officials considered an overly intimate and compromising relationship with investigator Sokolov and various White Russian leaders. While on the platform, Lasies confronted Wilton and pressed him on how fire and acid could have destroyed the family. Wilton, becoming uncomfortable, said he would return in a few minutes and when he did return stated: Commandant Lasies, even if the tsar and the imperial family are alive, it is necessary to say that they are dead!*

McNeal also mentions in her account that the testimony of Yurovsky that 12 people were killed and not eleven says that all were buried together. Yet Alexei and Anastasia/or Maria (as Dr. Maples and the Russians dispute) could not have been buried in the same location, if we are to believe what the official account of the Romanov's fate currently tells us, as McNeal alludes to quite rightly. McNeal also points out that Yurovsky would have had to be awake 75 hours to do what he said he did in his personal account found in documents held by members of his family as late as 1989. Discrepancies between his note and a copy his son had, McNeal says, namely the burial site location are evident. McNeal notes that there are even two accounts of who executed the Romanovs: Yurovsky and Pyotr Ermakov, an Upper-Isetsk commissar who says he did it. McNeal notes that the author, Edvard Radzinsky in his accepted account of the Romanov mystery, says Ermakov was a drunk and to be discounted yet there is no evidence of this according to McNeal. McNeal makes the excellent point that this is not the type of night or event one forgets details of over time or not. McNeal argues there is no consistency in documents or testimony on the number of executioners present; how they fit in such a small room; and, how many actual victims there were and whether or not and how they were sitting or standing. McNeal even points to the fact that Jemmy, the Grand Duchess Tatiana's dog, was found at the bottom of the mine according to Sokolov but she can find no mention of the pet being in the murder room account.

"What seems apparent," McNeal writes, "is that for several years after the disappearance of the family neither the Bolsheviks, nor the Allies, or various White factions could furnish conclusive evidence that the Romanovs had been murdered or had survived. Yet it is evident that both the Bolsheviks and their adversaries wanted the world to accept the fact that the family had been murdered. War makes strange bedfellows indeed."

McNeal also observes in a final passage that will be very important to Martin's account that:

> *For the most part, Rescuing the Czar consists of two diaries of two men: one a British intelligence operative and the other a Russian nobleman posing as a Bolshevik. Its description of the last days of the family is remarkably different from any other published version that had been made available to the world prior to Rescuing the Czar's debut. It proposed quite a different outcome: the successful removal of the family from the Ipatiev House by the British intelligence agent Charles James Fox who 'claims to be an American' but says he was 'born in Paris.' Fox's diary, which comprises the first part of the book, also covers his infiltration of the Bolshevik guard in Ekaterinburg one week prior to the events of that July summer night in 1918. In Rescuing the Czar, Charles James Fox alleges that the family was extricated from an underground tunnel by the British and taken into the British*

consulate, where they were secretly removed and hidden in Russia before being taken to Turkistan. Then, due to troubles in India, which was their intended destination, they traveled through Tibet where, with the aid of lamas, the behest of the Dalai Lama, they were guided on to China. They are supposed to have ended their flight in Chungking. Charles James Fox states that upon arrival in Chungking he turned them over to the commander of a British gunboat where they embarked on a trip down the Yangtze River to Woosung, twelve miles from Shanghai. The diary alludes to ships dressed with holiday flags and infers it was the holiday season – December 1918. Curiously, this date corresponds to the December 1918 telegram referencing he 'family seven times.' Fox's final notes revel the interaction he had with the commander of the gunboat: With his code word still ringing in my ears to be repeated to one man at Berlin, to another man in England, another in Japan, and to a dignitary in Italy, the mission I have undertaken shall have been successfully discharged, so far as history and public policy is concerned…' Rescuing the Czar indicates that the Imperial family's ultimate destination was Ceylon, where they supposedly arrived on an unmanned man-of-war accompanied by a wealthy tea merchant." One of the translators of the book, McGarry worked for Sir William Wiseman, head of British Intelligence in New York.

Rescuing the Czar, as McNeal and others acknowledge, has been dismissed by many as a money-making opportunity from film and a disinformation plan. "Yet, as McNeal notes, "the newly discovered documents reveal that there were several complex operations mounted in 1918 to save the Romanovs and that perhaps one may have succeeded, at least in part."

As McNeal says, "If *Rescuing the Czar* has any validity it indicates that in the final hours once again different plots to rescue the family collided - one being engineered by the German General Staff and the other involving a lone British Secret Service agent, the man we know as 'Charles James Fox', who claims to have infiltrated the Ipatiev House guard."

On page 262 of her book, McNeal asks the following key question:

> *Why this effort if HMS Kent had already secretly made its way out of Russia, less than three weeks before, with eight tons of the family's belongings? Why would Kolchak seemingly not know that the shipment of the initial twenty-nine cased that were secretly in transit in March? Unless the family has been taken out by the Kent in January [1919] and therefore the Kent had returned to collect their personal belongings.*

McNeal says that, "One man who may have known the whole story relative to the Imperial family was Breckinridge Long. At the bottom left of the 'Family' telegram of 30 December are Long's initials." McNeal continues, "We have seen how involved he was in the attempt to save the family from the very beginning; he ran his own secret service, 'known only to the president'; he recruited Jerome Barker Landfield; he was responsible for looking after British Foreign Secretary Balfour as well as Prince Arthur of Connaught and for the secrecy surrounding his presence in the United States; he was in constant contact with Sir William Wiseman of British intelligence; he dealt with the political aspects of the negotiations over the loans to China and the Chinese Eastern Railway; he reported directly to the President and was the President's right-hand man when anything sensitive needed to be handled. Even when he was brought back by President Franklin Roosevelt during the Second World War, he was again made responsible for 'the safety of influential refugees.' That this telegram should have been passed to him therefore comes as no surprise. Could Long, having been involved from the outset, be the man further to confirm that the rescue mission was a success? He may have done this on 17 and 18 January 1919," McNeal concludes.

"On the evening of the 17th," McNeal says, "Long met Mr. Debuabi, a representative of the Japanese embassy. Debuabi followed up the next day with a hand-delivered letter to Long confirming that the 'seven points' enumerated in the memorandum handed by the American ambassador to Tokyo to Viscount Uchida on 9 January 'are well understood by the latter.' The letter dated 18 January 1919, bore the letterhead of the Imperial Japanese embassy in Washington. In Long's handwriting he noted, 'Handed me by Mr. Debuabi of the Jap. Embassy. BL'. Yet it was not stamped in until 13 February 1919. And it was finally filed on 13 April 1921. Why was it filed two years and two months later? The significance of the letter may have been lost on his successor, as Long had resigned by then. The letter is supposed to have referred to the plan for supervision of the Chinese Eastern Railroad and the Trans-Siberian Railway. Breckingridge Long was shepherding the negotiations of the Chinese Eastern Railway in 1918 and 1919, thereby making its correspondence the perfect vehicle for messages regarding the seven members of the Romanov family. So the family' telegram may have informed Breckinridge Long that the completed rescue had occurred as planned and that the family were in the hands of the Japanese.

On the 6th of December [1918], another report that should be considered legitimate once again mirrored events in *Rescuing the Czar*, according to McNeal. The report, McNeal says, "emanated from Charles Crane's friend Nelson Page, was the American ambassador in Rome. Page wired the State

Department: For your confidential information. I learned that in the highest quarters here it is believed that the Czar and his family are all alive."

So, McNeal's questions, reasonably multiply as have ours queries:

> *Did the family really make it to Woosung as related in Rescuing the Czar? And did they sail away to a reasonably secure environment and new home in Ceylon, after the gunboat brought them to safety as Rescuing the Czar asserts? Was that the reason HMS Kent was called out of the Indian Ocean, during the war, merely to run sea trials just outside Hong Kong until it received the order to proceed to Woosung for only one day, then slip up the coast to Japan? Perhaps we have not totally come full circle. Does the evidence indicate that the allegorical account told in Rescuing the Czar demonstrates that the Imperial family could have been brought to safety out of Russia by a small international team? There is certainly intriguing evidence to support it. Even if Rescuing the Czar does not hold all the answers, it does stand as a roadblock to complete acceptance of the traditional view of the night of 17 July 1918. If nothing else, Rescuing the Czar may be the Rosetta Stone that has given us a glimpse into the world of intelligence activity and secret diplomacy that sometimes shapes the destinies of nations. In this case, the impact on Russia of this activity remains unclear. Still it is interesting to note that three men, who decades later would be the leaders of their countries, played significant roles in their respective governments in 1918 – Churchill, Director of Munitions; Stalin, one of Lenin's most able administrators; and Franklin Delano Roosevelt as Under-Secretary of Navy for the United States – and each was connected to events in Russia during this time-frame.*

McNeal's remarkably well-researched book was a tremendous contributor to the world's knowledge of the Romanov mystery, thus our need to extensively recount here what we have learned from her research since it is among the latest available to examine. To appropriately honor her work, we finish presenting McNeal's findings as context for Martin's story with this concluding passage:

> *What seems feasible is that the Allies did indeed work diligently to construct a method of finding anti-Bolshevik activities through the secret banking scheme established under Major Terence Keyes in Siberia, with the objective of overthrowing the Bolsheviks and potentially re-establishing a constitutional monarchy. Moreover the very men who were central to these efforts – Karol Yaroshinsky, Boris Soloviev and Sidney Reilly were all connected, at a time when Yaroshinsky was the financial benefactor to the family during the last days of their captivity in Tobolsk and Ekaterinburg. These men were also involved with Henry Armitstead and Jonas Lied, who had been paid through the British Secret Service for activities in Northern Russia that included building a house that appears to have been for the Tsar, which was stocked with supplied in increments of seven. This trail also led to the failed April and June attempts to gain the freedom of the family after what seems to have been a ransom paid to Lenin for their release. At the same time the Germans also appear to have engaged in their own bidding war for the Romanov family. Further, the story told by Parfen Domnin document regarding the planned overthrows and the Czech Legion's attempt to advance on Ekaterinburg also has more than a ring of truth.*
>
> *But did the family survive? Did one of the factions succeed in taking control of the family and were they taken to Lysva as the symbols found on the wall, in addition to the*

symbol of the Brotherhood of St John of Tobolsk (see plate section) would indicate? Did they subsequently meet their fate in the Perm/Lysva area, where in 1919 some obscure Bolsheviks were accused of the murder of the Imperial family and were summarily executed? We know practically nothing about this episode and therefore cannot adequately weigh it, as the event quickly and with little investigation disappeared from the pages of history.

Or did the family actually disappear by being evacuated through the tunnel and escape for a time via the route in Rescuing the Czar?

What can categorically be stated to have come from this research has been the deconstruction of the notion that King George V and his close allies did nothing to try to save the Tsar and his family. It is also now certain that they made attempts, albeit unsuccessful ones, to overthrow the Bolsheviks and give Russia the breathing space it deserved to determine whether it wanted a return to Tsardom in the form of a constitutional monarchy.

Two stories. From an outsider perspective that have successfully generated many whispers related to the Romanov mystery, as we know it, asking in essence, what if?

Recommended reading:

- Michael Gray, *Blood Relative: The Astonishing Story of the Survival of the Tsarevich*, Victor Gollancz, London, England, 1998, ISBN: 0-575-06608-3.

- Shay McNeal, *The Secret Plot to Save the Tsar: The Truth Behind the Romanov Mystery*, William Morrow, New York, NY, 2001, ISBN: 0-688-16998-8.

4 | Theories & Thistles

If Nicholas Romanov lived, as Martin Hutson insists, despite DNA evidence to the contrary, then where did he go after escaping Siberia?

- *Rescuing Nicholas*

The single, greatest impediment to proving Martin's story true is the declaration by British forensic experts that there is a 98.5% probability that the remains found in the Koptyaki forest meadow in 1991 were in fact those of the Imperial family.

Even more vexing is this question: If Nicholas Romanov lived, as Martin Hutson insists, despite DNA evidence to the contrary, then where did he go after escaping Siberia?

For another perspective on the Romanov mystery, consider now the perspective of another key insider: American Consul General for Siberia, Ernest Harris.

Harris' Ashes

So, what now of Martin's testimony that the Louisville *Courier-Journal* published an article in 1932 alleging that the American Consul-General in Siberia, Ernest Lloyd Harris, confirmed that the Tsar was aboard his "special" train?

The *Courier-Journal* article has not been located as of this writing but a similar sounding article in Montreal's, *The Gazette* on December 20, 1930, some two years earlier than Martin recalls, gives the whisper campaign about the Romanovs plight a little more humph.

Consuls are official representatives of a government serving in the territory of another government, serving to foster greater trade between their two countries and working to protect their own citizens working in that foreign territory.

A Consul-General is the highest-ranking Consul in a territory and generally has several Consuls reporting to him at a central location, such as an Embassy or Consulate. Consuls and Consul-Generals report to Ambassadors and Secretaries of State, who themselves represent their government with another head of state, as opposed to a territory, which is the purview of a Consul or Consul-General.

Harris was Consul-General in Irkutsk from 1918 to 1921. He was assisted by John Embry in 1918 and Embry's successor, Alfred Thomson in 1919. Harris held a law degree and at least two doctorates, with the law degree and one doctorate coming from the University of Heidelberg. He retired from the Foreign Service in 1935 and died in February 1946 in Vancouver, British Columbia, Canada.

Buried on page 14 of *The Gazette* in Montreal, dated Saturday, December 20, 1930, correspondent John MacCormac in a special cable to *The New York Times* and *The Gazette*, with a dateline Vienna, December 19th, leads with the following explosive headline by today's standards that got largely ignored then:

> *"American Diplomat Partly Confirms Gen. Janin's Story. Tells How Czarist Remains were Given Protection Of U.S. Flag. Had Trunk 21 Days."*

The Gazette article begins with the following opening:

> *How the remains of the murdered Russian royal family were taken from Vershne-Udinsk, in Russia, to Harbin, Manchuria under the protection of the American flag, were*

related today by Consul-General Ernest Harris, now in Vienna, who was the Consul-General in Siberia.

Vershneudinsk was a so-called buffer state established by the Bosheviks consisting of areas east of Lake Baikal and including the territories of Kamshatka and Sakhalin, according to published reports by Reuter at the time. Remember, too again, that Martin contends the evacuation trip included Harbin which is mentioned in this article.

Again, according to *The Gazette*:

Mr. Harris's story corroborates many statements of the French General Janin, in his book, which is being published in Prague. But although the Consul-General refused to enter into any controversy, it contradicts General Janin's account – at least as anticipated in the newspaper Cesko Slovo – in certain important particulars.

Mr. Harris, who had been in Russia since the outbreak of the Revolution, had headquarters at the time of the execution of the Royal family in a special train which changed its locations in accordance with the exigencies of the moment. He was a close personal friend of General Kolchak, White Russian leader, afterwards executed by the Bolsheviks, and as a result of his impartial distribution of Red Cross supplies he was also on good terms with Attaman Semenoff, Cossack General, and a prominent figure in the guerilla warfare being waged in Siberia at the time.

Mr. MacCormac in his special cable to *The Gazette* and *The New York Times* reports that Mr. Harris' story was as follows:

I was in Omsk during the entire summer of 1919, when the executions took place at Ekaterinburg. Sokoloff, the judge who under Minister Telberg conducted the investigation of the murder and the trial of the murderers, brought the remains of the Royal family to Vershne-Udinsk in a small car. He was accompanied by General Dietrich, who had resigned his post as head of the Kolchak forces and was leaving Siberia.

On the night of January 9, 1920, the English tutor of the Royal family for sixteen years, who had followed them from Petrograd to Toblsk, but had been left behind in Omsk when they were taken to Ekaterinburg, brought me a letter from General Dietrich. The letter asked me to take a trunk out to Siberia and turn it over in Harbin to Sir Miles Lampson, then acting British High Commissioner in Siberia and now Minister to Pekin.

Charles Sydney Gibbes was the British-born and –trained tutor to the Romanov children mentioned in *The Gazette* article. Gibbes was a graduate of the University of Cambridge where he was a divinity student. Gibbes and his French tutor counterpart to the Romanov family, you will remember from earlier information, Pierre Gilliard, directly assisted and supported the Sokolov investigation and even visited the Ipatiev House. He returned to the United Kingdom following the reported assassination and took up life as an Orthodox Monk. He died in 1963 and is buried in Oxford, England.

Sir Miles was a career diplomat for the United Kingdom who was born in August 1880 and educated at Eton, entering the Foreign Office service in 1903. His postings included Japan and China prior to being appointed Acting British High Commissioner in Siberia in 1920. Sir Miles died in September 1964 having also served his Majesty, the King of England, during World War II as the Ambassador to Egypt. His records are located at the University of Aberystwyth.

Harris relays to MacCormac that the trunk was "actually turned over to me by General Dietrich. I not only took it through Siberia, but also took Sokolov, who travelled generally in a small car attached to my own and was actually acting as custodian of the trunk."

Amazingly, Harris then admits to correspondent MacCormac that he never opened the trunk allegedly containing the Tsar's remains. Harris is reported as saying:

> *It was Sokoloff – now dead – who told me that it contained the remains of the Royal family and gave me an inventory of the contents. I never opened it myself. The trunk was in my possession from January 9 to January 30. I kept it under the table in my dining car carelessly tied up with cord as though it contained nothing of value, and many guests kicked their toes against it without suspecting what was in it. While General Semonoff frequently visited me on my train, he knew nothing of what it contained nor was it ever opened by his soldiers.*

Nikolai Sokolov died impoverished in France in 1924 from a heart attack following a long illness while trying to finish his investigative report on the Ipatiev House massacre. The full commission report by Sokolov is actually available for review in Washington, DC at the Law Library at the Library of Congress.

Harris contends that Sokolov stayed with him until the Harris party reached Manchuria station. "There," recounts Harris, "he left me, but I kept the trunk until at Harbin, Sir Miles arrived with four carriers and took it over personally.

I don't know directly what happened to it afterwards, but I understand that Sir Miles Lampson turned the trunk over to General Janin, who later published an article to the effect that he had given it to the Russian Ambassador to Paris."

Harris pleads that he does not wish to enter into the controversy brewing at the time over General Kolchak's death, but informs MacCormac that Harris and Kolchak "were warm personal friends."

From *The Gazette*, we get the following:

> *On the witness stand on February 6, 1920, the day before he was executed, General Kolchak said, 'Harris, the American representative, always gave me in a friendly way the utmost sympathy and extraordinary encouragement. He was the only one of the several American representatives who seriously wished to help u in the sense of looking after our wants.'*
>
> *In reply to the questions of the Prosecutor General Kolchak quoted me as saying that I would have welcomed his assumption of power if he designed it only as a temporary expedient, and recalled that in reply he had promised not to hold on to power a day longer than was necessary, or to abuse it where he wielded it.*

On the same page of the December 30th newspaper, General Janin, who is contacted by Correspondent MacCormac to confirm the former Consul-General Siberia's account, says that he had no knowledge of the disposition of the Tsar's remains. MacCormac reports:

> *I received in April 1920, at Harbin from the Russian General Dietrich, whose request it had been refused by the English representative, four boxes containing objects and documents relative to the inquiry which had been made into the assassination of the Imperial Russian family and some human remains picked up at the spot near Ekaterinberg, where*

the bodies were cut into pieces and burned," General Janin writes.

Not to be outdone by Harris in his astounding conclusions, General Janin tells MacCormac that he kept the Tsar's remains in his personal family chapel on his property at Serre Izard near Grenoble, France in four boxes that were provided by General Dietrich. General Janin says that he is awaiting a reply from M. De Giers, the former Russian Ambassador to Italy, as to what to do with the remains from there.

"I learned subsequently," says General Janin, "that his intention was to send them to General Wrangel in Crimea. I have no knowledge of what disposition was made to them ultimately."

A third article in the column below the story on General Janin, then goes on to report that the Grand Duchess Marie Pavlovna of Russia, first cousin of Tsar Nicholas II and Granddaughter of Tsar Alexander II (Nicholas' father), is quoted as saying in response to the Harris and Janin news articles that she was in London "when Judge Sokolov arrived with a few chests containing clothing and other effects of the nineteen members of the Imperial family murdered by the Bolsheviki." She says that the boxes were delivered in a period "that might have been in 1919-1920."

Notice in this testimony that tere are now nineteen members of the Imperial family murdered by the Bolsheviki. Not eleven, or five, or three.

"Whether it is true that the ashes are now reposing in General Janin's family vault or not – that I do not know," the Grand Duchess concludes after observing the turmoil within the surviving Romanov family members as to what to do with such relics and artifacts.

General Maurice Janin is a controversial figure in these accounts. Those loyal to Tsar Nicholas II and White Russian forces accused the French military leader, who was head of the French Mission in Siberia, of having betrayed Admiral Alexander Kolchak and turning him over to Bolshevik Revolutionaries at Irkutsk knowing they would execute him in due time. They did despite the alleged earlier pledge by Janin to guarantee the Admiral's safety.

General Janin would die in Paris in April 1946.

The conflicting whispers and theories that the Romanov tale continues to generate a century after their reported murder in Yekaterinburg raises a number of very important thistles to consider as Martin's story progresses and competing theories of their ultimate fate persist.

Thistles are thorny little plants that cause those who encounter them to bypass their more-prickly elements because they are annoying, they often frustrate, and sometimes they even hurt - an apt description of what one encounters when dealing with the Romanov mystery.

However, by being mindful of the prickly challenges thistles present and refusing to give up on better understanding one's subject, it becomes possible to get past the thistle's troublesome surface confrontations, if one wants to.

For clarity's sake, it is worth repeating here what the competing theories are surrounding the Romanov family fate, by person. It is also advisable to present the thorny little problems as well that each of these competing theories present when trying to conclusively determine what happened to Tsar Nicholas II on the night of July 17, 1918, and thereafter.

As we have just read in this chapter and the last, and not presented in any particular order of importance or credibility, we know the following:

- Russian investigator Nicholas Sokolov was the first to conclude in his official White Russian government capacity that the Tsar and his family and attendants were indeed murdered and probably buried nearby. Of course, a little Revolution in the area puts a great deal of pressure on one to characterize a desired outcome a certain way.

- Author Shay McNeal argues that the Tsar may have been rescued from Russia through a route that vastly differs from that propounded by Martin Hutson. McNeal believes the Tsar was assisted by a group of spies who were committed to securing his safe passage to England. As you will see in the following pages we will see many of those same spy names resurface through Martin's account as it is tested.

- The fictional Michael Gray believes that he is the son of the rescued Tsarvich Alexei, who was aided by a group of his father's cronies, some of whom were alleged spies as well. Gray, the pseudonym, says the family settled in Ireland at the invitation of King George V, the Tsar's very-much-look-alike cousin. Some of the names in Gray's account will resurface in Martin's story as well as you read on.

- American Consul Ernest Harris, who admittedly played a very serious game of cat-and-mouse during his tenure in Russia, contends that he escorted the Tsar's ashes out of Siberia on a train, therefore, it would be his position that the Tsar was very dead.

Reacting to Michael Gray's Perspective

Consider the following issues these problematic theories outlined thus far create, starting with the last passage first:

- *The Gazette* article from Montreal confirms that a "special train" was used by the American Expeditionary Forces in Siberia on behalf of Consul-General Ernest Harris to move around the Russian theater as needed. It is interesting to read a long-forgotten published report from Harris that both Judge Sokolov and Attaman Semonoff travelled with or visited Harris on the same train as the Tsar's remains, without knowledge that the remains were supposedly present. Why?

- Semonoff is theoretically one of two key White Russian leaders who would be somewhat interested, one would think, in knowing that his former monarch's ashes were on his train. In the article, Harris admits that he has a good relationship with the Attaman. One would also think Attaman Semonoff would have a very vested interest in helping protect and properly dispose of the ashes of his Imperial Highness and other family members if in fact such ashes were present. After all, Semonoff has military control of the area where Harris' "special train" is traveling. The question here is: why would Harris and General Janin go to such extraordinary lengths to spirit the Royal family remains out of Siberia, only to return them a year later through Russian diplomatic means?

- And why hand the remains over to General Janin, according to Harris' account, knowing that the General at least appeared to have betrayed White Russian Leader Admiral Kolchak by handing Kolchak over to the Bolshevik Red Russian revolutionaries on January 14, 1920?

- Why, too, would the U.S. Army or an American president agree to risk soldier lives to bring ashes of a dead Tsar out of war-torn Russia under such clandestine circumstances?

- Harris recounts how he turned over four boxes to Sir Miles Lampson, however, Martin's story claims AEF Siberia soldiers actually transferred only three boxes to the British team. Was there a fourth box or are the accounts here in error?

- Both the Martin Hutson and Ernest Harris accounts appear to confirm that Romanov family members, either dead or alive, were transferred to British officials at Harbin in China sometime between October 1919 and January 1920, depending upon whose story is accurate.

- The article on Consul-General Harris reports that 1919 was the assassination year of the Tsar but we clearly know that the actual assassination year was 1918. Was this an error on the part of the correspondent, or did Harris purposely mis-speak?

- Seven members of Royal family were reportedly killed at the Ipatiev House in Yekaterinburg, so why was only one box with purported remains delivered to Consul General Harris in Siberia? Were the multiple remains of the seven Romanovs mixed together in the box? Why do that? And if there were multiple known bodies in the bottom of the grave, why would those loyal to the late Tsar allow the remains to be mixed with those of servants, one would ask?

- How could the remains that Harris discloses to the reporter possibly have been in ash form when all previous evidence indicates that the bodies were chopped up and splashed with acid before being burned to some degree but most likely completely so that they would be ashes only?

- Harris reports that he was on the train with the Tsar's remains in his custody from January 9th to January 30th, 1920. Martin's timeline, as we have seen in earlier chapters, and will see again in passages to follow, places Martin with the Tsar on a "special train" sometime in or around mid-October to late November 1919 - at least a full month prior, if not more, to Harris' account.

- AEF Siberia notes in the National Archives do not appear to support Harris' account, according to records we have found to date. Moreover, we know from published reports and National Archive records on AEF Siberia that President Wilson directed all American troops out of Siberia in an order issued December 29th - 30th, 1919 and ordered by General Graves on January 8th. It appears highly unlikely that Consul-General Harris would have disobeyed his President's order given that he was a committed career diplomat, although it is entirely possible Harris and his team was in the process of evacuating Siberia via Vladivostok, as ordered. The only problem with this scenario is that Ben Johnson on the Railroad Company was reported on the last train out of Siberia back on November 8, 1919 – two full months prior for a trip that would only have taken a few weeks at most to complete.

- On the other hand, Sir Miles Lampson did ultimately serve as the Acting British High Commission to Siberia, following his actual encounter with Consul-General Harris under both scenarios. Was this a reward for Sir Miles' rescue mission role, even if the rescue was of Romanov remains?

- Is it possible that both the Martin and Harris timelines could have been accurate? Could a live Tsar and members of his family been spirited out of Siberia in October-November 1919 as Martin contends and then the Consul-General smuggled fake Romanov remains from the forest burial site Sokolov found near Yekaterinburg out of Siberia several months later for the benefit of public perception that the Tsar was dead? As Consul-General, Harris would have had, one would again assume, prior knowledge of the intended deception, especially when using his "special train" for these purposes. Remember from Martin's account, three boxes were removed from the "special train" in Harbin, not the four boxes described by General Janin, nor the trunk described by Harris, nor the four chests described by the Grand Duchess Maria.

- Harris' account of the Tsar traveling in his dining car also does not square with published reports about how the Tsar typically traveled on one his Imperial trains. It is described by numerous sources that the Tsar traveled in his personal car and that meetings were generally held in the salon car, as opposed to the dining car. The larger dining car, on an evacuation mission, would most likely have been occupied by many others riding on the train out of Siberia.

- Harris does not sound concerned that Semonoff's soldiers would search the contents of his car yet we know from previous accounts here that Consul-General Harris belligerently opposed soldier searches of his train as detailed in previous news accounts of an earlier search attempt by Russian soldiers.

- The Romonov children's English Tutor, Mr. Gibbes, writes extensively on his attempts to get the Tsar and his family out of Russia alive, if possible, and if dead for certain, but never re-tells the story provided by Harris and Janin's accounts. There were ample opportunities for Gibbs to corroborate the Harris account, but there is presently no evidence to support the record here.

- More interestingly, however, following the Tsar's assassination and Gibbes direct support of the Sokolov investigation Gibbes did serve as a secretary to the British High Commissioner of Siberia and may have remained silent because he was bound by some type of secrecy oath from his service. His participation in delivering a letter or messages to Harris directly or through intermediaries was entirely possible in the time frames mentioned here.

- Kolchak being a close personal friend of Consul-General Harris confirms the role Kolchak and his forces probably played in getting the Tsar (dead or alive) out of Russia. Clearly, an evacuation of the Tsar and members of his family would have been made much easier if Kolchak and his troops were assisting Allied Forces in their effort to rescue the Tsar and/or members of his family.

- Kolchak's testimony to Bolshevik prosecutors as recounted by Harris in the MacCormac article appears to confirm, at least partially, our theory that Wilson was looking to support the use of temporary power by Russian leaders as the President and his allies worked to restore the Tsar to power.

- Did the reported Romanov ashes ever really make it out of General Janin's chapel or were they in fact transferred to the former Russian Ambassador to Italy as Janin said? There is no record of such an event that we have been able to locate thus far. If the ashes were, in fact, transferred to the former Russian Ambassador as Janin reports, why did the Romanovs show up as decaying bones (as opposed to ashes) in the 1990s in the Koptyaki Forest?

- The Grand Duchess Maria in her remarks observes that 19 members of the Romanov family were killed in Yekaterinburg. We know from published accounts and even Judge Sokolov's on-site investigation at the Ipatiev House reports that seven members of the Romanov family and four others were murdered by Bolshevik soldiers on July 17, 1918 - not nineteen as said by the

Grand Duchess. Why did the Grand Duchess say, or even appear to think, that 19 people had been killed among her family in Yekaterinburg?

- Is it possible from the conflicting accounts of Martin, Harris, Janin and Grand Duchess Maria that many different effects, especially clothing and other relics of the Romanov clan could have been on the "special train" to Harbin. Martin specifically reports that once the Tsar and his family members were transferred to British officials in Harbin, he and his crew were ordered back to Vladivostok, rather than being allowed to take the more direct route out of area through Peking, for example. Rumors indicate that more of the Tsar's personal effects may have been smuggled out of Russia, including wealth like jewels, and this could have possibly been the purpose of "special train" continuing its dangerous journey on to Vladivostok.

Reacting to Shay McNeal's Perspective

- Clearly, as Shay McNeal reveals, there were indeed a number of very complicated rescue missions in the planning before and after the alleged July 17th assassination attempt, as indicated by her phenomenal research. Moreover, the intelligence network that would be needed to support such missions do indeed appear to have been in place with people who had credible connections to either President Wilson or King George V.

- Martin testifies in his audio statement that high-ranking officers from the United States, England, Canada, France,

Italy, Czechoslovakia and Japan were onboard Evacuation Train #28 when he first and last encountered Nicholas. McNeal documents the roles the same countries played in planning the rescue so could they have been one-and-the-same when it comes to Martin's story?

- As you will see in subsequent passages in this book, Martin will tell Hutson family members that according to his conversations with Nicholas that there was a safe house in northern Russia, as McNeal contends, and that Nicholas and his family were rescued by the British from the Ipatiev House through an underground tunnel with the help of troops loyal to the Tsar assigned to the House of Special Purpose detail, just as McNeal contends again.

- Did William Gibbs McAdoo, the former head of the United States Secret Service and Treasury Secretary, President Wilson's son-in-law, convince John O'Conor to remove his book, Rescuing the Czar from circulation in 1920 as McNeal contends? McAdoo was indeed connected in this mystery it would appear in a number of interesting ways: His own son-in-law was strongly connected to Vladimir Lenin on financial transactions, and McAdoo was head of the American Red Cross in Siberia at the time of the purported evacuation. Was Lenin complicit in the rescue of Nicholas by the Allied forces in Siberia?

- Was the DNA analysis conducted on the Romanov remains actually more inconclusive that was reported, and if so, why? There were indeed a number of very interesting and troubling aspects to the investigation that we soon explore in greater detail such as why were the skulls of the Tsar and his family stored under a citizen's bed for several years, how much were those bones contaminated during the long process of their examination, why was the chain of custody of the remains so badly interrupted if in fact they were known to be those of the royal family, and why would certain key tests not conducted and other evidence found if the remains were indeed those of the missing Romanovs?

- How would there have been a rescue mission through Tibet as McNeal speculates, if Martin's account of a rescue through Harbin was true? There are after all a number of consistencies in how the rescue missions were conducted like using boats to spirit the Romanovs away (remember the *USAT Thomas* and Kara Sea motorboats details). How do we square up these accounts with Martin's story? The evidence in McNeal's book appear to be very strong based on her earlier research.

Reacting to Michael Gray's Perspective

- Michael Gray's book has far too many friends, supporters and political cronnies of Tsar Nicholas II reported in and around Collon, Ireland, at the time that "Nikolai Alexandrovich" visits in 1948, to easily dismiss out of hand as being coincidental. The web of spies and faithful aides who could have helped the Imperial family escape their "death" in Yekaterinberg, is very significant and noteworthy. Unfortunately, nothing short of verifiable DNA evidence will prove whether or not

Chebotarev was in fact, Alexei and that Michael Gray is his son, the latest rightful heir to the Romanov throne. Is such DNA evidence from Gray's alleged father, the Tsarevich, possible even today?

- If Alexei did escape Russia via a Southern Siberian route through Constantinople, then what was the role the American Expeditionary Forces in Archangel playing there in the closing months of the war? And if Alexei finally escaped Russia in April 1920, where was he for the intervening some 33 months?

- Did the Trust of Kings really exist – it does come right out of Hollywood central casting – and if so, did President Wilson know of it, too? Did President Wilson have some obligation to the Trust of Kings that nobody has known about?

- The Red Cross figures yet again in to Gray's account of his alleged father and his friends who hung around him in Ireland. What is their story and what role did the American Red Cross really play in potential Romanov rescue missions?

Finally, add to these vexing questions above a few more inquires that we will need to deal with to understand the validity of Martin's story:

- President Franklin Roosevelt, as we have also seen through McNeal's accounts, seems to imply in his mind through, *The President's Mystery Story*, that the Tsar may have faked his death in order to live free of his domineering wife. More on this in a later chapter. We have seen from Tsarist history that Nicholas' family had pulled that trick before. Might they have done so once more in this case?

- Professor William Maples, before his own untimely death, did not believe that Alexei and Anastasia, and probably Nicholas himself, were in the Koptyiaki Woods grave as promoted by the Russian government. He believed the bones that we said to be the Tsar's did not fit the crime, to borrow the case of another great murder-mystery. His Russian forensic counterparts believe very strongly and adamantly that they did indeed find the Romanov family remains and consider the case closed, having affirmatively identified them as being the ill-fated Imperials.

- To the contrary, the Russian Orthodox Church does not appear, as of this writing, to believe that the Tsar's bones entombed in the Peter and Paul Cathedral in St. Petersburg to be them - or at least not all of them. The bones were placed in Saint Catherine Chapel in 1998 but no formal recognition of their validity has been forthcoming from the church since.

- Neither President Wilson, Ben Johnson of the Russian Railway Services Corp, nor Major General William Sidney Graves, ever confirmed in writing that their Siberian mission was also intended to rescue the Tsar. Official records confirming a mission, the mission, do not exist as far we know.

- It appears, thus far at least, that King George V, Kaiser Wilhelm II, and former British Prime Minister David Lloyd George might agree with Wilson, Johnson and Graves.

- On the other hand, as you will learn, former U.S. Secretary of War Newton Baker writing General Graves' forward for his 1931 book, *America's Siberian Adventure,* does allude to perhaps something else being afoot in that extraordinary episode.

On the flip side of the Martin Hutson coin, you will discover that Russian Historian Helen Rappaport concludes that Tsar Nicholas II and his family were all killed in Yekaterinburg, as do authors, Robert Massey and Peter King. The same can be said for author Peter King again through his outstanding research with colleague Penny Wilson in subsequent published work.

A mysterious book mentioned by McNeal alleging that the Tsar was rescued, printed in 1930, does not now seem to exist, or at least is lost to the ages on some wayward shelf where it has yet been located by modern-day librarians. Even the Library of Congress says it has two copies of the book, but cannot find them, thus far.

The wartime spy and journalist, Carl Ackerman of *The New York Times* wrote at the time that he thought there was a six-in-ten chance that the Tsar was murdered as stipulated. Would anyone take the resulting four-in-ten odds that he was not?

Wilson biographers extraordinaire A. Scott Berg and John Milton Cooper, Jr., whom you will soon meet in a following chapter did not indicate any such clandestine mission for President Wilson in their work on the subject.

The pretenders to the Romanov dynasty certainly have expressed their theories over time, but each in due course, has been discredited to one degree or another. Peter Kurth did outstanding research and due diligence on the story of Anna Anderson in Virginia. Was her DNA faked or was she really a Romanov as some contend even to this day?

William Clarke adds to the urgency of the mystery because of the sheer wealth that he has catalogued in lost Romanov assets that would be worth hundreds of billions of dollars today, assuming that any rightful heir or heirs could be found.

And, finally, there is the Ipatiev House that is no longer, not to mention Vladimir Lenin's Soviet Union itself. With so much evidence now long gone, or deeply tampered with over the years, to state it charitably, how in the world will we ever be able to know for certain that the Romanovs died or lived after that fateful July 17th date?

And, now of course, comes Martin's story. Although clearly, he will not profit from his story since, he too, has passed, how do we know with any certainty that his story is any truer than the others?

Perhaps it starts with a more detailed run-down on the players who may have pulled off a successful rescue of Nicholas as well as a revised time line on the opportunities they had to do so as we now know it all of these decades later?

It might help reconstruct events into a clearer understanding of just what happened to Nicholas and his family.

Recommended reading:

- Michael Occleshaw, *Dances in Deep Shadows: Britain's Clandestine War in Russia 1917-1920,* Constable, London, England, 2006, ISBN-13: 978-0786717897.

- Michael Occleshaw, *The Romanov Conspiracies: The Romanovs and the House of Windsor,* Orion Books, Ltd., London, England, 1994, ISBN-13: 978-1857974287.

Part II:
The Romanov Rescuers

5 | Aide's Covenant

"That was the biggest decision Wilson ever made, and much of what happened in the world since then has flowed from that decision."

- *John Milton Cooper, Jr., Woodrow Wilson: A Biography*

On December 28, 1918, Woodrow Wilson celebrated his sixty-second birthday in London, England at Buckingham Palace where he and his wife, Edith Bolling Galt Wilson, were staying as guests of King George V and his wife, the indomitable Queen Mary. World War I had formally ended just a few short weeks before on November 11th, when Germany surrendered to Allied forces in Reims, France.

Kaiser Wilhelm II had fled to the Netherlands, where he would live out the remaining years of his life in the peaceful exile that his first cousin, Nikolai Alexandrovich of Russia was not afforded, at least if you believe what history currently tells us.

Born on December 28, 1856, in Staunton, Virginia, to a devoutly Presbyterian minister family, Thomas Woodrow Wilson graduated with multiple degrees from prestigious academic institutions such as what would eventually be called Princeton University and attended a year of law school at Thomas Jefferson's University of Virginia.

Wilson's doctorate would be earned from Johns Hopkins University, where he would learn to speak German, a requirement for his degree. He would also later serve Princeton as its president and be elected Governor of New Jersey.

Serious, studious, and stern were all words that described Wilson, yet he engendered from those close to him, absolute loyalty, extreme confidentiality and political devotion on levels that have generated intense speculation as to why.

But Wilson was not devoted to President William Howard Taft, a Republican he successfully opposed for election in 1912 as a Democrat. Wilson won that race, not because of the strength of his own campaign, but because former Republican president Teddy Roosevelt decided to jump in and oppose President Taft, too, but as an Independent candidate who split the vote in favor of Wilson.

Apropos, Roosevelt called himself a "Bull Moose Progressive."

Woodrow Wilson's presidency was noted for guiding America through World War I, his advocacy of the League of Nation's, which was established through the 14th point of the Fourteen Points doctrine he famously pioneered, as well as passage of the landmark 19th amendment to the U.S. Constitution, in which women were given the right to vote in America.

Middle class reforms he pioneered would be the envy of any modern-day president now. Wilson created the Federal Trade Commission (FTC) and was credited with giving Americans their personal income tax through the 16th Amendment in 1913.

Witnessing in his youth the ravages of the Civil War, Wilson reportedly saw first-hand, Confederate General Robert E. Lee paraded through town in handcuffs following his surrender.

Wilson would know tragic personal suffering in other ways, too. His first wife, Ellen, with whom he had three daughters, died from kidney failure during his first term in the White House. As a couple, the Wilson's had previously suffered the indignities of an affair Woodrow Wilson had earlier in their marriage while traveling in romantic Bermuda.

When he arrived at the House of Windsor on that December day, with his second wife, Edith, herself a widow, Wilson was an understandably very tired man who had fought many political battles, not to mention, "the war to end all wars." Less than a year later, Wilson would suffer two serious back-to-back strokes, one of which would incapacitate the President, paralyzing his left side, leading eventually to passage of the 25th Amendment to the U.S. Constitution providing for an orderly succession in the event of a president's death or disability.

Wilson, who history has observed was the first and only president of the United States to earn a Ph.D., was also noted by his biographer, John Milton Cooper, Jr., to be the "next to last president to write his own speeches." Says Cooper: "No other president has combined such varied and divergent elements of learning, eloquence, religion, and war."

President Wilson's biggest decision of his two-term presidency was the fateful decision to go to war with Germany. Writes Cooper poignantly in his book, *Woodrow Wilson: A Biography*:

> *That was the biggest decision Wilson ever made, and much of what happened in the world since then has flowed from that decision. Unlike the other American wars of the last century, this one came neither in response to a direct attack on the nation's soil, as with World War II and Pearl Harbor and the attacks of September 11, nor as a war of choice, as with the Gulf war and the Iraq war, nor as a smaller episode in a grand global struggle, as with the Korean War and the Vietnam War. Many have argued that the United States joined the Allies in*

> *1917 because great underlying forces and interests involving money, ties of blood and culture, and threats to security and cherished values were 'really' at work. Perhaps so, perhaps not, but one incontrovertible fact remains: the United States entered World War I because Woodrow Wilson decided to take the country in.*

The question of ties of blood and threats to security, and even cherished values, were, as Cooper says, what was really at work in Wilson's decision, based on what we now know about Martin's story, assuming of course, that you believe what Martin says of his time with the Tsar.

Underlying forces and interests involving money will be left for validation by research from other authors, as you have seen already from Shay McNeal, Michael Gray, Michael Occleshaw, Greg King, Robert Massie, Helen Rappaport, and others. It would appear that these factors, too, were indeed evident.

Suffice it to say, that when President Wilson decided to go all in in World War I, he did so with a stealth competence and determination that we are only now discovering thanks to the uncovering of new archives in the post-Russian Revolutionary period that lasted until the fall of Communism and the Soviet Union during the Ronald Reagan administration. Martin's story appears to support this newfound evidence.

The Aide-Mémoire

Being a president who could write his own policy statements and speeches, especially having been Princeton University's 13th president as well, Woodrow Wilson would author a very quiet but now famous document that would change the course of history: *The Aide-Mémoire.*

The Aide-Mémoire, addressed to "The Secretary of State to the Allied Ambassadors," was an unsigned seven-page document President Wilson used to outline his policy and objectives for his new commander in the theater of war to follow as American ground troops entered Russia and Siberia in the aftermath of Tsar Nicholas II's earlier abdication. Ironically, and perhaps not unintentionally, it was signed and dated by the President on the same day that the Tsar was said to have been murdered with his family in Yekaterinburg – July 17, 1918.

According to Wilson:

> *The whole heart of the people of the United States is in the winning of this war. The controlling purpose of the Government of the United States is to do everything that is necessary and effective to win it. It wishes to cooperate in every practicable way with the Allied Governments, and to cooperate ungrudgingly; for it has no ends of its own to serve and believes that war can be won only by common counsel and intimate concert of action.*

Wilson continued:

> *It is the clear and fixed judgment of the Government of the United States, arrived at after repeated and very searching considerations of the whole situation in Russia, that military intervention there would add to the present sad confusion in Russia rather than cure it, injure her rather than help her, and that it would be of no advantage in the prosecution of our main design, to win the war against Germany. It can not, therefore, take part in such intervention or sanction it in principle. Military*

> *intervention, would, in its judgment, even supposing it to be efficacious in its immediate avowed object of delivering an attack upon Germany from the east, be merely a method of making use of Russia, not a method of serving her. Her people would not profit by it, if they profited by it at all, in time to save them from their present distresses, and their substance would be used to maintain foreign armies, not to reconstitute their own.*

Based on this philosophy, President Wilson said he was authorizing the use of two American forces in Russia - a force to be deployed in Siberia to the South and West, and a force in Murmansk and Arkhangelsk to the North and East. The forces in Northern Russia were affectionately nicknamed *the Wolfhounds* and *the Polar Bears* (the southern force did not have a nickname that stuck through time) but officially as the American Expeditionary Forces Siberia under the command of Major General William Sidney Graves.

Wilson appears to outline three objectives for the AEF in Russia according to his *The Aide-Mémoire.* These objectives, however, are not specifically listed in any order or clarity per se, but historians and political scientists appear to agree on their intent and evidence supports the various interpretations of Wilson's intent:

> *The first objective was to provide all possible assistance to the "Czecho-Slovaks" legion, to rescue their forces from Russian and German captivity and make their way back home through Siberia.*
>
> *The second objective was to safeguard US- and Allied-provided military supplies and equipment that had been sent*

to Russia prior to the Bolshevik Revolution when Russia was waging war against Germany.

· *The third objective was to provide the Russian people humanitarian assistance through relief programs provided by "a commission of merchants, agricultural experts, labor advisers, Red Cross representatives, and agents of the Young Men's Christian Association...."*

Clearly, President Wilson was still very much concerned about honoring his commitment to the early tenets of the principle of self-determination. The principle, whose name is credited by historians to British Prime Minister David Lloyd George, essentially says that nations, like Russia, should have the freedom to determine their own sovereignty and not be subject to external interference from other nations. This principle would be clarified and expanded upon when the League of Nations is proposed by President Wilson and its successor effort, the United Nations was established decades later.

It may be possible, based on what we know from Martin's story and other research to be outlined later in subsequent chapters, that Wilson actually may have had a fourth unstated objective in mind when he wrote his *The Aide-Mémoire* - rescue Tsar Nicholas II and restore his Imperial reign, if possible, assuming of course that it was the will of the people consistent with their right, in his opinion, to determine their own sovereignty.

A bold move such as this fourth unstated objective to rescue the Tsar would not be out of character for President Wilson. Another passage from one of his biographers, John Milton Cooper, Jr. alludes to this trait. "In 1914, he told his Princeton classmates at their thirty-fifth reunion, 'There is nothing that succeeds in life like boldness, provided you believe you are on the right side.'" As Cooper points out, boldness and thinking big clearly marked Wilson all of his life, "and those qualities helped make him the only president who rose to the top in two professions entirely removed from public affairs."

The question is: was there a fourth undisclosed objective in the *Aide-Mémoire*?

That Wilson would micromanagingly author such a groundbreaking document in such great secrecy from members of his Cabinet, was an amazing feat when one considers that Woodrow Wilson did not have a lot of foreign policy training prior to entering the White House. "Writing his own memos and speeches was not that unusual for the old college professor and Ivy League university president," writes biographer Cooper. "He wrote his own memorandum for how to wage war on his typewriter. That he would write *The Aide-Mémoire* would, therefore, not have been that unusual either, nor his decision not to consult Congress.

Cooper also says:

> *Wilson had to learn diplomacy on the job, and made mistakes, particularly in Mexico, where he originally did harbor some facile notions of promoting democracy. He learned hard lessons there, which he applied later in dealing with both the world war and the Bolshevik Revolution in Russia. Like others at the time, Wilson invested American intervention in the world war with larger ideological and purpose. But he had no illusions about leading a worldwide crusade to impose democracy. The most famous phrase from his speech to Congress in 1917 asking for war read, 'The world must be made safe for democracy' – perhaps for the most significant choice of the passive voice by any president. A year later, speaking to foreign journalists, he declared, 'There isn't any one kind of government which we have the right to impose*

upon any nation. So that I am not fighting for democracy except for those peoples that want democracy.

On July 6, 1918, therefore, according to notes found in the AEF Siberia archive, "President Wilson called the highest-ranking American officials together to deliberate on how to handle the three tasks at hand." Officials attended the meeting were reported to include "Secretary of State Robert Lansing, Secretary of War Newton D. Baker, Secretary of the Navy Josephus Daniels, Chief of Staff Peyton March, and Chief of Naval Operations Admiral William S. Benson."

According to a report on the encounter:

President Wilson proposed to the leaders that the United States and Japan would work together to cover the costs of supplying the Czechoslovak Legion. He also said that the United States and Japan would both station troops in Vladivostok to guard the Czechoslovak forces' safe passageway from Irkutsk to the Far East. Each country would send 7,000 soldiers for a total of 14,000 soldiers between The United States and Japan. The General Staff set aside the 27th and 31st Infantry Regiments that were stationed in Manila, Philippines.

Newton Diehl Baker, Jr., Woodrow Wilson's Secretary of War was an American Progressive. From 1912 to 1915, Baker was the Mayor of Cleveland, Ohio, before becoming Woodrow Wilson's Secretary of War in 1916. He was born in Martinsburg, West Virginia in December 1891. He graduated from Johns Hopkins University, where he met Wilson, and received his law degree from Washington and Lee University in 1894. He attempted to join the service in the Spanish-American War but was rejected due to poor eyesight. Between his service as Mayor of Cleveland and Secretary of War, Baker and a colleague founded the venerable law firm, Baker Hostetler, a firm that today comprises some 900 attorneys in 14 cities around the nation. Some of their most notable clients today include Bayer Corporation, the William Jefferson Clinton Foundation, the Ford Motor Company, Major League Baseball, Morgan Stanley, and Verizon.

It was Baker who recommended General Pershing be appointed Command-in-Chief of the American Expeditionary Forces in World War I and convinced President Wilson to keep American troops independent of the Allies against the Central Powers, specifically Germany, which not surprisingly, put him at odds with the influential British Prime Minister David Lloyd George, who did not appreciate the Secretary's perspective on American independence. Wilson biographers say that the 28th president hoped that Baker, whom he respected very highly, would succeed him into the White House. A Pacifist by nature from his early days on, Baker never formally ran for president, as Wilson hoped, including when urged to do so before Franklin Roosevelt ultimately received the Democratic nomination in 1932. He died at age 66 on Christmas Day in 1937 and is buried next to his wife, Elizabeth, in Shaker Heights, Ohio. Frederick Koppel in a Foreign Affairs profile of America at War under Newton Baker observed:

> *If I had to choose the one quality in his make-up which exercised the most potent influence upon soldier and civilian alike, it would be his courage, an undramatic but imaginative courage, broad enough to cover both a gallant recklessness and a philosophic fortitude. His effective support of the Selective Draft demanded that sort of courage, particularly from so recent a convert to its necessity. To set the pattern of American participation upon so vast and costly a scale took*

> *both imagination and courage. And certainly, to break all American tradition by giving the General in the field a free hand and protecting him from criticism meant both courage and fortitude. It was Pershing who kept Leonard Wood on this side of the Atlantic; it was Baker who silently received the resulting storm of protest.*

President Wilson's Secretary of State Robert Lansing was Secretary Baker's political polar opposite - he was a conservative Democrat. Born in Watertown, New York in 1864, Lansing was an Amherst University-trained lawyer but he rose to the Secretary's position having been an advisor as an acknowledged expert on International Law to the State Department at the outbreak of World War I. Lansing replaced the famed William Jennings Bryan as Wilson's Secretary of State following the sinking of the *RMS Lusitania* on May 7, 1915 when Bryan resigned during a series of protest letters that Wilson sent to Germany, which Bryan thought on at least one occasion were too biligerent. Lansing, on the other hand, supported Wilson's protests and advocated that the United States enter the war against Germany. During his early tenure at State, Lansing was credited with creating the Bureau of Secret Intelligence, which today is known as the U.S. Diplomatic Security Service and which would play a part in the Romanov rescue missions saga that will be soon be discussed here.

Lansing "was the most unsatisfactory Secretary," in President Wilson's cabinet according to Cooper's biography. Lansing was said by Wilson to be "good for a second place but unfitted for the first. That he had no imagination, no constructive ability, and but little real ability." Lansing was very independent-minded, did not fully support Wilson's League of Nations as being necessary for ensuring world peace, and was never fully trusted by the President despite the fact that

President was content to let Secretary Lansing handle other parts of the war effort, including Mexico, Latin America and parts of Asia.

Lansing was so unpopular with Wilson that Navy Secretary Josephus Daniels said, "Lansing was a Big Stick diplomat who believed in Dollar Diplomacy and in Force and had no part in Wilson's idealism and faith in real democracy." For his part, Lansing though that Wilson was too calm and too sobering. "Excitement," he was observed to say, "would see very much out of place at the cabinet table with Woodrow Wilson presiding."

A newspaper publisher from North Carolina, educated at what is now Duke University, Wilson's Secretary of the Navy, Josephus Daniels, was known to be a political progressive in the mold of Newton Baker. Like Baker and Lansing, Daniels went to law school, but unlike Baker and Lansing, chose not to practice law once admitted to the bar. Daniels was a vocal supporter of Wilson's during the 1912 presidential election, and was appointed Secretary of the Navy upon Wilson's electoral victory.

Born in 1864 in Easton, Pennsylvania, and a West Point Military Academy graduate who was a descendant of a signer of the American Declaration of Independence, Thomas Stone of Maryland, Army Chief of Staff Peyton March was the architect of that role in the military for presidents of the United States. However, General March would become deeply critical of President Wilson's decision to authorize the use of American Expeditionary Forces in Siberia as time went by, saying that its mission was a complete failure for those who planned it.

A native of Georgia, Admiral William S. Benson was the first ever Chief of Naval Operations and was responsible for overseeing the rapid expansion of naval operations during the early days of Wilson's entry into World War I.

The Aide-Mémoire was delivered to Major General William Sidney Graves from his commander-in-chief in a train station in Kansas City, Missouri on August 6, 1918. It was delivered in hush-hush secrecy worthy of a *James Bond* movie by U.S. Secretary of State Newton Baker. Graves, who was West Point-trained and who had proven himself in battle in Mexico under the command of the iconic General "Black Jack" Pershing, was appointed commander of the American Expeditionary Forces Siberia and was ordered to strictly follow the President's instructions in the Allied intervention.

Graves, writing in his memoire years later, said of the encounter, Baker said:

> *This contains the policy of the United States in Russia which you are to follow. Watch your step; you will be walking on eggshells loaded with dynamite. God bless you and goodbye.*

Graves was a politically adept soldier with great instincts. He was even also somewhat connected politically through his father-in-law, Senate Committee on Military Affairs Chairman, Republican Francis Warren of Wyoming.

Mexico had been a warm-up for Russia and Europe for Wilson. Black Jack Pershing had commanded U.S. troops there and was now headed to the war front in France and Germany to take on the Kaiser. Graves, when he received his orders to meet Secretary Baker in Kansas City, had been training 8th Division soldiers to deploy for duty in France. America's allies, especially in Europe, were pushing President Wilson hard to intervene in the war but the president was walking a political tightrope on this subject in the United States. Wilson was a big believer in the principle of self-determination. More to the point, he had campaigned in the 1912 presidential and 1914 mid-term elections on keeping America out of the war.

When the Tsar abdicated on the 15th of March 1917, President Wilson decided to support the Provisional Government in Russia. Unfortunately for Wilson and the Allies, however, the Provisional Government was soon overthrown by Vladimir Lenin's Bolshevik Revolutionaries. Their overthrow badly undermined Allied strategy for ending the war with Germany, especially when Germany and Russia ultimately decided to execute the Brest-Litovsk in late 1917.

Again, Cooper observes of circumstances: Congress would have voted against going to war had they been able to rely upon a secret ballot. The president's own allies in Congress, the progressives, loved the idea that the autocratic Tsar Nicholas II's reign had come to an end. They, and the American public, had little stomach for intervening in the coup against the Tsar.

But Germany was making Wilson's promise to stay out of the war very hard to keep. The U.S. had been sending supplies across the Atlantic Ocean to help stock the allies against the war. The German Navy sank the British passenger ship, the *RMS Lusitania*, with American passengers aboard, and another ship, the *Sussex*, forcing Wilson to conclude that he had no choice but to enter the war despite his previously stated neutrality.

On April 2, 1917, President Wilson asked Congress for a declaration of war on Germany, and received it almost immediately on April 4th, with six Senators and 50 Representatives voting against the measure. It was reported by A. Scott Berg in his biography of Wilson that nearly every American was wearing or holding an American flag as Wilson approached Congress to give his late evening declaration request on a night that offered a light rain.

Edith Wilson, Berg observes, said that the "audience settled into silence so deep, one could hear only the sound of people breathing." Berg said that the President appeared to be nervous at first. "He looked pale, his voice quavered, and his fingers trembled. 'There are serious, very serious, choice of policy to be made,'" Wilson Berg said, "'and made immediately, which it was neither right nor constitutionally permissible that I should assume the responsibility of making.'"

> *The present German submarine warfare against commerce,' he insisted, 'was nothing less than a 'war against all nations' and a 'challenge to all mankind.'*
>
> *Each nation, Wilson said, must decide for itself how to meet the challenge. 'Our motive,' he asserted, 'will not be revenge or the victorious assertion of the physical might of the nation, but only the vindication of right, of human right, of which we are only a single champion.' There is one choice we cannot make, we are incapable of making,' he said to the utterly still audience: 'We will not choose the path of submission - '*

The chamber, Berg notes, erupted in cheers. "Chief Justice White dropped the big soft hat he had been holding so that he could raise his hands in the air and clap. The applause spread from the floor to the galleries." Wilson signed the War Act on April 6th. He had tried to keep America out of the conflict for more than two and one-half years but the inevitable had happened.

Wilson, who clearly did not have a lot of foreign policy or war training in his record before he became president, was noted for delegating much of his war effort in Europe, Mexico and Russia to trusted subordinates while setting policies and directions for everyone else to follow. Cooper reports in his biography that Secretary of State Baker "took care of raising and training the army. No cabinet member enjoyed greater confidence and respect from Wilson than Baker, whom Wilson would stand by steadfastly."

The following account, Cooper wrote, sums up Wilson's preferred way of doing business:

> *Recruiting, training, arming and transporting troops to their battle theaters became a very high priority for Secretary Baker. In the meantime, the president and the War Department agreed to send over a commander of future forces at once. At the beginning of May, in consultation with the president, Secretary Baker tapped Major General John J. Pershing to lead what would be called the American Expeditionary Forces. As commander of the Punitive Expedition in Mexico, Pershing had the most recent field experience of any American general. Moreover, unlike the other possible choice, Roosevelt's close friend Leonard Wood, Pershing had refrained from publicly criticizing Wilson's preparedness policies and restraint in Mexico. He also possessed excellent political connections; his recently deceased wife was the daughter of a senior Republican senator, Francis Warren of Wyoming, former chairman of the Military Affairs Committee."*

Cooper says that General Pershing would see Wilson face-to-face for the first and only time during the war on May 24, 1917 when Secretary Baker took General Pershing to the White House, "where the president told the general he would have complete freedom in conducting operations. Wilson also reviewed Baker's final orders to the AEF commander on May 26, the day before he left for France."

Wilson, according to Cooper, believed that President Abraham Lincoln during the American Civil War, "had made mistakes in waging war." Wilson, Cooper said, "steeled himself to jump in fully and decisively. He meant to wage war with every resource at his command, and he meant to do it his way."

The Decision to Intervene

George F. Kennan was an American diplomat who was also known as being the father of one of America's most prominent foreign policies: Containment. His research and writing has been credited by International Relations experts as having inspired the (Harry S) Truman Doctrine, which sought to "contain" the expansion of Communism in Eastern Europe during the Cold War.

A University of Michigan missive on the decision to intervene, based on Kennan's work, notes: "Wilson had no plans to overthrow the new Bolshevik Government in Russia and considered it impractical to attempt to open a second front to oppose the Germans from within Russia," as some of America's associates proposed.

The article goes on to say that it was not clear on what the President wanted them to do with the policy to intervene in Siberia. The President's style of leadership, "which was secretive, excessively involved in small details and distrustful of professional members of his Administration," made the Wilson directive all the more difficult to execute, they argue. Moreover, the authors contend that Kennan agreed, concluding that "there was no coherent overarching plan to the Wilson administration's handling of the Russia intervention." They further contend that, "Neither Wilson nor anyone in his administration were quite sure what the Bolsheviks wanted and they compounded this ignorance by acting upon it." Kennan said, "The Wilson Administration had no plan other than to rescue foreign nationals, protect allied war aims and provide a small amount of humanitarian assistance."

According to the article again, "Lenin's rise to power had to be stopped, so the Wilsonians allied themselves," they argue, "to the anti-Bolshevik forces and attempted the overthrow of the Bolshevik Government. The intervention," they continue, "was a last desperate gamble to prevent communism in Russia."

From our perspective, the authors of the incendiary article, then ask a question, or make a statement, that we can agree with: "Those who believe the intervention was part of a clearly devised plan must determine what that plan was." We do believe that there was a plan that was not publicly shared, which of course is the purpose this book as will be outlined in later chapters.

The authors of the "Chaos Management" article conclude that, "Both Wilson and Lenin opposed secret deals," but as we have seen and will see in future chapters, that does not appear to apply to President Wilson, based on the evidence that we and other authors have uncovered in more recent years.

Even more astounding, the authors then go on to assert that in their estimation, there is a very clear objective when addressing the President's, *Aide-Mémoire*, which we quoted earlier: "The United States had no interest in intervention, its main goal was to defeat Germany and Wilson, the author of this message, felt that he spoke for the United States in this matter. The over-riding theme," they say, "that can be seen in U.S. Foreign Policy, following entry into the war, is the defeat of Germany and the rebuilding of a stable, peaceful, democratic world system."

Perhaps not, as we will see in succeeding pages.

And, then, they add this: "Wilson may have thought he was making history but he was only the figurehead of his class."

This clearly, from our research, was not the case - good or bad, it just simply is not true, as you will see.

To make matters more confusing, the authors of the article then conclude, wrongly in our opinion, "The United States would not support any policy that might return the Tsar to power. The relationship between the Wilson Administration and the new Russian leadership," they argue, "was not a simple one but a mix of converging ideals, opposing ideals, areas of agreement, areas of disagreement, suspicion, misunderstanding, revulsion and sympathy."

Perhaps true on some elements but clearly wrong when it comes to the main premise, at least from our perspective, reinforcing our belief that so much of the story behind the Tsar's supposed fate was manufactured simply for the purposes of making us believe "he died so that he could live."

The Wilson Inner Circle

In addition to Baker and Lansing, Woodrow Wilson had a very interesting cast of characters around him, too, like George V, advising or opposing his policy directives in the White House. These personalities would play a major role in helping the President shape his place in Martin's story - and, more importantly, world history.

William Gibbs McAdoo

Secretary of the United States Treasury William G. McAdoo - McAdoo was a generally unknown Secretary of the Treasury, but according to one historian, "in his lengthy career as a lawyer, entrepreneur, political organizer, Cabinet official, director of various regulatory agencies, Presidential candidate, spokesman for Prohibition, U.S. Senator, and shipping magnate,

McAdoo not only navigated the changes in American political culture and economic policy that dominated the early 20th century, but was an integral figure in creating those changes that culminated in the New Deal." Philip Chase in a doctoral dissertation on Secretary McAdoo summed up this central figure in the Wilson sphere as well as the Hutson story, with the following description:

> *During his lifetime (1863-1941), William Gibbs McAdoo was one of the most admired, respected, despised and reviled figures on the American scene. He was compared by various contemporaries to Jefferson, Hamilton, and especially Lincoln, while one admirer went even farther and consoled him after an election loss with the admonition "Our Savior said God: Forgive them (the voters), they know not what they do! Woodrow Wilson, his father-in-law, referred to McAdoo as "attractive and dynamic" but "lacking in the requisite powers of reflection to be President. Walter Lippmann described him as "a statesman grafted onto a promoter" but H.L. Mencken declared that "McAdoo was worth a dozen (Franklin) Roosevelts." Various political adversaries called him "mercenary and shoddy," "as cunning as that fabled rodent," and "at least a chosen companion of crooks, if not one himself." Arthur Schlesinger, Jr. praised McAdoo for being "tough and energetic" and lauded him for the powerful and dramatic speech that led to FDR's first nomination for President, but also called McAdoo "facile and plastic" and holding no principles except "an economic pseudo-radicalism."*

McAdoo was born on a farm in Marietta, Georgia, October 31, 1863, three months after the Battle at Gettysburg to put his times into perspective. He moved with his family to Knoxville, Tennessee, in 1877 when his father, a lawyer, became a professor at the University of Tennessee. McAdoo graduated from the University of Tennessee and then attended law school, did not graduate, but was admitted to the bar in 1885, the same year that he married his first wife, Sarah Hazelhurst Fleming. He and Sarah would have seven children. He practiced law in Chattanooga, Tennessee, remembering that Chattanooga was also Martin Hutson's hometown, and then moved to New York City about seven years later after reportedly loosing a great deal of his personal wealth trying to electrify the rail system in Chattanooga.

McAdoo's law practice centered on investment securities law. McAdoo then returned to Knoxville in 1895 to take over a bankrupt streetcar company that got him embroiled in litigation, which he eventually lost. In 1897, he gave up on his streetcar company ambitions in Knoxville and returned to New York City where he then played a leading role in building the Hudson River mass transit tunnels connecting Manhattan to New Jersey. McAdoo served as Vice Chairman of the 1912 Democratic Convention in Baltimore, Maryland that eventually nominated Woodrow Wilson on the 44th ballot.

Although his political career was a raging success, his personal life took a sad tumble. Sarah McAdoo died that same year. Known as being a political progressive, McAdoo supported Wilson's opponent through 43 ballots. He became Wilson's campaign manager and was tapped to be Secretary of the Treasury when Wilson was elected, serving from 1913 to 1918. "As Wilson's Secretary of the Treasury, McAdoo was most adept at taking institutions that had previously performed anemically, or had not even existed at all, and strengthened their regulatory reach in ways that most Americans would have considered impossible (not to mention undesirable) only a few years before.

At this time, McAdoo was following the political demands of the populace (and his own supervisor, Woodrow Wilson) but he was also leading many individuals into a realization of the power and effectiveness that strong governmental institutions could provide." McAdoo, then 50, married Wilson's youngest daughter, Eleanor Randolph Wilson, 24, in a Blue Room ceremony at the White House in May of 1914. They would have two daughters. As Treasury Secretary, McAdoo is reported to have provided the financing for America's role in World War I, unexpectedly selling more than $17 billion in war bonds with a stated goal of raising $2 billion during the process. He also served as Director General of the Railroads and Chairman of the Federal Reserve Board Ran during World War I.

As Treasury Secretary, McAdoo is generally credited by economists with helping avert a major recession by closing the New York Stock Exchange for four unprecedented months in 1914 when British and French investors were attempting to pull their investments out of the United States which would have depleted the U.S. gold reserves, which backed the currency of the nation at the time. It was thought that these European investors were seeking to fund their war efforts through greatly diminished U.S. assets and product prices.

McAdoo resumed his law career in New York in 1919, was an unsuccessful candidate for President in 1920, even though he led the nomination process on the first ballot. He would move again to California in 1922. In 1932, McAdoo was credited for helping to save Franklin Delano Roosevelt's ultimately successful presidential nomination with a speech that is reported to have ensured victory for the New York Governor. McAdoo married President Wilson's daughter when he was twice her age but divorced her in July 1934 when he was a

United States Senator from California for one term ending in 1938 after failing to regain his nomination.

Senator McAdoo surprisingly remarried some two months after his divorce degree was final to Doris Isabel Cross, a 26-year-old nurse. McAdoo was 71 at the time. McAdoo ran again for president in and led through the first 100 ballots but was ultimately not nominated by the Democrats. As a California attorney in his later years, McAdoo served as General Counsel and a 20 percent stakeholder for the renown film and television entertainment company, United Artists whom he helped advise during their formation, which included leading investors like Charlie Chaplin, Douglas Fairbanks and Mary Pickford. United Artists would eventually merge with MGM and then be purchased by eventual CNN founder Ted Turner's Turner Broadcasting System. Today, United Artists has morphed into United Artists Media Group, which is partially owned by San Francisco-based Hearst Corporation and distributes, ironically enough, the popular television show, *Survivor*.

Variously described by his doctoral dissertation biographer, Philip Chase, as "stubborn", a man who would "swim against the tide", "entrepreneurial", "skilled", "innovative", "bold", who could "inspire intense loyalty", McAdoo died from a massive heart attack while on a trip to Washington, DC on February 1, 1941 and is buried at Arlington National Cemetery.

It was said by his biographer, Chase:

> *And yet, despite his moralistic approach to many political questions, William McAdoo was probably closer in temperament and behavior to Franklin Roosevelt than he was to his political mentor, Woodrow Wilson. McAdoo never said an unfavorable word about Wilson, and until 1932 never said*

> *a favorable word concerning Roosevelt, but the eagerness to use power (in the public interest, naturally) and the necessity for forceful action without deep contemplation was always a McAdoo trait, and fits much better with the leader of the New Deal than with that of the New Freedom. As far as there was continuity between the Wilson and FDR years, it was because wartime regulation by the federal government showed a model of crisis management that could be adopted for another kind of crisis; and even if business leaders in the 1920s doubted the efficacy of federal intervention in the economic life of the nation, most of the citizens (at least by the 1930s) did not.*

Chase notes in his dissertation that McAdoo resigned his post at age 55 as Wilson's Treasury Secretary in November 1917 due to "reasons of physical exhaustion and the depletion of his financial resources." He also says, "a career that had already been uniquely 'crowded' was put on hiatus. Yet McAdoo would take on an even heavier role as head of the American Red Cross in war-torn Siberia and would immediately launch into his own presidential campaign the next year, 1920. Was he really exhausted, or simply needed by Wilson elsewhere?

Colonel Edward Mandell House

Even though he never served in the military and his title was honorary, the "Colonel" was considered to be one of the most influential Wilson foreign policy advisors during his Administration. Texas-born in 1858, House was a successful businessman and behind-the-scenes political king maker known for his clandestine capabilities.

A close friend of Wilson's during his days as New Jersey Governor, House served as the President's chief negotiator in Europe during peace talks. He was, says Wilson biographer A.

Scott Berg, "President Wilson's most trusted confidant. In access and influence, he outranked everybody in Wilson's cabinet, including the Secretary of State ...." But, at the Peace Conference in 1919, House had a falling out with the President and the two men went their separate ways. House was a very strong proponent for going to war against German but was said to have told President Wilson that he was 'not well fitted' to be a war president; 'he was too refined, too civilized, too intellectual, too cultivated not to see the incongruity and absurdity of war.'" House was also said to believe that Secretary Daniels and Secretary Baker were not suited for war either.

William Frank McCombs

McCombs was a college friend of President Wilson's who worked on his campaigns as a highly respected senior advisor and manager. McCombs had met Wilson at Princeton University where he took many of Professor Wilson's courses. Born in Arkansas, McCombs, like Wilson, had southern influences. Crippled in an accident at a young age, McCombs required the use of a cane but had a very keen intellect to offset his physical challenge.

But not all was well with the McCombs-Wilson relationship as time passed. Wilson did not offer McCombs a cabinet position and their relationship became very tense over time with McCombs actually opposing Wilson's run for president in 1920 before Wilson's strokes decided his fate. In a biography on McCombs through the state of Arkansas, it is noted that. "Although McCombs considered Wilson brilliant, he found him a cold, distant, insincere opportunist who used Congress to promote his own whims and who crushed those who disagreed with him."

Breckinridge Long

Long was the third Assistant Secretary of State for Woodrow Wilson beginning in 1917, whose given name was Samuel Miller Breckinridge Long. Long was born in Missouri, educated at Princeton University and became a lawyer after attending Washington University School of Law. He was a strong proponent for Wilson's League of Nations and worked hard for the President's re-election in 1916.

At the State Department, Long was responsible for Asian affairs and communications for the Department. He would also serve Franklin Roosevelt at the State Department during his presidency but would get into trouble over falsifying records, for which he was demoted. He was reported in various sources to have had a life-long love for race horses and sailing.

Charles Richard Crane

Crane was an American industrialist who had a strong passion for Russia, Eastern Europe and the Middle East. Introduced to you earlier by Shay McNeal, Crane was a close and early friend of Czeck leader Tomas Masaryk. Wilson used Crane extensively in the region.

More on these players will come to light in the chapters ahead but their introduction here provides a useful context for information that will be revealed through further research.

As the World War was closing, the elections of 1918 notes Cooper, "gave Republicans 38 new seats in the House, to give them a two-vote majority and 12 new seats in the Senate to give them a two-vote majority."

Cooper said that, "It was not considered a referendum on Wilson's foreign policy, as political observers and historians have concluded that if so the Republicans would have picked up far more seats. Like most midterm contests, this one turned chiefly on domestic and local issues rather than foreign affairs, event though a war was raging."

Incapacitated, paralyzed, broken, and not yet afforded the accolades that he might have been entitled to receive for potentially rescuing the former Tsar of Russia and his family from a brutal fate, Woodrow Wilson collected his 1919 Nobel Prize in 1920 for being "the leading architect behind the League of Nations," and, for ensuring "world peace after the slaughter of millions of people in the First World War."

Once out of office, the predictions for Wilson's presidency and role in the world started to flow. Jan Smuts of South Africa predicted that future Americans would "gratefully rank him with Washington and Lincoln, and his fame will have a more universal significance than theirs.' Smuts added, that hundreds of years hence, 'Wilson's name will be one of the greatest in history.'"

Berg also writes that Frank I. Cobb seconded Smut's opinion in a *New York World* opinion page article saying, "No other American has made so much world history as Woodrow Wilson,' he observed. "In drawing a sharp contrast to president Harding. Cobb reminded his readers that Wilson dealt almost exclusively with ideas. He cared little for party politics, and patronage bored him., as did the actual administration of government. He pronounced Wilson the most profound student of government among all the Presidents – with the exception of Madison, 'the Father of the Constitution.' Wilson's foreign policies had obscured the rest of his administration, he said, but his domestic policies alone guaranteed him an elevated position in American history."

Questioning What We Know

Again, if Martin's story is true, and all of these key players were available to President Wilson in assisting the AEF Siberian rescue mission, the story begs still more questions:

- Why would King George V not want to reveal that he did indeed rescue his cousins the Tsar and Tsarina of Russia, rather than be judged by history (until now at least) to have been so callous and uncaring a relative and monarch?

- Was the King's cast of trusted inner circle advisors capable of pulling off a successful rescue of the Romanov family after all?

- Did Parliament know what the King did? Or were they kept in the dark like Woodrow Wilson's Congress?

- What would be the consequences of this secrecy had it been revealed in a more-timely fashion?

- Why would President Wilson's legacy be void of such an intriguing political accomplishment if 28 did indeed aide V in plotting an evacuation?

- Was there more to the *Aide-Mémoire* than we have been led to believe?

- Did William Gibbs McAdoo play a more prominent role in Siberia for Wilson than history has indicated to date?

Recommended reading:

- A. Scott Berg, *Wilson,* G.P. Putnam's Sons, New York, NY, 2013, ISBN: 978-0-399-15921-3.
- John Milton Cooper, Jr., *Woodrow Wilson: A Biography*, Alfred A. Knopf, New York, NY, 1998, ISBN-13: 978-0-307-26541-8.

6 | Polar Bears & Wolfhounds

"The sending of this expedition was the last occasion in which the president reversed the recommendation of the War Department during my service as Chief of Staff of the Army ... almost immediately after the Siberian and North Russian forces had reached their theaters of operations, events moved rapidly and uniformly in the direction of complete failure of these expeditions to accomplish anything that their sponsors had claimed for them."

- *U.S. Army Chief of Staff Peyton C. March*

It was considered to be one of the more difficult decisions of Woodrow Wilson's presidency: the question of whether or not the United States should intervene in the civil war in Siberia following the Russian Revolution?

President Wilson's own departments of State and War argued very strongly against U.S. intervention in Siberia. Wilson, America's 28th president of the United States, ultimately decided he should indeed intervene, even though our country was winding down its involvement in World War I following an armistice with aggressor Germany, on November 11, 1918, a date we celebrate as Veterans Day in the United States and Armistice Day in the United Kingdom.

A Japanese occupation of Siberia was severely threatening American military and business interests in the region and more worrisome, nearly a billion dollars worth of arms and supplies were still sitting on the docks in Vladivostok at the end of the war potentially soon to become the property of either the Japanese or the Red Army, if American forces did not act to protect the property.

The Russians, who had previously signed the Armistice with Germany as well, were deeply involved in their own civil war between the Red Army, who was friendly to the Revolutionaries, and White Russians and other factions, who were friendly to the Tsar. A Czech Legion of some 40,000 to 50,000 stranded soldiers added to the tension in that troubled theater causing America's allies to press hard for U.S. aid and intervention.

Wilson, who was later to found the League of Nations, a first loose attempt at what would ultimately become the then-equivalent of today's United Nations, saw the Czech plight as a great excuse for America to intervene for cause. In fact, Wilson himself, personally, wrote the U.S. policy document outlining the American plan for intervention in Siberia. It was called, you will remember, the *Aide-Mémoire.* Ironically, the *Aide-Mémoire* was distributed to America's allies on the same day that Tsar Nicholas II and his family were purportedly executed on July 17, 1918.

The seven-page *Aide-Mémoire,* typed by the former president of Princeton University President Wilson himself, formally dictated American neutrality in Russia, but clearly outlined a military-supported mission in order to help restore political, financial and military stability in the region. Wilson approved of the use of up to 10,000 U.S. troops. It was the only directive that would be given his commander in Siberia, General William Sidney Graves.

A graduate of the U.S. Military Academy at West Point, Graves was a highly experienced officer trained in military intelligence. He commanded America's Eight Division, and the 27th and 31st infantries, the first troops of which arrived in

Vladivostok to a cheering crowd of White Russians on August 16, 1918.

Additional troops would eventually assist from the 12th, 13th and 62nd Infantries. Graves himself arrived in Russia on September 1st with an additional wave of 5,000 more troops. He made it to Siberia by the 4th of September. General Graves had been given a personal copy of the *Aide-Mémoire* by Wilson's Secretary of State, Newton Baker. The document, which did not contain President's Wilson's signature, was interpreted by Graves to mean that U.S. troops were not in Russia to fight Russians or any other faction. Bolsheviks and White Russian were to be treated equally, in his opinion.

While the mission was clear when President Wilson determined his preferred course of action, it was not so clear 90 days later when General Graves arrived on the ground in Siberia. The Czech Legion was no longer at risk from the Bolsheviks. The Japanese had more than 70,000 troops scattered throughout the region and unrest among the population was not as bad as it had been in previous months.

Even Congress was now questioning Wilson's decision to intervene. Logistical matters made things even worse in that the weather was horribly hostile to American troops; fuel, ammunition, supplies and food in general were short. Water-cooled machine guns froze in the inhospitable Siberian climate and were rendered useless. The American troops were equipped with M1918 (BAR) Browning Automatic Rifles, M1903 Springfield rifles, shotguns, and M1911 .45 caliber pistols. One's duty assignments dictated they type of weapon you were supplied in theater, it appears.

Wilson's Army Chief of Staff, General Peyton C. March, was becoming highly critical of the decision to commit ground troops to Siberia saying at the end of the mission: "The sending of this expedition was the last occasion in which the president reversed the recommendation of the War Department during my service as Chief of Staff of the Army ... almost immediately after the Siberian and North Russian forces had reached their theaters of operations, events moved rapidly and uniformly in the direction of complete failure of these expeditions to accomplish anything that their sponsors had claimed for them."

By the following spring, the 31st Infantry found itself distributed along the railroad lines from Vladivostok in the east to the Suchan Valley in the west. An Inter-Allied Railway Agreement had divided the 6,000-mile-long Trans-Siberian Railroad into three key sectors. The military's mandate from General Graves was to protect those sectors assigned to them from guerilla attacks by local insurgents, who were overwhelmingly sympathetic to Bolshevik Revolutionaries, and keep the railroad open for travel and communications, especially for American and White Russian forces. Duty included Vladivostok and Nikolsk-Ussuriski in the north.

General Graves' duties as the commanding officer of the American Expeditionary Forces Siberia did not come without great angst to the General and many of his troops. The General did ultimately receive the Distinguished Service Cross for his service in World War I and another for Russia. The Citation on Graves' DSC: "For especially meritorious service as assistant to the Army chief of staff and as commanding general of the American Expeditionary Force in Siberia." General Graves was also awarded the Order of The Rising Sun from Japan, the Order of Wen Hu, or the Striped Tiger, from China, the Crown of Italy, and the Czecho-Slovak War Cross. "Despite stinging rebukes and grossly unfair criticism from our own State Department and 'allies,' Gen. Graves faithfully carried out his orders, 'surrounded by ambitious commanders of many nationalities and confronted by many people made desperate [and] embittered by years of war.'"

One major conflict that is often cited in the literature surrounding the AEF Siberia relations in theater is an incident between General Graves and the U.S. Department of State over American recognition of Admiral Aleksandr V. Kolchak's White Russian government, which Graves strongly accused of mistreating people. An incident that is often detailed in historical accounts of the AEF Siberian mission had General Graves and officers in his troop blocking the delivery of rifles to the Admiral because Graves and some of his lieutenants believed that those same weapons might be turned against U.S. troops.

Secretary of State Baker had General Graves reporting to General John J. Pershing, the legendary commanding officer known to much of the military world as, "Black Jack Pershing," to head the Allied Expeditionary Force Siberia. On the other hand, Baker also insisted that the AEF Siberia forces be an independent fighting partner of the Allies against Germany, Red Russia and others, rather than permitting American troops to be used simply replenishment troops for British and French forces as those nations had recommended when attempting to lure the United States into intervening in Russia, as President Wilson ultimately decided.

Army Chief of Staff March, even though he was questioning Wilson himself for intervening, was nevertheless at the same time a Graves defender back home in Washington ecstatically praising Graves for his performance in Siberia: "the choice of the Commanding General of the Siberian Expedition was fortunate. Major General William S. Graves is particularly loyal, level-headed and firm. All these qualities were strained to the limit during the period of the American occupation of Siberia. Every possible attack was made upon him - diplomatic, newspapers and even military - and even our State Department. ..." Secretary Baker himself wrote of the criticisms that they were due to Graves' "sticking to the letter and spirit of his instructions."

In the end, sixteen Americans were awarded the Distinguished Service Cross, our nation's second-highest military award. Thirty more were killed in action and sixty soldiers were wounded in battle and skirmishes.

The Russians

There were Red Russians and there were White Russians, and often nobody could tell who was who. In fact, the Red Russians, who were supposed to represent the Bolshevik Revolutionaries led by Vladimir Lenin, were often a band of misfits who simply wanted the Tsar gone and reveled in the chaos that was post-Tsarist Russia. Their uniforms, if they even existed in those days of short supplies and no money, were a rag-tag group of colors, the only distinguishing feature was generally a red ribbon attached to their lapel signifying that they in fact considered themselves to be Red Russian.

Conversely, the White Russians had many of the same economic challenges, not to mention that "their" country no longer existed as they knew it, but they chose to wear a white ribbon on their lapel. As a consequence, it was very difficult in the days and weeks immediately following the Revolution and the Tsar's abdication to make heads-or-tails of who played what role until you were literally face-to-face with the other side.

This uncertainty and lack of clarity produced even great confusion in the battle theater so one could never really trust whom they were dealing with in those times. This bred great fear and mistrust, which of course, only made things worse for the participants, as we have seen, for example, in Martin's account of encounters with both sides.

The Red Army

Formed in January 1918, their official name was the Red Workers' and Peasants' Army, which was often shortened to be the Red Army. Lenin called them the "People's Militia." They consisted of men over the age of 18 who were class-sensitive and performed more manual work in the fields and factories where they labored. Their mission was to defend the achievements of the October Revolution and to advance the promise of Soviet socialism.

Their commanding officers were considered to be very poorly trained and said to have displayed even weaker leadership skills, thus their higher casualties and suffering economics. Communications and planning were often absent which lead, critics would say, to a very high death rate and remarkable battlefield losses.

"The poor leadership caused unbearable hardship, countless defeats, and the eventual breakup of the army as a whole. With every urge to return home on their mind, and their mentality for war running thin due to harsh conditions, Russian soldiers sometimes killed or deserted their Commanding Officers to escape service. However, soldiers who returned home faced their own civilian hardships that were brought by the growing intensity of the Russian Civil War. Revolutionaries of the Bolshevik movement, joined by Tsarist Officers and Cossack Warlords, patrolled the lands of Russia with the help of unorganized troops of ex-Russian soldiers on a mission to recruit new members to support communism, and to raid small cities and villages to feed and equip their ranks. This faction of military presence in Russia soon became known as the Red Army. The Red Army would face off against the White Army of the White Movement, which did not support the violent takeover of the Russian government, but supported absolute monarchy and the Tsar."

But in earlier days of World War I, the Red Army was considered to be an asset in the Allied forces defeat of the Kaiser's Germany, despite their poor training and high defeat rate, especially on the eastern front. Their morale improved under the Red Army, says essayist Lewis Siegelbaum, because the Soviets provided rations to the farmers who joined the Army or at least assisted in operating their farms while they were away. Just in case there was unhappiness or a desire to flee, the Soviet Red Army also had what was called Cheka brigades, which consisted of soldiers who would perform summary executions in the field of those who were considering desertion and of those who were captured in battles. Every unit in the Red Army also a political officer embedded in every unit whose job it was to override the unit's commander if they deemed that the unit commander's decision ran counter to the principals of the Soviet Communist Party. These officials, who also instilled great fear and second-guessing into the Red Army, were called the "politruk."

The White Army

While the Red Army struggled, more than just economically, the White Army enjoyed the strong financial and military support from the Allied Force, who was generally more sympathetic to the former Tsar and Provisional Government.

The White Russians were decidedly anti-Bolshevik but not as always so clearly pro-Tsarist in their consensus sentiments. Led by Alexander Kolchak, who was their Supreme Commander until his arrest in 1919 and then execution in January 1920, the White Russians were undoubtedly anti-Communist. Their forces, although quickly defeated in World

War I Russia, would hold together until World War II and even clandestinely until the fall of Communism under the Ronald Reagan Administration in the latter half of the 20th century.

The primary mission of the White Russians was to oppose the Red Russians and, if possible, restore the Tsarist monarchy or something similar. They were nationalistic in their perspective, they rejected ethnic separatism, and they opposed those who wanted separate nation-states within Russia, which they got with the Soviet Union and the post-Soviet Union that came with Mikael Gorbachev and Boris Yeltsin.

The Whites were decidedly conservative and highly patriotic. "The movement," says author Peter Kenez, "had no set plan for foreign policy; Whites differed on policies toward Germany, debating whether or not to ally with their forces. They wanted to keep from alienating any potential supporters and allies, and thus saw an exclusively monarchist position as a detriment to their cause and recruitment." Kenez said, "Some warlords who were aligned with the White movement, such as Grigory Semyonov and Roman Ungern von Sernberg, did not acknowledge any authority but their own. Consequently, the White movement had no set political leanings: members could be monarchists, republicans, rightists," and others. Among White Army leaders, Kenez said that, "neither General Lavr Kornilov nor General Anton Denikin were monarchists, yet General Pyotr Nikolayevich Wrangel was a monarchist willing to soldier for an elected, democratic Russian government. Moreover, other political parties supported the anti-Bolshevik White Army, among them the democrats, the Socialist-Revolutionary Party, and others who opposed the Bolshevik October Revolution of Lenin. But, depending on the time and place, those White Army supporters also exchanged right-wing allegiance for allegiance with the Red Army. "

Many of the White's leaders, not surprisingly, came from military leaders of the former Tsarist Russia. They, unlike the Reds, were well-trained, highly experienced in combat, and fairly well educated. They were generally better organized and had troops who followed orders and command. That is not to say, however, that after the Tsar's abdication there was not general lawlessness as a result. The Whites fought side-by-side with the Cossacks on the Southern Front of the post-Russian Revoliution. They also coordinated with the Czech Legion, who now controlled much of the terriory along the Trans-Siberian Railway between Simbirsk and Vladivostok, but were eventually pushed back to the far east until giving up that strategy in the 1920s after the AEF Siberia retreated from Russia and returned to the United States.

Although they eventually retreated after the American forces, in particular withdrew from Siberia, White Russians still maintained strong enclaves in cities such as Harbin, China, and San Francisco, California. Omsk and Vladivostok were also long-held White Russian strongholds. Colonel Semenov had autonomous control in Trans-Baikalia, while General Horvat commanded Manchuria, having been Tsar Nicholas II's military governor in the region previous to the Tsar's abdication.

Because the White Russians were able to control the southern regions between Simbirsk to Vladivostok, the British were able to focus on Northern Siberia and Russia, especially from Murmansk to Archangelsk. Kolchak, in turn, would take the city of Perm from the Bolsheviks and the Czech Legion with Kolchak's help would recapture Yekaterinburg.

So, with much going in their favor, why did the White Russians ultimately loose to the more disorganized and underfunded Red Russians?

Was Leon Trotsky, the Marxist Revolutionary, to be given credit as some have done? Or was Trotsky just a very lucky and timely beneficiary of a much broader decision made by Allied forces that led to the White Russians downfall?

Did the White Russians lose because they were made up of a group of folks who despised one another and could no longer function when the Red Russians were able to effectively use the Checka to keep their forces in line with threats and intimidation? The Checka was the Soviet secret police.

In either case, the struggle between Red and White Russian was epic. The future of Soviet Russia, or a more democratic society, rested upon their outcome.

The Allies

The Allied Force in World War I Russia during the so-called Intervention was an interesting mix of countries fighting the Kaiser's Germans. It coalesced into its final membership form by August of 1918 when 70,000 Japanese troops entered Russia along the Manchurian border and met up with the 60,000-strong Czechoslovak Legion, who had been fighting for several years already, a month or so later.

The Allies, whom Martin outlined from his own experience, comprised an admittedly odd pairing that included: Britain, Canada, Czechoslovakia, France, Great Britain, Italy, Japan and, of course, troops from America and White Russia aided from time-to-time by China. In addition to AEF Siberia force introduced earlier, the Allied Force enjoyed the following support:

Britain

Britain's troops were few since the country was fighting the war with the Germans on several fronts. Her 1,500 troops consisted of the 9th Battalion's Hampshire Regiment and the 25th

Battalion's Middlesex Regiment. First formed in 1881, the Hampshire Regiment was a British army infantry line that came from the Southeastern coast of England. Known as the "Die Hards," the Middlesex Regiment was also a British army infantry line unit that today is known as the Queen's Regiment.

Canada

Known as the Canadian Siberian Expeditionary Force, Canada's troops consisted of some 4,192 soldiers who reportedly saw little fighting and a lot of desk duty. Canadian Prime Minister Robert Borden sent his troops to Vladivostok in order to support his Crown's British troops even though he and Canada had little political or military interest in Siberia. In fact, there was considerable opposing Labour Party objections to the deployment, not to mention significant public opposition, as well.

Czechoslovaks

The Czech Legion consisting of volunteer troops seeking independence of Bohemia and Moravia from the Austrian Empire and Slovak land from the Kingdom of Hungary, was the most dominate force in Siberia during the post-Russian Revolution period in spirit. Although second in size at 50,000 troops to Japan's 70,000 troops, the Legion suffered great hardship during its tenure in Russia, including significant periods of imprisonment and the death of more than 4,000 of them, which began when they asked Tsar Nicholas II for permission to help him fight Austria-Hungary and Germany as the war broke out. The Czech Legion was instrumental in keeping the Trans-Siberian Railway open for White Russians fighting the Bolsheviks and Allied Forces, including the United

States, assisting them in their battle. In May 1918, tensions with the Bolsheviks provoked the Revolt of the Legions, leading to them helping the Allies open an Eastern Front to the War with Germany. Their plight led to the Allied intervention in the Russian Civil War.

France

France, also waging war on multiple fronts like Britain, only provided 800 troops to the Allied Force in Siberia.

Italy

Two-thousand four-hundred troops comprised the "Corpo di Spedizione Italiano in Estremo Oriente" and were ex-Italian prisoners of war, captured by the Russians from the Austro-Hungarian Army. The Italians were credited for playing a very important role in the intervention and saw combat in and around Harbin, Irkutsk and Vladivostok. They are often pictured with Allied troops on heavily-armored trains along the Trans-Siberian Railway that were strongly supported by them in concert with the Czech Legion.

Japan

Japan had interesting motivations to fight the war in Russia – they wanted to keep Russia from fighting them on a future date using Siberia as their base. They intervened at the request of President Wilson sending an initial force of 12,000 at the urging of Prime Minister Terauchi Tasatake. The force eventually grew to 70,000 troops on the ground. Like Canada, there was significant political opposition at home in the Diet to sending troops. Japan had declared war on German on August

13, 1914 under its treaty obligations according to the Anglo-Japanese Alliance. Allied control of the port of Vladivostok facing the Sea of Japan was seen by the Japanese as being of considerable military and security importance. Army Chief of Staff Yui Mitsue commanded the Japanese troops and did not yield operational control to the Allies as a condition of participating in the intervention. The Japanese would not withdraw from Siberia until October 1922.

Poland

Poland provided several thousand troops to the Allied effort in Russia.

With that context in mind, the battlefronts facing the AEF Siberian were set.

Questioning What We Know

- Why did the State Department and War Department not want to be in Siberia?

- Why did the AEF Siberia forces go to war even though World War I was ending and the Czechs had been freed, and Japanese expansion was in check, and American war supplies were under guard in Vladivostok?

- Why did the AEF Siberia forces withdraw so suddenly from Siberia in early 1920 if the White Russians were considered to be better equipped to win the Revolution?

Recommended reading:

- William S. Graves, *America's Siberian Adventure,* Peter Smith, New York, NY, 1941, ISBN-10: 0-844-61205-7 and Uncommon Valor Press, Kindle Version, 2013.

- Gibson Bell Smith, *Guarding the Railroad, Taming the Cossacks: The U.S. Army in Russia, 1918-1920,* National Archives, Washington, DC, Vol 34, No. 4. 2002.

7 | Reconstructing Timelines

Evacuation Train #28 is observed arriving on time in Harbin Rail Yard at 6:00 a.m. from Shan Hai Kuan, China.

- *AEF Siberia archives, September 27, 1919*

The American Expeditionary Forces Siberia played a highly influential role in Russia especially during the closing days of World War I when civil war pervaded the land and lawlessness ran amok. Without the tacit and unwavering commitment of her allies, America would most likely have failed in achieving her mission in Siberia and northern Russia whatever the formal objectives President Wilson dictated for his soldiers through the *Aide-Mémoire.*

Based on a wealth of information that has been compiled over the years in the official records of the American Expeditionary Forces Siberia, and other well-researched articles and manuscripts found elsewhere by many reputable and highly-respected authors, we can reconstruct the following facts by date and thus illustrate the significant milestones they represent to any Romanov rescue mission, not to mention the validity of Martin's version of events after Yekaterinburg.

Understanding the timeline of the AEF Siberia mission is critical to assessing the authenticity of Martin Hutson's recording.

The Lead-Up Years

From June 20, 1837, until her death on January 22, 1901, Queen Victoria of England was the reigning and perhaps dominant monarch in Europe and Asia. Wilhelm II of Germany, George V of Great Britain, and Nicholas II of Russia, in order of the births, were all Victoria grandchildren as we have seen.

Thomas Woodrow Wilson will be born in Staunton, Virginia in 1856 on December 28th. Wilhelm II will be born in 1859 in what was then called Prussia at the Crown Prince's Palace in Berlin on January 27th. Future British Prime Minister David Lloyd George, who would heavily influence King George V's decision on whether or not to grant his cousin Tsar asylum is born in 1863 in Manchester, England on January 17th.

AEF Siberia commanding general William Sidney Graves is born in 1865 in Mount Calm, Texas on March 27th. George V himself will be born that same year on June 3rd at Marlborough House, London. Three years later, in 1868, Tsar Nicholas II will be born on May 18th in Tsarskoye Selo, Russia. The Empress Alexandra will be born in 1872 on June 6th in Darmstadt, German Empire. Franklin Delano Roosevelt will be born on January 30th in 1882 at Hyde Park, New York.

The stage will be set for the ultimate Romanov mystery when Martin Hutson will be born about eight months after Queen Victoria passes.

The milestones to this story thus begin to unfold:

1889

William Sidney Graves graduates from the United States Military Academy at West Point beginning a very distinguished career in the Army that would ultimately lead him to Siberia.

1891

An assassin attempts to kill Nicholas II in Japan on April 29th, badly wounding the future Tsar after hitting him in the head with a sword.

1894

Nicholas is coronated Tsar of Russia upon the death of his father, Alexander III. Nicholas & Alexandra wed on November 26th, at the Grand Church of the Winter Palace in St. Petersburg, Russia, upon which Alexandra is also crowned Empress of Russia.

1895

Grand Duchess Olga Nikolaevna is born to Nicholas and Alexandra on November 15th at Tsarskoye Selo in Russia.

1897

Grand Duchess Tatiana Nikolaevna is born on June 10th at Petergof, St. Petersburg, Russia.

1899

Grand Duchess Maria Nikolaevna is born on June 26th at Petergof, St. Petersburg, Russia.

1901

Edward VII succeeds Queen Victoria and is crowned King of England. He reigns until his own death on May 6, 1910. Grand Duchess Anastasia Nikolaevna is born on June 18th at Petergof, St. Petersburg, Russia. Martin Hutson is born on August 3rd in Chattanooga, Tennessee. Woodrow Wilson becomes President of Princeton University.

1904

Tsarevich Alexei Nikolaevich is born on August 12th at Petergof, St. Petersburg, Russia.

1910

George V begins his reign as King of England upon the death of his father, Edward VII, on May 6th.

1911

Woodrow Wilson is inaugurated Governor of New Jersey on January 17th.

1913

Woodrow Wilson is inaugurated the 28th president of the United States on March 4th. On March 14th, Franklin Delano Roosevelt is appointed Wilson's Assistant Secretary of the Navy serving under Navy Secretary Josephus Daniels.

1914

Beginning June 26

Gavrilo Princip unexpectedly and violently kills Archduke Franz Ferdinand as well as his wife in Sarajevo igniting the twentieth century's first world war. A Serbian national and valued member of the Serbia Black Hand Society, Princip shoots the Ferninands in what many will see as an act of unwarranted terrorism. The Black Hand Society Princip belonged to was reportedly designed to unite all of the South Slavic territories and had been in existence since 1901, the same year that Queen Victoria died. The Archduke's assassination, in turn, provided the Archduke's Austro-Hungarian Empire the pretext to attack Princip's Serbia in order to quell what the Austro-Hungarians considered excessive Slavic nationalistic feelings among its subjects. Russia, being allied to Serbia and the European powers through treaties and self-defense agreements, was conflicted over being members of two groups in the skirmish - the Triple Alliance composed of Germany, Austria-Hungary, and Italy, and the Triple Entente, or the Allies as they were termed, consisting of Great Britain, France, and Russia. Austria-Hungary wanted very much to punish Serbia for Princip's actions, which in turn, is credited by historians with forcing Russia's political hand in the unfolding crisis. Several weeks after the assassination, Tsar Nicholas II ordered a general mobilization of his troops to deal with the crisis. If Nicholas' Russia chose to honor its alliance with Austria-Hungary, Germany would have to mobilize its own troops in response, but Germany, at the time, did not want to start a two-front war with Russia and France, if at all possible. On the other hand, Germany's treaties were important to Germany so Germany looked to conduct an opening attack against France in the event of war since Germany did not believe that Russia could mobilize quickly, or at least as quickly as France could. By advancing through Belgium and Luxembourg, Germany believed that it could attack France quickly and decisively leaving it time to deal with Russia in the aftermath. In other words, the race to war was quick and decisive.

August 1

Germany mobilizes its armed forces and demands free passage for its troops through Belgium. Belgium refuses Germany's demand two days later, and Germany, of course, disregards Belgium's refusal of its demand and attacks instead. An 1839 treaty by Great Britain's to guarantee Belgium neutrality forces a very reluctant Great Britain to intercede in the dispute. Great Britain protests Germany's violation of Belgium territory but Germany refuses to stop its aggression. Great Britain has little choice in the conflict, due to its honor code, but to declare war.

August 17

Russia invades East Prussia greatly surprising Kaiser Wilhelm's Germany. Germany, for its part, decides to destroy Russian General Alexander Samsonov's Second Army, unexpectantly taking 120,000 Russians prisoner in the meantime.

1916

March 4

Woodrow Wilson is inaugurated to his second term as president of the United States.

July

The war is not going well. Great Britain incurs at least 57,000 casualties in a single day of battle and the war thus rages on.

December 7

David Lloyd George becomes Prime Minister of England.

1917

January 7

Great Britain shares a telegram from Germany to Mexico with the United States advocating that Mexico join Germany in attacking the United States if Woodrow Wilson's United States ends its neutrality in World War I, as was regularly requested by the Allies, especially Great Britain. The United States is purposefully moving slow on entering the war.

February 1

German Kaiser Wilhelm II orders unrestricted_submarine warfare against the Allies in an effort to apply intense pressure on the Entente powers. President Wilson chooses to end diplomatic relations with Germany as a result of the Kaiser's actions.

March 8

Food riots break out in Leningrad, which has now been renamed Petrograd by the Russians.

March 14

The Russian Provisional Government is established by the Duma, Russia's Parliament, after Tsar Nicholas II's Imperial Guards revolt. The streets in Russia are littered with Russians killed in fighting, including police and military personnel who are ordered to surrender their swords. The United States ambassador to Russia, David R. Francis, reportedly welcomes the Tsar's downfall as a chance for democratic reforms to be implemented in Russia, but will later have reservations about that support.

March 15

Tsar Nicholas II abdicates in favor of his brother, Michael, who ultimately refuses to take the throne from his abdicating brother. Tsar Nicholas II is held prisoner by Bolsheviks at Alexander Palace in Tsarskoye Selo. The Tsar's net worth at the time is reported to be worth some US$900 million - which is $13.7 billion adjusted to early 21st century value.

March 16

Two American ships, the *City of Memphis* and the *Illinois,* are sunk by German U-boats in fierce Atlantic Ocean battles.

March 22

The United States government formally recognizes the Provisional Government in Russia hoping that in doing so it will help ease the pressure for America to intervene in the war since the United States does not feel the American people are ready to participate.

April 2

President Woodrow Wilson formally asks Congress to declare war on Germany.

April 4

Congress approves President Wilson's request for a declaration of war against Germany.

April 6

President Wilson signs the War Act against Germany.

April 16

Russian revolutionary leader Vladimir Lenin arrives in Petrograd, the former St. Petersburg.

April

The United States mobilized it forces and dispatches an American Expeditionary Force (AEF) to France under the command of General John (Black Jack) J. Pershing.

May 17

Russian Marxist leader Leon Trotsky arrives in Petrograd from New York City. The Provisional Government in Russia asks for American assistance in helping run the Trans-Siberian Railway. John F. Stevens and five railway experts, including one Benjamin O. Johnson of North Dakota, are sent to

Vladivostok in May 1917. Stevens concludes that American aid is indeed required because the Trans-Siberian Railroad is incapable of distributing the necessary supplies required to support people there.

August

Russia agrees to the offer for American assistance in August. Stevens' plan calls for twelve American railway personnel units to be created with superintendents, dispatchers, trainmasters, travelling engineers, mechanics, and telephone experts. Ten of these fourteen-man units will operate the railway under Steven's plan between Vladivostok and the Russian city of Omsk.

August 7

The first American Red Cross mission arrives in Petrograd. "It ministered to all in need, even cooperating with the Bolsheviks when necessary to ensure the safe delivery of supplies." The first lady's cousin, Dr. Raymond Teusler, heads the American Red Cross mission in Vladivostok. To supplement military supplies, the Red Cross is reported to furnish the AEF soldiers with socks and other winter clothing. Critical aid was also furnished to the Russian people, White Russian soldiers, and Czechoslovakians as well as the AEF, according to archived records. The Red Cross is reported to be running relief trains carrying food, clothing, and medicine to stations located along the Trans-Siberian Railway. Three sanitary trains and one dental train are also reported to be circulating through the area. A Red Cross anti-typhus train is reported to be shuttling between Vladivostok and Perm bathing 105,000 people and disinfecting 1,000,000 articles of clothing in the reported process. Red Cross support personnel are not universally offered, however, according to these same records.

Dr. Teusler, who is decidedly pro-Kolchak, is even later accused of being the virtual Surgeon-General for Kolchak's army. Little or no help was provided to the Reds during this time according to a report filed by the Wolfhounds. Another concern regarding the use of such non-military agencies by the Red Cross and others arises during the AEF's operations in Siberia, again according to official records of the Wolfhounds. The Wolfhounds report that the Red Cross, the YMCA, Knights of Columbus, and Russian Railway Service Corps personnel all wore uniforms similar to the US Army, creating, of course, much confusion. These individuals, it should be noted however, were not subject to Army regulations thus many foreigners had difficulty differentiating between the groups, it was reported. In the end, improper action by certain civilians had a negative impact on the U.S. Army's image with the Army having no way to correct the error. This problem was common enough for a few soldiers to use alleged lack of recognition as an excuse for not following an officer's orders, according to reports on the Wolfhounds' operations.

October

The Chief of the American Red Cross Mission to Russia, Raymond Robins, visits a Russian unit near Stalna and records in his diary, "The war is dead in the heart of the Russian soldier." Shortly after this visit, Mr. Robins reportedly has a revealing discussion with British General Alfred Knox concerning the Bolsheviks. The Russian Revolution's Bolshevik government signs a peace treaty with Germany causing the Entente powers to worry about a collapse of the Russian front. Germany is permitted to shift troops and war material from its eastern front to the west but Germany also decides to stockpile huge amounts of supplies that had been accumulating at Murmansk, Arkhangelsk and Vladivostok. More than 50,000

Czechoslovak Legion troops are reported to be fighting on the side of the Allies. The troops are reported to now be behind enemy lines and attempting to fight their way out through the east to Vladivostok along the Bolshevik-held Trans-Siberian Railroad. Great Britain and France decide they should militarily intervene in the Russian Civil War against the Bolshevik government. The British and French are reported to be very short of troops so they again formally request help from the Americans. The British have approximately 1,500 troops in Siberia at this time. The 9th Battalion, Hampshire Regiment and the 25th Battalion, Middlesex Regiment are among those troops reported in the Siberian and/or northern Russia theater. The Canadian Siberian Expeditionary Force, commanded by Major General James H. Elmsley, comprises 4,192 soldiers. It is also reported that Italy's Corpo di Spedizione Italiano in Estreme Oriente made of Alpini troops is supported by 2,500 ex-Italian Prisoners of War, who had fought in the Austro-Hungarian Army, and are now enrolled in the Legione Redenta in the Irkutsk, Harbin and Vladivostok regions. Japan is asked by President Wilson to supply 7,000 troops as part of an international coalition of 25,000 troops, including an American expeditionary force. Japan agreed to send Wilson 12,000 troops but under the command of Japan only, specifically Chief of Staff Yui Mitsue. It is reported that, "In political terms, the Bolshevik doctrines of class warfare, world revolution and the overthrow of capitalism were already well-known in the west."

November 2

Knox reveals his feelings toward the Bolsheviks in a conversation that is held at the Hotel Europe in Petrograd where he reportedly said, "I'll tell you what we do with such people. We shoot them."

November 11

"On 11 November 1917, just four days after Lenin and his fellow Bolsheviks seized control of the Russian capital, over 200 railway men in St. Paul, Minnesota, said goodbye to their families and boarded a train for San Francisco. Members of newly formed Russian Railway Service Corps (RRSC), a unit of experienced railway men formed to improve operations along the Trans-Siberian Railroad, the longest continuous railway on earth. Although they were uniformed similarly to U.S. army officers and were organized as a military unit, they had the legal status of civilian employees of the State Department. Not until years later would an act of Congress qualify them for military benefits." The RRSC came to Siberia at the request of Alexander Kerensky's Provisional Government, which was subsequently ousted from power by Lenin and his followers. Though ostensibly politically neutral, the Corps, in fact, worked closely with anti-Bolshevik forces and played an important role in the Allied military expedition in Siberia in 1918-1920. At first tolerant of the American railroad men's presence, since it hoped for U.S. recognition, the Bolshevik government came to view the RRSC as enemies of the state."

November 18

Colonel George H. Emerson with 350 railway personnel accompanying him sail from San Francisco, California, for Vladivostok, Russia, on the *U.S. Army Transport Thomas*. Due to the Russian Revolution, the *Thomas* does not land at Vladivostok.

November 19

Montana's Ben Johnson and his men departed for Vladivostok aboard the *U.S.S. Transport Thomas.*

December

Arriving in December, Johnson finds the port in great turmoil and decides to divert to Nagasaki, Japan, for eight months instead.

December 14

The *Thomas* arrives at its alternate destination, Nagasaki, Japan. It is reported that the *Thomas* cannot wait out the civil disturbances by anchoring in the Vladivostok harbor for fear of being iced in. Stevens decides to travel to Harbin, Manchuria, to confer with the Chinese Eastern officials to ascertain if he could put his men to work there instead.

December 15

The Bolshevik-German Armistice is agreed to.

1918

January 8

President Wilson outlines in much greater detail America's war plans to a skeptical Congress.

January 12

The first Japanese cruiser arrives in Vladivostok, Russia.

February 27

Permission is also granted so the Russian Railway Service Corps to begin its movement to Harbin. The Railway Service Corps will use Harbin as its headquarters since the Trans-Siberian Railroad is a critical element and key component in any decision to intervene, if needed. Harbin and the railroad's control is deemed to be of paramount importance in supporting any operations in Siberia. The existence of the

Railway Service Corps with its mission to supervise the operations of the rail line, in itself, is reported to be supportive of any decision to intervene, if required. The Bolsheviks also attempt to overthrow the Provisional Government but fail. Lenin flees to Finland to avoid capture and imprisonment.

March 3

The Bolsheviks sign the Treaty of Brest-Litovsk with the Germans. The Czech Legion declares its neutrality toward all political groups in Russia and starts moving toward Vladivostok for subsequent transfer to the Western Front. As the Legion departs the general area of Kiev, it is forced to hold off advancing German units. German and Czech units have battled for railway station control near Bachmach as the Czechs attempted to "entrain," it is reported. After losing approximately 100 to death and 200 more to wounds, while inflicting serious losses three times that on the Germans, the Czechs defeat the Germans and begin their long journey East.

March 26

The Bolsheviks agree to permit Czechs to return to Europe via Vladivostok. The Bolshevik government agrees to allow the Czechs to cross Russia providing all weapons except one rifle for every ten men surrendered. The Legion has now grown to approximately 45,000 strong and requires 65 trains to move eastward when they move.

April

Allied forces decide to officially intervene in Siberia, especially Japanese forces protecting shopkeepers. Ben Johnson joins Colonel Emerson and four other RRSC members in Harbin on special assignment to Vologda, the junction of the Trans-Siberian Railway and the Moscow Archangel Railway, where

Ambassador Francis has moved his headquarters from Petrograd as a result of the Brest-Litovsk crisis. Johnson and his team inspected rail terminals and travelled only by day whenever and wherever possible.

May 5

Two lead infantry regiments under the command of the Legion's Chief of Staff, General Milo K. Dietrich, reach Vladivostok. The remainder of Dietrich's troops are scattered over 4,500 miles of railroad as far west as the Volga River due to minor "bickering" with numerous Bolshevik officials, railway system inefficiency, and a lack of locomotives, it is reported.

May 26

Johnson and his party arrive in Irkutsk where significant hostilities between Czechs and Bolsheviks break out in full force and intensity.

May 27

Colonel Emerson and his men attempt to mediate a Czech-Bolshevik dispute for some two weeks.

June 8

The American Consul General at Irkutsk, Ernest Harris, orders an end to mediation efforts in the region due to full-scale civil war which breaks out unexpectedly. Emerson and his men resume their planned journey to Vologda getting as far as the Urals where they are advised by Bolshevik authorities that they will not be allowed to communicate with Ambassador Francis.

June 29

Open, unrestrained fighting breaks out between Dietrich's Czechs and the Red Army in Vladivostok. The Red

Army loses and a White Russian government is ultimately installed. Thirty-one Marines from the *U.S.S. Brooklyn* land in Vladivostok on 29 June 1918 to protect the American consulate and participate in Allied patrolling of the city."

July 6

President Wilson convenes a conference of his advisors and against the significant advice of his Department of War agrees to send 50,000 American troops as the American North Russian Expeditionary Force. This force is also known as the Polar Bear Expedition. Wilson also agreed to send 10,000 U.S. troops as the American North American Expeditionary Force Siberia.

July 16

The U.S. State Department agrees to allow overall Japanese command of the war effort for the time being but nobody appears to have informed the War Department of this decision. Evidence in the AEF Siberia records indicate that President Wilson was aware of this determination. Wilson says that the chain of command for the 20-month duration of the expedition would remain President Wilson through Secretary of War Baker to General Graves."

July 17

Tsar Nicholas II is reportedly assassinated in Yekaterinburg. President Wilson signs the *Aide-Memoire.* A series of reports indicate that the War Department had been vigorously opposed to any new war endeavor not focused on France. It is reported that Secretary Baker was greatly surprised by President Wilson's decision to intervene in Siberia. Baker, it will also be reported, would later write that the intervention in Russia was the only military decision Wilson determined personally during the course of the war that he was aware of. Army Chief of Staff, General Payton March, recommends to Secretary Baker that Major General William Sidney Graves, the commander of the 8th Infantry Division at Camp Fremont, be selected to command the AEF Siberia expedition. Graves is said to be well-known to both men, having served as March's Secretary to the General Staff just prior to taking divisional command in July 1918. Upon completing the *Aide-Mémoire,* President Wilson was under pressure to choose a commander that would lead the American Expeditionary Forces (AEF) into Siberia. However, it was noted that President Wilson was not about to choose any random commanding officer; he wanted an officer that had specific qualities and that would strictly adhere to his orders and the guidelines of the Aide-Memoire. During his Presidency, it is said that President Wilson did not maintain a strong relationship with his military advisors. Although he trusted their knowledge on military strategy, logistics, and specific tactics, Wilson, it is reported by many ultimately expected them to follow and implement his orders on matters of foreign policy and conflict. President Wilson had a reputation for expecting his military advisors to respect and obey his final orders, even if they disagreed with those orders. Sounds like almost any American president. This mentality was a struggle for the established military officers to deal with. Chief of Staff General Payton March noted in that the initial meeting between the military officers to discuss the role of the United States in the Allied intervention in Siberia, President Wilson entered the meeting and addressed the military officers as if they were a class of pupils and he was the teacher. General March also noted that President Wilson never attended one of the weekly meetings that were held by the War Council during his Presidency. President Wilson was confident over his military officers' capabilities, and also his authority over them.

Therefore, he seldom took the time to oversee their activities. President Wilson did not utilize the military power that came along with his title as commander-in-chief, nor did he attempt to influence military directives, appointment of officers, or military strategy." General March recommended General Graves to command AEF Siberia "without hesitation."

July 29

Vladimir Lenin declares that a state of war exists between Soviet Russia and the Allies.

August

"During August, 1918 General Graves coordinated logistics for the operation directly with General C.A. Devol, the Army's departmental quartermaster in San Francisco. Graves, Devol and the U.S. War Department agreed to bypass the Quartermaster General in Washington to supply the expedition. As Devol's responsibility also included U.S. Army Alaska, he had access to the cold weather equipment Graves' forces would need. Graves also insisted that food be supplied from San Francisco. As a result of this relationship and the regular runs of the U.S. Army Transport Service ships tied dockside to the Trans-Siberian Railway, support for the operation was superb." Medical care was also reported at the time to be excellent. "With two hospitals present, physicians were present with almost every company-sized detachment deployed. That these doctors also treated the local peasantry contributed much to General Graves' "operational fires." Plans also reportedly included a nine-day voyage from the Philippines to Vladivostok aboard US Army transport ships. Additional augmentation was reported to include a field hospital, ambulance support, engineers, and communications support. The plan apparently called for dispatching the two regiments in early August to arrive at Vladivostok around the 20th of August. It was reported that two groups of 3000 men each would be sent from the U.S. Pacific coast as reinforcements. One group, it was reported, would sail in early August and arrive at Vladivostok near the end of August while the second group would reportedly sail from the United States once transports were available. The War Department reported that it expected to complete troop deployments to bring the AEF to full strength by mid-October.

***August* 3**

Britain's 25th Battalion, the Middlesex Regiment in Hong Kong, was ordered to Vladivostok but the orders were cancelled before the battalion moved out. In June 1918, the battalion was again alerted. It departed, it is reported, in July and landed at Vladivostok. A lack of artillery support was compensated for courtesy of the Royal Navy. Commodore Payne of the *HMS Suffolk* at anchor in Vladivostok outfitted two armored trains by removing weapons from the *Suffolk*. The trains, it is reported, were each fitted with two twelve-pounder naval guns and two machineguns. The dependence on the Trans-Siberian Railroad made armored trains essential. All forces used them as will be seen in later paragraphs. Also on August 3rd, General Graves met Secretary Baker in the waiting room of the railway station in Kansas City, Missouri. Baker was running late but handed Graves a sealed envelope, which merely consisted of the *Aide-Mémoire,* saying it is reported, "Watch your step, you will be walking on eggs loaded with dynamite. God bless you and goodbye." Graves understood both the strategic objectives and limitations contained in the 17 July 1918 document at first reading.

Reports from the Wolfhounds note that War Department cabled the Commanding General, Philippine Division, to send the 27th and 31st Infantry Regiments to Vladivostok on the first available US Army transports. A field hospital, ambulance company, and telegraph company were said to to accompanying the regiments. The U.S. Transports, *Warren, Merritt,* and *Crook* were all designated for use. The telegram named Graves as the AEF Siberia commander and stated that 5,000 men would be sent from San Francisco to Vladivostok to complete the regiment's authorized strengths. Graves was also cabled instructions for the Philippine Division. It was reported that the U.S. War Department instructed Graves to select 5,000 men from the 8th Division at Camp Fremont for service with the AEF Siberia and he was told that additional instructions would include taking his "Chief of Staff, Assistant Chief of Staff, necessary intelligence officers, and such members of his division staff" as he deemed necessary.

August 5

The U.S. Department of State issues a press release explaining the American decision to intervene in Siberia. The Department contends that reopening the Eastern Front was "explicitly not a reason for intervening because such action would not aid Russia. Supporting this type of operation," they argued, "would use up valuable resources needed by the Russian people. Intervention was needed, however, to help the Czechoslovakian forces under attack from Austrian and German prisoners as well as steadying any self governing actions undertaken by the Russians." The State Department announcement further states, "that the United States, France, and Great Britain would land troops near Murmansk and Archangel in northern Russia with the United States and Japan landing troops in Siberia." Very clearly, the announcement promises non-interference in Russia's internal politics. In addition to armed forces, the United States makes its intention known that it will, "send a commission of merchants, agricultural experts, labor advisors, Red Cross workers, and representatives from the Young Men's Christian Association (YMCA). Other reports contend there were numerous additional reasons that influenced the Allied decision to intervene in Siberia. "Great Britain and France were openly anti-Bolshevik. Japan sought raw materials and land for population expansion. The United States wanted to help the Russian people find democracy, save the Czech Legion, and protect military and non-military supplies. It is noted that unfortunately, different reasons motivated each country. This precluded a coordinated operation from taking place since each Allied commander had to follow the dictates of his country regardless of the impact on the other Allied forces, the reports indicated.

August 6

General Graves receives a cable that updates him on the Philippine Troops that would be at his disposal for Siberia.

August 7

The 27th Infantry under the command of Colonel Henry D. Styer sailed from the Philippines aboard the USATs *Crook. Warren*, and *Merritt*.

August 8

General Graves meets U.S. Secretary of War Newton Baker in Kansas City, Missouri, at the train station and is personally handed President's Wilson *Aide-Mémoire* with instructions for waging the Siberian campaign.

August 9

Colonel Sargent receives a confidential letter of instruction from Headquarters, Philippine Department, ordering him to prepare the 31st Infantry for movement. The 31st at the time totaled 43 officers and 1346 enlisted men. Rather than going to France to fight Germans, Sargent was told that the 31st was being sent to Siberia, "a place few American knew much about." Smalser reports, "Forces were alerted on 3 August and began movement within 10 days. The combat forces, according to Smalser, were the 27th and 31st Infantry Regiments in the Philippines. Both, it was reported, contained primarily long-term professional soldiers but were at less than 50 percent of authorized strength, requiring 5000 individual replacements from Major General Graves' 8th Division at Camp Freemont. It was reported that these were mostly young draftees from the Pacific Coast states and it was observed in reports that General Graves built his American Expeditionary Forces Siberia staff from officers and headquarters detachments sent from Camp Freemont and the Department of the Philippines.

The situation was, not surprisingly, described as chaotic. Russia had suffered the heaviest casualties of any participant in the First World War and after three years of poor leadership, mind-numbing hardship, and one defeat after another, its army had fallen apart. Many Russian units shot or abandoned their officers and simply went home. For most, going home was short-lived because few could survive outside the warring factions in Russia's civil war. Ill-disciplined soldiers led by Bolshevik revolutionaries, Czarist officers, and Cossack warlords roamed the land, forcibly recruiting new members and looting the country to feed and equip themselves. By the summer of 1918, the opponents had coalesced into two main factions, Bolshevik Reds' and monarchist "Whites."

Western Allies, it was also reported, feared Russian revolution would sweep across Europe. War-weary people had become susceptible to revolutionary influences. German troops occupied nearly a third of their territory. Anti-war Bolsheviks controlled Moscow and St. Petersburg. Supplies sent to aid Russia's war effort were left unguarded on the docks at Murmansk and Vladivostok. Vladivostok alone accumulated 725,000 tons, valued at $750,000,000. Former German and Austro-Hungarian prisoners of war, Czechs and Slovaks drafted into Austro-Hungarian war. Czech government pledged to join the war against German if the allies would help get its men home. President Wilson agreed to do what he could.

Japan wanted to expand its empire into the Asian mainland. Japan had joined war against Germany but because it wanted Germany's Pacific territories. 70,000 Japanese troops entered Siberia. Allies therefore decided to occupy Russia's ports, ostensibly to prevent stranded war material from falling into hostile hands.

Major General William S. Graves, a Texan who had been decorated for bravery during the Philippine Insurrection in 1900 and served with General 'Black Jack' Pershing on the Mexican border, was selected to lead the American component of the allied expeditionary force. After serving with distinction on the Army staff, Graves had just assumed command of the 8th Division at Camp Freemont, California when he was summoned by coded message to meet Secretary of War Newton D. Baker at the Baltimore Hotel in Kansas City. The message gave no reason for the meeting and Graves did not know if he would be returning to California afterwards. He hastily departed Camp Freemont by train, meeting the Secretary in Kansas City as ordered. Baker conveyed the President's orders that Graves take two infantry regiments then stationed in the Philippines (the 27th and 31st) to Vladivostok. Most of his staff and 5000 fillers would be drawn from the 8th Division. (The 8th Division was organized around the 8th, 12th, 13th and 62nd Infantry Regiments.)

It was reported that earlier in 1918, President Woodrow Wilson had sent other service agencies to assist in Siberia. Reports also indicate that these agencies included Colonel George Emerson and his 350-man Russian Railway Service Corps, who were "instrumental in keeping the Trans-Siberian Railway operational." Also present, it was noted, were the American Red Cross, the Young Men's Christian Association and the Knights of Columbus." Reports say that these agencies "were not under Graves' controls but there was considerable cooperation, especially with the railway group. Military attaches and War Department observers were located in Harbin, Manchuria and Omsk, Siberia. State Department representatives included Ambassador Roland Morris in Tokyo, Consul General Ernest Harris at Irkutsk and Consul John Caldwell in Vladivostok."

August 10

The 3rd Battalion 31st Infantry was withdrawn from Corregidor to the Cuartel de Espana in Manila to prepare for departure. The remainder of the regiment, it is reported, was moved by barge on the Pasig River from Fort McKinley to Manila.

August 12

The regiment's main body and 115 tons of baggage, ammunition and regimental property is reported in the records to have left Manila aboard the *USAT Sherman*, while the *USAT Crook* took the regiment's horses and a 50-man caretaker detachment. The remainder of the regiment was transported aboard the *USAT Logan*. En route to Vladivostok, the transports stopped to refuel in Nagasaki, Japan. It is also noted that the 31st Infantry under Colonel Frederic H. Sargent sailed from the Philippines aboard the *USAT Sherman* for Vladivostok.

August 14

Graves, with the first of his California-based troops, leaves Camp Fremont on two trains for the transport dock at Fort Mason, San Francisco. This group, it is then reported, left the same day on the *USAT Thomas*. Colonel Robinson is reported to be accompanying General Graves as his Chief of Staff with a Major R.L. Eichelberger as his Assistant Chief of Staff on board as well. The battleship, *USS Oregon*, and the U.S. gunboat, *Vicksburg*, accompanied this element as well, it is reported.

August 15 – 21

Beginning in mid-August, the first of some 3,000 American troops disembark at Vladivostok, Russia. These troops are assigned guard duty along segments of the railway between Vladivostok and Nikolsk-Ussuriski in the north of Russia, according to Wolfhounds accounts. The *Warren* and *Crook* arrived at Vladivostok on the 15th. The *Merritt* docked the next day on the 16th of August.

August 16

According to reports: "Colonel Henry Styer was the 27th Infantry commander and senior of the two regimental commanders. Styer had landed in Vladivostok on 16 August and cabled Graves on the 19th concerning the situation as briefed to him by the Japanese forces on the ground. The Japanese were planning a general Allied offensive north of Khabarovsk against 15,000 Bolsheviks and German prisoners then west to Irkutsk along the Amur River to rescue the Czechs there from 40,000 enemy with the objective of relieving the Czechs before the onset of winter. The arriving Americans were expected to participate under Japanese command. The facts were that instead of the 7,000 to 10,000 troops envisioned by Wilson (and agreed to by the Japanese), there were nearly 72,000 Japanese troops on the ground at the time of Graves' arrival. They had also placed a 12,000-man division in control of the Chinese railway zone in Manchuria."

Mid-August

The RRSC team returns to Vladivostok and Russian officials give permission to the team to work in Harbin along the Chinese Eastern Railway.

August 21

The 31st Infantry sets up a tent camp east of the city in Gornastaya Valley. Several days later, four companies are dispatched to the north to establish strong points alone the Trans Siberian Railroad. "On arrival in Vladivostok, a detachment of roughly platoon size was drawn from the 31st to serve as guards with the 117th Hospital Train. Among them was Private Cesar Pares. Over the coming months, Pares would travel as far as Irkutsk on the Trans-Siberian Railway, picking up sick and injured American and allied soldiers and scores of desperate civilian refugees. More than a few times, bands of Red and White bandits blocked the rail line in hopes of extorting food and weapons." "The Trans Siberian Railway extended 4,700 miles from the Ural Mountains to the Sea of Japan. From Cheliabinsk, just east of the Urals, it passed through Omsk, Krasnoyarsk, and Irkutsk, then skirted Lake Baikal and proceeded to Chita. Shortly beyond Chita two branches continued to the sea at Vladivostok, the chief port of the Russian Far East. The Chinese Eastern Railway, the shorter southern branch, intersected the Chinese frontier at Manchurian Station, crossed Northern Manchuria through Harbin, the line's center for administration, and reached the Russian frontier again at Podgranitsa, a few hours from Vladivostok. The other, more circuitous branch made a great loop along the northern side of the Amur River to Khabarovsk and then due south to Vladivostok." Meanwhile, the remainder of the AEF continued to sail for Vladivostok. The 31st Infantry, it is reported, arrived. The *Vicksburg* left and the *Thomas* and returned to San Francisco. The *Oregon* left with the *Thomas* the next day. "Afterwards," according to the Wolfhounds report, "the troops manned two Browning machine guns and two one-pounder cannons on deck for self protection. After arriving at Vladivostok themselves, the 31st Infantry Regiment established a garrison camp east of the city, it was reported. The 31st Infantry arrived without its organic field transportation so they were not available for field service immediately upon arrival. A later ship brought the transportation assets they required. The tent camp in Gornastaya Valley served as the regiment's main base with detachments being sent out to guard various points along the railway. The base camp was reportedly moved a short time later from Gornastaya Valley to brick barracks on the edge of Vladivostok that the Russians had built after fighting the Japanese in the area in 1904-1905. Other than posting guard elements at various places in the area, little significant activity occurred between August and October, according to official reports.

August 29

The 31st Infantry's first combat action occurred at Ugolnaya, a small town some twenty-five miles north of Vladivostok, when a patrol came under fire from local partisans, inflicting the first American casualties on Siberian soil.

End of August

The Czech Legion now controls the Trans-Siberian Railroad from the Volga River to Vladivostok. They have established friendly governments in the cities along the railway.

September and October

The United States, France, Great Britain, Italy, and Japan recognize the Czechoslovakian National Council as the government of a co-belligerent nation fighting the Central Powers with its army in Russia an Allied army.

Early September

Emerson and Johnson are reported to have arrived back in Vladivostok after Czechs had destroyed more than 100 bridges as well as numerous depots, water towers, and other railway facilities. "Johnson played a major role in the repair work, taking charge of repairs from Irkutsk to the Ural Mountain front. His efforts gained the admiration of Czech military leaders, especially that of General Jan Syrovy, with whose troops Johnson had been early in July as the prepared to attack Ekaterinburg, the city in the northern Urals in which Tsar Nicholas II and his family were confined as prisoners of the Bolsheviks. Shortly before the general armistice of 11 November 1918, Johnson was awarded the Czechoslovak War Cross in recognition of 'conspicuous service' the only American to be thus honored during the First World War." The good relations Johnson was said to have enjoyed with the Czechs "were no doubt enhanced by his ability to communicate with them without an interpreter. Nearly all of the Czech officers spoke French and, as Johnson wrote to a friend back home in Livingston, his own command of that language was good enough 'so we get by.'" It was reported that initially, "he had great difficulty communicating with Russians, but he spent many of his evenings during the spring and summer of 1918 struggling with the Russian language and his progress was such that by the middle of August he was able to report, 'I felt very proud lately to have a boss ask me to do some Russian interpreting for him.'"

September 1

General Graves arrives in Valdivostok, Russia with Companies A, B and I. These companies were sent to Harbin, Manchuria, to guard the spur of the Trans-Siberian Railway that passed through a region of China where government no longer ruled. M Company, consisting of Chinese, British, and Japanese troops were sent to the Suchan coalmines with Lt. Col. Sylvester Soring, commanding. F and G Companies were assigned to guard the rails at Spasskoye. Major Fitzhugh B. Allerdice was the commander. L Company was assigned guard duty on the important railway tunnel in Radzolnoye. Captain Francis G. Bishop was the commander. Headquarters, supply, machinegun, along with companies C, D, E, H, and K remained at Vladivostok the remainder of 1918, it was reported. At about this same time, Czech troops took over a large segment of the Trans-Siberian Railway between Lake Baikal and Yakutsk while General Graves' son, Major Sidney C. Graves, the Executive Officer of the 3rd Battalion 31st Infantry, received the Distinguished Service Cross for service in France.

September 2

The *Thomas*, with Major General Graves on board, docks at Vladivostok. General Graves immediately visits with Japanese General Kikuzo Otani to achieve an agreement "whereby Graves would retain command of American forces but would cooperate with the Japanese within the limits of the *Aide-Memoire*. "

September 5

Japanese troops linked up with a vanguard of the Czechoslovak Legion and then were joined a few days later by British, Italian and French contingents and then trekked westward beyond Lake Baikal where Japan stopped and refused to go farther, it was reported.

September 6

Four days after the Graves-Otani meeting, the Japanese "cancelled their major offensive and began a consolidation of forces at Khabarovsk."

September 11

Graves receives word from Czech authorities "that their campaign along the Trans-Siberian Railroad from Vladivostok to Samara was a success, and that they had been able to suppress uprisings from the German and Austrian prisoners of war effectively along the way."

September 14

Additional trips by the US Transports like Martin's *Great Northern* supporting AEF Siberia delivered the remainder of the forces as needed. The USATs *Warren* and *Crook* disembarked Ambulance Company Number 4 and Field Hospital Number 4 from the Philippines. The Ambulance Company set up operations at Ulysses Bay. The field hospital established an evacuation point at Khabarovsk. A total of seven officers and 129 enlisted men were included in the two medical elements. The field hospital at Khabarovsk was upgraded to a 100-bed hospital by November, when the 27th Infantry's medical detachment combined with Field Hospital Number 4.

September 29

Replacements from Camp Fremont arrived at Vladivostok aboard the USATs *Sheridan* and *Logan* offloading an additional 3,682 soldiers. This group, reportedly, included an evacuation hospital, a medical supply depot, air ordnance-detachment, dental and veterinary elements. These replacements were also reportedly used to bring the two regiments up to full strength, form an AEF headquarters detachment, and organize a replacement battalion. The headquarters detachment contained one officer and sixty-four enlisted men. The replacement battalion consisted of six officers and 250 enlisted men. An Intelligence Section was formed from the officers and men arriving on the *Sheridan* as well as the earlier groups. The recent arrivals from the *Sheridan* included sixteen members of the Military Intelligence Division, Washington. Four officers and fifty-one enlisted men had arrived earlier and were assigned because of their knowledge of Slavic languages, Japanese, or German, it was said. A detachment of one officer and eighteen enlisted men from the Corps of Engineers were assigned for mapping. Another group of eighteen enlisted men was assigned to the Intelligence Section from the Signal Corps for communications support. With the fifteen clerks assigned, this section totaled 123 soldiers.

October

"Due to heavy casualties from Bolshevik offensives, shortages of supplies, exhaustion, the harsh Siberian winter, and lack of Allied support, the Czechoslovak Legion finally collapsed in October 1918," it was reported. "After the Czechoslovak Legion collapsed, the reason to keep the AEF in Siberia dissipated. However, the State Department was doing everything it could to redefine the role of American forces in Siberia to prevent their extraction. The State Department seemed to become increasingly anti-Bolshevik; however, the conditions of President Wilson's *Aide-Mémoire* prohibited the United States military from meddling in Russian political sovereignty. General Graves was skeptical of the State Departments (sic) new feelings toward Bolshevism. He didn't see the use of American forces in Siberia anymore, and felt that an American presence was only delaying the clash of various political extremist groups in Russia."

October 11-17

Reports from this period say that, "Because Graves was uncomfortable with the information he was getting from the interior and probably also about Japanese intentions, he visited the 'front lines' at Khabarovsk in early October. This visit confirmed the decision on courses of action he had developed during September in Vladivostok. His conclusions were: 1) all organized resistance in Siberia had disappeared, 2) Japanese intentions were to control the railways, and with them, the economies of Siberia and Manchuria, and 3) the French and English were trying to get the Allies committed to some act that would rehabilitate the eastern front; the means to this end appeared to be the overthrow of the Bolsheviks." It was reported that Graves, "kept Secretary Baker informed by cable and was instructed, in turn, not to place any U.S. forces west of Lake Baikal and, if the Czechs withdrew westward, to keep the railroad open. When communications opened in the interior, he learned from Colonel Emerson of the Railway Service that the Czechs controlled the railway all the way to Irkutzk. As a consequence, in consultation wit (sic) General Otano, Graves decided to employ his force to protect the railroad junctions from Vladivostok to Khabarovsk, to guard war stocks around Vladivostok and to employ a combined Japanese-American force in the Suchan coal mining district to keep fuel flowing to the railroad. The deployments commenced in October and were effected by company-size elements from both regiments with a battalion at Suchan. He also sent companies to protect the Chinese Eastern Railway Headquarters at Harbin, Manchuria (and to watch the Japanese) and run the POW camp at Krasnaya Retshaya. The military objective was to protect these assets from all belligerents, not just the Bolsheviks." Interestingly, "Graves' military objectives and policies did not sit well with the other Allies, who were growing in number daily. What had begun as a 15-20,000-strong Japanese-American expedition would grow, likely because of distrust for each other's intentions, to 72,000 Japanese, 9000 American, 2000 Italian 1600 British and 4200 Canadian. It was in the European best interest to overthrow the government that took Russia out of the war and British and French representatives, notably British General Alfred Knox, launched a diplomatic and media campaign against Graves. Knox was Chief of the British Military Mission to Siberia, had been a long-service attache' to Russia and was strict Czarist."

It is further reported in the archives that in October 1918, General Graves allowed *New York Times* correspondent, Carl Ackerman to join him on an inspection of the US troops guarding the Trans-Siberian Railroad.

October 15

The dispatch to British Foreign Secretary Arthur Balfour from Siberian High Commissioner Sir Charles Eliot states that witnesses saw the Romanov Imperial train depart Yekaterinburg on July 17th following the alleged assassination with the window shades closed. It is thought that the Tsar and his family was on board, it is said.

October 25

Italy's "Black Battalion of Death" detachment arrives in Vladivostok.

October 26

Canadian contingent arrives in Vladivostok. Joins General Janin of France and General Knox of Great Britain and General Otani of Japan.

October 1918 – March 1919

Reports from this period of time say: "The situation was relatively calm from October 1918 through March 1919. Few significant actions took place. MG Graves reported as early as 31 October that few troops were required in Siberia. In a letter to General Peyton March and the Army Adjutant General, MG Graves pointed out that the Japanese already had 60,000 soldiers stationed east of Lake Baikal. The presence of such a large number of soldiers was a source of discontent for the Russian people. Graves also noted the difficulty he had dealing with Russians allegedly friendly to the Allies."

November 9

Kaiser Wilhelm II flees Germany and goes into exile in the Netherlands.

November 11

World War I ends at the 11th hour on the 11th day of the month – Armistice Day as it would later be noted by King George V a year later.

November 18

Admiral Kolchak declares himself "Supreme Ruler" of Russia. Lenin and his men do not agree to the self-declaration.

December 31

Official reports indicate that the 31st Infantry grew to 3589 men from initial troop force of 1562. "New troops," it was reported, "were given a heavy dose of individual and squad training, marksmanship, and forced tactical marches in a replacement battalion before being assigned to their companies." It was also reported that, "One of the early replacements was Private Forrest Moore of Los Angeles, who was assigned to H Company in October 1918. In a letter to his mother, Moore describes the barracks and food as good, the locals as friendly, and the men of H Company as "men who really know how to soldier." Moore later served at the Suchan mines where the Bolsheveks captured him. Not everyone shared his view of the barracks and food." The first three months of 1919, were reportedly "extremely cold but Army winter clothing was surprisingly suitable for Siberia's climate. It consisted of some woolen shirts and trousers, a woolen jacket, a three-quarter length sheep lined overcoat, muskrat cap, muskrat gloves, and heavy four-buckle overshoes. Troops were equipped with an M1903 Springfield rifle, an M1918 Browning Automatic Rifle (BAR), or an M1911 .45 caliber pistol, depending upon their duties. All of these weapons, as shown by the year of fielding in their model designators, were still fairly new at the time, representing the state of the art in infantry weapons. Soldiers who fought in Korea 30 years later would still be using the BAR and trusty .45 caliber pistol would remain in service for over 70 years." It was also reported that, "Soldiers and most leaders remained uncertain of their mission, causing occasional disconnects between policies and actions. Some believed their primary responsibility was to help the Czechs fight their way back home. Others assumed they were to round up German and Austrian prisoners of war running loose all over Siberia. Most believed they had been sent to fight the Bolsheviks, derisively nicknamed, "Bolos" by American troops."

1919

January 9

The Inter-Allied Railway Agreement is authorized and approved permitting great use of the Trans-Siberian Railroad by the various parties operating in the region.

January 31

H Company of the 31st Infantry is positioned east of Vladivostok.

March

More replacements arrive, some coming from as far away as France. The Red Russian "ideologue" Yakov Ivanovitch Triapitsyn demands the withdrawal of all Allied Forces soldiers from the Suchan Mines region. The U.S. 1st Battalion's Executive Officer, Major William N. Joiner, leads C, D, E, and L Companies from nearby Shkotovo to Suchan to immediately bolster the mine guard. Companies H & K, as well as detachments of the Machinegun and Headquarters Companies, are sent as reinforcements as well. Lt. Alf Thompson, is the Regiment's signal platoon leader and orders repairs on the telegraph lines that have been cut by Russian partisans.

March 23

H Company moves to the Suchan Mines region to replace M Company as part of the mine guard. However, subsequent orders keep both companies at Suchan.

April

The Allies agree to assume responsibility for the rail line's security and operation. "The 31st Infantry was assigned the main line from Vladivostok to Ussuri, the branch line to the Suchan mines and the mining district, and also provided a small operational reserve of two companies at Vladivostok."

April 1

The requirement for continuous railway operations as a means of transportation and communication made cooperation between the United States and the Allies is deemed essential to mission success, according to records. Conferences are held between "the intervening nations' representatives to divide responsibility for operation of the railroad. Roland S. Morris, US Ambassador to Japan, represented American interests at these conferences." The representatives of the intervening nations decide to form a "Special Inter-Allied Committee" to supervise both the Chinese Eastern Railroad as well as the Trans-Siberian Railroad. "Each power with military forces in Siberia had a representative on the committee. The chairman was a Russian. Two special boards were also formed. The Technical Board was composed of railroad experts from the nations with military units in Siberia and was charged with technical and economic management." Records reflect that John F. Stevens, the US railway expert with the Russian Railway Service Corps, had been elected the board president in early March. The second board was the Military Transportation Board, whose function it was to coordinate military rail transportation. "After much discussion among the various representatives, the commanders agreed 14 April to divide the rail line into sectors to be guarded by military forces." The sectors for each nation are reported as follows:

AEF Sector 1: Vladivostok (inclusive) to Nikolsk-Ussuri (inclusive) with the Suchan Mine branch line - 144 miles.

AEF Sector 2: Spasskoe-Udinsk (inclusive) to Useuri (inclusive) - 70 miles.

AEF Sector 3: Verkhne-Udinsk (inclusive) to Baikal City (inclusive) -265 miles. This sector was later enlarged to include Verkhne-Udinsk to Mysovaya (inclusive) which added 102 miles to the length giving a total sector size of 316 miles.

April 14

Major General Graves issues orders for AEF Siberia elements to assume their designated guard posts.

April 21

Graves publishes a proclamation to the Russian people where he explains his views concerning the necessity for AEF Siberia soldiers to guard the railway. Graves points out that guarding the railway is in the best interests of the Russian people regardless of their political affiliation. Graves notes that the Allied Forces, as a group, have decided that the guard mission is necessary and confirms that the AEF's purpose is to "protect the railroad and railway property and insure the operation of passenger and freight trains" in each of the AEF's sectors "without obstruction or interruption." Graves goes on to promise that the Allies will treat everyone equally regardless of "nationality, religion, or politics." Graves also states that, "interference with traffic will not be tolerated." Kolchak supporters, it is reported, are said to be upset about the lack of any anti-Bolshevik opinion being included in the statement. It is noted, that the deployment of the AEF units "resulted in combat between the Americans and the Bolsheviks." It is explained that, "The White Russians and Allies principally controlled towns and villages. The railroad linked these power centers. The Bolsheviks occupied rural areas. Since the railroad supported the White Russians, the Bolsheviks felt they had to interdict it. American attempts to protect the railroad, whether to help the Russian people survive or to aid the Allies, forced the AEF into conflict with the Reds. Fighting and American casualties were inevitable."

May 21 – 23

Troops from the 31st Infantry "roust an ill-disciplined band of Bolshevik partisans out of town of Maihe on the Suchan spur." No American casualties are reported.

Summer

Ben Johnson of the RRSC visits Yekaterinburg and the room where the Romanovs are said to have been murdered. It is reported that, "Although he and other members of the Emerson party en route to Vologda a year earlier had been for a brief time in the vicinity, they had not been able to enter the city itself. Johnson now made up for that missed opportunity by taking time not only to interview a number of Russians who had been in the city when the imperial family was killed that summer but also to tour the house – and stand in the very room – where the executions were carried out."

June

H Company is only 31st Infantry unit now left in the area around Spasskoe, according to reports.

June 21

Three H Company men, Corporal Harlan S. Daly, Private Harold Bullard, and Private Forrest Moore, are captured by Red Russian troops while fly-fishing in the shallow Suchan River waters on a "warm summer day." Private Eastland W. Reed of H Company and Lt. Custer Fribbley of the Quartermaster Crops are captured as well and marched from Novitskaya. An Allied Forces patrol is sent out to find them as Colonel Gideon H. Williams, commander of Allied Mine Guard dispatches a detachment of the 31st Infantry to recapture them as quickly as possible.

June 22

The 31st Infantry enters the village of Novitskaya at around 8 o'clock pm with a 110-man detachment from M Company led by Lt. Gilpin Rumans. They are reportedly ambushed by a larger force of Red Russians and troops are killed. Private First Class Dee P. Craig of H Company is killed in the fighting. H Company presses its attack and captures Red Leader Sergei Samushenko. "In the suchan area, the 'truce' was broken on 22 June by a local Bolshevik leader who intended to disrupt the railway. Five 31st Infantry sodiers (sic) were taken hostage while fishing. The AEF G-2, Lieutenant Colonel Robert Eichelberger (later MacArthur's 8th Army Commander as a Lieutenant General) negotiated their release while ambushes of Americans occurred in two locations in the Suchan, resulting in 29 Americans killed. Openly challenged, General Graves ordered the 31st Infantry over to offensive action."

June 23

M Company returns to Suchan without the captured Americans.

June 24

A Company reaches Romanovka with 21 men to reinforce others. Colonel Robert L. Eichelberger, is the Siberian AEF G-2 Intelligence Officer.

June 25

Sergei Lazo's Reds fire on Company A so E Company at Novo Nezhino, which is described as being down the rail spur come to help. K Company with a "Hospital train arrived." Lt. Sylvian Kendall recalls, "The ground was strewn with blood-soaked bodies of American soldiers." Captain Oscar C. Frundt is listed as the medical officer in charge of the Company K hospital train. Gunfire continues when the hospital train arrives, it is reported, and wounded are taken aboard the train. The train attempts to returned to Vladivostok where a blown bridge stopped the train from crossing the gorge with the wounded soldiers.

June 26

C & D Companies are attacked by larger forces at Sitsa. Sgt. Ralph Cranford of Franklin, Pennsylvania is listed as the acting platoon leader and ultimately receives the Distinguished Service Cross for his actions. The Red Russians are reported to be engaged in "heavy telegraph line cutting and blowing up bridges" along the rail spur between the Suchan mines and main trunk of the Trans-Siberian Railroad line. The cut lines leave the Americans unable to call for reinforcements, or move quickly along the spur line, opening them up to ambush while on foot. It is noted that resupplies are harmed as well. General Graves goes on the offensive again ordering that partisans be chased out of Suchan and Shkotovo by Allied Forces.

June 30

The 31st Infantry is reported to have 109 officers and 3,411 enlisted men in its ranks.

July

Skirmishes, as they are described, continue throughout the Shkotovo area. A "stiff fight" occurs at Vladimir Alexandrokskoye on American Bay. Troops are picked up by the *USS Albany* and B Company is removed from Harbin. Company K fights against Red Russian partisans at Olga Bay with the British cruiser *HMS Carlisle*. A "three-axis advance" is reported through the Suchan Valley with the Army "capturing the villages then turning them over to Admiral Knight's marines and sailors for garrisoning."

July 2

Major Sidney Graves, General Graves' son, leads M Company and two machine gun squads in a counter offensive at Frolovka, where Red Rusians are believed to have their headquarters. Troops led by the younger Graves secure the town and are assisted by M Company on the ridge nearby. H and D Companies defend Suchan.

July 3

C & D Companies attack Red partisans at Kazanka, while H Company defeats another attack on Suchan.

July 5

Colonel Williams takes Companies D and M, as well as a machinegun, a medical detachment, and a Japanese rifle company, to pick up supplies at Vladimiro on American Bay. Vladimiro is described as being some 25 miles from Suchan.

July 10

H Company marches to Vladimiro-Alexandrovskaya "to escort the remaining sixty wagon loads of supplies to Suchan." No fighting is reported.

Late July

Approximately 1,400 Japanese troops enter the Suchan valley area. They have no contact with partisan forces until they are joined by Russian troops from Nikolsk.

August 6

"A partisan ultimatum" given to Colonel Williams sparks the next combat action in the region. According to records, "A local citizen told COL Williams on 6 August that the partisan band in the area forbade the Americans to bring any additional beef cattle to Suchan. This ultimatum displeased COL Williams. Therefore, he detailed CPT O.R. Rhoads to take a force to destroy the partisans. CPT Rhoads selected 2d Platoon, H Company for the task. LT Leslie commanded the 2d Platoon. Since he had only thirty-six fit soldiers, M Company provided a few reinforcements. LT Resing of M Company was detailed as a guide. The total force was composed of three officers and approximately forty enlisted men."

August 7

Captain Rhoads leads his force from Suchan to the Novo Litovskaya valley on an evening mission. The final battle in Suchan is also reported to occur when Company H annihilates a thirty-man partisan platoon, "prompting a Bolshevik withdrawal from the area. An estimated 500 Bolsheviks were killed in the month-long offensive."

August 8

The Rhoads platoon rested passes through the valley seeking information on the partisans. Captain Rhoads stops at Novo Litovskaya in the late afternoon to purchase eggs. He has discovered no information concerning partisan activities but just after Captain Rhoads leaves the village to march toward the Eastern Bay beach, a local citizen confidentially tells Captain Rhoads that the partisans are ten miles away on the Novo Litovskaya River where it emptied into Eastern Bay. Rhoads is reported as continuing in that direction until "his point element sighted the partisans." More of the description of the encounter:

> *The partisans were on a flat piece of ground about fifty yards wide along the river edge close to the river mouth. The river broadened here so it resembled a bay. Its mouth closed to a small size where the river met the Eastern Bay. The actual river mouth was about three feet deep and fifteen feet wide. The partisans were between a log hut and the water's edge. CPT Rhoads' force was about 500 yards from the river mouth when it spotted the partisans. The Americans were able to deploy without alerting the partisans. Rhoads sent one automatic rifle team to cover the left flank and two such teams to cover the right flank. One squad was detailed as a reserve. The remainder of the force moved one squad at a time to within twenty feet of the river bank which was fifty yards from the water line. These maneuvers surrounded the partisans. The Americans had three directions cut off with the river behind the partisans.*

Captain Rhoads, through his interpreter, reportedly called on the Bolsheviks to surrender but they responded by attempting to escape or take cover. "Some ran for the log cabin. Some jumped in the river to swim away. Others tried to run around the American flanks. A few partisans slipped between the American platoon and right flank automatic rifle teams but were later killed or captured. The battle started at 1800 and lasted ten minutes. Of the thirty partisans, six were captured (two severely wounded), seventeen were killed, five drowned or were killed in the river, and two escaped. No Americans were injured. Corporal Charles Frankenfeld wins the Distinguished Service Cross for his actions.

August 10

The Battle of Troitsa occurs in North Russia with Allied Forces defeating the Red Army, thus securing evacuation positions for Allied troops.

August 11

Captain Rhoads' platoon returns to Suchan. Relations with the Japanese detachment there are reported to not be good. An M Company detachment is still in town to act as a point of contact for supply operations through America Bay. "The Japanese signal officer told the American sergeant in charge of the detachment that he had to pay for all messages with money or food. The sergeant refused. CPT Rhoads was treated discourteously by the detachment commander. The provocations were so severe, one of the 2d Platoon's squads wanted to kill several Japanese soldiers. They had tried to injure CPT Rhoads.6 After returning to Suchan, CPT Rhoads was again alerted to prepare an expedition to attack the partisans. However, before he could set out, AEF Headquarters directed that all Americans leave the Suchan mine area.

August 14

AEF Headquarters Siberia orders Americans troops to meet the *USAT Merritt* in America Bay on 18 August.

August 15

The 1st Platoon, H Company, departs Suchan in the morning using wagons gathered from the area.

August 17

Supporting Martin's story that his company, H Company, did burial detail, the archives note the following: "The last Americans, except for a burial detail guard (a platoon from H Company), left at 0600…." It is reported that, in all, five wagon trains moved the Americans for this particular mission.

August 18

Rough weather, it is noted, prevents the *Merritt* from unloading the burial detail on board until today even though it arrived 16 August. This is the burial practice day detailed in an earlier chapter.

August 19

The Americans leave Suchan because it is determined that they cannot adequately defend the rail lines on the spur so the mines are closed due to conflict. Having no legitimate reason to keep their garrisons in the valley, Allied Forces march to America Bay boarding the *USS Merritt* for the remainder of the evacuation trip to Vladivostok. Cossack Whites are reported to fill the "vacuum" left by the withdrawing Allies. "Unfortunately, the platoon left at Suchan had exhumed and then reburied the American dead when the burial detail failed to arrive. When this H Company platoon reached the bay, an M Company platoon was sent back to Suchan with the burial detail to exhume the bodies again. This group the brought the bodies to America Bay. The *Merritt* completes loading and sails at 2130 that evening.

August 20

The *Merritt* arrives at Vladivostok at 1000. American participation in the Allied Mine Guard is deemed finished. However, it is observed that other operations will be conducted in the Suchan area as time progresses. 18-year-old Martin Hutson thought he was recruited to go to Mexico but is instead informed that he will be going to Siberia.

August 21-24 +/-

Hutson is at Fort Ogelthrope and ships out to San Francisco, via train.

August 23

The last of the Americans and their General leave North Russia.

August 23-26 +/-

Hutson travels to Fort McDowell in San Francisco, via train and spends 3 to 4 days.

August 26-30+/-

Hutson ships out for Hawaii and Vladivostok, Russia.

September

"Shortly after the visit to Ekaterinburg, Johnson was confronted with an unanticipated challenge that taxed his energy and expertise to their limits," according to accounts. "The forces of Admiral Aleksandr Kolchak, leader of the White movements against Bolshevism, suffered disastrous reverses near the Ural Mountains, prompting a massive eastward retreat across the Trans-Siberian Railway." The accounts from Village Green provide this interesting observation:

> *Johnson and a handful of other RRSC officers had charge of this movement through Omsk, and during September 1919 they directed the passage of some 45 trains a day. Then, in October, with the demoralization of the Kolchak forces complete and amidst an outbreak of typhoid fever and smallpox, the Allies ordered the evacuation of all Allied troops from Siberia. RRSC personnel were instructed to cease all other activities and assist the troops to Vladivostok. Johnson left Omsk with the last Allied train on 12 November and the Bolsheviks occupied the city the next day.*

September 2

Russians in the presence of Japanese troops arrest an American Captain and a corporal at Iman, 250 miles north of Vladivostok. Neither was said to have passports at the time.

September 2-6 +/-

Hutson is aboard the *USST Great Northern* and arrives in Hawaii.

September 3-7 +/-

Hutson ships out for Vladivostok aboard the *USAT Great Northern*. Spends 14 days at sea.

September 7

General Graves' chief of staff, Colonel Robinson, is dispatched to meet with Russian General Rozanov.

September 9

The British retreat to Arkhangelsk.

September 17-21 +/-

Hutson arrives Vladivostok.

September 20-24 +/-

Hutson spends three days at the hanger in Vladivostok. Is assigned to H Company, 31st Infantry.

September 26

President Wilson suffers a series of strokes that leave him incapacitated.

September 27

Evacuation Train #28 is observed arriving on time in Harbin Rail Yard at 6:00 a.m. from Shan Hai Kuan, China. Chapter 14 discusses this in detail.

September 29

The Czech Legion receives orders to leave Siberia.

October

Company H occupies Shmakovka.

October 1

Allied forces evacuate Murmansk.

October 2

Colonel Fred W. Bugbee assumes command of the 31st Infantry from Colonel Sargent. President Wilson suffers another very serious stroke that leaves the left side of his body paralyzed.

October 14 - 22

The United States government decides to support Kolchak's forces by supplying rifles in several shipments to be delivered to the Warlord. One of these shipments includes 45,000 rifles on a train guarded by forty-five men of the 31st

Infantry under the command of 1st Lieutenant Albert E. Ryan. As the train enters the 27th Infantry sector, "the operation ceased being routine." Lt. Ryan left Vladivostok at 0100 on the 14th of October. He had reportedly planned to leave the afternoon before but mechanical delays interfered. "Mechanical problems, wrecked trains, and local hostility slowed his journey," it was said. It is noted that stops en route provided the Americans with several opportunities to bathe and purchase food. The train is reported to have reached Harbin on October 20th. Ryan arrived at Manchuria Station at 1900 on the 22nd of October.

October 24

At 0500, Lt. Ryan arrives at Chita and stops to purchase beef for his troops. "At 1000, the Russian lieutenant presented a telegram" to Lt. Ryan "that the Russian claimed to have just received from his headquarters. The telegram authorized the Russian to give 15,000 rifles to Semenov. Since Lt. Ryan's orders were "to deliver the entire trainload to Kolchak's army," Lt. Ryan reportedly refuses "to part with the 15,000 rifles unless orders from AEF Headquarters to do so "arrive. The Russians threaten to take the rifles by force but that does not dissuade or distract Lt. Ryan from his position, it is noted. "Furious telegram traffic" between Colonel Morrow, Major General Graves, Semenov, and Japanese and Russian representatives confirm Lt. Ryan's orders and they all express support for Lt. Ryan's opinion. Ryan prepares for a fight with the Russians and constructs fighting positions under the train cars, which are now barricaded on the track to prevent the theft of any of the cars.

October 25

Similar to an incident recounted by Martin, a Russian armored train pulls along side Lt. Ryan's train at 0245. "A Russian company with four machineguns" approaches the station at 1000 but do not attack. At 1325 that afternoon, the Russian lieutenant returns to the station and tells Lt. Ryan that the matter is settled. Semenov agrees to allow the train to continue on its way. Being ever so cautious and skeptical, Ryan refuses to take down his barricades until the Russian armored train has pulled completely away. By 1700, it is reported that the Russians have departed. At 2215 that evening Lt. Ryan and his team finally leave Chita.

October 27

Ryan transfers the rifles to Admiral Kolchak's forces at Irkutsk.

As 1919 Progressed

As 1919 progresses, "The State Department also came to be aligned against Graves." Graves' reports to Washington on the atrocities committed by Kolchak's warlords which he felt were weighing against recognition of the Omsk government, something the local State Department representatives and Foggy Bottom's Russian Bureau desired as much as the British and French. "Complaints from both Secretary of State Robert Lansing and British Prime Minister Lloyd George were repeatedly rebuffed by President Wilson: ..."

November 1-5 +/-

Hutson has spent six weeks at the church outside of Vladivostok training with other troops from Company H.

November 8-12 +/-

Hutson learns Wig Wag in preparation for shipping out to Irkutsk.

November 12

The RRSC's Ben Johnson leaves Omsk on last Allied train.

November 13-19 +/-

Hutson travels to Irkutsk arriving at the train yard for guard duty.

November 13

Bolsheviks occupy the city of Omsk.

November 16-21 +/-

Hutson guards the train at Irkutsk train yard.

November 16

A Czech leader named Alexander Gaida, a Lieutenant in Admiral Kolchak's Siberian Army, leads an insurrection at Vladivostok.

November 17-22 +/-

Hutson meets Nicholas and spends week with him talking two hours a day for a week.

November 22

A train guard detachment is ambushed near Razdolnoye.

November 31- December 3 +/-

Hutson has spent a 2nd week with Nicholas traveling to Harbin via Chita.

December

Ben Johnson is promoted to the rank of Colonel and designated Emerson's successor both as commanding officer of the RRSC and as chief inspector of the Chinese Eastern and Trans Siberian Railways. Johnson, it is noted, has become responsible for formally overseeing the drawn-out process of evacuating Allied forces from Siberia.

December 1-4 +/-

Nicholas is transferred to another AEF contact in Harbin, China, according to Martin's story.

December 4

H Company under Captain Rhoads' command moved from Vladivostok to Shkotovo to reinforce the garrison. Major Thomas Arms is noted as commanding the provisional battalion, and sends Company H to Fanza to reinforce Company C.

December 5

H Company, which is listed as comprising only 100 soldiers now, reinforces the Fanza garrison. Thirty of its soldiers occupy Baritznaya. Forty occupy Kishmish.

Christmas

Christmas 1919 is not recorded as being a quiet one for the Americans in Shkotovo. At approximately 0100 the 28th, Americans hear several shots in the Russian barracks. "Thinking it was a typical drunken brawl, no one worried. However, at 0200, the Russian garrison commander arrived at the American headquarters and was very excited. At least one-half of the 800-man Russian garrison had deserted. Four or five Russian officers had been murdered.

December 29-31

General Graves is formally notified to begin preparations to withdraw from Siberia. Graves issues orders to his units to begin concentrating their locations so that they can begin moving to Vladivostok.

1920

January 5

H Company moves to Shkotovo where Shkotovo had difficulty using the railroad. The Bolsheviks have destroyed two railroad bridges between Romanovka and Novo Nezhino and the Americans therefore are forced to "requisition" over 100 local wagons on sleds in order to move. Twelve miles of track are reported to have been destroyed.

January 8

AEF is formally withdrawn from Siberia. Departure begins from Shkotovo District where two partisan attacks also occur.

January 9

Cossacks attack the 27th Infantry.

January 10

The troops in the area are all reported to be well concentrated at Shkotovo. Train engines to move the entire body of troops are reported difficult to find. Only one engine near Ugolnaya is eventually obtained. Russian railroad officials protest its seizure but a four-man guard detail guaranteed its security. The Americans used the engine for seven days. This incident is also consistent with a story shared in Martin's account.

January 14

All Spasskoe-Ussuri sector troops are reported to be in Vladivostok and begin departure for Camp Barry in Manila.

January 16 – February 25

American and British Red Cross units depart with the Lake Baikal echelons and begin arriving in Manila through February 25th.

January 18

All troops from the Shkotovo sector are reported moved to Vladivostok.

January 25 – February 3

General Rozonov's Russian White Army is overcome in Amur Province by a combined force of Social Democrats and Bolsheviks, formally ending White Russian opposition in Siberia. Rioting and looting is reported to break out in Vladivostok in anticipation of a Red Russian takeover. Companies A, C, I and L establish police patrols in the city. Companies E and H patrol outside of the city.

January 31

A Bolshevek government is formed in Vladivostok and a large parade is reported held to celebrate their accomplishment.

February 3

American patrols in and around the city are ordered to be discontinued.

February 7

Admiral Kolchak is executed by Bolsheviks in Irkutsk, the same town where he was said to have been married.

February 15

The first units of the 21st Infantry leave Vladivostok and continue to do so for 45 days. The *USAT Crook, Dix, South Bend,* and *Great Northern* carry "Polar Bears" back to Manila where their odyssey began.

February 15 - April 1

The 31st Infantry departs in groups from Siberia on the *USAT Crook, Dix, South Bend,* and *Great Northern* transport ships. The 2d Provisional Battalion consisting of A, C, E, H, and I Companies depart first and arrive at Manila on the 5th of March. Each echelon reportedly stay at Camp Barry temporarily before moving to Fort McKinley.

April 1

The last contingent of the 31st Infantry leaves Siberia:

> *The 31st Infantry had carried out its orders with courage, humanity, and dignity. Sixteen members of the regiment had been awarded the Distinguished Service Cross, 29 were killed in action, 8 died of wounds received in action, and 52 were wounded, testifying to the valor of a generation of Americans fighting in a far-off, miserable place to accomplish an unclear mission."*

"Allied intervention ends."

April 17

The entire regiment is assembled at Fort William McKinley. Major General William Sidney Graves becomes the Fort McKinley commander.

June

The last train load of Allied soldiers reached Vladivostok. The RRSC departs for home.

July 30

All Allied forces but the Japanese have sailed for home or other locations.

August 26

Franklin Roosevelt serves his last day as Assistant Secretary of the Navy.

By end of year

James P. Smythe publishes the controversial, *Rescuing the Czar,* which later goes missing from book shelves.

1921

March 3

Woodrow Wilson's last day as president of the United States. He will remain in Washington, D.C.

1922

October 22

British Prime Minister David Lloyd George's last day in office.

Mid-November

Ben Johnson finally leaves Russia. Various reports say the following of that time:

The American tenets of self determination and self government – so ably expressed in the 'Fourteen Points' – yet so misunderstood by our Victorian friends, were to be set in stone by AEF Siberia. There were only two alternatives for the Russian people – autocracy under a White Russian government or collectivism under the Bolsheviks – and the majority of Russians favored Bolshevism during the AEF Siberia's tenure in Russia. However distasteful Bolshevism was, it was what the people wanted and Wilson's principles demanded they be allowed to have it. Graves served Wilson, and the furtherance of American principles, well here."

AEF Siberia put 9000 soldiers in harm's way for 20 months in the subarctic misery of World War I, half of them young draftees. That Graves only lost 35 killed, 52 wounded, 135 dead to disease and 50 to desertion is truly remarkable. This reflects favorably on the leadership, discipline and training provided by AEF Siberia.

Although esteemed in the eyes of many – President Wilson, Secretary Baker, Peyton March, Robert Eichelberger and the soldiers of AEF Siberia (who continued to hold reunions well into the 1970's) – William Graves' personal reputation would be pilloried for decades. His 1931 book, America's Siberian Adventure, is a defensive treatise on policy written as though the operation was a disaster. Graves' son, in the next generation, would devote much effort to clearing his father's name. Graves' superiors, to their credit, did not sacrifice him to political expediency, although there was considerable pressure to do so. Graves went on in the 1920's to command the 1st Infantry Brigade, the 1st Infantry Division, VI Corps, the Panama Canal Division and the Department of the Canal Zone until his voluntary retirement in 1928.

Washington warned General Graves that the Japanese Strategy was likely to keep the various Russian forces apart and oppose any strong Russian central authority, but to support a number of weak Russian forces which could not form more than a screen for Japanese Action.

1928

William Sidney Graves retires from the Army. Baroness Sophie Buxhoeveden publishes a biography on Empress Alexandra, her friend, whom she is accused of betraying to the Bolsheviks at Yekaterinburg. Harriet von Rathlef-Keilmann publishes, *Anastasia: The Survivor of Ekaterinburg.*

1929

Sergei Makin publishes, *How We Tried to Rescue the Tsarista.*

1930's

December 30, 1930

The American Consul General for Harbin, Ernest Harris, is quoted in the *Montreal Gazette* as saying that he escorted the Tsar's ashes out of Siberia on an AEF train.

1931

Retired Army Major General William S. Graves publishes his memoire, *America's Siberian Adventure.* Future Russian president Boris Yeltsin is born in Butka, Russia on February 1, 1931.

1932

Martin Hutson alleges that he saw an article in the *Louisville Courier-Journal* in quoting Consul Ernest Harris as saying that he, Harris, saw the Tsar alive long after reported assassination on a similar train. Martin says that he asks the U.S. State Department if he can speak with Consul Harris but is told that the Consul is not available.

March 4, 1933

Franklin Delano Roosevelt begins the first of four unprecedented terms as president of the United States.

November 16, 1935

President Roosevelt's *Mystery Story* is published by *Liberty*.

January 20, 1936

King George V dies at Sandringham Castle in Norfolk, England.

1940's

February 27, 1940

Major General William Sidney Graves (Ret.) dies in Shrewsbury, New Jersey.

June 4, 1941

Wilhelm II dies in exile in Doom, Netherlands.

March 26, 1945

Former British Prime Minister David Lloyd George dies in Wales.

April 12, 1945

President Roosevelt dies in Warm Springs, Georgia.

1950's

1956

Yul Brynner stars in the motion picture, *Anastasia,* with the actress Ingrid Bergman, who wins the Academy Award for Best Actress, for her portrayal of Tsar Nicholas II's youngest daughter.

1960's

1965

Dr. Zhivago is released in movie theaters and wins five Academy Awards for the landmark film telling the story of the Russian Revolution.

1970's

1971

Robert Massey publishes the epic *Nicholas & Alexandra* which, wins more than just rave reviews for its compelling storyline. Martin Hutson records his story as "An Episode in My Life: 1919-1920" with family members. Martin dies shortly after that recording date on August 1st in Harlan, Kentucky.

1975

Guy Richards publishes, *The Rescue of the Romanovs.*

1976

Anthony Summers and Tom Mangold publish, *The File on the Tsar.*

July 27, 1977

The Ipatiev House is destroyed by Boris Yeltsin.

1979

Nine bodies believed to be the Tsar, Tsarina and other members of his family are physically found in a grave at Koptyaki Road, 12 miles from Yekaterinburg to the northwest. They are found by two amateur sleuths who are reported to remove three skulls, taking two to Moscow and placing one under a bed.

Alexei and one daughter are reported missing and is not certain if the missing daughter is Anastasia, Marie or Tatiana.

1980's

1980

The amateur sleuths reportedly re-bury the skulls at the Koptyaki gravesite.

1983

Peter Kurth publishes, *The Riddle of Anna Anderson*.

1990's

1991

Romanov gravesite re-opened and the bodies are reportedly exhumed.

July 10, 1991

Boris Yeltsin becomes President of Russia.

May 10, 1992

The Sunday Times of London carries the eye-popping front-page banner headline: "Remains of Tsar and Family Found in

Forest." The bodies of Alexei and a daughter are reported to be missing.

July 25, 1992

University of Florida forensic anthropologist, Dr. William Maples and his team arrived in Yekaterinburg to examine the Romanov remains checking into the Hotel October, a hotel that was formerly used only by high Communist officials.

September 15, 1992

Pavel Ivanov board a jet in Moscow and carries with him in a British Airways travel bag, femur pieces carefully wrapped and sealed in polyethylene from each of the nine alleged Romanov skeletons that had been lying on examining tables in the Yekaterinburg morgue that then Secretary of State James Baker, III, had previously visited.

January 24, 1993

The Times of London carries another eye-popping headline: "Great Tsar's Bones Hoax.

April 1993

Dr. William Hamilton, the Gainesville, Florida medical examiner, accompanies Dr. Maples on his second trip to Yekaterinburg this time with a film crew from the television show, Nova, a Public Broadcasting System production of their popular science program, *Unsolved Mysteries.*

August 1993

The bones are identified as Romanovs by the Aldermaston team lead by Dr. Peter Gill, where Prince Philip sent his blood sample.

1994

Michael Occleshaw publishes, *The Romanov Conspiracies.*

February 1994

Dr. Peter Gill, Pavel Ivanov, and others put their findings in print in their own words, publishing a description of their work in Nature Genetics, the authoritative journal of their profession. Their findings and article have never been challenged or even mildly criticized in print or orally, by another DNA scientist."

1995

Robert Massey publishes, *The Romanovs: The Final Chapter.*

1997

The Walt Disney Company releases an animated version of the Anastasia story grossing more than $140 million to date at the box office and from home video rentals.

1998

Michael Gray publishes, *The Astonishing Story of the Survival of the Tsarevich.*

July 17, 1998

The remains of Tsar Nicholas II, are entombed in the St. Catherine's chapel at Peter and Paul Cathedral in St. Petersburg, Russia along with those also said to be Alexandra, Olga, Tatiana, Anastasia and the four attendants who are believed to have perished with the Romanovs: the Tsar's physician, Dr. Eugene Botkin; his valet, Alouzy Tropp; the family cook, Ivan Kharitonov; and, the Tsarina's lady-in-waiting. Alexei is still missing according to Russian officials who claim that the Tsar's daughter, Maria, is missing as well.

December 31, 1999

Boris Yeltsin ends his run as President of Russia.

2000's

2001

Shay McNeal publishes, *The Secret Plot to Save the Tsar.*

2003

Greg King and Penny Wilson publish, *The Fate of the Romanovs.*

April 23, 2007

Boris Yeltsin dies in Moscow at age 76.

August 23, 2007

The second Romanov grave is said to be found containing Alexei and the missing second daughter.

2008

Helen Rappaport publishes, *The Last Days of The Romanovs.*

2014

Helen Rappaport publishes, *The Romanov Sisters.*

2016

Russian Orthodox Church asks government officials for more testing to assure the identity of Romanov found remains before interring them in the Cathedral of St. Peter and St. Paul with the rest of the family. Russian authorities approve the request. Russian president Vladimir Putin announces that he would like to restore Tsars to Russian life.

2018

Russia will host the FIFA World Cup with the Tsarist murder city, Yekaterinburg, serving as a venue site. The 100th anniversary of the alleged assassination occurs three days after the final match on July 17th.

Questioning What We Know

Knowing now how the AEF Siberia mission unfolded, especially in context with the other events surrounding the Romanov mystery over the years, and Martin's episode taken into account in the timeline as well, a number of new questions arise:

- The archives material on the AEF Siberian expedition demonstrate that burial detail practices occurred in and around the time that Martin Hutson was "in-theater." Were these sessions related to Martin's mission?

- On November 22, 1919, a train guard detachment is ambushed near Razdolnoye. This incident also falls within Martin's timeframe of events. Was this the time when the Nicholas evacuation train was attacked and burned?

- And, the incident in which a single train was commandeered by AEF forces in early 1920, is that related to Martin's story as well?

It would appear, for the moment at least, that the timeline for the AEF Siberia's activities and Martin's account are plausible based on this detailed reconstruction of events related to the Romanov mystery.

Recommended reading:

- David Bullock, *The Russian Civil War, 1918-22*, Oxford, England: Osprey Publishing, 2008, ISBN-10: 1846032717.

- Betty Miller Unterberger, *America's Siberian Expedition, 1918-1920*, Duke University Press, Durham, NC, 1956, ASIN: B000NZZWDW.

8 | Warring Cousins

On a personal side, Wilhelm, who has been Kaiser since 1888 when his father died of throat cancer after only a few weeks on the throne, is feeling belittled by Nicholas because his grandmother, Queen Victoria, does not appear to like him as much as she apparently likes "cousin Nicky."

- *Michael Balfour, author of The Kaiser & His Times*

George Frederick Ernest Albert governed a monarchy steeped in intrigue: He was second cousin to the warring Tsar Nicholas II of Russia and first cousin to Kaiser Wilhelm, II of Germany. He was the grandson of the fabled Queen Victoria and prodigal son of Edward VII, a former Prince of Wales.

When his elder brother (he was the second-born son) died from pneumonia related to a worldwide flu epidemic that swept Britain in 1891-1892, he married his fiancée, Princess (later the much-celebrated Queen Mary) Mary of Teck, who herself was born at Kensington Palace. He was father to George VI and Edward VIII, who controversially abdicated the throne to marry an American divorcèe.

He changed the family's royal name from the very German-sounding Saxe-Coburg-Gotha to what we know it to be today - Windsor. He is the grandfather of the reigning British monarch at the time of this writing, Her Magesty Queen Elizabeth II.

Born in 1865, the same year that Abraham Lincoln was assassinated in America, His Royal Highness (HRH) George V, as he would later be known, was a naval officer of the first order, similar to many other members of his own royal family past and present, and eventually became a member of the House of Lords. He was crowned King at the famous Westminster Abbey in 1910 after his father died and soon inherited a war in July 1914 waged by yet another grandson of Queen Victoria, herself of German ancestry.

As the father of six, a heavy smoker, he preferred to rule by executing existing laws rather than creating new ones. He was popular for personally visiting the front lines of the war hundreds (not tens) of time and for being on hand in places one would not expect a monarch to visit.

Recognizing after the fall of both first cousins that monarchs were unpopular, George V permitted Ireland to a break away and become a free state while India took steps to independence during his reign with his permission. Australia, Canada, New Zealand and South Africa followed suit.

The King's Cast

King George V was and has been largely criticized by historians for not doing more to help save the Tsar from his alleged brutal murder in 1918. At one point, the King had promised his cousins political exile in England, only to withdraw that offer before exile could be achieved.

The King had a number of players around his inner and governing circles who would play a major role in the Tsar's abdication and reported murder, among them the following:

David Lloyd George – was England's Prime Minister from late 1916 to 1922. Prior to having been Prime Minister, Lloyd George was Chancellor of the Exchequer, which is the equivalent of the U.S. Secretary of the Treasury – the money man, if you will. He was a lawyer by training, a skilled politician through experience, and an agnostic when it came to his religious beliefs, which no doubt must have bothered the highly spiritual Woodrow Wilson immensely, despite his other liberal political leanings. Born in England to Welsh parents, English was Lloyd George's second language. He was happy that the Tsar's reign ended but was in favor of giving the Tsar sanctuary in Britain, if need be, or in a neutral country, preferably. Despite this, Lloyd George was roundly blamed for much of the 20th century as having been responsible for the King's decision to keep the Tsar and his family in the Urals, where they reportedly were murdered. Lloyd George and Woodrow Wilson clashed on numerous occasions at the 1919 Paris Peace Conference that gave the western world the Versailles Treaty, reinforcing understanding around the world that the two political Allied leaders did not actually or frequently see eye-to-eye. Historical profiles of Lloyd George say he was a known womanizer despite being married for a long time.

Sir William Wiseman – head of British Intelligence in the United States was the acknowledged liaison between King George V and Woodrow Wilson, especially through Wilson confidant Colonel Edward House. A banker and intelligence officer, Sir William was in later years a partner in a respected American investment firm for four decades. Wiseman spent a notable week on vacation with the American president and Colonel House in August 1918.

Arthur Balfour – was the British Foreign Secretary under Prime Minister David Lloyd George, but a former Prime Minister himself during the reign of Edward VII in the early 1900s. Balfour distrusted America's concept of equality and was said to be a highly self-obsessed person.

Prince Arthur - Arthur William Patrick Albert was the Duke of Connaught and a trusted confidant of his nephew, King George V. He was also the 10th Governor General of Canada from 1911 to 1916. His godfather was Wilhelm I, the World War I Kaiser's father. His wife was also heavily involved in the Red Cross.

Sir Thomas Preston - was head of the British Consulate in Yekaterinburg when the Tsar and his family were reportedly shot.

Kaiser Wilhelm II

He was the third cousin in our story, the eldest grandson before Nicholas II, his second cousin married to his first cousin, and another first cousin, George V.

The war was not yet really a day old but Kaiser Wilhelm II, whose non-regal name is Friedrich Wilhelm Viktor Albert, the Emperor of Germany and King of Prussia, and Nicholas II, the Tsar of Russia, two already storied grandsons of Queen Victoria of England and thus first cousins, were trading telegrams. The telegrams have been described as being "frantic" in nature.

Wilhelm, who was born in 1859 in Potsdam outside of Berlin with a withered arm from a difficult birth that caused Erb's Palsy in Potsdam, is worried that Nicholas will be drawn into the newly declared war by Germany and Austria-Hungary on Serbia in retaliation for the assassination of the Archduke Franz Ferdinand, who was a close personal friend, and his politically unfortunate wife a month earlier by a Serbian nationalist in the capital city, Sarajevo.

Germany had a mutual protection treaty with Austria-Hungary while Russian had a similar agreement with Serbia, thus the diplomatic and military impasse the two cousins now found themselves facing as heads of state of their respective empires. Nicholas was escalating the tensions by mobilizing his troops in response to the newly declared war against Serbia by Germany fearing, too, that the Kaiser was using the Archduke's assassination as a pretext of sorts to launch a war that would shore up its power in the Balkan states region.

On a personal side, Wilhelm, who has been Kaiser since 1888 when his father died of throat cancer after only a few weeks on the throne, is feeling belittled by Nicholas because his grandmother, Queen Victoria, does not appear to like him as much as she apparently likes "cousin Nicky." He pleads:

> *In this serious moment, I appeal to you to help me," writes Tsar Nicholas II to Wilhelm in a telegram dispatched at wrote one o'clock in the morning of July 29th, the day after war is declared. "An ignoble war has been declared to a weak country," Nicholas says. "The indignation in Russia shared fully by me is enormous. I foresee that very soon I shall be overwhelmed by the pressure forced upon me and be forced to take extreme measures which will lead to war.*

Wilhelm in a message that crossed that same early morning hour to Nicholas, expresses deep concern and reservations about the impact Austria's declaration will have in Russia and urges calm and consideration as a response from Nicky. Receiving the Tsar's telegram in the meantime, Wilhelm taps back that:

> *I ... share your wish that peace should be maintained. But ... I cannot consider Austria's action against Serbia an 'ignoble' war. Austria knows by experience that Serbian promises on paper are wholly unreliable. I understand its action must be judged as trending to get full guarantee that*

> *the Serbian promises shall become real facts ... I therefore suggest that it would be quite possible for Russia to remain a spectator of the Austro-Serbian conflict without involving Europe in the most horrible war she ever witnessed.'*

"I foresee that very soon I shall be overwhelmed by the pressure forced upon me and be forced to take extreme measures which will lead to war, Nicholas responds. "To try and avoid such a calamity as a European war I beg you in the name of our old friendship to do what you can to stop your allies from going too far. Nicky." He also writes the Tsar on the 29th:

> *Thanks for your telegram conciliatory and friendly. Whereas official message presented today by your ambassador to my minister was conveyed in a very different tone. Beg you to explain this divergency! It would be right to give over the Austro-servian [sic] problem to the Hague conference. Trust in your wisdom and friendship. Your loving Nicky.*

Wilhelm, who was 29 when he ascended to the Prussian Kingdom throne, seeks to assure Nicholas that his government is working to broker an agreement between Russia and Austria-Hungary, but he warns Nicholas that if Russia were to take military measures against Austria, war would essentially be the unavoidable result. On July 30th, Wilhelm writes to Nicholas:

> *I have gone to the utmost limits of the possible in my efforts to save peace .... Even now, you can still save the peace of Europe by stopping your military measures.*

Nicholas replies the next day:

> *It is technically impossible to stop our military preparations which were obligatory owing to Austria's mobilization. We are far from wishing for war. As long as the negotiations with Austria on Serbia's account are taking place my troops shall not make any provocative action. I give you my solemn word for this.*

Austria's Emperor, Franz Josef, rejects the Kaiser's offer to mediate with Austria-Hungary, alleging that the Kaiser's offer has come too late since Russia is already mobilizing troops on the Serbian front side of the country and seems intent to do battle. Germany delivers an ultimatum – end the mobilization within 12 hours, or else Germany will begin its own mobilization that will result, most likely, in war. Russia remains silent in response to the ultimatum and the Kaiser orders a mobilization in response. The world is at war but does not yet fully appreciate that fact.

Tsar Nicholas II presses Wilhelm nonetheless for assurance that his mobilization does not necessarily mean war in itself but Wilhelm is highly dismissive of cousin Nicky:

> *I yesterday pointed out to your government the way by which alone war may be avoided .... I have ... been obliged to mobilize my army. Immediate affirmative clear and unmistakable answer from your government is the only way to avoid endless misery. Until I have received this answer alas, I am unable to discuss the subject of your telegram. As a matter of fact I must request you to immediatly [sic] order your troops on no account to commit the slightest act of trespassing over our frontiers.*

Wilhelm had seven children with a wife who died after 21 years of marriage and a second wife who outlived him. His mother had raised him to be inclined toward the British culture but history says that Wilhelm actually preferred Germany's more autocratic rule, as opposed to Britain's more democratic rule, causing great tension with his parents. Tension would also exist with governmental leaders in Germany who objected to the Kaiser's active participation in government and with other Western governments who would be embarrassed by his failure to appropriately support foreign policy initiatives such as the Boxer Rebellion (in which he was very late to the game of putting down an anti-western rebellion in China, yet very brash in his charge to his troops to go in an do battle when battle was essentially no longer needed); and, the Moroccan Crisis in which he appeared to take sides against France in Morocco's quest for independence.

Historians have said that both sides of Wilhelm's family suffered from various forms of mental illnesss, which may explain, they say, his own apparent emotional instability at times. Wilhelm's "concerns" included the driving need to create a German navy that would rival that of Britain and Russia, least they decide to invade his country. He reportedly craved his grandmother's approval and intensely disliked and distrusted his British royal family members. In fact, the historian David Fromkin, says that Wilhelm, who was highly intelligent, very impatient, and at times appeared irrational, actually had a love-hate relationship with Britain that was fueled by his own dislike for his English-born mother. Writes Fromkin:

> *From the outset, the half-German side of him was at war with the half-English side. He [Wilhelm] was wildly jealous of the British, wanting to be British, wanting to be better at being British than the British were, while at the same time hating them and resenting them because he never could be fully accepted by them.*

Proof, some say, of the Kaiser's anti-British viewpoint before it became clear with World War I, was an interview that became known as the *Daily Telegraph* Affair in October 1908, in which Wilhelm, among other highly incindiary comments emotionally referred to the Engliash as being, "mad, mad, mad as March hares" asking, "What has come over you that you are so completely given over to suspicions quite unworthy of a great nation?" He went on to imply that Germans, therefore, cared nothing for the British, let alone the French, the Russians, and the Japanese, all of whom he ended up fighting in World War I.

To make matters worse, perhaps in keeping with the paranoia that some historians alleged the Kaiser exhibited, it is also clear from correspondence available all these years later that the Kaiser believed that England, Russia and France had previously agreed among themselves to use the Austro Hungarian-Serbian conflict as a pretext for waging a war of annihilation against Germany, knowing that Germany had treaty obligations that compeled them to support Austria. He said:

> *Our dilemma over keeping faith with the old and honourable Emperor has been exploited to create a situation which gives England the excuse she has been seeking to annihilate us with a spurious appearance of justice on the pretext that she is helping France and maintaining the well-known Balance of Power in Europe, i.e., playing off all European States for her own benefit against us.*

At home, Wilhelm was being marginalized by his own generals. The Schlieffen Plan, which called for Germany to attack the perceived weaker France if Britain might enter the war, was designed to help keep the war a one-front affair potentially, while Russia figured out what it was doing. Unfortunately, for Germany, the Plan was a failure so Field Marshall Paul von Hindenburg, who the famed dirigible was named for, and General Ericj Ludendoff took control of the war strategy while Wilhelm was dispatched to perform the more ceremonial duties of state.

As the war winds down, President Wilson makes clear that the Kaiser will not be welcome in negotiating the peace between the Allies and Germany. Wilhelm lost significant political and military support within his own government as a result and abdicated on November 9, 1919 – two days before the Armistice with Germany, fleeing to the Netherlands, who agreed to provide him political asylum. His family's 400-year rule had ended, too. The Treaty of Versailles sought to prosecute Wilhem for war crimes, but Queen Wilhelmina refused to extradite Wilhelm despite strong calls to do so from Allied forces.

British Prime Minister David Lloyd George, in one of his more theatrical moments, called for the Kaiser to hang, but King George V, smartly, rejected that idea although he did lable his first cousin as possibly the "greatest criminal in history." Wilson himself did not see value in extraditing Wilhelm, agreeing with Queen Wilhelmina that prosecuting Wilhelm would be internationally destablizing and, therefore, might possibly destablize world peace.

Unlike his cousin Nicky, Wilhelm was permitted to remove twenty-three railway carriages of furniture including a car, a boat and an assorment of other household goods from the Kaiser's New Palace at Potsdam, the last great Prussian baroque palace.

Was there a special deal in place that made for a safe asylum in the Netherlands, connected somehow to an asylum deal for Nicholas II and his family?

Wilhelm II died in 1941 and is buried in the Netherlands, never returning to Germany, as he wished, at least until the monarchy is restored.

Questioning What We Know

- So, did Wilhelm II help rescue Cousin Nicky?
- Did Wilhelm have an agreement for safe asylum of his own at the end of World War II, which permitted him to go to the Netherlands?
- Was there an asylum agreement between the cousins for Nicky's safe passage?
- Was George V's ruling style sensitive to criticism like that which was reportedly offer by the Prime Minister?
- Did George V have an inherent distrust for his "trusted advisors" similar to President Wilson?

Recommended reading:

- Dennis Judd, *The Life and Times of George V*, Weidenfield & Nicholson, London, England, 1993, ASIN: B00120FKVC.
- John van der Kiste, and Coryne Hall, *Kaiser Wilhelm II: Germany's Last Emperor*, Sutton, Gloucester, England, 1996, ISBN-13: 978-0750919418.

9 | Wilson's Boys

One of the most dashing men ever to wear the uniform, John Joseph "Black Jack" Pershing was the most accomplished and celebrated American soldier of the early 20th century

- *The American Experience,* WGBH Boston/PBS

He was called, *Black Jack.* General Black Jack Pershing, that is, and ironically enough for this book, Pershing was of German ancestry.

A graduate of the U.S. Military Academy at West Point in 1886, John Joseph Pershing was a Missouri boy who did good in school, earned his appointment, rose to the highest cadet rank possible, was remembered for his extraordinarily strong leadership skills, and earned the respect of a grateful nation through his service in World War I. His service saw some of the most storied battles in American military history: The Apache and Sioux Wars of the late 1800's, The Cuban War and the Battle of San Juan Hill, the Russo-Japanese War, The Moro Rebellion, the Mexican Revolution where his forces which included General William Sidney Graves defeated the famed Pancho Villa in 1915, and then as Commander-in-Chief of the American Expeditionary Forces in Europe and Asia.

A member of the 6th U.S. Cavalry in the early years of his military career, Pershing would become an expert marksman in pistol and rifle. He was called, *Black Jack,* because of a not-so-nice more derogatory nickname he picked up from cadets he later taught at West Point, who thought he was too strict and rigid. They called him that because he was a white officer who commanded African-American troops when he led the famed segregated 10th Cavalry Regiment. It was a nickname that stuck and became well known and respected by the time of the Tsar's reported assassination in 1918.

Pershing's exploits on the battlefield led to his award of the Distinguished Service Cross, the Distinguished Service Medal, the Silver Star, the Purple Heart, and France's Légion d'honneur, their highest medal for service. He also earned a law degree in 1893 while teaching military science and tactics at the University of Nebraska at Lincoln. Pershing's citation for his Distinguished Service Cross reads:

> *The Distinguished Service Cross is presented to John J. Pershing, Brigadier General, U.S. Army, for extraordinary heroism in action against hostile fanatical Moros at Mount Bagsak, Jolo, Philippine Islands, on June 15, 1913. Brigadier General Pershing personally assumed command of the assaulting line at the most critical period when only about 15 yards from the last Moro position. His encouragement and splendid example of personal heroism resulted in a general advance and the prompt capture of the hostile stronghold.*

In 1921, Pershing was appointed U.S. Army Chief of Staff by President Warren G. Harding, and rose to the prestigious position of General of the Armies by act of Congress before retiring in 1924. He was the only person in American history to be promoted to General of the Armies during his lifetime, a rank that was awarded George Washington in 1976, long after his death, of course. Pershing is credited for training America's great World War II generals, including: Omar Bradley, Dwight David Eisenhower, George C. Marshall, and George S. Patton.

Pershing's wife was Helen Frances Warren, daughter of a powerful and influential United States Senator, Francis E. Warren, a Republican from Wyoming who also chaired the Senate Committee on Military Appropriations. President Theodore Roosevelt was a great fan of Pershing earlier in his career so when he was promoted to the rank of General over many other more senior officers, reports indicate that accusations flew that Pershing's promotion was as a result of his political connections, not his military accomplishments and ability.

Helen and their three daughters would die in a tragic fire at the Presidio in San Francisco in August 1915. His six-year-old son, Warren, survived the fire, which was caused by the lacquered floors at the famed military installation not far from the Golden Gate Bridge.

During his service in the Philippines from 1909 to 1912, Pershing commanded Fort McKinley, located near Manila, which would be extensively used by AEF Siberia during the Tsar's disappearance and reported assassination.

During the Mexico war, Pershing commanded the Mexican Punitive Expedition consisting of 10,000 soldiers and chased Villa's troops deep in to the country, but failed to capture him. The Expedition was ill-equipped and ill-prepared for the battles, and received very little direct support and aide from the Mexican government, a lesson that would not be lost on Pershing in future battles, including Siberia.

When Pershing took over command of the U.S. troops in Europe during World War I, President Wilson gave the General great leeway in conducting his missions through a very "hands-off" philosophy that would mark his own career and not surprise, as we have seen earlier in the profile of President Wilson, those who served him closely. Command of the troops was to have gone to General Frederick Funston, according to most historical accounts, but General Funston suffered a heart attack just weeks before the declaration of war and died. Pershing was selected by President Wilson who valued his discretion and loyalty. According to Wilson biographer, A. Scott Berg:

> *And so, Secretary Baker and Wilson turned to General John J. Pershing, then fifty-seven years old. Tall, stiff-backed, and square-jawed, with a manicured mustache and a commanding voice that he used as little as possible, Pershing consistently had displayed leadership as he had risen through the ranks: with the 6th Cavalry, fighting Apaches and Sioux; commanding the 10th Cavalry – a regiment of the African American "buffalo soldiers", which earned him the nickname "Black Jack"; teaching at West Point; fighting in Cuba and the Philippines: and serving in diplomatic postings in Japan and the Balkans before leading the 8th Calvary in the punitive expedition along the Mexican border.*

The Mexico expedition had been a politically stressful event in Pershing's military career because there was not consensus in Washington on Capitol Hill or at the other end of Pennsylvania Avenue either as to how to solve the safety issue along the very long U.S.-Mexico border. Pancho Villa and his bandits were crossing the border at will and the U.S., which had a small presence there was not really in the position to prevent or end the unauthorized incursions into U.S. territory. Villa was at war with the Mexican government and disliked the Americans for appearing to endorse their leader Carranza.

On Newton Baker's first day in office as Secretary of War, Villa and 1,500 bandits rode three miles inside the border and attacked a small town in the American state of New Mexico, Columbus. Seventeen Americans were killed, according to an account by Berg, only half of whom he notes were soldiers. American troops from the 13th Cavalry in turn chased Villa's bandits five miles back inside Mexico killing 75 of them in the process but discovering papers that Villa had dropped detailing his true mission, Berg writes, "Kill all the Gringos." Gringos, of course, being a derogatory Spanish word for "foreigners."

Wilson authorizes a "punative expedition" whose sole objective is to capture Poncho Villa dead or alive. Wilson had not consulted either Carranza's Mexican government, or even secured the recommendation of his own general in the area, before sending in U.S. troops. Not surprisingly, Carranza strongly objected to the violations of his own border but agreed to cooperate with Wilson so as to avoid a war with the United States. One of Carranza's Colonels, however, not on the same page with his de facto leader, as he was being described by the U.S., said that he would attack U.S. forces if they did go inside the Mexican border. Wilson, from his perspective, did not view the American "invasions" as an intended infringement on Mexican sovereignty – he wanted to stop a bandit who was clearly not going to stop raiding cities and towns inside the U.S.-Mexico border.

Into this potentially volatile political and diplomatic mix, Wilson sends in Pershing, who takes 5,000 U.S. soldiers with him and does cross the U.S.-Mexico border to pursue Villa who is now much farther inside Mexico hiding from the Americans. The political debate continues in Washington, with Secretaries Baker and Lansing arguing that the U.S. should withdraw, while Colonel House and other Cabinet secretaries argue to go all in.

Wilson decides to stay in but his political opponents on Capitol Hill call him tentative and indecisive and ask if that will serve American interests in Europe? Carranza, meantime, is also being criticized by his own side for permitting the American incursions and is accused of being a traitor for allowing a foreign army to occupy their territory. Pershing's and Carranza's troops do attack one another in a small Mexican village called Carrizal, some 75 miles inside Mexico. Nine U.S. soldiers are killed and another 25 are taken prisoner by the Mexicans, led by a local commander who is not apparently cooperating with Carranza's collaboration strategy. Villa continues to evade Pershing.

Wilson holds strong against going to war with Mexico over the Carrizal incident even though there are strong calls to do so from Capitol Hill, and from within the White House itself. Wilson, Berg says, is worried about U.S. intelligence that indicates that Germany is trying to cause a war between the U.S. and Mexico on its southern border in order to protect their own submarine warfare in the Atlantic Ocean, on the United States' eastern shore.

Wilson is criticized for doing too much in Mexico and not enough in Europe and he is criticized for not doing enough in Mexico and ignoring Europe all together. The Mexican impasse with Villa is eventually addressed by Congress who authorizes the National Guard in the United States to fund and place 100,000 troops along the border to protect American interests.

Berg says of the Congressional action:

> *Without capturing Villa, Pershing's men served as mostly scarecrows at the border, reservists from all walks of life playing soldier for a few months and enjoying their military excursion. For Mexicans – even those who disapproved of Villa – the eleven-month expedition remained an unforgiveable incursion.*

Either way, Pershing was no clearly Wilson's man. He did what he was ordered to do and he did it without question.

Another story that is recounted in Berg's biography tells the story very nicely as to why Wilson was so impressed with Black Jack Pershing. Wilson, aboard the *U.S.S. George Washington* steaming to London for a Christmas 1919 meeting with King George V, asks his advisors to remember something about the General as well: It is said that "he asked everyone gathered if they would remember one story: 'that not five months prior, General Pershing's AEF had joined the French at Château-Thierry, where they were ordered to retreat with the French army. The American commander tore up the orders and commanded his divisions to advance instead, thereby saving Paris and gaining momentum to win the war. 'It is not too much to say that at Château-Thierry we saved the world,' Wilson told his advisors, 'and I do not intend to let those Europeans forget it. They were beaten when we came in and they know it .... They all acknowledged that our men at Château-Thierry saved them. Now they are trying to forget it.'"

At the end of Woodrow Wilson's second term as president, when he knew he would not seek election again because of his debilitating strokes, Pershing was encouraged to run for the office himself. He declined to actively campaign for the office that was eventually won by fellow Republican Warren G. Harding of Ohio.

Published in 1931, Pershing's autobiography, *My Experience of War*, won the Pulitzer Prize for history the following year. He passed away at age 84 in 1948 in Washington, DC, a resident of the Walter Reed Army Medical Center. His body lay in state at the U.S. Capitol, a rare honor few non-presidential Americans are afforded by our nation and he is buried under a very simple headstone next his beloved, "Doughboys" of World War I at Arlington National Cemetery next to two grandsons, who also served.

The American Experience through WGBH/PBS probably summed it up Pershing's career best noting in their profile of the General many years later:

> *One of the most dashing men ever to wear the uniform, John Joseph "Black Jack" Pershing was the most accomplished and celebrated American soldier of the early 20th century. But to a young Douglas MacArthur entering West Point in 1899, the name John Pershing most likely elicited fear and loathing, not admiration. That summer MacArthur joined Company A, where stories about their recently departed tactical officer -- Pershing, known to the company as "Lord God Almighty" -- had already become legendary.*

George Hutson

George Hutson was Martin's older brother and a valued Black Jack Pershing aide in World War I. He served his country and the General in Europe with the American Expeditionary Forces earning the Distinguished Service Cross near Le Channel, France, eleven days after the Tsar's purported murder in Russia. His citation reads:

> *The President of the United States of America, authorized by Act of Congress, July 9, 1918, takes pleasure in presenting the Distinguished Service Cross to Private George R. Hutson (ASN: 1550465), United States Army, for extraordinary heroism in action while serving with Battery B, 76th Field Artillery, 3rd Division, A.E.F., near Le Channel, France, 28 July 1918. After he, himself, his commanding officer, and 32 comrades had been wounded by a bomb from an enemy plane, Private Hutson remained at his post, assisted in laying his piece, and directing fire on the enemy.*

Born in Tullahoma, Tennessee and raised in Knoxville, the injuries he sustained in the war would dog him the rest of his life, but George R. Hutson was proud of his service to his nation, and that of his little brother, even if they could not talk openly about their exploits.

Unlike Martin, George could be mildly more flambouyant in style only. He liked dapper clothes and especially his hats - Fedora hats. Because of his disability, George never married and never had children. As for George's personality, he was very serious in demeanor and was known for being precise and thorough - a stickler, as they say, for detail and perserverance.

William Sidney Graves

William Sidney Graves, who commanded the American Expeditionary Forces Siberia with all of the authority of a president of the United States, it would seem, was a West Point man, through and through, a graduate of the class of 1889.

He was born in Texas to a Southern Baptist minister's family. He would rise to the rank of Major General in the United States Army and earn some of his nation's most coveted battle awards: The Distinguished Service Medal, the World War I Victory Medal, and he would be recognized for top honors from Japan, Italy and Czechoslovakia. He would serve in the Spanish-American War, the Philippine-American War, World War I and the Russian Civil War. He commanded the 1st and 8th Infantry Divisions and, of course, commanded the American troops in Siberia.

Graves was also a family man. Graves' wife, Katherine Pauline Boyd, Kate as he called her, was the niece of his commanding officer, Henry C. Merriam, an Army General who was also a Medal of Honor recipient for his service with African-

American troops during the U.S. Civil War between the North and the South. They married in Colorado while he was posted at Ft. Logan, and had four children, one of whom died as an infant. Their son, Sidney Carroll Graves, would follow in his father's footsteps graduating from the United States Military Academy at West Point himself and commanding troops along side his father in Siberia, earning a Distinguished Service Cross. He would also marry one of Teddy Roosevelt's relatives. This is somewhat ironic, if you think about it as you read further in this book, as Assistant Secretary of the Navy during the Siberian Adventure, Franklin Delano Roosevelt, also married a Teddy Roosevelt relative, not to mention was one himself.

Coincidence?

There are other very interesting familial connections throughout General Graves' story as well, as you will learn, involving President Wilson's relatives and the American Red Cross in Siberia. Is there more than just a loose connection here? We shall see.

In the meantime, for our purposes in this chapter, Secretary of War Newton Baker says of Graves, ". . . I knew him to be a self-reliant, educated and highly trained soldier, empowered with common sense and self-effacing loyalty, the two qualities which would be most needed to meet the many difficulties I could foresee. Now that this strange adventure is over, I am more than ever satisfied with the choice of the American Command. A temperamental, rash, or erratic officer in command of the American force in Siberia might well have created situations demanding impossible military exertions on the part of the Allies and particularly of the United States, and involved our country in complications of a most unfortunate kind.

General John J. Pershing was introduced to Graves' capabilities during his service in the Spanish-American War where he participated in various battles and skirmishes against Philippine insurgents. Newton Baker and Woodrow Wilson noticed Graves' devotion to duty and his famous discipline while he was stationed in Washington, DC doing stints as Secretary to the General Staff and as Assistant Army Chief of Staff. Several secret missions to Great Britain and France helped lay the groundwork for Wilson and Baker to take America into World War I.

Two news worthy events occurred during his career that were interesting background pieces for understanding General Graves' experience and perspective:

> *The Great San Francisco earthquake of 1906 leveled much of that great city and resulted in the deaths of more than 700, although the U.S. Geological Survey, when reporting on the event which they say is one of the most significant in American history, says the earthquake itself, prior to the fire, was probably under-reported by a factor "of 3 or 4." Graves was sent to San Francisco by the army to help maintain law and order, as well as clean up and rebuild the city. The Army had a major presence there at the Presidio and nearby Angel Island. He would later serve as commander at San Francisco's Ft. McDowell when he received orders to take command of the American Expeditionary Force Siberia.*
>
> *The Court Martial of Billy Mitchell was an extraordinary event where the famed aviator, who was a recipient of the Distinguished Service Cross and the Distinguished Service Medal, was accused and eventually convicted of insubordination after accusing Army and Navy leadership of being essentially treasonous for not building aircraft carries instead of battleships in 1925. Mitchell is often called the "Father" of the United States Air Force and even had the World War II workhorse B-25 named in honor of him,*

years after the court martial, interestingly enough. It was the B-25 that Colonel Jimmy Doolittle and his band of raiders used to bomb Japan during World War II. Graves and Douglas MacArthur were both judges on the 12-judge Mitchell court martial that lasted some seven weeks and earned many headlines in newspapers across the nation.

In his 1931 book, *America's Siberian Adventure,* Graves strongly criticizes the White Russian leadership in Siberia for their many atrocities. His official papers reside at Stanford University's Hoover Institute but a read of the book is quite fascinating – both for what it says and what it does not say.

The forward itself by former Secretary of War Newton Baker explains how Siberia came about and the decision to recommend Graves to the President:

At a third conference the President told me that he was satisfied with the soundness of the War Department's view but that, for other than military reasons, he felt obliged to cooperate in a limited way in both proposed expeditions. The reasons moving the President to this determination were diplomatic and I refrain from discussing them.

Like so many other times when examining the AEF Siberia campaign, and General Graves' leadership of those forces, questions get raised. What, for example, does Secretary Baker mean when he writes that he will refrain from discussing the reasons President Wilson was moved to authorize the Siberian intervention?

The book by General Graves, after all, was designed specifically to set the Siberian record straight since many were openly criticizing the mission in the 1920s. The non-military reasons were very clearly diplomatic. Was the reluctance to talk about the reasoning behind the decision to intervene because the Siberian mission included a previously unwritten Tsarist rescue component for King George V as well?

Baker then adds fuel to the fire with this: "Detached from its world implication, the Siberian Adventure seemed mystifying. Indeed, even General Graves himself has 'never been able' to come to any satisfying conclusions as to why the United States ever engaged in such intervention." That is somewhat odd in its own right as well. If you review the three stated goals of the *Aide-Mémoire*, as President Wilson outlined them, General Graves' service should be deemed a wildly successful mission. The Czech troops were liberated in the end, Japanese expansionist ambitions were thwarted in the end, and valuable American supplies were kept out of the hands of the Germans and Red Russians until they were judged no longer detrimental to American and Allied war objectives.

Even if the there was a fourth, and as far as we still know unwritten, objective for intervening in Siberia, the Tsar and his family appear to have been rescued as well. Why would Secretary Baker, therefore, believe that General Graves would not be able to satisfy his conclusions as to why the United States ever engaged in that intervention, especially if you take at face value, which is a conservative exercise here, that General Graves was the type of West Point-trained Army officer who would not (and apparently previously did not) question his orders from the President and General Black Jack Pershing?

In fact, in that same forward where Baker makes his astonishing comments about being mystifying and not wanting to comment on other presidential motives, Graves himself alludes to another mission perhaps in his book dedication?

To the Honorable Newton Baker, former Secretary of War whose cooperation, support and sense of justice made it possible for American troops to perform their duties without anxiety as to the consequences of misrepresentation and hostile criticism.

What misrepresentation could General Graves be considering here? The Siberian intervention was President Wilson's decision and the direct order of the Commander-in-Chief to his commanding officer in Siberia, as outlined in a very direct document called the *Aide-Mémoire*? The AEF Siberia troops were neutral, but armed force was certainly permitted and even expected by American political and military leadership to defend themselves where needed under battle conditions, which certainly existed at the time of World War I and the Russian Revolution.

The Siberian Expedition put very simply started with a conspiracy - a Bolshevik conspiracy to overthrow the Tsar of Russia, a Red Russian conspiracy to murder him and his family in Yekaterinburg, an Allied conspiracy to rescue the Romanovs from Russia, and a decades-long conspiracy by western governments to bring an end to Lenin's Soviet Union once and for all.

At the center of it all, whether he liked it or not, was General William Sidney Graves, the commanding officer of the American Expeditionary Forces Siberia, who by all accounts did his job, in the best traditions of the Army. The controversies Siberia generated then and still do today would remain a daily part of his existence even after General Graves retired from the Army in 1928.

Although General Graves died on February 28, 1940, at the age of 74, he remains at the center of the discussion to this day nevertheless.

Questioning What We Know

- Why did George Hutson have so much influence that he could convince General Black Jack Pershing to select Martin for a special role in Siberia with Nicholas II?
- Why was Black Jack Pershing so determined to help rescue the Tsar in such a risky mission from Siberia?
- Would General Graves have been trained to perform such a mission while at West Point?
- What was the true purpose of the Kansas City train station meeting with Secretary Baker?
- Was there an earlier connection between General Graves and Secretary McAdoo?
- Why did General Graves never really come forward and set the historical record straight when it came to the true success or failure of the AEF mission in Siberia relative to Tsar Nicholas I.

Recommended reading:

- Douglas B. Craig, *Progressives at War: William G. McAdoo and Newton D. Baker, 1863-1941,* Baltimore, MD: Johns Hopkins University Press, 2013, ISBN 1 4214 0718.
- Donald Smythe, *Pershing: General of the Armies,* Indiana University Press, Bloomington, IL, 1986, ISBN-13: 978-0253219244.

PART III: ESCAPING SIBERIA

10 | SPECIAL TRAIN #28

"Train 28 arrived on time at 6:00 am. Stevens arrived at 9:17 am."

- A.J. Carr, Traffic Inspector, Harbin Rail Yard

Nicholas' Imperial Trains, like that which was used to evacuate the former Tsar and his family members according to Martin, were magnificent. Ornate. Luxurious. Regal. Adjectives do not adequately represent in themselves just how special these trophies of the Russian empire were, nor do these particular adjectives tell the true story of the role they played in the Tsar's death - whether he truly died as history dictates, or as said earlier, "died so that he could live."

Their interiors were palatial. The finest linens, the splendid china and crystal, the intricate fabrics, the wood inlays, the mesmerizing photographs and personal family touches, the Tsarist blue hues of the cars themselves adorned by the Romanov crest, accented by Indian teakwood or trimmed in gilded gold leaf, were all on display throughout the coaches that composed the Tsar's Imperial Train.

The curved ceilings sported paddle fans the length of the car. The windows were many and permitted great amounts of sunlight to enter the cars creating an airy sense of freshness with sparkle. Heavy curtains were swept back into ties that would permit the windows to be covered if desired when the outside world was not wanted inside the Romanov's kingdom. Like the modern day Air Force One, this mode of stately transportation bespoke of the prestige of its occupants and their role in governing a country as massive as Russia.

Consider this description of the Imperial Trail from *Royal Russia*:

> *The design of the train, its materials and facilities envisaged a special, heightened system of security. To ensure comfort, the newest technical achievements of advanced European countries were taken into account, studied and used. The interiors were remarkable for their lavish décor. The walls and furnishings were upholstered in stamped leather and varicolored silks; the floors were covered with carpets; the furniture of red beech and satinwood was decorated with carving and elaborate inlays.*
>
> *The carriages had the chased ormolu coats-of-arms between the windows. The walls and furnishings were upholstered, mainly in English cretonne with plant ornaments; silk fabrics and leather were amply used. The panels, ceilings and furniture, made of polished oak, walnut, white and gray beech, maple and Karelian birch, were covered with linoleum and carpets. The carriages intended for the Imperial family were particularly comfortable. They were provided with everything necessary for convenient life and fruitful work.*
>
> *Originally a bimetallic bath (of copper outside and silver inside) was installed between the studies of the Emperor and the Empress. It was made in Paris and had several reflectors at the sides, to evade the splashing of water when the train moved. Later the train interiors were upholstered and provided with furniture in the Art Nouveau style produced by Robert Meltzer.*
>
> *The sleeping-car incorporated the studies of Nicholas II and Alexandra Feodorovna, dressing compartments with*

wash-basins, compartments of the lady-in-waiting and of the valet, and a wardrobe. The Empress's compartment had a bed with carved decorations suspended on belts as a hammock. The compartment was separated from the study by a screen of blue silk with a flower pattern. All the draperies, the bedspread and the upholstery of armchairs and chairs were in blue silk with matching patterns; a carpet on the floor had a design of flowers and leaves against a birch green ground. The furniture was of Karelian birch and cedar. The richly carved desk was upholstered in gold-stamped leather; on the desk were a silver writing set of twelve articles, a lamp, a blotting-pad and a paper-case; numerous family photographs and icons adorned the walls.

It was on the Imperial Train that the Tsar's official abdication was signed, formally ending three hundred years of rule by a single family. It was also here that the Tsar and his family made their fateful trip to Yekaterinburg, clearly not the same joyous occasion such as when they traveled to the Crimea or Tsarkoe Selo for vacation. The trains themselves, two of them, were ordered built by Nicholas II's father, Alexander III.

By the time of the Russian Revolution, Nicholas II's entourage would make up eleven carriages that were constantly being updated or replaced as time and resources permitted. The typical carriages traveling the royal route were the:

- The Empress's saloon car
- The Tsar's private study and sleeping car
- The children's cars
- The church car
- The kitchen car
- The dining car

- The luggage car
- The workshop car
- The servant's car; and,
- The railway servicemen's car.

Royal Russia, who maintains an excellent archive on the Imperial Trains, says that during World War I a shorter version of the royal train was used by the Tsar. His aide-de-camp, Colonel Mordvinov, is said to recall: "'The Imperial train was not large. In its center was the Emperor's carriage, with his bedroom compartment and study, and next to it was, on one side, our retinue carriage of eight compartments and, on the other, a dining-car with a compartment for receptions. Further on there was a kitchen with a buffet, a carriage used by a traveling military office; the last service carriage was occupied by railway engineers and the head of the railway line where the train was to go.' The royal train was accompanied by another one intended for the retinue, which followed it with an hour interval," they write.

The Tsar's private car was where his private world revolved. Here he slept and ate and held small, private meetings if needed. Royal Russia's description of the Tsar's carriage is much as Martin retold to his family years before: "The study of Nicholas II," as *Royal Russia* describes it, "was provided with furniture of Karelian birch and beech upholstered in brown leather. On the table, also upholstered in gold-stamped leather stood a bronze gilded writing set of twelve objects. Books, magazines, maps, albums and photographs were also kept there. The study was illuminated by gilded bronze sconces; the floor was covered with a cherry-colored plush carpet." They add, "The carriage used for meals and receptions consisted of the two sections: the dining-compartment itself with a small buffet for snacks, where people gathered for meals and tea, and the compartment where headquarters assemblies and receptions were held."

More descriptions from Royal Russia add to our understanding of the environment in which Martin said he resided for two weeks in 1919:

> *The décor of the dining compartment was sustained in warm brown tints; its furniture was made of bright polished oak, the chairs were lined in brown leather and fastened with copper nails, the tables and the mirror shelves were covered with brown cloth and the floor with a grayish-blue carpet; the satin curtains were of the same color. The dining compartment was lit by two bronze chandeliers with ball-shaped shades of frosted glass and table lamps. The walls of the dining compartment were decorated with a portrait of Empress Alexandra Feodorovna and the icon of The Vernicle in a silver mount with enamel decoration.*
>
> *The saloon had soft mahogany furniture in the Art Nouveau style. The walls, sofas, armchairs and chairs were lined in striped pistachio curtains; a plush carpet on the floor had a checked design. The saloon was illuminated by bronze sconces mounted on the walls and table lamps with silk shades. The interior was embellished with porcelain and glass vases, a clock of black marble and coloured stone, an ash-tray of red stone and Dutch porcelain. A portable crystal ink-pot with a silver cover stood on one of the tables; a special table was intended for various games: dominoes, chess, draughts, bezique, etc.*

The *Royal Russia* descriptions provide important first-hand evidence of the Imperial Trains used by the Tsar and his military because the various carriages from the Imperial trains themselves no longer physically exist. Ironically, they were destroyed during World War II. They had been in an outdoor museum at the Peterhof Museum at Alexandria Park where they were taken in 1929 for public display.

Three other carriages for an Imperial Train built for the Nicholas II's father, Emperor Alexander III for an earlier trip with the sovereign of Finland, when they were opening a rail line connecting St. Petersburg with Riihimäki, Finland, do amazingly still exist in the Grand Duchy of Finland. It includes the Emperor's car, the Empress' car, and a lounge car all on display for the public today but it is said that the other carriages from the royal train were destroyed, too.

The museum in Finland describes the carriages as:

> *The oldest car of the train is the Emperor's car which was built in Germany in 1870. The interior of the car was decorated with luxury materials. The walls and the furniture of the reception area of the car were covered with dark green leather, the ceiling is decorated with silk. Wooden decorations are made of American walnut tree and the carpeting is of wool plush.*
>
> *The Empresses' car and the lounge car were built in 1870's in the Finnish Railway's repair shop in Helsinki. The decoration of the Empresses' car is blue silk and the lounge car and it's furniture are decorated with red silk. The outside of all the three cars was painted dark blue and decorated with golded imperial emblems. The cars were later modified and improved in many parts like in the heating system, illumination and the toilets.*

The Finnish Railway Museum says, "The Imperial cars survived mainly for two reasons. They were built by the Finnish Railways and kept from 1914 in Kaipiainen train shed instead of earlier storage site in St. Petersburg. If the train had been left in town, it would have most certainly been destroyed during the Russian revolution in 1917 like happened to all other imperial trains in Russia."

Train #28

Evacuation Train #28, as it was known, was clearly a "special train." It was more than a symbolic train - it was a train of great importance according to Martin, which like the President it represented, the 28th president of the United States in this case, was fully aware of and sensitive to its purpose in the envelope of time that was World War I.

Special trains were those trains that carried RRSC executives or Allied Forces officers and U.S. State Department personnel. The use of "special trains" had to be approved in advance, according to documents at the National Archives II, in College Park, Maryland, by Colonel Benjamin O. Johnson. Johnson had approved many other such special train requests, according to the documents examined from that time period.

In reviewing the train schedules from that period of time in the National Archives' section on the American Expeditionary Force Siberia, there is only one mention of Evacuation Train #28 that we have found to date. It is noted in type as opposed to handwriting by A. J. Carr, the Traffic Inspector at Harbin Rail Yard, that Train #28 was in the yard on September 27, 1919 having arrived "on time" at 6:00 a.m. from Shan Hai Kuan. The train was classified as a freight train, meaning that it clearly did not have passenger cars attached at the time. The weather was said to be "clear and warm."

Shan Hai Kuan is located in the northern-most section of China where the Great Wall begins at the Pacific Ocean. The pass in the Great Wall of China here is today an extremely popular tourist stop known as the *First Pass Under Heaven*. Kuan is the first entry into Manchuria on the way to Harbin. The rail line divides at Harbin with another line heading over to Vladivostok and the second spur to Port Arthur, the Russian military base where its navy is located.

It is interesting to observe that little other information on Train #28 was marked down in Mr. Carr's report to Mr. Johnson. Many other trains were observed in the log and make reference to the number of passengers on board, freight, weight, and many other relevant details that are missing on the Train #28 report.

Another intriguing note is attached that observes that Russian Railroad Service Corps Chairman Stevens also arrived in Harbin Yard that same morning on another train that pulled in at 9:17 a.m. No departure information for Train #28 is noted, nor is there any mention on which train Colonel Stevens used to depart Harbin. Harbin, remember is the headquarters for the Trans Siberian Railroad, so it is possible that he did not depart but remained in Harbin. There are detailed passenger lists of who got on and off of what train by date but a review of those records has not been possible thus far because the records are offsite being digitized by a private contractor for the National Archives. Those records will not be available for at least a year, according to Archivist Eric S. Van Slander.

The AEF Siberia files do contain several folders that are marked "Special Trains." A handwritten note in one such file, as old as the other documents in its box's care says, "File Destroyed." The note is handwritten on a piece of paper that dates itself to 1919 like the other documents surrounding it in Box 1, Entry 846 from the RG43 group. No one knows what happened to the file or why it was "destroyed."

Another supporting note to Martin's story comes from McNeal who outlines in her book examined earlier that the movement of the Tsar and his party from Toblsk to Yekaterinburg took place on two trains "bearing Red Cross flags" in late July 1917. "The family's sleeping cars were supplied from the rolling stock of the Chinese-Eastern Railway," writes McNeal. "In total, two trains were required to move the large contingent of retainers, as well as the Tsar's aide-de-camp, General Tatischev; Prince Valia Dolgorukov; the children's tutors, Pierre Gilliard and Charles Sydney Gibbes; the court physician, Eugene Botkin; the Tsarina's personal lady-in-waiting, Anastasia Gendrikova; the Tsarina's reader, Ekaterina Schneider; another lady-in-waiting, Baroness Sophie Buxhoeveden; parlour maids, Anna Demidova and Elizaveta Ersberg; Ivan Sednev, the children's servant the cook, Kharitonovl a valet, Alexander Volkov; and Alexei's companion, N.G. Nagorny, a sailor."

National Archives records also note that the Railway Committee consisted of one representative from Japan, the United States, Great Britain, France, Italy, Czechoslovakia, Russia and China. These countries parallel those that Martin said had officers on his Evacuation Train in October 1919, perhaps helping explain how and why such officers would come to find themselves aboard Train #28 at that particular time. It was indeed a coordinated effort, it would appear.

Martin's conversations recounted to members of his family that were not recorded from that fateful trip through Siberia yield some additional fascinating clues to the probable Romanov fate. These recollections are based on what we as family heard Martin say in the years long after the Romanov rescue mission:

> The Tsar's Escape: Martin was told by Nicholas that he and his family escaped the Ipatiev House in Yekaterinburg with the help of the British Embassy there

and members of his own guard who were mixed in with the Bolshevik soldiers.

The Tsar's Safekeeping: According to Martin, Nicholas told him that he and members of his family had been kept at a safe house built by the British and the Americans. Martin believed that safe house to be in the Archangelsk/Murmansk region of Russia. Nicholas thought that he and his family would live out the rest of their lives in Russia at that location.

The Decision to Evacuate: Nicholas says he, his wife and daughter were sent to Irkutsk where Martin meets him for the first time when the British and Americans decided to evacuate Archangelsk and Murmansk when Red Russians began to gain dominance over the territory. The mass confusion and chaos created by the massive Allied withdrawal offered useful coverage for the Romanov family to flee the area undetected.

Many Helping Hands: Nicholas told Martin that he was very much aware of how many people were helping his escape. Nicholas said that he understood German, Russian and Chinese leadership supported his rescue but that he was warned by British officials after the Ipatiev House that many troops would not be supportive and would try to kill them, so trust no one.

A Very Dangerous Mission: Martin said that his Lieutenant was very worried all of the time about how dangerous their mission was and kept talking about all of the things that could go wrong between Irkutsk and Vladivostok. The Lieutenant, Martin said, kept saying that to succeed all they had to do was their job one day at a time. Martin said that he talked with Nicholas about the dangers several times, but that Nicholas preferred to focus on other topics when the danger to him came up in conversation. He was full of faith that God would prevail. Martin said that there was a lot of training for each element of the mission - and threats were made many times to keep quiet and not talk about what they were doing in Siberia.

<u>On Why He Was Selected For The Mission:</u> Martin said he was selected for the rescue mission by his brother, George, because he could be trusted to keep his mouth shut and do as he was instructed. Martin said that he and George talked about it many times after that but neither brother realized how harrowing it would actually be to be in Siberia with Nicholas.

<u>The Missing Romanovs</u>: Nicholas told Martin several days into the trip east that his other children had escaped through Europe, although he did not distinguish for Martin whether that escape was between south or west) and showed to Martin no outward concern for their safety while on the train with the AEF Siberia troops.

<u>The Original Plan:</u> Nicholas told Martin that the original plan was to escape through Russia through Finland but that that plan did not ultimately work out. Martin did not know why for sure but thought it might have been because of colder-than-normal weather in summer season that made travel for the Romanovs too difficult.

A Backup Plan: Martin said that the Consul General on board his train discussed the viability of a back up plan to send the Romanov family members on a British warship from Vladivostok to San Francisco, if needed during the trip east through Siberia. The Consul General, Martin said, was very worried about being betrayed. The plan, Martin understood from overhearing conversations among the officers was that a train would then take the Romanovs to Chicago and then on to New York accompanied by a trusted British "emissary." Martin said that he understood the plan would then be for the royals to London from there.

A Flock of Decoys: Martin's Lieutenant told him that there were a number of "decoy missions" underway to rescue the Tsar ir order to confuse Red Russian troops who continued to actively search for the former monarch after their escape from Yekaterinburg.

Another Ben: Martin said that heard the American Consul General talking about another Ben (since my name was Ben, too) helping the Allies with executing the mission but he was also worried if Ben could pull off the rest of the mission that lay ahead. Martin said that the American Consul General, whom he never called by name himself, ever said the last name of the other Ben either.

Controversial Leadership: Martin said that the American Consul General on board his train had a substantial ego and was not a particularly friendly or engaging person. He said the other dignitaries on the train were not certain that the American Consul General could be trusted and was often prone to being subversive in executing his tasks. Martin said that he believed this was the American Consul General's standard operating procedure because he was a trained U.S. intelligence agent.

Identifying the Romanov Daughter: Martin said that even though he spent a significant amount of time with the young Romanov daughter, he did not know her name for certain because they were never introduced by name, nor did her mother or father ever say her name out loud in his presence. Over time, Martin came to believe that the young daughter might be the Grand Duchess Anastasia because he saw photos of her years later when the Tsar's photos of his family were eventually published in the United States. Martin says that he never received any kind of confirmation as to the daughter's identity. But, he says she appeared to be essentially his age, was light and funny, intelligent and well-centered. She spoke fairly good English, and he thought French, too, although Martin did not speak French himself. He described her as being blond with blue eyes and very pretty. He said that she had a little bit of the devil in her but in a good way, not a bad one.

Identifying the Mysterious 14-Year-Old Boy Onboard: Likewise, Martin never learned the identity of the 14-year old boy he encountered from the train in the Vladivostok gun battle, which is described in his audio account. Martin often wondered if the boy was Alexei. The Tsar's photos years later looked like him and led Martin to believe it might be possible that it was Alexei, but he did not understand why the boy would have traveled in the back of the train rather than with the family in the royal cars. Moreoever, Martin said there were only three burial boxes removed from the train containing live Romanovs when the transfer to British authorities took place in Harbin. Martin says Nicholas never indicated that his son might be on board Train #28 and had specifically said earlier that the other members of his family had escaped in another evacuation mission.

<u>Differing Demeanors:</u> Martin said that he and Nicholas talked about how relieved the former Tsar was to be done as ruler of Russia as well as how much he was looking forward to a quiet life. Alexandra on the hand, Martin said, was full of anxiety about the whole abdication and did not want the Romanov rule to be over. Martin said the former Empress talked during tea about how much she enjoyed working with people and being at the center of activity.

<u>Missing A Life Abandoned:</u> The Empress shared with Martin stories of their life together, especially at their summer home, but did not mention the palaces or other locations described beyond just "home." The Empress, Martin said, had wonderful memories of the children playing and large parties held late into the evening that were elegant and simple at the same time.

<u>A Close Couple:</u> Martin said that it was clear to him that Nicholas cared for Alexandra a great deal, and Martin said that she was an attractive woman who was very kind to him - very concerned about what he liked and did not like and his childhood and family back home. She thanked him for his bravery and devotion to duty

and wished that he would express the same to his fellow soldiers when the opportunity presented itself.

Disguises That Worked: Martin said that the Empress told him in one session that it had been easy for the Romanov women to blend in to the people in general because they disguised themselves as Red Cross nurses. Martin said that Alexandra told him that this was how they moved around without being recognized before and after abdication. To help Nicholas hide better, Martin said that he was instructed to teach the former Tsar how to speak English with a decidedly southern accent. Martin said that they did this every day together.

On The Royal Cousin: Nicholas told Martin that his cousin would be guaranteeing the family's safety in England after a long time spent negotiating and planning how this escape would unfold. Nicholas was also certain that his other cousin, Wilhelm II, would have had to have agreed to an escape in order for the British to have been successful at the Ipatiev House. Nicholas wondered if the Bolsheviks, and not Lenin by name or mention, had been aware of the plan, too. Nicholas said that there had been a tremendous lack of discipline and focus by the Bolsheviks in Yekaterinburg, which increased the odds of success that they would indeed escape alive.

The Imperial Wealth: Nicholas did not talk about the royal wealth or treasure onboard the train with him but Martin said that he saw evidence of the jewels and gold on the train while traveling east to Vladivostok. Martin said that Nicholas and Alexandra, at separate times, were very concerned about what might have been left behind in their rush out Russia. Martin said that a lot of the wealth had been removed from the train west of Lake Baikal and was sent by wagon along another route so that if the train was captured the "inventory" would get to safe hands.

On Accommodations: Martin described Evacuation Train #28 several times and what it was like traveling through Siberia. Rugged. Desolate. Frigidly cold. He said that he would bed down at night in a compartment below the floor of the traincar. He could hear the tracks below as the train's wheels rolled over them, and while noisy, it was oddly comforting, too. The stops along the way put Martin on edge but while they were moving, he thought, the team was safer than not. Martin said that the Tsar lived in a box in the middle car when not meeting with him or the Consul General for fear of being detected by a rogue person and under directive from the Allied leadership as a condition of his passage. The train itself was surprisingly clean and comfortable. Every task was highly planned and coordinated. No attention to detail, Martin said, was overlooked or ignored. Assumption was their enemy on this mission.

Unannounced Transfer: When the three Romanovs were transferred to British officials in Harbin, Martin says that there was no advanced notice to him and some of his fellow soldiers, including his trusted Lieutenant. Martin thought the Harbin stop was just like any other. They had practiced removing burial boxes on other occasions but the actual transfer plan was not shared with him in advance of it occurring. Martin said that it was very quick and there was no time for good-byes with the Imperial family.

Romanov Sightings: Martin said that he did not think any of the reported Romanovs he heard about over the years were the real deal because they did not look like the people he had seen, even though he recognized that they would have aged. Martin was of the opinion that the surviving Romanovs stayed out of sight and did not knowingly surface and would not have for fear of assassination despite the passage of time.

Martin would never see the royal family again, nor would he ever have contact with them.

Diciphering Who Was Who

So, who was the youngest Romanov aboard Train #28 according to Martin's story?

To help dissect the personalities involved, one only needs to consult Helen Rappaport's wonderful new profile on the royal family in her outstanding book, *The Romanov Sisters: The Lost Lives of the Daughters of Nicholas and Alexandra*. To make clear for the record, however, Rappaport, based on years of independent research, believes very strongly that the Romanovs did indeed die on July 17, 1918 and did not survive the Ipatiev House massacre as some now believe.

Most likely, as you will see in the personalities Rappaport describes below, the Romanov daughter was indeed, Anastasia. By a pure process of elimination alone, Anastasia fits Martin's description. She was blond-haired and blue-eyed. Close in age to himself, at 17, Anastasia was young, too, and although her 22-year-old sister, Olga, was blond-haired and blue-eyed, too, Olga was not known for being light and fun-loving as Martin said the girl he encountered was throughout the week he spent with her. The next youngest sister to Anastasia was Maria, who would later be rumored to be one of the missing bodies from the Koptyaki Woods burial site but Maria was described as being dark-haired, not blond.

To set the stage for better knowing the Imperial Family's personas, and to help you draw your own conclusion on which sister this was since she was never named to Martin, Rappaport starts her story when the Romanov's home, Alexander Palace, which was opened to the public after the rise of the Soviet Union. In telling of the event, Rappaport notes that:

> *As visitors were conducted from room to room . . . they could not avoid an increasing sense of Nicholas II, not as the despotic ruler painted to them but rather as a dull family man, who had crammed his study and library – where he received his ministers on matters of important state business – with photographs of his children at every stage of their development from babyhood to adulthood: children with dogs, on ponies, in the snow, by the seaside, a happy family smiling to the camera for home-made photographs taken on the Box Brownies that they took with them everywhere. Even in his private study the tsar had a table and chair where his invalid son could sit with him when he was working. This, the hub of now defunct tsarist power, could not have appeared more unremarkable, more domestic and child-friendly. Was it really the last home of 'Nicholas the Bloody'? The tsar and tsaritsa's suite of interconnecting private rooms further testified to their three consuming passions: each other, their children and their devout religious faith.*

The Romanov's presence in Alexander Palace, was everywhere, Rappaport notes. "On every shelf and table top in her private sitting room the tsarita had set out yet more knick-knacks and photographs of her children and her darling Nicky."

Continuing her detailed description of the residence, Rappaports says:

At the far end of the corridor toward the gardens, the cupboards in Nicholas's dressing room still held his neatly pressed uniforms and, nearby, the Great Library of glass-fronted bookcases was full of carefully ordered French, English and German books bound in fine Moroccan leather of the kind that he often sat and read aloud to his family in the evenings.

Alexandra Feodorovna Romanov
Born, June 6, 1872, age 46 at the time of Yekaterinberg

Of Empress Alexandra herself, one of the four Hesse sisters who were the daughters of Britain's Princess Alice, the second daughter of the daring Queen Victoria and her husband Prince Louis, Rapport writes the following account:

... these four princesses of the house of Hesse and by Rhine were considered by many to be 'the flowers of Queen Victoria's flock of granddaughters', celebrated for their beauty intelligence and charm.

Rappaport continues:

In July 1862, aged only eighteen, Alice had left England heavily veiled and in mourning for her recently deceased father Prince Albert, after marrying Louis at Osborne

House. By the dynastic standards of the day it was a modest match for a daughter of Queen Victoria, but one that added another strand to the complex web of royal intermarriage between European first and second cousins. During her long reign Victoria had orchestrated the marriages of all her nine children, and remained meddlesome enough into old age to ensure that, after them, their children and even their grandchildren secured partners befitting their royal status.

Alexandra's mother, according to Rappaport, was an admirer of the famed nurse, Florence Nightingale. She says, "Alice would have liked to take up nursing, having more than demonstrated her skills during her father's final illness in 1861. If this was not to be then there were other ways in which she was determined to make herself of use in her new home. With this in mind, she embraced a wide range of philanthropic activities, including regular hospital visiting and the promotion of women's health, fostering the establishment of the Heidenreich Home for Pregnant Women in 1864."

Princess Alix, as the former Empress was then known, was Princess Alice's sixth child, " . . . a pretty, smiling, dimpled girl who loved to play," Rappaport writes. "They called her Sunny and from the start her grandmother looked upon her as a golden child. Alicky was 'too beautiful … the handsomest child I ever saw', thought Queen Victoria, and she made no attempt to disguise her favouritism."

Rappaport says that Nicholas, "Nicky," was 16 and Alexandra, "Alicky," was 12 when they first met in Russia at the marriage of Alexandra's sister, Ella, to a third cousin. "The shy schoolgirl had become a slender, ethereally beautiful young woman and Nicky was deeply in love," Rappaport observes. Although, she also reports that gossip was circulating around family and friends that "Alix might be marriage material for

Prince George, which was reportedly encouraged at least at one point by Queen Victoria."

Rappaport notes on Alexandra's appearance that:

> *Alix could not have looked more beautiful or serene that day – tall and statuesque in her while-and-silver brocade dress, the train heavily trimmed in ermine and the imperial mantle of cloth of gold across her shoulders, her lovely figure complemented by her limpid blue eyes and her wavy reddish gold hair enhanced by the diamond-encrusted wedding gown. British envoy Lord Carrington was deeply impressed: 'She looked the perfection of what one would imaging an Empress of Russia on her way to the altar would be', he informed Queen Victoria. Other witnesses noted the commanding stature of the princess alongside her shorter and rather delicate-looking consort; to all intents and purposes she appeared to be the one with the physical strength, a woman of considerable presence, 'much above the traditional level of Duchy Princesses.'*

Alexandra is described by Rappaport as being "English through and through," and with "English habits, English sentiments and a no-nonsense English approach to family life bred in the bone by her mother and grandmother before her." Even though it is said that Alexandra "might have embraced" Nicholas' Russian Orthodoxy religion with "all her heart," this English background and Russian marriage "would have served her well had she remained within the familiar sphere of her Western-European bloodline, but Russia – despite the seductive beauty of its landscape, which she already loved – was unknown territory, a country legendary for its turbulent history and for the overpowering wealth and grandeur of its court."

As for each of the children, we find these descriptions:

Olga Nikolaevna Romanov
Born, November 15, 1895, age 22 at the time of Yekaterinberg

Olga was described as having her mother's and her grandmother Alice's altruistic spirit, according to Rappaport. She was known to be highly sensitive to the plight of others and very proud of her status as the oldest of the Romanov children. Described as being very curious ad asking a lot of questions, those with first-hand knowledge of the Grand Duchess also inform Rappaport that Olga could be grumpy, as well, demonstrating surprising flashes of anger on occasion. Olga was a musical child who loved to play piano. Their Cambridge University-trained English tutor, Sydney Gibbes, said Olga was clever like her younger sister, Tatianna, and a "dreamer," among the children. Her favored status with her grandmother, Queen Victoria, was evident when Rappaport notes, "The moment her new great-granddaughter was born, Queen Victoria, as godmother, took it upon herself to ensure that the baby had a good English nanny and promptly set about recruiting one."

Tatiana Nikolaevna Romanov
Born, June 10, 1897, age 21 at the time of Yekaterinberg

Tatiana was said to be pale-skinned, slender, having darker auburn hair with grey eyes when many of her other sisters had eyes that were bluer. Described by Rappaport as, "Arrestingly beautiful," and "'the living replica of her beautiful mother', with a naturally imperious look enhanced by her fine bones and tilted-up eyes." Tatiana was more emotionally cautious and reserved, like her mother, as compared to her siblings. She was not considered to be temperamental like Olga, instead preferring to be exceptionally polite. Rappaport found her to be a natural-born organizer with a very methodical mind and down-to-earth manner that her sisters, in particular, it was said, could not match. In fact, Rappaport found that her sisters even called her 'the governess.'

Maria Nikolaevna Romanov
Born, June 26, 1899, age 19 at the time of Yekaterinberg

Maria Romanov was noted by Rappaport as being the more shy sister, yet having a strong physique backed by a more boisterous personality. Clumsy. Pretty with "a peaches-and-cream complexion." Noted for her "rich brown hair" and, "eyes that shone 'like lanterns'," these were terms used to describe the third sister in the Romanov clan. A warm smile masked a not especially bright child, it was written. She had a talent for painting and drawing and earned the natural affection of those she knew as well as those she met. Her sisters nicknamed her, "Mashka," writes Rappaport, who also says that she was "possibly Nicky's favorite." Gibbs noted in his writings on the Romanov children, says Rappaport, that Maria was sweet and compliant, remaining the most self-effacing, consistently loving and stoical personality among the Romanov sisters, inviting, she writes, the least amount of comment or criticism. "Maria was the archetypal, holesome Russian girl: 'kind hearted, cheerful, with an even temper, and friendly.'

Anastasia Nikolaevna Romanov
Born, June 18, 1901, age 17 at the time of Yekaterinberg

Anastasia had the dominating personality in the family, described by Rappaport as being a force of nature, afraid of little to nothing, the least Russian-looking in the family. "Nastya," as her family called her, had dark blond hair like her sister, Olga, and sported the same blue eyes of her father but the beautiful features of her mother's side of the family. Anastasia was at all shy like her sisters, nor did she like to do what she was told to do by others, thus being one of the least accommodating Romanovs. Very Highly humourous, fun-loving, and often a rule-breaker, according to her biographer, Anastasia was often said to be distracted, inattentive, and considered by those in the know of not being particularly academically bright. Rappaport found that Anastasia would be the one to take her punishment in stride, often being found to be the instigator in controversial family and friend events, in fact, considered to be spiteful when dealing with other children. Gibbs is said to have found that she had "effervescent charm" and a "quirky intelligence." "Always happy" "Endlessly inventive." The constant playfulness and challenge to authority in the classroom soon began to grate: 'She wasn't serious about anything.' Gibbes agreed with Klavdiya Bitner that Anastasia was the 'only ungraceful member of the family.' The Empress' honorary lady-in-waiting, Baroness Buxhoeveden, whom the family referred to as Iza, and another aide, Trina Schneider, described Anastasia as "irrepressible" and, "a clown."

Alexei Nikolaevich Romanov
Born, August 12, 1904, age 13 at the time of Yekaterinberg

The Tsarevich, Alexei, was described by Gibbs in Rappaport's account of the family, as being "painfully shy." He was said to have a mind of his own and a strength of personality "equal to Anastasia." Alexei loved military ceremony, not surprisingly considering that he often accompanied his father to state affairs. His physical frailties were well reported here and elsewhere. He was described in Rappaport's book, as having "large blue eyes and head of golden curls the little tsarevich was the most beautiful of babies. They named him Alexey after the second Romanov tsar, Alexey I (who rules 1645-76), and father of Peter the Great, the naming coming from the Greek meaning 'helper' or 'defender.'"

Rappaport produces evidence in her book, that the four Romanov sisters all spoke good English, which is to be expected since that received tutoring from Englishman Gibbes and a Scotsman, John Epps. They were also taught French by their tutor, Pierre Gilliard, while Olga and Tatianna, were reported to have learned German as well. Alexei's English was reported to have been poorer than his sisters.

The British historian also reports the following on the Romanov's nursing experience that was relevant to Special Train #28:

> *When Russia went to war in the summer of 1914, it was faced with a desperate shortage of nurses. With massive losses of almost 70,000 killed or wounded in the first five days of fighting, the Russian government predicted that at least 10,000 nurses would be needed. Stirred by patriotic duty, legions of the fashionable and aristocratic ladies of St. Petersburg – or rather Petrograd, as the city was quickly*

renamed – as well as the wives and daughters of government officials, and professional women such as teachers and academics, rushed to do medical training and embrace the war effort. By September [1914], with the need for nurses increasingly acute, the Russian Red Cross had reduced the usual year- long training to two months. Many women did not make the grade and with it the right to be called sestry miloserdiya – sisters of mercy – as nurses were termed in Russia.

From the day the war broke out, Rappaport writes that, "the tsaritsa was determined that she and her two eldest daughters should play their part; in early September they began their Red Cross training, taking on the self-effacing titles of Sister Romanova, numbers 1, 2 and 3. Although Maria and Anastasia were too young to train they also were to play an active role, as hospital visitors. No one represented the female war effort in Russia more emotively than did the tsaritsa and her daughters through the two and a half long and dispiriting years of war that preceded the revolution of 1917.

Nicholas Romanov, II
Born, May 18, 1868, age 50 at the time of Yekaterinberg

Of Nicholas' personality, Rappaport adds this about the former Tsar:

With the millstone of duty lifted from him, Nicholas sat quietly and dined with his mama, went for a walk, packed his things and after dinner played a game of bezique with her. He signed the declaration of abdication at 3 o'clock that afternoon and finally left Pskov at 1 a.m. 'with the heavy sense of what I had lived through,' heading back to Mogilev to bid

> *farewell to his military staff. All around him he saw nothing but 'betrayal, cowardice and deception'; there was only one place that he wanted to be and that was with his family.*

And added later in her book, perhaps percipiently from our perspective:

> *'Now that I am about to be freed of my responsibilities to the nation,' Nicholas had remarked to the commander of the Tsar's Escort, Count Grabbe, 'perhaps I can fulfill my life's desire – to have a farm, somewhere in England.'*

In order to transfer the Romanovs to the British under the scenario Martin reveals, the British Navy would have had to have at least one ship in the area of the planned evacuation.

Onboard Train #28

With that said, many of the personalities onboard Train #28 appear to fit their subjects, as Martin describes them, remembering that not a lot of information was available in the days when Martin recorded his account, the only real exception being the release of Robert Massey's epic, *Nicholas and Alexandra*.

The Empress, Rappaport even notes in her biography, "liked to have afternoon tea at around five in the mauve boudoir, where she liked to have Nicky to herself if she could and the children only came by invitation, in their best frocks ....

These other passages from Rappaport's book on the Romanov sisters also lend credibility to Martin's account from more than 40 years ago:

The British ambassador, Sir George Buchanan, had been in an agony of frustration since the beginning of the year: 'I shall not be happy till they are safely out of Russia,' he had said . . . ."

By the time George's Foreign Secretary Arthur Balfour was instructed on 24 March (6 April NS) to suggest that the Russian government 'make some other plan for the future residence of their imperial majesties', far too much precious time had been lost. A powerful, grassroots opposition to any evacuation had escalated, particularly among the pro-Bolshevik executive committees of the Petrograd and Moscow soviets. Any attempt to get the family out by train would have been blocked by the heavily politicized railwaymen of Petrograd, who, according to Izvestiya (the new organ of the Petrograd soviet), had already 'wired along all railway lines that every railway organization, each station-master, every group of railway-workmen, is bound to detain Nicholas II's train whenever and wherever it may appear.'

In August 1917, when the family left for their imprisonment time in Tobolsk, Rappaport reports the following: "When the family arrived at the station – their cars surrounded by a mounted escort of Dragoons – they had to walk down the heavy moist sand of the railway embankment to get to their train, which had been mocked up with flags and placards proclaiming it was part of a 'Red Cross Mission.'

Elsewhere rumour was rife that the train was heading all he way out to Harbin in Manchuria – a destination already becoming a refuge for White Russians fleeing the revolution. Perhaps Kerensky had this in mind as an ultimate destination, but for now the objective was to get the Romanovs beyond the tentacles of Petrograd's militants.

Anna Demidova, in her diary, wrote of the trip: "Later that day when the train pulled up at a rural halt, she heard questions being asked of one of the guards by a railway official: 'Who's on the train? 'An American Red Cross Mission.' 'Then why does no one sow themselves and come out of the wagons?' 'It's because they are very sick, barely alive.'

Nevertheless Nicholas was grateful for any news; Sydney Gibbes noticed how he 'would read through a newspaper from beginning to end, and when he had finished, would start again.' He was rereading his old diaries too, which he found 'a pleasant occupation' and a distraction from his interminable routine.

The impact of their collective and individual personalities made the Romanov family members a force to be reckoned with whomever it was that encountered them, Martin included. Rappaport remembers this:

After they had gone (to Tobelesk), a dejected Mariya Geringer (senior lady-in-waiting) spoke of her still lingering hopes for them (the Romanov sisters). Perhaps the girls would be lucky somewhere in exile and find decent, ordinary husbands and be happy, she said. For her, and for other loyal retainers and friends left behind, the memory of those four lovely sisters in happier times, of their many kindnesses, of their shared joys and sorrows – the 'laughing faces under the brims of their big flower-trimmed hats' – would continue to linger during the long, deadening years of communism.

There was also this particularly haunting passage in Rappaport's "Romanov Sisters" book that is as striking now as it probably was then for any had met one or more of the grand duchesses, as it was, too, for Martin, we know:

> *As the three young women passed him, the engineer was struck by how 'everything was painted on those young, nervous faces: the joy of seeing their parents again, the pride of oppressed young women forced to hide their mental anguish from hostile strangers, and, finally, perhaps, a premonition of imminent death ...Olga, wth the eyes of a gazelle, reminded me of a sad young girl from a Turgenev novel. Tatiana gave the impression of a haughty patrician with an air of pride in the way she looked at you. Anastasia seemed like a frightened, terrified child, who could, in different circumstances, be charming, light-hearted and affectionate." That engineer was, forever after, haunted by those faces. He felt – indeed he hoped – 'that the three young girls, momentarily at least, sensed that was imprinted on my face wasn't simply a cold curiosity and indifference towards them.' His natural human instincts made him want to reach out and acknowledge them, but 'to my great shame, I held back out of weakness of character, thinking of my position, of my family.'*

Montana's Ben Johnson

The Trans Siberian Railroad was run by a man from Montana, Benjamin Johnson.

Livingston, Montana is a non-descript little town in America. It is non-descript by design, not happenstance. Residents prefer quiet anonymity. A hard day's work is reward enough among town folk here. No need to draw too much attention to oneself. Discretion was, and is, still a highly prized value here.

Benjamin Oliver Johnson was the typical Livingston resident. Quiet. Competent. Hard working. Discrete. He was a civil engineer by training – a graduate of the Worcester Polytechnic Institute where he earned a Bachelor of Science degree. Ben was described as being capable and efficient, kindly and courteous to all, loyal to his employers, and fair to any who had to deal with him.

A 39-year-old railroad worker when the World War I broke out, Johnson was Superintendent of the Northern Pacific Railway. He was the second of five children of a Swedish immigrant couple who preferred the peaceful and quiet life that Livingston, Montana had to offer its people. They had fled Massachusetts for Montana with young Ben a generation before trying to avoid military service themselves. But Ben had tried to enlist in the Army in France in June 1917 but poor eyesight and teeth undid his bid for military service.

When Great Northern Railroad General Manager George H. Emerson called for volunteers to go to Siberia to operate the Trans Siberian Railroad for the United States Army, Johnson jumped at the chance to serve his country. He had spent $600 of his savings to fix the teeth that had kept him out of service in France and was ready to go when this mission called. The Army was looking to find railroad men from the Dakotas and Montana to serve in Siberia for the Allied Forces where "long hauls and the rigors of the climate most closely approximated the conditions under which the men would have to function in Siberia." The group was organized militarily but also reported to the U.S. Department of State in a unique bicameral role.

Colonel John E. Stevens would have supervisory authority for the operations of the railroad in Russia, reporting to the Secretary of War's office. The Provisional Government in Russia had requested American help in operating the Trans Siberian Railroad when it fell into a serious state of disrepair following the Tsar's abdication. Poor management and antiquated equipment were to blame but conditions for the railroad where good otherwise, except for the Red Revolutionaries who were sabotaging operations at every opportunity. Colonel Stevens, who hailed from New York City, had an outstanding record in railroad operations having organized the staff for the successful construction of the Panama Canal and was thus a natural choice to lead its operations during War.

On the day that Ben and his family left Livingston, the *Montana Record-Herald* reportedly "ran an editorial praising his decision to serve the nation 'in a capacity that will have a vital influence in the winning of the war' and paying tribute to his many contributions to the Northern Pacific and its patrons:

> *While he is away in Russia driving spikes and struggling with the difficult language of that country, he can be sure that there are many hundreds at home in Montana who are betting that he will lead the percentage columns in both.*

Two hundred men left their families behind and boarded trains with Ben for Siberia via San Francisco on November 1917 thus beginning 11, their collective Siberian Adventure. Their official role was as executives as the newly formed Russian Railway Service Corps (RRSC). Over time, the Bolsheviks would come to view the RRSC as enemies of the state. Johnson would begin his service as a Major.

By the end of April, 1918, Johnson and members of his RRSC team found themselves in Harbin. Wilson was in the process of sending General Grave over to Siberia to command the war and to say things were in disarray would be an understatement. To illustrate the state of affairs in Siberia, consider the following passage from Giffin's account of Johnson and Emerson in the theater:

> *On 26 May, the same day that the Emerson party reached Irkutsk, hostilities between Czechs and Bolsheviks*

broke out in full force. Within two weeks most of the railway from a point west of Samara (later renamed Kuibyshev), on the Volga, to somewhat west of Irkutsk--a distance of roughly 2,500 miles--was wrested from Bolshevik hands either by Czech forces or by various indigenous anti-Bolshevik organizations that took advantage of the Czech action to seize points independently and establish a number of anti-Bolshevik governments.

Beginning on 27 May and continuing for nearly two weeks thereafter, Colonel Emerson and his men attempted to mediate the Czech-Bolshevik dispute, taking part in numerous conferences between representatives of the two sides and encouraging a cessation of hostilities. During the negotiations the Americans repeatedly passed blindfolded from the lines of the one group to the other. On 8 June, Ernest L. Harris, the American consul general at Irkutsk, ordered an end to the mediation efforts when it became apparent that the crisis was not a series of misunderstandings but a full-scale civil war. Harris feared that the mediatory efforts might be misconstrued as an attempt at American interference in the developing strife between the Bolsheviks and the so-called Whites, the name widely used by that time as a blanket designation for the various Russian counterrevolutionary groups moving to establish their own governments in eastern Russia.

Considering Harris's concern, it is ironic that within a matter of weeks President Wilson would use the Czech-Bolshevik conflict to justify American intervention. Wilson came to believe that only by sending American troops to Siberia and the Russian Far East could the way be cleared for the Czechs to reach Vladivostok and depart for the western front. In effect, the Czechoslovak Legion provided a solution to the dilemma that confronted the President. The British, French, and Japanese governments were exerting strong

> *pressure to cooperate in salvaging a front in Russia against the Germans. But American participation conflicted with Wilson's belief in self-determination. He deeply loathed the Bolsheviks for their Marxist ideology and antidemocratic practices, yet he was committed to the principle that the Russian people should determine their own fate. By convincing himself that the Czechoslovak forces required assistance, Wilson could at once justify intervening in Russian affairs and soothe his conscience.*

Johnson's role in Siberia grew quickly and substantively. He played a major role in repairing damage to the rail lines caused by the Czech Legion and he gained the admiration, according to Giffin, of Czech military leaders, especially General Jan Syrovy. Johnson had reportedly been with Syrovy's troops in early July 1918 as they prepared to attack Yekaterinburg. Yekaterinburg was the city in which Tsar Nicholas II and his family were confined as prisoners by the Bolshevik Revolutionaries. So much so, that Johnson was ultimately awarded the Czechoslovak War Cross in recognition of his "conspicuous service" - the only American to be honored thus so during the First World War.

Says Giffin, "The good relations Johnson enjoyed with the Czechs were no doubt enhanced by his ability to communicate with them without an interpreter. Nearly all the Czech officers spoke French and, as Johnson wrote to a friend back home in Livingston, his own command of that language was good enough 'so we get by.' Initially, he had great difficulty communicating with Russians, but he spent many of his evenings during the spring and summer of 1918 struggling with the Russian language and his progress was such that by the middle of August he was able to report, 'I felt very proud lately to have a boss ask me to do some Russian interpreting for him.'"

In the Summer of 1919, Johnson would visit the very room in which the Tsar was said to have been assassinated in Yekaterinburg at the Ipatiev House. He would remain in Russian until November 1922 – some five years after he first left Montana - when the very last of the American forces and personnel would leave, too. He would be highly honored for his service by his alma mater, the French government who would award him the Chevalier of the National Order of the Legion of Honor for helping French nationals escape Siberia, and the Chinese who would award him the second-class Chia-Ho decoration and the Japanese who would bestow their Imperial Order of the Sacred Treasurer.

According to Giffin, who has written the definitive short biography on Ben Johnson of Montana:

> *Upon his return to the United States Johnson moved his family from Montana to Minnesota to be near his relatives. Although his mother had died while he was in Russia, his father still worked the farm outside Winchester and a brother and two surviving sisters lived nearby. He was offered the presidency of Worcester Polytechnic Institute but turned it down, explaining that he was 'a railroad man, not a college man.' From 1923 until February 1932, when high blood pressure attributed by his doctor to the harsh conditions in Siberia forced him to retire, he was employed in various executive capacities by the Northern Pacific, working out of the company's main offices in St. Paul. According to his daughter, Frances Bishop, 'he got into trouble in some circles' during these years, 'because he believed the Bolsheviks were doing the best they could, considering the circumstances, and commented publicly that `although things are in a mess now, Russia will come out of it.' Bishop also cites his sympathy for the Bolsheviks as the reason he turned down an offer of*

$35,000 from Collier's Magazine for two albums of nearly 800 photographs given him by the Czechs in 1922. The albums included a number of gruesome photographs of Bolshevik atrocities, and Johnson felt that their publication would 'show only the anti-Bolshevik side of things,' noting pointedly that 'there were also atrocities committed by the Whites and their supporters.'

When one views the records of the American Expeditionary Force Siberia at the National Archives outside of Washington, DC, one can see first hand the role Ben Johnson played in running the Trans Siberian Railroad. If a memo in its browning frayed condition is not addressed to him it is certainly signed by him. Nothing happened on that railroad that Ben Johnson did not know about. Troop movements, by train number, date and weather condition included. Departure and delay time properly annotated in detail.

Given this later day evidence that has since been declassified, it is clear that Ben Johnson played a very prominent role in the rescue of the Tsar and his family, if indeed one occurred as argued by Martin Hutson, among others. In fact, like Wilson at the global level, Johnson may be that unsung hero at the ground level who ultimately orchestrated the Tsar's escape on the trains in Siberia.

Questioning What We Know

- Did the Romanov sisters find happiness in exile as the dejected Mariya Geringer wished?
- Was Anastasia onboard Train #28 with Nicholas and Alexandra?

- Was Alexei?
- Who was the French-speaking lady onboard the train, and the 30-year who sat with her and the Empress?
- Why were the records in the National Archives on Train #28 destroyed as the file indicates?

Recommended reading:

- Helen Rappaport, *The Romanov Sisters: The Lost Lives of the Daughters of Nicholas and Alexandra,* St. Martin's Press, New York, NY, 2014, ISBN: 978-1-250-02020-8.
- James P. Smythe, *Rescuing the Czar,* California Printing Company, San Francisco, CA, 1920, ISBN-13: 978-1438518831.

12 | Red Cross, Red Spies

"The Red Cross was unable to cope with the demands of World War I and in effect was taken over by these New York bankers. According to John Foster Dulles, these businessmen 'viewed the American Red Cross as a virtual arm of government, they envisaged making an incalculable contribution to the winning of the war.' In so doing they made a mockery of the Red Cross motto: 'Neutrality and Humanity.'"

- *John Foster Dulles, in the 1950 book American Red Cross quoted by Wall Street and the Bolshevik Revolution*

The American Red Cross had extensive operations in Siberia during World War I. But who knew that some of their operations might have included spying for Allied forces against both the Germans and the Russians? Who knew that the American Red Cross in Siberia might not be neutral or, perhaps, as humane as they were reported to be in popular opinion?

Red Cross Expeditions

Charles Lewis was a physician in the United States military who served in Siberia and worked in Russia and China through the auspices of the American Red Cross. Dr. Lewis' first expedition came in 1915 when he and others on his team were sent to investigate the treatment of Austrian and German prisoners of war. The second expedition, Lewis reports, was in 1918 as he was assisting the Czechoslovakian army as it was trying to make its way to the Western Front by transiting Siberia and departing Vladivostok by the now-all-too-familiar seaport in that Allied-controlled city.

According to Dr. Lewis:

> *The American Red Cross had complaints made to it of the manner in which the Austrian and German prisoners of war were treated by the Russians. The reports were very critical of Russia in the treatment of her prisoners. The American Red Cross requested the American Minister in Peking to send some one to Siberia to investigate the conditions. Dr. Reinsch, the Minister, asked Mr. Ogilvie and me to go up to Siberia to see how the conditions were. We left Peking about the first of January, 1915, and went to Harbin where we got into communication with Mr. Caldwell who was the American Consul at Vladivostok. We then got in touch with the Consul, Mr. Moser, of Harbin, and through him made requests of the Russian Government at Petrograd for the privilege of visiting the prison camps. We went from Harbin to Vladivostok with the object of visiting the prisoners. There were prisons outside of Haborovsk and we made the same requests through the Consul and waited there for a week or more for a reply but never got one. In the meantime we tried to see the prisoners but could not. At each place we had to give up in despair and go to another place to try. In Vladivostok we read many letters from German officers who were prisoners. The greatest complaints were that they had to sleep on concrete floors and had no books to read. They complained that they had no Victrolas or anything of that kind for amusements-things that prisoners would not get anywhere. Mr. Caldwell had given us these letters. We found that the Russians had no*

intention of treating the prisoners badly. It was only characteristic Russian mismanagement.

On leaving Vladivostok, Dr. Lewis reports on an accident that typified incidents in Russia:

> *We took an express and started for Irkutsk hoping to have better success in seeing the prisoners there. On the way from Vladivostok to Harbin about six or eight hours before reaching Harbin we were taking our lunch in the dining car. When I had a piece of pineapple about half way to my mouth I lost the pineapple. The waiter was knocked down. Our train had hit a military train ahead of us. The man in charge of the switch station had forgotten to close the switch and our train ran in to the back of the military train on a siding. Behind boxes of heavy cannon on flat cars there were four or five wooden cars (Paluchkas) full of soldiers. These cars were all smashed to kindling wood. I gave first aid to twenty-seven passengers. Passengers vacated part of the second class car for an operating room. We had plenty of splint wood to fix these men up. There was one man who had a leg almost off. The nerve was the only thing which was holding it. This I clipped off with my knife. The blood vessels were frozen full of icy blood which stopped the hemorrhage. These I tied. We had only a few proper first aid materials. I took an ordinary piece of twine and tied the arteries that I could get hold of. We tore up tablecloths, etc., and in about two hours had the men all attended to. There was one aristocratic Russian General along. The only way I could communicate with the Russian women was to give them their orders in German. This high Russian came and told me 'Deutsch ist verboten.' Indeed there was a sign in the car to that effect. He said there was a fine of two hundred rubles for speaking German. I mentioned that I*

was giving first aid to his soldiers. The ladies said, 'Never mind, these men must be looked after.' So he said it was all right, and we got them fixed up. Two surgeons were sent on a special train from Harbin. They came in a very dignified and orderly way and gave me a vote of thanks for what I had done. A special committee met the train and thanked me. We took the wounded on to Harbin. The engine was somewhat damaged and we had to get a new engine to take us through, which had to come back from Harbin. Then we went on to Irkutsk. At this station we met a very interesting man, Witte, a nephew of the old Witte.

During his second expedition to Siberia for the Red Cross, Dr. Lewis says that at the beginning of World War I, "the Czecho-slovaks being Slavs were not willing to enter the war and fight against their brother Slavs (Russians), but were compelled by the Austrians to go to war with them against the Russians." He says, "A great many of them, just as soon as they came to battle with the Russians, surrendered to them." Lewis writes in his report that near the end of the war in the spring of 1918, the Czech army consisting of about 60,000 soldiers made their first attempt to go to Vladivostok with a collection of arms, guns and cannons that he said also included aeroplanes.

"They could not fight against Germany and Austria, as they would have liked to do, because of the German-Austrian element in Russia," Lewis says. "So," he reports, "they made an effort to get to Vladivostok and to the Western Front through Vladivostok and by sea."

The American Red Cross, Lewis observes, "took pity on the Czecho-slovaks who had no equipped medical corps for their army. The American Red Cross appointed a number of commissioners to go to Siberia to organize a medical corps to help the Czecho-slovaks, and Roger Greene of the Peking

Branch of the American Red Cross, wrote and asked me to join this medical corps. Permission was given by the mission and I went to Harbin." Lewis reports that the date was August 23, 1918. His location: Harbin.

"Some of us doctors have been asked to join an officially organized American Red Cross Hospital Unit to work among the Czechs in Siberia and along the Chinese Eastern Railroad," Lewis writes. "Those of us who have responded to the call are here and are working upon organization now" he reported.

> *We went to Harbin about the fifteenth of August. I made a first or investigating trip with one of the American engineers, in his private car to Hailar. He was Major in the Engineer corps of sixty engineers who were sent by the American Government to keep the Chinese Eastern railroad in good operation. We went to Hailar to see what buildings were there that could be used as hospitals, and I found a number of Russian barracks, which with a little expense could be cleaned and put into good condition. There were buildings there to hold 2,000 beds, and at Buketu also room for about 5,000, with quarters for doctors and nurses. These were base hospitals where the men could be brought from the fighting front into these hospitals. There was a good deal of fighting at Irkutsk and around Lake Baikal.*

Dr. Lewis continues providing "color commentary" on the events of that day in Siberia:

> *Captain Gaida was the man who brought a whole army around the lake. The German-Austrian prisoners of war joined with the Bolshevists and fought with the Czechoslovaks and White-Russians. I was sent with our unit to open the hospital at Buketu. This was about August 25th. We had five*

American nurses to organize a hospital, also Dr. Hiltner, of Shanghai. Most of the nurses were from mission hospitals. We selected some Czechoslovaks who could speak English to act as our interpreters. Then we got assistants. Czecho-slovaks were the most capable men I have ever run across. I had them as assistants and dressers. Their army outstripped any other army. They would do almost anything you asked them. Each Regiment had an orchestra. I don't know where they got their instruments.... In our hospital in Buketu we had about 200 beds. We had plenty of surgical instruments from Japan. You could use the hemostats for at least a month before they would not close. The knives would hold an edge at least over night! We had a quantity of supplies made up by American Red Cross Branches in Shanghai, Peking, and Tientsin. Foreigners in China assisted in every way possible in the making of bandages. Here we had a number of patients but not as many as expected, because as soon as Captain Gaida cleared the railroad line around Lake Baikal there was no more fighting. The Czecho-slovaks had gained complete control of the Siberian and Chinese Eastern Railroad. Therefore, this hospital was not used for a war hospital but was still kept and used as a convalescent hospital.

"On the first of October another unit was made up. I was to be the head. This unit was composed of ten American nurses, mostly from mission hospitals, and four doctors. Their train started from Vladivostok. I joined the train the first of October and we were exactly a month going from Buketu across Siberia to Cheliabinsk and north to Ekaterinberg, where the Czar and his family were murdered, and to Tumen. By this time Czecho-slovakia had joined with Kolchak's White-Russian Army and were fighting against the Bolshevists, so we were going to establish a hospital in west Siberia in order to look after them....

In one city about half way to Yekaterinburg, Lewis reports that they had about 250 beds in their hospital. "The music hall in that building" he said, "was a beautifully furnished room with great chandeliers and galleries at both ends, and great stage. That hall held exactly 100 beds. I had charge of that surgical ward. It had a big piano. Every two or three nights we had the Regimental Band of about seventy pieces, in the gallery. This would fill the hall with music. The leader of the band had been the bandmaster to the Czar. Dick, my interpreter, had a great deal of dignity. He was about twenty-five years old. He had been a prisoner four or five years, had learned English very well, was a graduate of a high school. He danced all the Russian dances. His name was Richard Charles Schwerdlick. He said, 'Call me Dick for short.' He said that from the time he was a small boy he was always taught to look on and to think of Russia as a great bear from the north that would come down and wipe Germany off the map and help the Czechs."

"In 1918 the war was over and the Czecho-slovaks ceased fighting," Lewis wrote. "There were a few English soldiers who belonged to an artillery group who were assisting the Kolchak army with a couple of ten-inch guns, and who came to us as patients. He said of the time:

> *After the Czechs ceased fighting and we had no more Czech wounded, then we took in the Russian wounded, for the Reds and Whites continued to fight. Russian patients were the most obstreperous, the hardest to manage and the dirtiest patients I have ever had to do with. The Chinese were far easier. A great many of them had only a finger shot off and were malingering to avoid continuing in the war. The Russians were the worst complainers.*

The Red Cross in Siberia

The late U.S. Secretary of State, John Foster Dulles said of the American Red Cross in Siberia and elsewhere that, "The Red Cross was unable to cope with the demands of World War I and in effect was taken over by these New York bankers. According to John Foster Dulles, these businessmen 'viewed the American Red Cross as a virtual arm of government, they envisaged making an incalculable contribution to the winning of the war.' In so doing they made a mockery of the Red Cross motto: 'Neutrality and Humanity.'"

Clearly, we now know from records released over the past ten decades since the Tsar was reportedly assassinated, there was another mission for the Red Cross in Siberia - a secret mission - a political mission that would directly support a military one at that, too. Some of Woodrow Wilson's staunchest contributors, political supporters and American patriots have been linked to American Red Cross activities in Russia: Cleveland H. Dodge, president of Phelps Dodge in New York City; Henry B. Davison of J.P. Morgan; George Hill, president of American Tobacco Company; Harry Hopkins, who would later become a very close advisor to President Franklin D. Roosevelt; Alexander Legg of International Harvester.

Questioning What We Know

- Was it common for the American Red Cross to function as a shield for Allied or U.S. intelligence agents in foreign wars such the Russian Revolution?

- Were the Bolsheviks aware that the American Red Cross was heavily populated with intelligence agents?

- Was the American Red Cross working closely with the Red Crescent, the Empress' benefactor, to help spirit the Romanovs out of Siberia?

- Was the American Red Cross even aware that the U.S. military was so heavily represented within their ranks and around their operations in Siberia?

- Was President Wilson's relationship or persuasion over the American Red Cross that dominate that he could direct the humanitarian organization to participate in the Romanov rescue without Congress' knowledge, too?

- Does the American Red Cross have official records of these military and State Department officials playing such a role in the AEF Siberian mission?

- How does such work with intelligence agencies not compromise the American Red Cross' efforts in that case?

Recommended reading:

- John Albert White, *The Siberian Intervention*, Princeton University Press, Princeton, NJ, 1950, ASIN: B0007EGUTO.

Part IV: Un-Redacting History?

12 | Hyde Park Mystery

"All his life, FDR loved knowing secrets no one else knew ...."

- Ken Burns, *The Roosevelts: An Intimate History, Episode 6*

Hyde Park is one of those very quaint villages in upstate New York where you would hardly expect to learn that the world once centered here. But when Franklin Roosevelt lived, and Eleanor too, it certainly did. Their lasting mark on the world and contribution to world peace thankfully persists to this day. The political impact of his public policies, and her humanity and humility then, still resonate today in countries around the world.

The Roosevelts were a very influential family. They had wealth and privilege. Like the Fords, the Carnegies, the Vanderbilts in their day - the Kennedys, the Bushes, more recently. They were a family who made money but did great public good, too. They believed in public spirit. They believed in public service. They believed in humankind. They had familial ties back to the days of the American Revolution.

Franklin Delano Roosevelt, FDR to a generation of Americans whose very lives rested on his accomplishments, would one day himself be the 32nd president of the United States. He was the only White House occupant to be elected four times, after having previously served Woodrow Wilson as his Assistant Secretary of the Navy, a position that was considered to be the second highest ranking civilian post available in the service, other than, of course, Commander-in-Chief. FDR served in this capacity from 1913 to 1920, when AEF Siberia was ordered by Wilson to come home.

Roosevelt served as Assistant Secretary of the Navy under the Secretary Josephus Daniels. Both Daniels and Roosevelt had been big Wilson supporters in the 1912 presidential election and were awarded their posts for their political loyalty, even though Wilson, it was reported, did not completely trust Daniels. Wilson cipher name for Daniels, was, "Neptune."

Always the optimist, fortified with copious amounts of great public and private courage, FDR as he was called, loved the sea. His childhood home at Hyde Park even overlooked the astonishingly beautiful Hudson River Valley in the Empire State. He was a known casual sailor who took joy in navigating any body of water – large or small. In any weather - cold or warm, stormy or calm. One of his boats was called, the *New Moon*. His library collection of naval stories was said by Roosevelt to be 10,000 titles strong. He even wrote a book about his hero, John Paul Jones.

Although he did not work closely with, or really know very well at all, Winston Churchill in World War I, Roosevelt would certainly make up for this status in World War II, when he and Sir Winston would together defeat Hitler's Nazi Germany and the Empire of Japan, two foes he knew well from his earlier 20th century service. In his aptly named biography of Roosevelt and Churchill chapter, "Two Lions Roaring at the Same Time," the historian and editor Jon Mecham writes:

> *In later years, Churchill would not recall meeting the American visitor. Roosevelt certainly recalled meeting Churchill, however, and long remembered Churchill's*

> *brusqueness. 'I always disliked him since the time I went to England in 1917 or 1918,' Roosevelt said to Joseph P. Kennedy, the American Ambassador to Britain in a conversation in 1939. "At a dinner I attended he acted like a stinker.' Roosevelt and Churchill would not be in contact again for another twenty-one years.*

This passage is an extraordinary admission because Roosevelt, as Assistant Secretary of the United States Navy with command over the ports in question such as Vladivostok, Russia, and Churchill, who was in charge of munitions for King George V and former head of the British Admiralty, could have or even should have encountered each other much earlier in history, given their small roles in Tsar Nicholas II's brush with history.

It is all the more symbolically astonishing to know, as recounted in Mecham's superb biography as it opens, when he recounts how Roosevelt, Churchill and Soviet leader Joseph Stalin were "sitting in the Grand Ballroom of the Livadia Palace, a former summerhouse of the Russian czars" in February 1945 in the Crimean coastal town, Yalta, as they were negotiating Europe's post-war reorganization.

As Assistant Secretary of the Navy, Roosevelt had responsibility for the operations of the service branch during World War I in both Europe and Russia. For example, it was Roosevelt who championed the creation of the United States Naval Reserve in order to make available more forces, on short notice, in the event that the Navy needed help from her troops. Nothing could have happened in either place - Russia, San Francisco or England - without his direct knowledge - including any potential rescue of the Tsar and his family, especially where they were to be spirited out of the country they once ruled by sea.

In McNeal's book, *The Secret Plot to Rescue the Tsar*, the author rightly observes that:

> *If nothing else, Rescuing the Czar may be the Rosetta Stone that has given us a glimpse into the world of intelligence activity and secret diplomacy that sometimes shapes the destinies of nations. In this case, the impact on Russia of this activity remains unclear. Still it is interesting to note that three men, who decades later would be leaders of their countries, played significant roles in their respective governments in 1918 – Churchill, Director of Munitions; Stalin one of Lenin's most able administrators; and Franklin Delano Roosevelt as Under-Secretary of Navy for the United States – and each was connected to events in Russia during this time-frame. In the paperback edition of The File on the Tsar, Summers and Mangold note that: Pressed on the matter (of the Romanov's fate) in the House of Lords, Lord Goronwy-Roberts made two curious remarks. Asked whether he was absolutely satisfied that three daughters of the Tsar are not still alive, he replied: 'No. Nor do I think anybody else is absolutely satisfied about that.' He also suggested that this book, 'The File on the Tsar', be placed with the official material on the case in the Public Record Office.*

McNeal then makes a very interesting observation that we wanted to explore: President Roosevelt, she said, "piqued my interest, when I learned that in the 1930s he had told an aide that he had a mystery story whose ending he could not solve and that he wanted to write for years but had never had time to undertake the task. His aide responded that if the President would share his storyline with him he would engage six writers to work out the ending for the President. The aide subsequently invited the best mystery writers in American to take part and commissioned them to contribute to a book called, *The President's Mystery Story*. Roosevelt provided them with the beginnings of a tale about a Russian man who was wealthy, well-known and wanted to disappear with enough of his fortune to live on, but be perceived as dead. His story's character seemed to mirror that of the Tsar. The President appeared genuinely intrigued by the thought that a man could die but continue to live and he wanted the writers to explain what would happen to a man who falsified his own death. Why would Roosevelt have conjured up such a yarn unless he was puzzling over something about which he had some first-hand knowledge but had lost the track? McNeal says that:

> *On May 12, 1935, President Roosevelt had dinner at the White House with a few friends, including Fulton Oursler, the editor of the popular weekly magazine, LIBERTY. Always a great fan of mystery novels, the President during the course of the evening confessed that he had formulated an idea for a mystery story but that he could not figure out the ending. At Oursler's urging, the President described the plot. Oursler suggested several possible endings, but the President dismissed them as flawed. Oursler then proposed that he serialize the President's mystery plot in LIBERTY magazine, using leading mystery writers of the day to advance the story chapter by chapter. Oursler thought that the mystery writers could solve the plot, and if not, then the readers of LIBERTY would do so. The President reportedly laughed and told Oursler, 'Go ahead. The idea is yours – and theirs. Now see what you can do with it.'*

Asked about the McNeal report, the FDR Library says, "that serialization began in the November 16, 1935 issue of *Liberty* as "The President's Mystery Story . . . Plot by Franklin D.

Roosevelt." The first installment was written by Rupert Hughes. Succeeding installments were written by Samuel Hopkins Adams, Anthony Abbot (a pseudonym for Oursler), Rita Weiman, S.S. Van Dine, and Jon Erskine.

"Following the publication of the last *Liberty* installment, Farrar and Rinehart published the serial in book form. In October 1936, Republic Pictures released a film very loosely based on the plot called "The President's Mystery." The FDR Library told us, "We do not have any documentation as to what the President thought about the movie, nor was he involved in the production.

"In 1967, the serialization was republished in book form by Prentice-Hall as THE PRESIDENT'S MYSTERY PLOT, by Franklin Delano Roosevelt and Rupert Hughes, et al. It includes an excellent introduction by Arthur Schlesinger, Jr. describing the history of the mystery plot, all of the original chapters from *Liberty,* and a new final chapter written by Erle Stanley Gardner of Perry Mason fame. Schlesinger also mentions that the 1936 movie received rather poor reviews since it did not adhere very closely to the original plot and serialization.

While President Roosevelt did not write any of the serialization himself, he did provide the underlying plot for the mystery. He was considered a substantial enough contributor to have received $9,000 from LIBERTY and $72.27 from Farrar and Rinehart, it is said. All of the money was donated to the Georgia Warm Springs Foundation, which treated polio sufferers, and where the President would end his life in 1944.

In fact, *Liberty* Editor Oursler says that the story came about in the following manner, after pressing the President on his idea for a story:

> *'All right!' he (FDR) exclaimed. 'You brought it on yourself. Here in a nutshell is the idea. The principal character in my story is a man of considerable wealth. Perhaps he has six*

or seven million dollars tied up, as such fortunes naturally are, in a variety of investments – stocks, bonds, and real estate. My millionaire is not an old man – just over forty and wise enough to feel that his life is only beginning. But he's tired, fed up with his surroundings and habits. Perhaps, too, the sameness of his middle-aged routine has begun to wear him down. Furthermore, he is disheartened at the hollowness of all the superficial friendship surrounding him. The men at the club smile and slap him on the back but they go away to do him in the eye. Finally he has an ambition, a dream. So, in the trite old expression of another generation, he would like 'to get away from it all.' Only in this case there is a difference – he would like also to get away with it all. Yes, my man plans to disappear. His purpose in vanishing from the scene in which he has played an important and successful part is twofold. First, he wants to find a new world for himself, one in which he will no longer be bored. He wants to start life afresh – he's finished with his present career because he feels he has exhausted its possibilities. Second, and equally important, that dream he has – he would like to make a certain experiment in some small city where, in his new identity, he will not be recognized. To carry out this laboratory experiment, which if successful would become nation-wide and benefit all the people, he will need five million dollars. The dream will cost money, you see, and moreover he feels that he has a right to live well and enjoy, in his new environment, the fruits of his labors in the old. In other words, he wants to vanish – but he wants his money with him when he goes. Now, this man has an estate of six or seven million dollars. If he leaves a million or so behind him he will have made ample provision for his wife and the others dependent on him. That ought to be easy. But it's not – the problem is not so simple as it seems. How can a man disappear with five million dollars in any negotiable form and not be traced?

A detailed read of *The President's Mystery Story* is indeed uncanny for its parallels with the Tsar's story, especially in light of Martin's contribution to what we might now know about his fate. The lead character in *The President's Mystery Story* is a very conflicted and unhappy fellow named Jim Blake. Blake is married to a very domineering wife, of Russian background, Ilka, who does not love him. In fact, Ilka is having an affair with one of Jim's friends, under his nose, much as was rumored about the Tsarina's infatuation with Gregori Rasputin. According to the story, Ilka is not blame for the Russian revolution. "The Noblemen who fled with her soon squandered what cash they carried away, and soon pawned and lost what jewels they smuggled out."

Blake spends the early part of the story trying to figure out how to get out of his unhappy marriage. "The solution came to him in a flash, as he says smoking in the club car" of a train he was riding into New York City. "He would simply cease to be James L. Blake. Why not? Instances of total change of personality, occurring accidentally and pathologically, were well known," he reasoned. "Why not deliberately, then? That was it! He would disappear! And he would take most of his money with him, too."

The President's mystery story continues to unfold, "To be *and* not to be - that was his question. To be gone and to stay; to die out of the twisted life he led and yet to go on living moving about as a ghost of sort, recognizing but unrecognized.

It seems that Blake reasoned his fate this way: "First, when he ran away, he must get himself a new personality, make a complete physical transformation.... Second, he must manage to carry off five or six million dollars, leaving Ilka a million or two to keep her quiet .... Third, he must select a new residence where he could carry on an important life, doing philanthropic work without having his connections with the old life traced."

Blake decides to acquire a new personality as well as a new voice and a new look, thanks to advancements in plastic surgery medicine. So, Blake hires a ventriloquist by the name of Vaurot to teach him a very short period of time how to speak differently. Blake says to Vaurot, "I have a considerable capacity to work. Suppose we allot twelve hours a week to it. Uninterrupted in your flat." Of course, Vaurot does not think it is possible to change ones voice convincingly in just two hours a day over the course of a week, but Blake manages, impressing Vaurot.

Blake discovers Ilka's murder plot by impersonating her lover one evening on the phone in an attempt to see if he could be convincing as someone else. He flees on train, the Roosevelt team describe as "in flight to a new life."

Paralleling the Tsar's story, as Martin tells it, Roosevelt's inspired character, Jim Blake, hides out for two long months while he undergoes his transformation. "Two months that were a kind of death, and in-between existence, a gap separating one life from another."

You have to read the story yourself, but 202 pages later you learn that Blake changed his name, fell in love with his secretary, disappeared into the background but through necessity had to contact a governmental friend of his, the governor of his state in this case, to save him from an ultimate fate that was unacceptable. In the end, he was able to fade in to the background again very successfully thanks to the Governor's loyalty, or at least once the Governor was convinced that Blake was how he thought Blake should be.

And, you have to love this last irony from the President's mystery book, on page 150: when family and friends believe that Blake is dead, a victim of a suicide car-off-of-the-cliff accident, a now plastic-surgery-altered lead character attends his own funeral disguised as another man. The name of the church his funeral is held in? The Collegiate Church of St. Nicholas on Fifth Avenue. Was that coincidental irony on Roosevelt's part? The Church of St. *Nicholas*?

So, could FDR have been talking about Tsar Nicholas, II, when he conjured up this murder mystery at the prodding of his friend, Mr. Oursler? Do you see the similarities in the story, remembering that FDR's account here comes half a century before the world would know what happened to the Tsar, or so they were led to believe.

Ironic that Ilka would be Russian nobility. Ironic that she would have attempted to spirit jewels out of Russia in a way remarkably similar to that proposed by the Tsarina, Alexandra. Ironic that the main character would want to die to live and would need the help of his Governor friend, as opposed to cousin King? Either way, a reviewer at the time, Frank S. Nugent said of the film related to the book: "In its melodramatic way, 'The President's Mystery' is a well-constructed essay on one means of achieving a more abundant life, and it is an interesting picture as well."

FDR was Assistant Secretary of the Navy when Martin says the Tsar was spirited out of Russia with the help of the United States Navy in Vladivostok and San Francisco. Did FDR know more than we were told about the Tsar's fate? Did he take millions and attempt to disappear by train as Jim Blake did in *The President's Mystery Story?* Did llka's story mirror that of Her Royal Highness Alexandra?

Did Roosevelt know what had really happened to Tsar Nicholas II and his family? Was this his way of telling folks that he did?

Most likely, the answer to this question is, yes. It was

the FDR way.

The talented documentarian, Ken Burns, in his PBS epic on, *The Roosevelts: An Intimate History,* says of Franklin Roosevelt in episode six that, "All his life, FDR loving knowing secrets no one else knew . . . ." Burns was referring in a segment known as, *The Common Cause,* that FDR was rendevouzing with British Prime Minister Winston Churchill who was onboard his naval vessel, the *HMS Prince of Wales,* off of Newfoundland, Canada, when folks in the United States thought that he was vacationing on Cape Cod aboard his presidential yacht, *Potomac,* which was deceptively and intriguingly flying the presidential standard even though the President himself was not on board. FDR even writes to one of his trusted aides with delight at the slight of hand.

It was just one of many times that FDR would prove knowingly deceptive and secretive, when events warranted in his mind.

That he would also use the same *Liberty* media outlet as a political tool to achieve his public relations objective was not a first in this case, either. Years earlier when he was running for his first of four terms as president, FDR placed a bogus account from his physicians saying that he was in excellent health when in fact he was not in order to keep his Republican opponents at bay on the potentially volatile issue.

Questioning What We Know

- The obvious question: Did Franklin Roosevelt know something more about the Tsar's potential rescue that history now tells us?

- Was *The President's Mystery Story* Roosevelt's story about Nicholas Romanov?

- What role did Franklin Roosevelt really play as Assistant Secretary of the Navy in coordinating the allied extraction of the Romanovs using naval vessels?

- Did Roosevelt work then, too, with his future compatriot in World War II, Sir Winston Churchill, the then-British Secretary of War?

- What do the archives at the Roosevelt Library in Hyde Park, New York, tell us about this remarkable rescue mission?

- Is there a hidden record of the event?

Recommended reading:

- Roosevelt, President Franklin Delano. *The President's Mystery Story,* The Franklin Delano Roosevelt Presidential Library & Museum, Hyde Park, NY.

13 | Brilliant Consequences

"...The President's complete disregard of the Senate following on top of his very tactless appeal to the country to return a Democratic Congress, has made him just about as thoroughly and completely unpopular in his own country as a president has been or could be."

- *Wilson by A. Scott Berg quoting a diplomat's wife watching the President's Sixth State of the Union speech*

Nothing sums up better, Wilson's problem with the United States Congress as a result of his decision to bypass them on the trust plane than this passage from A. Scott Berg's wonderful biography of Woodrow Wilson simply titled, *Wilson*:

By the time Wilson tried to rally the Congress behind him in his sixth Annual State of the Union, the lawmakers felt marginalized. He entered the overflowing chamber on December 2, 1918, to what one onlooker called an 'ominous silence.' Even delivering a patriotic speech did little to thaw his audience. Starting with an evaluation of the nation's war effort, Wilson attributed most of it success to 'the mettle and quality of the officers and men we sent over and of the sailors who kept the seas, and the spirit of the nation that stood behind them. He singled out various bureaus and constituencies that had contributed to the nation's success- especially America's women. He spoke of the specific challenges ahead as the country returned to a peacetime economy. Still, little received applause, even when his supporters trued to incite ovation. Secretary Daniela found the Congressional reserve nothing short of 'churlish.' But one diplomat's wide, who viewed the proceedings through her opera glasses, wrote in her diary that 'the President's complete disregard of the Senate following on top of his very tactless appeal to the country to return a Democratic Congress, has made him just about as thoroughly and completely unpopular in his own country as an president has been or could be."

So what if Woodrow Wilson did not inform Congress of all of his activities in Siberia, if in fact there was an undisclosed fourth objective in the Aide Memorie to rescue Tsar Nicholas II for his cousin King George V? Does that constitute a presidential lie on Wilson's part? What would have been the consequences for his presidency if the Tsar's rescue mission had been discovered by members of Congress who did not support the President's objectives, assuming of course that there was in fact a rescue mission?

History is replete with presidential lies, if you want to be that harsh about calling these statements lies. Presidential "lying" is not necessarily an uncommon occurrence, fortunately or unfortunately, depending upon how you view it. In fact, George Mason University public policy professor, James Pfiffner, suggests in a superb 2013 *Washington Post* article on "Presidential Lies and Consequences," that there are in fact different categories of presidential lying to consider. Professor Pfiffner says these are:

"Justifiable lies, such as to protect national security; minor lies, such as campaign exaggerations; lies to prevent embarrassment, such as John F. Kennedy's denial that he had

> *Addison's disease; lies to cover up important facts, such as Ike and the U-2 or Richard M. Nixon and Watergate; and finally, at the top of the list, lies of policy deception. That would include things like Lyndon B. Johnson and Vietnam, Nixon and Cambodia and Ronald Reagan and Iran-Contra."*

Eric Alterman, in his 2004 book, *When President's Lie*, looked at four specific presidencies and the untruths that were told relating to foreign policy matters. He focused on Franklin D. Roosevelt's undisclosed promises to Russian leader Josef Stalin during World War II, John F. Kennedy's unrevealed negotiations with Soviet Union boss, Nikita Kruschev, Lyndon B. Johnson's limited Gulf of Tonkin incident information to further justify excursions in Vietnam, and Ronald Reagan's clandestine arms sales to Iran to pay for Nicaraguan Contra operations Congress directly forbid.

Somewhat paralleling Wilson's Siberian adventure, Alterman examines in great and fascinating detail FDR lying, he says, to Congress and even to his closest aides about a number of off-the-record agreements FDR made with Stalin at their summit in Yalta with British Prime Minister Winston Churchill in attendance. Sound familiar?

Former Richard Nixon White House Counsel from the Watergate era, John W. Dean, writing a review of Alterman's book observes, "that Roosevelt also wanted Stalin to cooperate with his efforts to create the United Nations, accomplishing what Woodrow Wilson had failed to do with the League of Nations. Stalin, whose troops were in Poland and Eastern Europe, wanted to keep what his army had won. Accordingly, Roosevelt and Stalin concluded several agreements--among them Roosevelt's acceptance of ongoing Soviet dominance of Poland and the rest of Eastern Europe--which were known to only a very few people, and never fully reported to the American public."

Dean, who had his own personal experience of deceptive commanders-in-chief to draw upon, also astutely notes that Alterman felt the presidents writing of the book in his review:

> *Believed themselves to be acting on the basis of patriotic necessity when deceiving the nation. Roosevelt thought he was 'preserving the postwar peace'; Kennedy felt his lies were necessary to prevent war with the Soviets; Johnson believed his dishonesty would prevent the spread of Communism in Southeast Asia; and Reagan held similar beliefs about Central America. Alterman points out, 'ex-presidents Reagan and Bush are nationally admired and, to many people, beloved figures, subject to nary a mention of the lies and crimes described in detail' -- perhaps because the Cold War ended on U.S. terms, granting Reagan and Bush a kind of historical pardon. Ironically, 'ex-President Jimmy Carter, who earned a reputation for being painfully honest in public life, enjoys no such cachet in the media or insider political establishment.'*

Dean continues:

> *For Alterman, of all the lies a president may make, none are less unforgivable than those 'relating to matters of war and peace,' the 'most sacred and demanding of presidential duties...where the presidential words carry the greatest power.' He explains that presidents must play "great power politics" on the world stage, while American citizens do not understand the world in these terms. Stated a little differently, in the real world 'deals must be struck and compromises made on behalf of larger purposes,' and rather*

than explain all this to the American people, 'presidents tend to prefer deception over education.' [Presidents lie] because they believe the lies they tell serve their narrow political interest on the matter in question. Moreover, US presidents, like so many politicians the world over, have demonstrated a remarkable psychological felicity for confusing their own good fortune with that of the nation's. While appearing to be honest is generally considered better than its opposite, this is hardly the same thing as actually being honest. Hence, truth telling has no independent instrumental value. Hence, if a president believes a lie to be necessary to maintain or improve his political fortunes, the lie is told. The truth is fine too, but if a lie works better, well that is generally considered fine too. As Peter Teeley, press secretary to Vice Presidential candidate George Bush, explained after the 1984 Bush/Ferraro debate, 'You can say anything you want during a debate, and 80 million people hear it.' If the press then points out an error, 'So what? Maybe 200 people read it, or 2,000, or 20,000.'

So, for Wilson, 80 million people did not get the opportunity to hear him say anything about a potential rescue of Tsar Nicholas II mission using U.S. troops in Siberia because there was no information delivery system like Bush-Qualye/Ferraro debate nearly 7 decades later. Clearly, we are talking about matters relating to war and peace in Wilson's case, as Alterman notes, but the motive for lying, if in fact he did lie, is less clear in Wilson's instance it would appear.

David Wise in his examination of the politics of lying published in 1973, and Carl M. Cannon in an outstanding essay on untruth and consequences in *The Atlantic*, says that it may be because "Presidents prevaricate for the reasons other people do: pathology, politeness, paternalism, convenience, shame, self-promotion, insecurity, ego, narcissism, and even, on occasion, to further a noble goal."

Wise further believes that Presidents "also have burdens not felt by most of us—keeping the nation safe, for one. High-level statecraft, he says, "requires a talent for telling divergent groups of people what they want to hear. This is not, Wise wryly concludes, "the best recipe for truth telling, particularly in times of war or national peril. All lies, unlike all men, are not created equal. Philosophers from Aristotle to Niebuhr have made moral distinctions among falsehoods, whether 'white lies' told for social convenience or to spare feelings, 'excuses' that are only half true but that rationalize our own behavior, lies told during a crisis, lies told to liars, paternalistic lies told to protect those we care about, and lies told for the social good—also known as 'noble lies.'"

Says Cannon, "All lies, unlike all men, are not created equal. Philosophers from Aristotle to Niebuhr have made moral distinctions among falsehoods, whether 'white lies' told for social convenience or to spare feelings, 'excuses' that are only half true but that rationalize our own behavior, lies told during a crisis, lies told to liars, paternalistic lies told to protect those we care about, and lies told for the social good—also known as 'noble lies.' The presidential scholar Richard Norton Smith points out that Thomas Jefferson's own interpretation of the Constitution's limits on presidential power probably didn't allow for the Louisiana Purchase. Yet in office, having sworn to uphold that Constitution, Jefferson couldn't resist stretching the words and doubling America's size for a few million dollars. "And talk about a turnaround—it was Nixon who went to China," Smith added. "It's often the flip-flop, in pursuit of interests that transcend ideological consistency, that puts a president on Mount Rushmore."

So, perhaps, Wilson was telling one of those "noble" lies, if we want to ascribe to him the most-noblest of intentions? After all, one can make the argument that it was indeed for the purposes of keeping Americans safer, based on the evidence we can find to date.

That said and that assumed, what would be the consequences of Wilson not telling Congress about a rescue mission?

The Consequences, Then

The consequences then of Congress, and Parliament, not knowing what the President and the King were up to would be dramatic.

For example, had the Tsar been restored to power in Russia in the early days after the end of the Revolution, when Lenin was struggling to keep the wave of communism going, there might never have been a Soviet Union. The Soviet Union for nearly 70 years menaced much of the world as it practiced its philosophy, sometimes brutally and often deftly.

More immediately, for Russia, too, the Red and White Civil War might have ended sooner. Stalin's atrocities from famines to forced labor gulags, to his notorious prisons and prisoner executions might never have happened.

World War II would most definitely taken on a more determined face avoiding perhaps the eventual Cold War of the 50s and 60s, as well as the division of Berlin and the Iron Curtain of Eastern Europe.

On the other hand, the space race between Russia and the United States might not have resulted in mankind landing on the moon, especially if there had been no motivation for America to race its able competitor, the Soviet Union.

There might not have been a near-nuclear war over Cuba, either.

Had Congress found out about the Wilson omission, there may very well have been impeachment proceedings of the President, especially in his more frail and vulnerable days. If Wilson had been impeached, or nearly impeached, would there ever have been a Nixon and Watergate? How about a Clinton and Lewinski scandal. There most certainly might never have been a League of Nations or even perhaps a United Nations.

The most evident consequence of the Wilson-George decision is, we believe, that Romanovs lived and they lived in a peaceful exile somewhere under the banner of their cousin, the King of England. Trust in government was not eroded and governing was not made more difficult then because Congress did not find out about the secret mission or missions to save the Tsar.

FDR might never have been president due to his role as Wilson's Assistant Secretary of the Navy. Would the Great Depression have happened? Would America have moved toward more equal and civil rights?

We will never really know what the consequences of Wilson's actions might have been had history known of his daring deeds.

Recommended reading:

- Eric Alterman, *When Presidents Lie*, Viking, New York, NY, 2004, ISBN-13: 978-0670032099.

14 | Dead Man's Tale

"It was not until far more than half a century after the alleged Yekaterinburg massacre, that the remains of nine bodies, not the expected 11, would eventually be exhumed from a shallow mass grave four-and-one-half miles from Four Brothers ... "

- *Rescuing Nicholas*

The assassination of the Tsar and his family, as reported by eyewitnesses such as lead executioner Yakov Yurovsky, was particularly savage. With Czech and anti-Revolution White Army troops rapidly approaching Yekaterinburg (the White Army regained control of the city eight days later) to find the Imperial family, despite rampant rumors swirling that the family had long ago escaped their captivity, Yurovsky would later state that the Tsar was shot in the head at point-blank range at his Ipatiev House prison and died immediately, while members of his royal household, including the Tsarina, his daughters and his son were shot sometimes dozens of times, repeatedly stabbed, head-crushed with rifle butts, kicked and then mutilated beyond facial recognition.

Their stripped and now naked bodies were also reportedly desecrated and then dumped in an abandoned, flooded mine shaft 12 miles north of the city a day later after being unceremoniously hauled by horse-drawn cart through swamps and mud in a heavily forested area known as Four Brothers. Hand grenades, acid, lime and fuel oil were used on the bodies to collapse the mine and further hide the identity of the bodies and cover up the crime.

In early 1919, some six months after the suspected assassination, Nicholas Sokolov, a 36-year-old professional investigator for White Russian Admiral Alexander Kolchak looking in to the family's suggested demise, found evidence of grenade explosions at Four Brothers, along with traces of two bonfires, horse-trampled earth, and burned wood still floating on the surface of one mine shaft known as Ganin's Pit. Sokolov and at least two of Alexi's tutors assisting his search for the family found a variety of artifacts, but no bodies: the recognizable military belt buckle that once belonged to the 13-year-old Tsarevich, an emerald cross that had belonged to the Tsar's mother and was often worn by the Tsarina, six sets of women's corsets, the Tsar's physician's eyeglasses and false teeth and "a few charred bones, partly destroyed by acid but still bearing the marks of an ax; revolver bullets; and a severed human finger, slender and manicured as Alexandra's had been."

The searchers also found Anastasia's beloved King Charles Spaniel, Jemmy, in the pit as well. When Yekaterinburg fell again to the Red Russians a short time later, Sokolov fled with a suitcase contained what he said was proof of a murder. The evidence was taken by Sokolov to Vladivostok, then to Harbin, China, by French General Janin. Sokolov took the Box back from Janin and went to Japan, where he met up with General Rozanov and his family. The Box was eventually taken to Europe where is was protected for years and eventually examined in greater detail itself.

Allied governments, including Great Britain and Germany, would not dispute the Tsar's death. Official condolences and condemnations would be issued. Subsequent investigations would abound but prove inconclusive. In response to German concern about the fate of the German-born

Alexandra, one such intriguing inquiry, for example, triggered on an October 15, 1918 dispatch to British Foreign Secretary Arthur Balfour from Siberian High Commissioner Sir Charles Eliot, stating:

> *"On July 17, a train with the blinds down left Ekaterinburg for an unknown destination and it is believed that the surviving members of the Imperial family were it .... It is the general opinion in Ekaterinburg that the empress, her son and daughters were not murdered."*

Were members of the royal family truly on board that train as the British dispatch claimed, or where Romanovs lying at the bottom of the pit in or around Four Brothers as their reported assassins contended?

A 1935 interview with an allegedly dying (throat cancer) Peter Ermakov, who together with Yakov Yurosky, had participated in the murder and disposal of the bodies, denied that any bodies even now existed. The interviewer, Richard Halliburton recounts Ermakov's remembrance, even though Ermakov would not die after the interview and in fact lived another 17 years:

> *"We built a funeral pyre of cut logs big enough to hold the bodies, two layers deep. We poured five tins of gasoline over the corpses and two buckets of sulfuric acid and set the logs afire....I stood by to see that not one fingernail or fragment of bone remained unconsumed....We had to keep the fire burning a long time to burn up the skulls....We didn't leave the smallest pinch of ash on the ground...I put tins of ashes in the wagon again and ordered the drive to take me back toward the high road....I pitched the ashes into the air – and*

the wind caught them like dust and carried them out across the woods and fields."

Ermakov was a highly suspect individual. He was known to drink heavily and claimed falsely, he would admit, that he and not Yurosky had killed the Tsar.

It was not until far more than half a century after the alleged Yekaterinburg massacre, that the remains of nine bodies, not the expected 11, would eventually be exhumed from a shallow mass grave four-and-one-half-miles from Four Brothers by Alexander Avdonin, a geologist by training but an amateur archeologist in practice, and a small team of five assistants who had been privately searching for the martyred Romanovs. The location was Koptyaki Road, 12 miles from Yekaterinburg to the northwest, near grade crossing 184, some 700 feet in the direction of the Isetsk factory near the railroad tracks that pass six miles between the road and the factory. The year was 1979.

Adding to the controversy of the find, of course, is the fact that Avdonin and his influential Russian filmmaker supporter and former policeman, Geli Ryabov, did not maintain the scientific and forensic integrity of the burial site or of the remains themselves during their discovery. Three skulls, for example, spent a significant amount of time with Ryabov and at least one skull in Avdonin's home, having been removed from and then reinterred at the site while they unsuccessfully sought assistance in testing their authenticity and identification. Moreover, their discovery of the Romanov remains would not be announced until 1989 when Ryabov alone announced the discovery in a media interview and then gave even more information in yet another interview a short time later. The 10-year or so delay was ostensibly attributed to fear of retribution by repressive Soviet agents, even though Avdonin and Ryabov had sought help from local officials, on earlier occasions at least, and did not seem that concerned.

When the gravesite was officially opened by government officials in 1991, with the permission of President Yeltsin who had assumed office following the fall of the old Soviet Union after 74 years of rule, archeologists the world over were horrified to learn that heavy machinery was used to exhume the bodies rather than more sensitive, evidence-protecting tools of their trade. The contamination of the gravesite with heavy machinery was eerily reminiscent of the demolition of the Ipatiev House where the Tsar and his family were murdered. Later known as the Museum of the People's Vengeance, the Ipatiev House at 49 Voznesensky Prospekt was demolished in July 1977. The order to destroy the former merchant's Mansion, where the Romanovs had spent the last 78 days of their lives, allegedly, was given by then-local Communist Party Chair and later Russian President Boris Yeltsin. Today, in post-Soviet Union Yekaterinburg, the Church of the Blood stands on the old Ipatiev House site and is, not surprisingly, a major attraction in its own right.

The DNA Controversy

Noted DNA experts from Russia, the United Kingdom and the United States would argue years later over whom was actually found at the site - not to mention, whom allegedly was not. The nine were said to be that of Nicholas (50), Alexandra (46), Olga (22), the Tsar's physician Dr. Yevgeny Sergeyevich Botkin (54), the Tsarina's court maid, Anna Stepanovna Demidova (40), the Imperial family's cook Ivan Mikhailovich Kharitonov (48), and the Tsar's valet, Alexi Yegorovich Trupp (61). Less clear to scientists was whether or not two of the bodies were Tatiana (21) or Marie (19), or Tatiana or Anastasia

(17). Alexi was not among those found in the shallow mass grave, although he would be reportedly found about 70 meters away.

The Empress Alexandra was first cousin to Germany's Kaiser Wilhem, II. As pointed out many times now in this book, the Tsar was the cousin of England's King George V, Queen Elizabeth, II's, grandfather. King George V was also first cousin to the Empress Alexandra and the Empress was the granddaughter of Queen Victoria of the United Kingdom. The Queen's husband, Prince Philip, the Duke of Edinburgh, was also related through Princess Alice of Greece, making Prince Philip the Empress' grandnephew. Relatives of these royals would offer samples of their own for DNA testing that would ultimately conclude that the bodies were in fact the Romanovs, who would eventually be honorably entombed at Peter and Paul Cathedral in St. Petersburg.

> *"DNA testing in the 1990s by geneticist Peter Gill of the University of Strathclyde in Glasgow, Scotland, indicated that the remains were those of the czar and czarina and three of their daughters. For comparison samples, researchers used DNA from Britain's Prince Philip, whose grandmother and the czarina's grandmother were sisters, and from indirect descendants of the royal family.... Russian authorities enlisted the help of geneticist Michael Coble of the Armed Forces DNA Identification Laboratory in Rockville, Md., the world's largest mitochondrial DNA testing facility, specializing in identifying the remains of U.S. soldiers."*

The regional government in Yekaterinburg had called in outside forensic scientists to verify the veracity of the find. The American team was led by Dr. William Maples of the University of Florida. Maples, who would die five years later in 1997 from brain cancer, and his team took issue with their Russian counterparts concluding that remains of the Tsarevich Alexi and the Grand Duchess Anastasia were in fact missing from the gravesite. The Russian team of scientists agreed that Alexi was missing but they argued that Anastasia was in the grave – it was the Grand Duchess Maria who was missing, the Russians argued.

The bodies in the mass grave, also known as Grave #1 located in a "small clearing on the former Koptyaki road about two hundred yards from the Ekaterinberg-Perm railway line," yielded the following information:

> Body #1 believed to be Alexandra's maid, Anna Demidova because she was considered to be "a fully matured" woman with poor teeth and orthopedic evidence indicated a life of stooping or bending over frequently, as would be expected of a chambermaid. Her skull was reported to be missing facial bones. Anna was described as being tall and statuesque.
>
> Body #2 was believed to be the Tsar's physician, Dr. Yevgeny Botkin. The skeleton, whose torso was still partially intact, appeared to be that of a tall male with very distinctive facial features similar to those attributed to Dr. Botkin. The skull showed an entry wound in the left forehead and an exit wound in the right temple. Upper teeth were missing but lower teeth were found, which the scientists concluded were consistent with Sokolov's earlier claim that he had found the good doctor's upper denture.
>
> Body #3 was concluded to be the Grand Duchess Olga, the Tsar's eldest daughter. The skeleton was consistent

with being a fully developed female as evidenced by her pelvic structure. Dr. Maples estimated that the body was in her early twenties when she died. Her wisdom teeth were fully rooted, consistent with a mature person. An entry wound was found on the left jaw, which pierced the nasal palate and exited her right forehead. Dr. Maples believed that the gunshot indicated she was lying on the floor at the time of this wound based on "such a trajectory." This skeleton had an usually prominent forehead, similar to that which Olga was seen to have in photographs. Her skull also featured an "uncommon protruding bone structure in the back of the head. This feature, called wormian bones and found in only 5 or 6 percent of the population, strongly suggested a sibling relationship between the three younger women, and a mother-daughter relationship" between bodies #3, #5 and #6 with body #7. Her legs had been cut in half making height estimating more difficult but an examination of her arm bones led Dr. Maples to conclude that this person was just under 5′ 5″.

Body #4 was deemed to be that Tsar Nicholas, II. The most distinguishing factor found on his skeleton was orthopedic deformation consistent with frequent and sustained horseback riding, which His Royal Highness was known to do. His skeleton showed him to a mature male, fairly short in stature. The middle of the skull was missing but had with wide sloping features and a jutting jaw similar to that he was known to exhibit. A computer-imposed calculation also found similarities between the skull of the victim and photographs on the Tsar, thus allowing Russian scientists to agree that body

#4 was indeed that of the now-confirmed late Tsar Nicholas, II.

Body #5 was the smallest and youngest of all, female, about 5 foot 7 ½ inches tall. Dr. Maples and Dr. Levine, assisting him, concluded this was a relatively young person at the time of her death because her third molar teeth were not completely developed, nor was the sacrum in the back of her pelvis. Dr. Maples, thinking that the body was too tall to be that of the Grand Duchess Anastasia, however, judged the body to be that of the Grand Duchess Maria, because Dr. Maples believed this person to be in her late teens or early twenties at the time of her death. The Russians, however, concluded that body #5 was that of the Grand Duchess Tatiana. Dr. Maples found evidence that this body was in the process of developing wisdom teeth but the body showed signs of extensive abuse by her executioners. Half of the middle of her face was missing, according to scientists examining her more than a half century later.

Body #6 was considered by team to be Grand the American Duchess Tatiana because her skeletal development was considered to be between that of bodies # 3 and #5. The Russian team, on the other hand, believed that body #6 was in fact the Grand Duchess Anastasia. Dr. Maples estimated this body to be about 5' 5 ½" in height. Dr. Maples also noted that this skeleton featured the broadest bone structure of the youngest bones recovered from gravesite #1. Tatiana had a very slight bone structure, especially compared with Maria and moreover, body #6 had a fully formed collarbone, which is inconsistent with a younger female, such as Anastasia would be expected to possess at the time of her alleged death. The Russian process of using photographic superimposition led them to argue that positive matches on the skull of body #6 meant that in their opinion, body #6 was that of Anastasia and not Tatiana. Dr. Maples, however, took issue with the way the skull had been glued back together by Dr. Abramov before he superimposed the photos. According to Dr. Maples, doing so created variations, he said, that would lead to wrong conclusions. Moreover, argued Maples, when using computers to superimpose photographs, one can manipulate the skull "until it fits the photograph." The highly lauded Professor Richard Helmer of the Institute of Legal Medicine in Bonn, Germany, in September 1993, on the other hand, spent fives days in Moscow reviewing Dr. Abramov's process and announced that "this was the best superimposition program he had ever seen." Helmer's credibility in this determination was aided by the fact that he was also president of the Craniofacial Identification Group of the International Association of Forensic Sciences and was recommended for his opinion by Dr. Maples. Abramov would argue to Dr. Maples that some of the bones might have been mishandled and valid height identification, which Dr. Maples relied upon for his determination, might have been therefore compromised.

Body #7 was a deemed to be the Tsarina Alexandra because it was that of a middle-aged female, with lower teeth containing both platinum and porcelain crowns with other teeth featuring gold filings. The dentistry was similar to that found in the United States at that time, but according to Dr. Maples, also practiced in Germany, the Tsarina's home country. Her ribs showed signs of possible bayonet damage.

Body #8 was considered to be the cook, Ivan Kharitonov, a middle-aged male whom scientists also concluded has been thrown into the grave shaft first because it exhibited the most damage.

Body #9 was found resting under body #4 and was that of the oldest male victim, consistent with the Tsar's valet Alexi Trupp. Because the bodies were in contact with one another, Dr. Maples instructed that each fragment of the two bodies needed further and individual DNA testing to conclude their identity.

The Russian medical team included Dr. Vladislav Plaksin, who was the chief medical examiner of the Russian Ministry of Health. Nonetheless, controversy would persist as to who was missing. Alexi for certain because of the skeletons then present were of mature, middle-aged males, none a young male – but was it Anastasia, Marie or Tatiana?

A chilling passage from Robert K. Massey's, *The Romanovs: The Final Chapter*, described the scene as follows:

> *"The pit was only three and a half to four feet deep, beneath that level a layer of rock had prevented a deeper hole. The searchers quickly found a box containing three skulls, which Avdonin and Ryabov had reburied eleven years before. It was intact and unchanged. Digging wider, they encountered more skulls, ribs, leg bones, arm bones, vertebrae. The skeletons lay in disarray, one on top of another, at all angles, as if the bodies had been dumped into the pit at*

random. The bones were various shades of gray and brown; some had a greenish tinge. The fact that they were not grievously deteriorated was ascribed to the pit having been dug in clay, which prevented air reaching the bones. The skeleton at the bottom of the pit was the most thoroughly destroyed. Here the explanation seemed to lie in the broken pieces of large ceramic pots with screw-on lids believed to have contained sulfuric acid. Once the pots were placed in the hole and shattered by rifle fire, acid spread across the bottom of the pit, consuming the flesh and damaging the bones it encountered.

"The pit revealed no traces of clothing; this was consistent with the accounts of both Sokolov and Yurovsky; both had written that all the victims' clothing had been burned before the bodies were thrown down the Four Brothers mine shaft. Fourteen bullets were collected from the grave. Some had been embedded in the bodies; some probably were a result of the firing at the pots of acid.

"More terrible was the evidence of what had been inflicted on the human beings to whom these skeletons and bones had once belonged. Some of the victims had been shot while lying down, said Dr. Koryakova ('There are bullet wounds through the temples'), they had been bayoneted, their faces were smashed in by rifle butts, their jaws broken ('the facilial parts of the skulls are destroyed'), many other bones were broken, and finally, they had been 'crushed as though a truck drove over them.' In the course of her career, Dr. Koryakova has exhumed many prehistoric settlements in western Siberia and unearthed a large number of skeletons. 'But never,' she told the Sunday Times, 'so many that were so badly damaged – so violated. I was ill.'"

In 1998, Avdonin wanted to see if his scientists could find the other victims nearby. Maples had been replaced by Dr.

Anthony Falsetti following his death as well as another added assistant, Peter Sarandinaki. Another reknown forensics expert from the University of Colorado, Dr. Diane France from Necrosearch, traveled to Ekatrinberg to engage in yet another search of the gravesite. Necrosearch specialized in finding and identifying difficult to find and determine remains, especially in controversial and high-profile cases such as this one. Falsetti and France confirmed for scientists at the time that they agreed with Dr. Maples' conclusion that the Grand Duchess Anastasia was missing from the grave, and not Grand Duchess Marie, as the Russians believed, siting evidence that all of the skeletons were tall to have been Anastasia, who was reported to have been around 5′ 1″or 5′ 2″ at the time of her alleged execution. Consider this account to from one of the leading late-Tsarist historian teams of the time, Greg King and Penny Wilson reported:

> *"In winter, 1917-1918, standing next to Olga in a photograph, Anastasia is at least 2-3 inches shorter. She cannot have been, then, at the time of the murder, anything more than five-one or five two; thus, far too short to fit any of the skeletal remains found."*

Grave #2 was found August 23, 2007, a very short distance away from the mass grave exhumed in 1991, and contained two partial skeletons. Consistent with Yurovsky's account of the murders, the site appeared to match the bonfire location described in his report to Soviet officials. Archeologists identified the male skeleton as being between 10 and 13 years of age. Alexi was one month shy of his 14th birthday at the time of the Ipatiev House incident. A female skeleton was found next to him, which was estimated to be between the ages of 18 and 23 years old. Independent DNA testing by the University of

Massachusetts Medical School, and not that of Maples' University of Florida labs, concluded that in fact the remains were those of two of the Tsar's family. The sister's actual identity was determined by scientists to be that of the missing Anastasia.

Major American media concluded that Red Army Bolshevik Revolutionaries had indeed killed all of the Tsar's family in 1918:

> *"(CNN) -- One of the most enduring mysteries of the 20th century has been put to rest: DNA analysis of bone fragments has proven that two of Czar Nicholas' children believed to have escaped were killed with their royal family during the Russian Revolution. The chemically damaged and burnt remains were found in the Romanov family's makeshift grave outside the city of Yekaterinburg, Russia, in 2007. In 2008, scientists used bone and tooth fragments to identify the remains as those of the two missing children of Czar Nicholas II: 13-year-old Crown Prince Alexei, the emperor's only son and heir to the throne, and his sister Grand Duchess Maria, about 19.... The drama surrounding the Romanovs has been the subject of many books, movies and documentaries. Several women have claimed that they were Anastasia, Nicholas' youngest daughter, contending that they escaped the executions. The body of one impostor, Anna Anderson, was cremated when she died in 1984. DNA tests showed she was not related to the Romanov family."*

British scientists deemed that Prince Philip was an exact match to the Empress' DNA.

The Tsar's bones did not themselves yield and exact match because it had a mutation that could not be conclusively linked, but nonetheless had a very high probability of being a match at 98.5%.

There are a number of very troubling aspects to the identification process. Just look at the following sample from two key works that are equally long and troubling:

From Robert Massey:

Why did Dr. Maples himself feel compelled in the end to attack Dr. Gill's ultimate findings, administrative procedures, and scientific competence on dealing with the Romanov remains?

Why was the Maples team chosen by Yekaterinburg government officials to conduct the DNA analysis over a blue-ribbon team that was initially assembled by the United States Government consisting of the FBI and the Armed Forces Institute of Pathology based at Walter Reed Army Medical Center in Washington, DC? Then-Secretary of State James A. Baker, III, had visited the Romanov bones had been asked to assist in the Russian identification effort. Even, Dr. Richard Froede was, as Robert Massey points out in his book, *The Fate of the Romanovs,* the lead medical examiner as well as a past president of American Academy of Forensic Sciences. Maples, for his part, again as pointed out by Massey, was actually a forensic anthropologist - a doctor who Maples notes deals with bones more than human remains, especially in a murder-mystery situation. Maples was a forensic anthropologist, he dealt with bones.

The U.S. government team could clearly have done the actual DNA match. Maples was not in a position to do that. In the end, it was the British who ended up doing the DNA match. Why? Surely they would know that this switch would generate speculation that was done so that the British could replace Prince Philips' DNA sample? After all, this was a highly charged political controversy of an international scale. Why do that and open yourself up to the charge? One of the proposed leaders of the team said of the episode to Massey, 'From the point of view of forensic investigation, we are probably the best the U.S. has. We could have offered much more, particularly in the way of DNA analysis, because Maples couldn't do that, and it ended up being done by the British. We have one of the few labs in the world capable of doing mitochondrial DNA, so we could have done it here, in house. We're a huge pathology lab with state-of-the-art equipment both here and at the FBI.' Did the British have mitochondrial DNA capability at the time, too? The answer is yes according to Aldermaston and Peter Gill, according to Massey.

From Michael Gray:

Starting with the discovery of the Romanov remains, Gray details a conversation with Vladimir Bolshakov, a local historian, he says spoke of residents in the area seeing a group of people tampering with the grave area one month before Geli Ryabov, the 'discoverer' of the site in 1979, dug up the bones. Gray also says that Ryabov himself, was 'a graduate of the Moscow State Institute of Law, a holder of the USSR State Prize for criminal investigation, a former employee of the interior ministry department better known to us as the KGB, and an assistant to Soviet interior minister Shchelokov – hardly the credentials of a paragon of disinterest.' Gray notes that 'Ryabov and his associate Alexander Avdonin had special permission to work in the Central State Archive, his alone, at the height of the Soviet era, points strongly to state involvement in, or at least knowledge of, their enterprise.' He adds, critically and somewhat cynically, 'Similarly, it is difficult to believe that Boris Yeltsin, at that time the autocratic Communist Party boss in Ekaterinburg, then known as Sverdlovsk, would not have been aware of Ryabov's and Avdonin's excavations on the Koptiaki Road. Accounts of the official discovery of the bones in 1991 – twelve years later – by Lyudmilla Koryakova, an Ekaterinburg archaeologist, savoured of heavy continuing official involvement.'

Nikolai Sokolov, who had produced the most authoritative contemporary investigation of the fate of the Tsar's family for the White government in 1918, had apparently made a minutely detailed search of this very same site in that year without finding anything; yet no one has every questioned the thoroughness of his methods. The Russian government's initial refusal to release Imperial dental records and the government's later refusal to examine part of a bandage that was soaked in the Tsar's blood from an 1892 attempt on his life in Japan before he became Emperor of Russia adds to the impression that Boris Yeltsin was possibly a party to any forgery related to the Tsar family remains.

Despite contemporary Bolshevik accounts that the Romanovs were finished off by bayoneting, there were no scars on the bones. Professor Alex Jefferies of Leicester University, the founding father of DNA testing in Britain, went on the record as saying that if bones had been switched with those of close relatives, it would be very difficult to tell them apart. Taking all of these factors together, it became obvious that the truth about the bones was neither pure nor simple.

Two types of DNA exist within the human body – nuclear or genomic DNA and mitrochondrial DNA. Nuclear DNA is inherited from both father and mother, where mitrochrondrial DNA is inherited from the mother alone, passing unchanged through the female line down succeeding generations. Mitrochondrial DNA, said Gill, gives a more reliable result than nuclear DNA precisely because it remains unchanged. Prince Philip's mitrochondrial DNA, inherited from his mother and ultimately – like that of his material great-aunt, the Tsarina – from Queen Victoria, had apparently matched the Tsarina's skeleton perfectly. Since five of the skeletons appeared to be a family group comprising a mother, father and three children, and could be shown to be so by their nuclear DNA, it seemed reasonable to assume that these bones were those of the imperial family. Only one cloud hovered on Gill's horizon. Apparently mitrochondrial DNA from the Tsar skeleton did not match donations from two living relatives, Irina Sfiris and the Duke of Fife. Gill explained this away as a mutation or heteroplasmy, claiming that Tsar had two kinds of mitrochondrial DNA in his blood. Because of this supposed mutation, Gill identified the bones as those of the imperial family with only a 98.5 per cent degree of certainty. Such a mutation, however occurs only once in every 120 generations – a period of 3,000 years – which make it very long odds against it happening in the Tsar's case. The mutation argument did not seem to carry a great deal of conviction; but the alternative would have been to announce that the 'Tsar' did not match his own relatives.

Dr. Michael Badden, who worked with Maples blasted the Gill conclusion as 'nonsense.' He said that with "DNA it's either 100 per cent or it isn't.

This, our course, raises a number of very interesting questions: why does everyone believe that a 98.5% probably, based on these scientific terms, is such great odds, as widely reported in the media at the time? Why did the Tsar's DNA not match his other relatives, and why was this fact not disclosed at the time? Was it reasonable to conclude that the once every 3,000 years period would conviently work this time? Why were there no bayoneting scares on the bones, despite eyewitness accounts from July 17, 1918 that bayonets "finished off" many of the Romanovs? Why was this not disclosed? Why was the attack bandage from the Japanese assassination attempt not analyzed? Why were Imperial dental records not released for independent inspection? Why were so many bones missing from the gravesite yet still others in such good shape to analyze? Why, so many things in an investigation of this political and historic magnitude?

More from Gray:

Maples had a problem with the uncovering of the bones. For one thing, he never actually saw the bones in the ground; when he arrived they were laid out, washed, on mortuary tables in the morgue in Ekaterinburg. Twenty tons of earth had been sifted through, he said, and there was not a single trace of Alexei or the missing Grand Duchess. As for the remains that had been found, the impression that nine complete individuals were present in the burial pit was entirely misleading. More than half the total number of bones nine bodies would possess were missing - over a thousand bones in all. Half of the backbone of the skeleton Maples presumed to be Grand Duchess Tatiana, for instance, was absent. Also, though adipocere or 'grave grease' - a fatty substance generated by decomposing bodies - had been present in the ground around the remains, no bioforensic tests by enterologist had been carried out at the site.

To a layman's mind it seemed that if large bones like vertebrae were missing, this probably indicated that the skeletons had, at some time in their history been moved. Bill Maples admitted to me that the bodies might well have been buried not in 1918 but at some time after that. He even conceded that, if these individuals had been killed and buried only two years later, the skeleton identified as that of Anastasia would have exhibited more signs of maturity, with bones in the skull fusing, for example, and that this would go some way towards bridging the gap between his interpretations of the discovery and that of the Russian scientist Sergei Abramov, who had developed the technique of computerized imaging of skulls, had claimed that the missing girl was Maria, while Maples maintained it was Anastasia because all of the girls' skeletons were mature, whereas in 1918 Anastasia had still been only seventeen and not all of her cranial bones would have fused.

Maples was also concerned that the DNA evidence was based on a single sample from the Duke of Edinburgh, something he considered to be bad scientific technique.

We also learn the following from Michael Gray's in-depth examination of the Romanov DNA controversy, which is supported by other scholars as well. For example, the labatory of Dr. Marie-Claire King at the Berkeley campus of the University of California finds indications are Princess Sophie's mitrochondrial DNA did not match that of the Duke's DNA. Robert Massie concludes that the Tsar's skeleton may not be the Tsar after all, based on Princess Sophie's DNA results. We also know that sample contamination is highly likely in the case of the Romanov remains for two reasons: 1) chain of custody issues where the bones were never properly handled; and, 2) that the bones very likely got contaminated, too, from laying around in the open for extended periods of time on the tables in the morgue and being touched by people such as then-Secretary of State James Baker, III, or the first discoveres, Ryabov and Avdonin.

Since, February 1998 when the Romanov examinations were occurring, we have learned, too, that mictrochinrial DNA has a number of shortcomings, which were published, according to Gray, in the American Association of the Advancement of Science. Dr. Bill Shields of New York State University, Gray says, reports that up to thirty percent of folks who produced matches had no actual family link. He says that one in three who were said to be related where actually not related at all, leading Dr. Shields to tell Michael Gray, we are informed, that mitrochondrial DNA is not as reliable as first thought.

What comes next, according to Gray is equally interesting to our purposes here, since Martin was told by the Tsar that Alexei escaped Russia and was alive and well after July 17, 1918. Michael Gray writes in his book that he decided to have his own DNA compared to that of the Yekaterinburg remains.

> *Though I had many reservations about the Ekaterinburg bones – since, as this chapter has already made plain, so much that cast doubt on their authenticity was coming out of Russia – I decided that it might just be worth comparing my own DNA to that of the remains. I knew that if the bones were a hoax, this might not produce any meaningful answers. Indeed, one of the possibilities was that the bones might well have been chosen not to match the real Romanovs: if such bones could be officially authenticated and buried, this would pre-empt any subsequent claimants to the lineage, who would inevitably fail to match the standard thus falsely established. Alternatively, as we have just seem the bones might be those of people close to, but not of, the immediate imperial family – perhaps those of Romanov relatives, as many émigré groups were now asserting.*

So, here, then, are the often-disputed, and still highly-controversial DNA facts as we now know them:

- Burial ground was forensically unsound – violated at least three times by amateurs

- Collection of artifacts not proper

- Assassin accounts of destruction of bodies are inconsistent

- Improper documentation and storage of Romanov bodies in the Russian morgue

- DNA on Tsar was not fully conclusive

- Superimposition of Anastasia by Russian scientists was suspect

- Anastasia buried at Cathedral was 5′7″, too tall to have been Anastasia

- Bones tested for DNA were not in proper custody

- DNA testing by British appear to have been valid and proper

- Alexei had hemophilia. DNA tests today at deCode Genetics could identify that presence?

- Born November 1884, Empress bones would have been 107 years old – replaced for DNA sample? Tsar May 1868 = 124 years. Olga November 1895 = 97 years. Maria June 1899 = 92 years. Tatiana June 1897 = 94 years. Anastasia June 1901 = 91 years. Alexi August 1904 = 87 years.

- Employment of doubles was common in Tsar's world.

- The existence of a second imperial 'blue' train too. Look-alikes could easily have been substitiuted for the Tsar and his family in July 1918. Anna Anderson was believed by Alix Hill to be a double, for example, too.

- Duke's secretary was involved in debunking Anna Anderson, an effort waged by Lord Mountbatten, in 1995, 10 years after her death. The mitrochondrial DNA did not match that of Prince Philip. It was said that she was Fransiska Schwankowska, a deranged Polish factory worker.

- Scientists matched Anna's mitrochonrdrial DNA to that of Karl Maucher, Schwanska's great-nephew. Sample was at Martha Jefferson Hospital in Charlottesville. "Another sample of Anna Anderson's blood, taken in 1951 in Germany by Professor Stefan Sandkuhler was tested by Professor Bernd Hermann of Gottingen University, and it did not match the Virginia sample.

- Gill himself has admitted that one of these samples - Charlottesville or Gottingen - has to be false." So, the question to ask is, was it switched? Contaimnated?

Questioning What We Know

So, we know from the DNA controversy that there are many more questions than answers available on the true nature of the reported Romanov remains. For example, we can ask the following of the experts:

- This case certainly presented the forensics team with a lot of challenges going into the examination of the remains in St. Petersburg. We know from reports that the American forensic team led by Dr. Maples and then Dr. Falsetti following Dr. Maples' death had some serious misgivings about whose bones were whose during the joint examination into the Romanov remains. We know for instance that Dr. Maples was of the opinion that Alexei and Anastasia were missing from the main grave site while Russian counterparts were of the opinion that Alexei and Maria were missing. Are there now any new perspectives among the American forensic team on this dispute now that more time has passed since the "discovery" of the remains?

- The Russian Orthodox Church, as of this writing, has recently asked their government to allow more testing of remains of the two remaining Romanov children before agreeing to inter them at the Cathedral with their parents and siblings, assuming that they are related. It would appear that the church is of the opinion that the remains may not in fact be members of the Imperial family. Do they have a right to be concerned?

- DNA evidence linked to that sample from Prince Philip is said to have been 98.5% probable that the remains were indeed those of the missing Romanov clan. Was that 98.5% probability a valid conclusion at the time? Dr. Maples and Dr. Falsetti were one of the few American scientists to ever get a chance to personally analyze the bones said to have been taken from the gravesite. What would be their observations today about the whole Romanov controversy now that we are approaching the 100th anniversary of the reported assassination at Yekaterinburg?

- So, the controversy over the Romanov remains deepened a little and was made worse by the fact that when King Richard III was found a few years ago under a parking lot in London, his DNA match was reported at 99.99% certain. Why was this not the case with Nicholas? Would it be reasonable to expect that there would have been a higher match percentage with the Romanov tests?

- Would there be more or less possibility now that Martin's story might be true from a more modern day forensic perspective? What could be legitimately right about this account from Martin Hutson and what could be legitimately wrong?

- If in fact there are eventually reasonable grounds to further question the remains as being Romanov, is there any modern testing that could be done, or should be done, now that might better determine the true identity of these various remains? In other words, how confident should the public be in the DNA conclusions about the Romanov remains? Are they the real Romanovs? Could medical teams have done something different to get a more reliable probability reading on the remains? Would those same forensic experts do something different in the process that would have made the 98.5% probability declaration from Dr. Gill less assailable in the court of public opinion?

More specifically, we can and should also focus on the following discrepancies and questions:

- Clearly, there have been significant chain of custody issues with the Romanov remains - the Koptyaki burial site appears to have been disturbed at least three significant times without proper forensic handling, including the final excavation by Russian authorities, before being sent to Petersburg - a period from 1979 when Avdonin and Geli said they found the first nine bodies and 1979 and when the 2nd grave containing the reported Anastasia was found. What impact would this have on the 98.5% declaration and its validity from a forensic perspective?

- Dr. Maples was troubled by the potential contamination of the Romanov remains while laying out in the mortuary, unprotected it was said, washed, on gurneys in the examining room, handled by a number of outside observers including then-U.S. Secretary of State James Baker. Would washed bones have had a negative impact on the examination? How were the bones cleansed? What impact would this have on the 98.5% declaration and its validity from a forensic perspective?

- Was there potential contamination of the Tsar's skull while kept under the bed of the first discoverers Avdonin and Geli - a two-year period it has been reported? Russian authorities even reportedly found the three skulls in a box at the bottom of the pit when they finally formally unearthed the remains in 1991. What impact would this have on the 98.5% declaration and its validity from a forensic perspective?

- It has been rumored that the Tsar's skull was missing evidence of the sword wound from the Japanese assassination attempt and expected blade wounds in general if you are to believe the Ipatiev House and Koptyaki forest accounts. Was such evidence missing when you examined the Tsar's remains? What impact would this have on the 98.5% declaration and its validity from a forensic perspective?

- Knowledgeable observers have criticized the Russian forensics on the Romanov remains for a wide variety of reasons including the allegation that Nicholas' bandages from the Japanese assassination attempt were never tested for a DNA match with the late Tsar, nor were his dental records compared, etc. Is the information that the bandages were never tested true to the best of our knowledge? Were members of the American forensics team able to compare the Tsar's dental records with the reported Romanov remains? What impact would this have on the 98.5% declaration and its validity from a forensic perspective?

- Bones of the Tsar were said by Dr. Maples to be too tall for Nicholas Romanov's reported stature. Do bones typically grow in the grave over a 70-year period? Could it be that the Tsar's reported remains might have been switched at some point between 1918 and 1991? What impact would this have on the 98.5% declaration and its validity from a forensic perspective?
- Dr. Maples was reportedly concerned that the Koptyaki gravesite did not conatin enough bones in the grave for the 9 reported victims found in grave #1. In fact, it has

been reported that up to 1,000 bones were missing. What impact would this have on the 98.5% declaration and its validity from a forensic perspective?

- Dr. Maples was reportedly concerned that the Koptyaki grave bottom was devoid of many of the human fat deposits that would be expected of a site that contained nine reported victims. It was also reported that an Enterologist should have performed bioforensic tests of the site as part of the Romanov inquiry but as best as we can tell at present those tests did not occur. Were such tests conducted? Should they have been? What impact would this have on the 98.5% declaration and its validity from a forensic perspective?

- It was reported that only 14 bullets were found in the Koptyaki meadow grave along with some acid pots in the bottom of the pit. The observation was that the bullets were probably as a result of troops shooting down into the pit to rupture the acid pots in order to further disfigure and cover-up the Romanov remains. Based on official reports from the Ipatiev House murder, would it not be reasonable and even logical to believe that there should have been far more bullets found in the clay bottom pit if in fact the Romanovs were killed in a hail of gunfire in that now infamous basement room if history is to be believed? Would it not have been reasonable to expect that the bodies might have, or should have, yielded more bullets in the bottom of the pit, especially if the bottom was clay? What impact would this have on the 98.5% declaration and its validity from a forensic perspective?

- It has been reported that Tsar Nicholas II's DNA did not match a mitrochonrial DNA sample provided from his direct relatives, including relatives who shared maternal connections. Nevertheless, Dr. Gill announced a 98.5% certainty saying that mutations that occur once in every 3,000 years probably happened in the Tsar's case. Is that a reasonable or even logical assumption to make? What impact would this have on the 98.5% declaration and its validity from a forensic perspective?

- It has been reported that no testing was done for the Hemophilia gene on Empress Alexandra or the Romanov Grand Duchesses or even Alexei that we know of to date. Is that accurate information based on what what the public was told when Dr. Gill announced the 98.5% probability finding? If so, what impact would this have on the 98.5% declaration and its validity from a forensic perspective?

- It has been reported that no radio isotopes testing was performed on the Romanov remains to see if they might have post-atomic bomb contamination which would have indicated a possibility that the remains lived or existed beyond 1945. There were a lot of rumored sightings of Romanovs in that time frame. Should such isotope testing have occurred? What impact would this have on the 98.5% declaration and its validity from a forensic perspective?

- It has been reported that no reputable independent examination of the Romanov testing records have been released to relevant and appropriate interested parties outside of Russia since the inquiry began. Is that true based on what the public has heard? Were members of the forensic team, especially the Americans, ever granted such independent review opportunities by Russian officials? If so, what impact would this have on the 98.5% declaration and its validity from a forensic perspective?

- Dr. Maples and his team was reported to believe that it was Anastasia who was missing from the Koptyaki grave site formally excavated in 1991. The Russians believed that it was Maria who was missing from that grave. Would team members, especially Dr. Falsetti, still believe that it was Anastasia who was missing from the grave found in 1991?

- It has been reported Prince Philip's sample might have been switched for misleading purposes when U.S. authorities did not test the DNA results, while Great Britain did instead. The British should have known that British testing of the sample, without independent verification would generate such speculation. It has also been written that Dr. Jeffries said that it would be hard to tell from DNA samples if some other Romanov relative was used instead of Nicholas II if a switch did indeed occur, as some have rumored. Is that concern about an illicit switch valid and if so, what impact would this have on the 98.5% declaration and its validity from a forensic perspective?

- It has been reported that Dr. Maples was concerned that there was only one sample from Prince Philip tested. Is testing from a single sample only considered to be a problem in forensic medicine? Should more samples have been tested before concluding the Romanov remains were in fact from the Tsar and members of his family? What impact would this have on the 98.5% declaration and its validity from a forensic perspective?

- It has been reported that the bayoneting scars that should be evident on the remains from the Ipatiev House massacre were missing. Is that true? If so, why might such scars turn up missing? Could they have disappeared over time? What impact would this have on the 98.5% declaration and its validity from a forensic perspective?

- It was reported that when Dr. Maples expressed concern about the larger size of the Tsar's bones during his examination, it was explained by a Russian authority that the Russians might have made a mistake when they measured the bones. Was the American forensic team permitted to measure the Romanov bones independently and if not, why not? If so, what impact would this have on the 98.5% declaration and its validity from a forensic perspective?

- It was reported that body #9, the Tsar's valet, was found on top of body #4, the Tsar's body, thus raising concern that more DNA testing would be required and was instructed by Dr. Maples. Is is true that Dr. Maples instructed for more testing? If so, did that extra testing occur? If not, what impact would this have on the 98.5% declaration and its validity from a forensic perspective?

- From the perspective of experienced forensic scientists, if official reports from the time of the Romanov assassination indicate that Sokolov made a very minute, detailed search of the site and found no bodies in 1918, is it reasonable to conclude that amateurs found the site in 1979 without the benefit of Sokolov's information from Ipatiev House participants or more professional experience? Could the burial site found in 1979 been manufactured to fit the reported murder scenario? What impact would this have on the 98.5% declaration and its validity from a forensic perspective?

- Grave #1 was reportedly found by Russian officials in 1991 after having been initially discovered in 1979 by Geli and Avdonin. Grave #2 was reportedly found in 2007. Witnesses reportedly saw grave tampering the month before the official find in 1991. Was this information ever made available to the American and British forensic teams and was there any evidence of this found during either of their examinations? What impact would this have on the 98.5% declaration and its validity from a forensic perspective?

- Yakov Yurovsky said that the Tsar was shot in the head at point-blank range and that he was shot by soldiers dozens of times, repeatedly stabbed, the Tsar's head was crushed with rifle butts, mutilated beyond facial recognition, hand grenades were exploded on him in the burial pit, the Tsar was dosed with acid and lime, and burned with fuel oil. Did the American or British forensic teams see evidence of each one of these elements in the Romanov remains? Was evidence of any of these claimed elements missing from their results? What impact would this have on the 98.5% declaration and its validity from a forensic perspective?

- At least one murder witness at the time said that Anastasia's beloved King Charles spaniel, Jemmy, was killed and throw into the pit with the Romanov family, burned and dosed with acid and lime, as well. Did the American or British forensic teams see any evidence of the dog in the Romanov remains they examined? What impact would this have on the 98.5% declaration and its validity from a forensic perspective?

- Peter Ermakov, whose credibility has been questioned by officials and historians, said that when he and the Ipatiev House assassins destroyed the Romanov remains they stayed until "not one fingernail or fragment of bone remained unconsumed" using a funeral pyre. If that was true, why were bones found in the grave that were examined by the American and British forensic teams? Also, Ernest Harris in his 1930 interview said that he escorted the Romanov ashes out of Russia on an American train through Siberia which leads some level of credibility to Ermakov's account. Would a funeral pyre have reduced the remains to ashes as Ermakov alleges, without one unconsumed fragment of bone remaining in the ashes? Ermakov also alleged that he threw the ashes into the air and the wind "caught them like dust." Regardless of whether or not Ermakov threw the ashes into the air, would Harris have been able to accumulate the ashes to transport them based on forensic experience? What impact would this have on the 98.5% declaration and its validity from a forensic perspective?

- Body #7, reported to be the Tsarina, was said to have had porcelain and platinum crowns. Was dental technology sufficient in 1918 to create that possibility? Did the American and British forensic teams have the opportunity to compare the remains on body #7 with the Tsarina's dental records? Was there any evidence that the crowns were generated in the years after 1918? What impact would this have on the 98.5% declaration and its validity from a forensic perspective?

- Criticism that the Romanov remains should have been examined by qualified medical examiners versus forensic pathologists has been alleged? Does that really make a difference in the case of the Romanov remains? Can one point to any insight as to what would motivate someone to allege this in the Romanov case? What impact would this have on the 98.5% declaration and its validity from a forensic perspective?

Let's take a look at these questions and any possible answers we might uncover from the experts. There are way too many questions for something that was said to be 98.5% certain.

Recommended reading:

- Dr. William R. Maples and Michael Browning, *Dead Men Do Tell Tales,* Doubleday, New York, NY, 1994, ISBN-13: 978-0385479684.

15 | From The Bones of a Tsar

"Is it really them?"

- *Rescuing Nicholas*

So, what about this Hutson family lore passed down through the generations? Was Martin telling the truth, as we have been looking to prove? Was it lore or was it historically significant fact.

Here is the new factual evidence on what we now know about the Romanov saga, based on Martin's story:

- Woodrow Wilson did authorize a fourth, unwritten objective to the AEF Siberia mission, which was delivered to Major General William Sidney Graves by the President's Secretary of War, Newton D. Baker at the secret meeting in the Kansas City train station. That objective was to rescue the Tsar, and if possible, restore him to power as the reigning monarch of all Russia. If not possible to restore Nicholas to power, then the mission was to return Nicholas safely to the British, who would give he and his immediate family members political sanctuary in the United Kingdom.

- The ultimately successful rescue of the Romanov family was planned personally by George V, the King of England, Alexandra's first cousin and Nicholas's second cousin, and Woodrow Wilson, the 28th President of the United States, at a Christmas week meeting in 1918 at Buckingham Palace. The planning occurred once the Allied leaders realized that the former Tsar and his family were in safe hands for the time being and capable of being extracted from Russia with the help of the AEF Siberia Forces.

- Martin V. Hutson was recommended for the Romanov rescue mission by his older brother, George, who was an intelligence aide to AEF commanding officer, General John Joseph "Black Jack" Pershing, who suggested Martin to his commanding officer in Siberia, Major General William Sidney Graves. George Hutson would earn the Purple Heart while serving with General Pershing in the Black Forest of Germany.

- Special Evacuation Train #28, so designated in recognition of its special role on behalf of the President of the United States, and disguised as an American Red Cross train even though it was once the Imperial Train of Russia, did exist according to notes found in the National Archives in Washington, D.C., and was in position at the times necessary to coincide with the special mission. Morever, very important dignitaries from England and the United States and commanding officers from Allied countries such as Canada, Czechoslovakia, Italy and Japan were on tha train as well, including the Consul Generals of the United State and Great Britain. The American Red Cross in Siberia and Russia was participating with Allied Forces in hosting US and British intelligence operatives in theater.

- We know that the Romanov escape route wound its way east through Siberia along the Trans Siberian Railroad, controlled by an American company – The Russian Railway Services Corporation - from Irkutsk, Russia to the Tsar's transfer in disguised burial boxes with his wife, the former Empress Alexandra, and an unnamed younger daughter in Harbin, China. Harbin was the headquarters of the American railroad company operating the Trans Siberian Railroad. The rescue mission was conducted by American and Allied officials principally in October, November and December 1919.

- We know that Private First Class Martin V. Hutson spent two hours a day for two weeks talking to the fomer Tsar, Nicholas II, in person aboard his private carriage on Evacuation Train #28. Martin also spent a week personally talking to the former Empress Alexandra and a young daughter in the car ahead of the former Tsars. Martin was teaching Nicholas a Southern dialect to his fluent English and was responsible for providing personal protection services to the former Tsar.

- We know that an American soldier tried to kill Martin in Irkutsk at the end of his first period guarding the train that carried the former Tsar and Empress of Russia. We also know from detailed records on the American Expeditionary Forces Siberia that the timelines and corresponding events for Martin's mission are consistent.

- We know from Martin's conversations with Nicholas that he and his family escaped the Ipatiev House with the direct help of the British Ambassador in

Yekaterinburg, members of the Tsar's former Imperial Guard, and British intelligence agents operating in the neighborhood where the reported assassination was said to have occurred.

- We know from Martin's conversations with Nicholas that three other people were killed in his place and their bodies chopped up and burned to disguise their identies from Red Russians.

- We know from Martin's conversations with Nicholas that the other members of his family were evacuated earlier through western Russia by members of British intelligence. We know that the former Tsar and his family were held in a safe house until their evacuations during the confusing and chaotic Allied retreat from Archangelsk.

- We know that the British took protective custody of the Tsar in Harbin under the command of Sir Miles Lampson and that the Hutson mission, for the most part, took place in November-December 1919, sixteen months after the Tsar and his family were reportedly brutally murdered in Yekaterinburg at the now-razed Ipatiev House.

- Much of the former Tsar's personal treasure, in the form of gold and jewels was placed on wagons in Chita, Russia and separated from the train for fear of discovery by Red Russian troops who were attacking in the region with frequency. The remaining personal items, which still included personal wealth and important items was taken to Vladivostok after the former Tsar and his family were transferred to British care in Harbin, China.

- We know from Martin's conversations with his commanding Lieutenant Humphries that the plan was for the British to take the former Tsar and his family from Harbin, China, up river by boat, to Vladivostok, where they would depart for Japan and then San Francisco. Once in San Francisco, at Fort McDowell, the Romanov family would be escorted by train to New York City, via Chiago, and then taken by naval vessel to London, England and sanctuary.

- We know that King George V and President Wilson hid details about the Romanov rescue mission from their Prime Minister and Parliament and Congress, respectively. We also know that key trusted operatives of the two world leaders were the area at the time of the Romanov family disappearance and Hutson rescue mission, including: William Gibbs McAdoo, the President's son-in-law who was head of the American Red Cross in Siberia and former head of the United States Secret Service; Benjamin Johnson, a top executive of the American company operating the Trans Siberian Railroad for the Russian government and a Colonel in the United States Army who oversaw train movements in Irkutsk and Harbin; Franklin Delano Roosevelt, a future President of the United States, who as Assistant Secretary of the Navy at the time of the the Romanov evacuation in Vladivostok controlled the movement of all naval vessels in and out of that eastern Russian port city; and,

From earlier research that has been conducted extensively by other authors cited in this work, especially the historian Shay McNeal, we now know there has been a wealth of supporting evidence that indicates, related to Martin's mission:

- That Allied Intelligence officials were operating in the same theater of operations at the time of Martin's rescue mission of the Romanovs including British and American secret intelligence agents such as the famed spy Sidney Reilly; William Wiseman, the head of British Secret Service in the United States; U.S. Major General Ralph Van Deman, the father of American intelligence services; and, Thomas Masaryk, the future president of Czechoslovakia.

- Private financing was being provided to the United States and Great Britain, for expenses like the Romanov safehouse in Archangelsk/Murmansk, by private donors like American industrialist Charles Crane, because Congress and Parliament had not specially authorized such a rescue mission for the Romanovs.

We also now know years later that the DNA evidence on the Romanovs that was once reported to be 98.5% certain is not so certain after all.

- American forensic scientist team leader, Dr. William Maples, argued until his untimely death that the bones said to be Nicholas' were not in fact Nicholas', in his opinion, because they were too large and did not contain the knash-marks that one would expect to find on his skull from a much earlier near-fatal assassination attempt in Japan.

- Dr. Maples also questioned Russian determinations that concluded that the Grand Duchess Anastasia was found in the Koptyaki Wood burial pit because he said the bones of the then-17-year-old were too mature to be that of Anastasia.

- The DNA conclusions were suspect, too, because they were contaminated by the handling of others, without protective gear such as incidents seens in photographs of Russian pathologists handling the remains without gloves and facemasks, and former U.S. Secretary of States James Baker visiting the Romanov remains on an official visit, also without proper protective gear.

- The DNA conclusions have also been called into question because western experts have not been able to personally review and inspect the evidence independently using scientifically valid standards for such analysis.

Forensically, the validity of the Romanov remains are also called into question by the following known facts repeated in this work:

- The burial site was disturbed and opened on at least three occasions before DNA and forensic evidence could be assured and protected.

- The chain of custody of the bodies and evidence were never maintained by proper Russian authorities.

- The latest DNA techniques were not used in determining the proper identity of the Romanov remains.

Moreover, here is the new circumstantial evidence on what we now know about the Romanov saga, based on Martin's story, as well:

- Woodrow Wilson's *Aide-Mémoire* was signed, ironically, on the exact same day as Nicholas II's reported assassination in Yekaterinburg – July 17, 1918. Was this a coincidence?

- If indeed the three stated objectives of the *Aide-Mémoire* had been fulfilled before Wilson sent the AEF Siberia troops to Russia, why did he go ahead and send them anyway?

- Franklin Roosevelt would pen a fictional story, entitled, *The President's Mystery Story,* as President telling the remarkably similar story about a wealthy man with Imperial Russian connections who dies so that he can live, vanishing from society without a trace. Was this coincidence or did the then Assistant Secretary of the Navy know more about the Romanov saga than he ever admitted?

- The fact that the late Queen of England's favorite granddaughter and her treasured great grandchildren's murders did not generate far greater consternation and even action from British officials at the time of their disappearance.

- The credible sighting of the former Empress in Perm several months of the alleged Yekaterinburg murders as reported by a high ranking British diplomat and continued searches by Red Russian officials for members of the Romanov family months after they were said conclusively to have died.

- The existence of top Allied diplomats and officers aboard Evacuation Train #28 which was reported by the Consul General of the United States to have had the Tsar aboard. Even if the Tsar was indeed in ashes form as Consul General Harris would disclose more than a decade later, why so many officials aboard the train with a dead man's ashes?

- The sightings of the former Tsar in English villages and Irish towns such as Collon, in the late 1940s.

- Martin's similar descriptions of whom he ultimately thought might have been the Grand Duchess Anastasia and the Tsarvich Alexei near Vladivostok – were they?

Clearly, in order to pull off a successful, let alone unsuccessful, rescue mission of this caliber, one will need to have several critical elements all in play at the same time to ensure vitory:

1. Incentive. One would have to have a valid reason, an incentive, to authorize such as a risky mission. We know that George V wanted to rescue Cousins Nicky and Alix but that he was under tremendous pressure from his Prime Minister, David Lloyd George, not to intervene in

bringing Nicholas to England, for fear that it might jeopardize his own hold on the monarch in England since monarchs were not the most popular among their publics in that era, we were told. President Wilson, on the other hand, wanted a stronger ally in King George V of England, especially when he is telling Congress and the public back home that the United States should support self-determination in these cases, in order to avoid entry into unnecessary war. The two leaders were motivated by helping each other win the war against Germany and believed that they needed to restore the Russian monarch to power if possible, in order to maintain the world order in Asia and Europe. In other words, the reason for intervening was evident based on what we now know.

2. Plan. One must have a viable plan for achieving such a risky objective. We know that there had been several previous Romanov rescue attempts prior to Martin's mission thanks to the excellence sleuthing provided by the historian Shay McNeal. The Buckingham Palace planning session was held once it was clear that the Tsar was safe in Allied-controlled territory. This fact is bourne out, most likely, in McNeal's passages on the mysterious "Times 7" telegram to the President by General Graves. The brilliance of the plan was reinforced by the decision to split the Romanov family into two separate groups for evacuation, especially given that Red Army officials were reported long after July 17th to be searching for members of the Imperial Family. The use of the American Red Cross enabled both the transportation of the family east out of Siberia, the longer route few would have expected the Allies to have

selected given the turmoil in the region, as well as cover, because the former Tsarina and her older daughters had long and expertly served as Red Cross nurses and would have, therefore, been able very credibly, to walk the walk, too. Because the also spoke reasonably fluent English and French, the Romanov women, had they been detained, would have been very effective at masking their true identities. The retreat of Allied forces from Archangelsk and Murmansk provided excellent and effective cover as well because of the tremendous confusion that existed along the rail lines as literally thousands of military personnel and war refugees fled en masse. And, finally, transferring the Tsar and his remaining family members in burial boxes would not necessarily draw attention either since it was a regular occurrence aboard the hospital trains that frequented the Trans Siberian Railroad, especially from Irkutsk to Vladivostok. Harbin was a great transfer city selection because the city was in Chinese-controlled territory, for the most part away from the Red Russians, but it was also under significant Allied command and control because of it being the headquarters for the Russian Railway Services Corps managed by Benjamin Johnson.

3. Surprise. One would need the element of surprise. We know that this occurred, if in fact, you subscribe to the determination that the British Ambassador spirited Nicholas and his family out of the Ipatiev House with the help of the former Tsar's Imperial Guard who had reportedly infiltrated the Red Russian command in Yekaterinburg. McNeal's research makes a very credible argument for this conclusion and Martin's story reinforces from his late 1919 conversation with the "late"

Tsar that this was what indeed happened that permitted the larger escape from Russia altogether. Congress had been very vocal in its opposition to entering the war on the side against Germany and Russia, at least until the RMS Lusitania was sunk. With that done, even, America was a reluctant warrior on the western and eastern fronts and appeared to have no stomach for ongoing, long-term conflict. Red Russian armies most likely did not believe that American forces in Siberia would travel all of the way west from Vladivostok to help rescue the Tsar, let alone finance that rescue through private sources such as Charles Crane, when Conrgess objected so strongly. The use of the American Red Cross trains was so blatant that it did not merit much serious consideration to the Red Russians when it came to rescuing Nicholas and Alexandra, if in fact, they believed they were alive in the first place. The abandonment of Archangelsk and Murmansk, further helped confuse the situation ensuring an even greater element of surprise in the end.

4. Accomplices. One would need to have a large group of highly trained and discrete accomplices available to pull off this plan. With that said, McNeal's book, as well as even Smythe's tome, prove that there were many accomplices in play in and around Yekaterinburg and throughout Siberia when Martin's mission was unfolding. The White Russians, former Imperial Guard, and many of his friends and relatives were first amongst those accomplices operating in the region at the time the Romanovs vanished from history. Allied Forces, more importantly, were operating very widely in that area as well and were deeply diverse comprised of Americans,

British, Canadians, Cxecks, Italians, Poles, Chinese, Japanese, and some others.

5. Means. One would have to have the means to support their plan, especially of Congress and Parliament are not willing to do so. Without question, as we have seen in much of the previous scholarly research done on the Tsar's disappearance, there was at the time of the Huston Project a tremendous network of USA and British spies in place to help execute the plan. Benjamin Johnson, Breckingridge Long, Major General Kuhn, Major General Ralph Van Deman, Jerome Barker Landfield, Raymond Robins, Sidney Reilly, Charles James Fox, Captain George Hill, Sir Samuel Hoare, and many others have been documented here and elsewhere to have been operating in and around Yekaterinburg and eastern Siberia at the time *Hutson* claims to have unfolded. There was also significant political support among key players back and abroad which reinforced the means necessary to make such as mission work: Prince Arthur of Connaught, Tomas Masaryk, Sir Thomas Preston, Colonel House, William Wiseman, Mansfield Cummings, Jonas Lied, the Emperor of Japan, and many others not documented here. Furthermore, you had more than just the intellectual means available in these folks, but you also had the financial means available through the Charles Cranes of the world, not to mention the promise of the Tsar's own wealth carried with him out of Russia aboard trains and wagons, which only added to confusion when assets were going in all directions as the evacuation emerged.

6. Executives. One must have a very competent and talented team of people available to execute the plan at the highest level, once a plan has been devised. That happened in form of Secretaries Baker and McAdoo, General Pershing and General Graves on the U.S. side, and Franklin Roosevelt for the all-important Navy.

7. Financing. One must have all of the necessary financing available to pay for an operation of this magnitude. And, again, thanks to works like McNeal's, we know that that financing was indeed available from people like Charles Crane, and institutions like J.P. Morgan and the Bank of England. Congress did not need to know, because Congress was not funding King George's expedition to Siberia. The President was permitted by Congress to help win the war with England but we know from the research documented here in this work, that much of the financial support most necessarily came from and through England, proving in even greater depth that King George V did not abandon his cousins Nicky and Alix in the greatest hour of peril, as the British might say.

8. Evidence. Finally, one must evidence that the mission worked. Martin Hutson provides that evidence, which we have been able to document, for the most part, detailing who and how this rescue mission was executed. Martin's own recorded statement as well as the DNA controversy itself over the Romanov remains demonstrates that this family tale recounted in *Hutson*, is most likely more than just family lore.

It is certainly clearer, based on the trail of evidence that Martin has uncovered for us through his leads, that all of these elements for success appear, at least to us, to be highly evident. Taken into context, then, it does not seem so surprising then that the British, with the encouragement and support of their American allies, would have elected after all, despite public opinion and political opposition at the time, to rescue Nicholas Romanov and his family from Revolutionary Russia.

In his book, *The Romanovs: The Final Chapter*, Robert Massie writes the following about what he calls, "The Imposters" to the Romanov saga, conspiracy, or mystery, one of whom one could clearly argue might be Martin, absent the information we have presented in the pages above:

> *"The mysterious disappearance of the Russian Imperial family in July 1918 created fertile soil for the sprouting of delusion, fabrication, sham, romance, burlesque, travesty, and humbug. Since then, a long, occasionally colorful, frequently pathetic line of claimants and imposters has glided and stumbled across the century. Their stories have a common beginning: among the executions in Ekaterinburg there allegedly existed a man, or men, of compassion - even Yurovsky was assigned this role - who secretly helped one Romanov, or two, or perhaps the entire family escape. A recurring motive in many of these impostures was the belief that Tsar Nicholas II left a fortune behind in a foreign bank."*

To this point, we do know that it was true that Nicholas and Alexandra had both been very adamant that they would not contemplate any rescue of the Imperial Family that involved the family being separated or having "to leave Russian territory." Helen Rappaport had a very reinforcing passage on this thought in her book on the Romanov Sisters. That said, then, how did the Allies convince Nicholas & Alexandra to do just that - split up the Romanov family and leave the Russian territory for England?

Consider this, too: In leaving Tobolsk for Yekaterinburg, Rappaport also reported: "It was clear to the four sisters that their mother could not travel without one of them to support her. Olga's health was still poor and she was needed to help nurse Alexey. Tatiana must take over the running of the household; even Gibbes asserted that she was 'now looked upon as the head of the Family in the place of the Grand Duchess Olga.' After discussing it among themselves, the girls agreed that Maria should accompany their mother and father, leaving court jester Anastasia to 'cheer all up.'" Why, then, might Martin think that it was the court jester Anastasia on board Evacuation Train #28 when Maria might have better been the one to accompany her parents, especially her ailing mother, Alexandra, across Siberia. But remember, too, Martin did not report that Alexandra appeared to be ill. To the contrary, he thought her quite beautiful and engaging. Maybe that, too, had been a smokescreen to through their pursuers off the trail had they been discovered fleeing Russia?

Perhaps, the passage from the Hutson-skeptical Rappaport would support Martin's perspective? Rappaport quoting Alexandra's maid, Mariya Tutelberg: "Don't make my pain worse, Tudels. This a most difficult moment for me. You know what my son means to me. And I now have to choose between son and husband. But I have made my decision and I have to be strong. I must leave my boy and share my life - or my death - with my husband. In the case of Martin's story, the first part of the passage from Rappaport would be supported by the quote, unless you stop to consider that Martin thought in the end that Alexei might have been on Evacuation Train #28 to

Vladivostok, too. Did Alexandra get it both both ways, when the story is finally told?

Was Martin's testimony just another one of those "Imposters" stories, as Massie so rightfully describes them? Why would Martin take time to record "an episode in my life" not long before he too would pass? There was no financial benefit to be gained for him so late in life. Is it fair to subject Martin's memory to the threat that he might have been just another one of history's pretenders by re-telling this story now through family as he had hoped to do?

Why even Martin in the first place? Why was he there, if the story is true? Why was an inexperienced and unworldly 18-year selected to work directly for a Major General of the United States, a protégé himself of the remarkable iconic General Black Jack Pershing, who himself was answering directly to the president of the United States?

Was Evacuation Train #28 a real mission? Woodrow Wilson was indeed the 28th president of the United States, so stranger things have happened in American history. Was the Tsar or any members of his family really on board? Did King George V give his cousin political sanctuary somewhere in the United Kingdom after all? Was the other cousin, Kaiser Wilhelm involved, too? We believe the answer to these questions is: yes.

Was General Graves an even bigger American hero than history originally thought for bringing the Tsar out of Russia, and then not talking about it despite the judgmental criticisms he took over the years for his leadership in Siberia? Once again, we believe the answer to this question is: yes.

Can this eyewitness account hold up to scrutiny? Does it matter, today? Yes.

In listening to Martin's recordings, which do not mention specific dates but do acknowledge time periods by days and weeks that we can reconstruct, and by examining his Army enlistment papers reflecting an induction at Fort Oglethorpe, Georgia, on August 20, 1919, we can construct the following timeline for Martin's movements and his extraordinary encounter with the person he ultimately believed to be the last Tsar of Russia:

- Martin spends two to three days at Ft. Oglethorpe after enlisting before moving on to Chattanooga, Tennessee for his trip to Fort McDowell in San Francisco, California.

- McDowell had been the former command of Major General William Sidney Graves before taking over command of the American Expeditionary Forces Siberia at the invitation of President Woodrow Wilson in a message delivered personally by Secretary of War Newton Baker in Kansas City, Missouri.

- Chattanooga to San Francisco by rail takes Martin two days to accomplish.

- Martin then spends three to four days at Ft. McDowell preparing for his trans-Pacific trip to Vladivostok himself. This makes it sometime between September 3rd and September 6th, 1919.

- On September 9th, the British are in the process of retreating to Arkhangelsk, home of the AEF Siberia Polar Bears. Is the former Tsar in transit now to Irkutsk?

- San Francisco to Hawaii, en route to Vladivostok on the *U.S.S. Transport Great Northern,* is a seven-day process, where Martin then spends another one to two days on shore leave eating pineapple and candy.

- Hawaii to Vladivostok takes another fourteen days to complete, placing his arrival in Russia somewhere around September 17th to September 20th, 1919, based on his account, thus far.

- Martin spends the next three days in the dirigible hanger in Vladivostok before moving to the old church where he begins close order drilling with Company H of the 31st Infantry for another six weeks.

- In the meantime, Evacuation Train #28 is en route from China to Harbin, being recorded in the Harbin Rail Yard on September 27th, as noted in Chapter 14.

- On September 29th, the Czech forces are ordered out of Siberia creating mass confusion in the region during their evacuation process. Cover for evacuating the Romanovs has been set.

- Allied Forces themselves evacuate Murmansk on October 1st. adding to the regional chaos and distraction.

- Ben Johnson leaves Omsk on November 12th. He is evacuating eastern Russia as well.

- Martin learns Wig Wag as instructed by Lt. Humphries and makes his way west by train from Vladivostok arriving in Irkutzk somewhere around November 13th at the earliest and November 18th at the latest.

- We know from information presented in Chapter 22 that the last Americans have now left Northern Russia and are working their way east on the Trans Siberian Railroad toward Vladivostok, Russia

- For the next three days, Martin guards the Red Cross steel Pullman car in the rail yard at Irkutzk before learning who is on board the train he is protecting in the frigid cold while deadly and threatening gun fire surrounds him.

- Sometime around the middle of November 1919, more than a year after his alleged murder in Yekaterinburg, Martin meets Nicholas aboard the Red Cross' Evacuation Train #28.

Several other interesting occurrences are worth repeating here as Nicholas and Martin head east toward Harbin, China:

- Harbin, China is the headquarters for the Russian Railway Services Corps, which operates the Trans Siberian Railroad under Ben Johnson and others.

- American Consul General Ernest Harris is onboard the train, as is a Japanese General and high-ranking Colonels from England, Italy, and Czechoslovakia, all of whom have been witnessed by Martin to be sitting in the car with Tsar Nicholas II.

- Martin has described Nicholas as weighing 150 pounds, which is consistent with historical accounts of the former Tsar's physical stature at the time. The Tsar is also reported to have spoken fluent, perfect English and was reported to be fluent in many other languages as Martin learned.

- Martin says the train sat in the Rail Yard at Irkutzk for seven days before finally departing.

- As Evacuation Train #28 made its way east, it took a route through Chita, Russia on its way to Harbin, China, where Martin says Nicholas and others in his party were off-loaded in wooden coffins disguising them as American war dead.

- This part of the trip, Martin says, took another five to seven days putting the Tsar's transfer to the British subjects of his cousin, King George V, at Harbin around the end of November - first of December, 1919.

Un-Redacting History

So, history un-redacted tells us, at least based on this first-hand eyewitness account from a young American soldier who was there, that the Tsar and members of his family did indeed escape Russia alive more than a year after their reported deaths at the hands of Red Russian troops at the now-razed Ipatiev House in Yekaterinburg. U.S. Army Private First Class Martin Van Buren Hutson of Tennessee was that eyewitness to Tsarist history and the actual last days of the Romanov Dynasty.

Martin Hutson contended that the Tsar, his wife the Tsarina, and a daughter, probably Anastasia, escaped Russia through Harbin, China with the direct help of Allied Forces Siberia on American Red Cross Evacuation Train #28, designated in honor of the 28th president of the United States, Woodrow Wilson, who helped King George V of England save his first (Alexandra) and second (Nicholas) cousins from a certain death at the hands of Bolshevik Revolutionaries.

Martin Hutson's testimony is that the Tsar, his wife, a younger daughter, and an attendant were smuggled out of China by American forces with an American Consul General on board through China, and were handed over to British troops who then evacuated the family to London through the United States.

Martin further testifies that the remaining Romanovs, the Tsarevich Alexei and three sisters, safely escaped with their grandmother, the Doweger Empress, through Central Europe months before. Martin said he based that conclusion on first-hand conversation he had with Tsar Nicholas II in and of Russia before he disappeared yet again into history cloaked by knowing heads of government in England, the United States, Germany and Russia.

It would appear from records and the eyewitness recording from Hutson himself, that the Tsar and his family were actually taken away from the Ipatiev House in Yekaterinburg alive on an Imperial Train staffed by members of the British and American Red Cross, under the direction of another American who was the brother-in-law of the president of the United States and former head of the United States Secret Service. The Tsar's wife and at least one daughter was mascaraing as Red Cross nurses, a role they performed in real life before the Red Russians came to town.

The President of the United States, Woodrow Wilson, had authorized American intervention in the Russian civil war during the last days of World War I, through the American Expeditionary Forces Siberia. His justification and command, which was taken without the approval of his own Departments of State, was outlined in a document known as the *Aide-Memoire*, approved ironically enough on the same day as the Tsar's alleged assassination, July 17, 1918.

The Trans-Siberian Railroad that the Tsar and his family traveled in the autumn of 1919, according to Hutson, was controlled by an American company and an executive named Ben Johnson. Johnson had visited the assassination site in Yekaterinburg prior to the departure. His train would travel more than 4,000 miles from west to east under the protection of the train company hired to operate the railroad safely and American soldiers who were onboard to assure that attacks would be repelled.

The Tsar and his family would be removed from their train in a small town called Harbin, a town that served as headquarters for the Trans-Siberian Railroad. They were in coffins that were reported to be American dead and other boxes that were said to be rifles being transported in secrecy to Russians who were fighting Vladimir Lenin. Their train was labeled Evacuation Train #28.

Removed on wagon, from Harbin, the Tsar and his family moved by the *U.S. Transport Merritt* from American Bay to Vladivostok on a trip that began, we believe the record now shows, in November 1919. From there, the Tsar and his family traveled from Vladivostok to Manila, the Philippines and then on to San Francisco's Fort McDowell. From Ft. McDowell, they made their way to New York City and eventually on to London, where they were eventually given political refuge by the Tsar's own cousin, the King of England, George V.

Hutson was selected for his special duty at the age of 18, on the recommendation of his 21-year-old older brother, who was working in intelligence for the iconic American commanding officer, General Black Jack Pershing, who had worked with Major General Graves in Mexico. He arrived in Vladivostok aboard the *U.S. Transport Great Northern* in September 1919 and departed aboard the *U.S. Transport Crook* in January 1920.

With that established, again for emphasis, here is what we may now know about the official record on Tsar Nicholas II and the Romanov family:

Conclusion #1: Nicholas Lived

Further scrutiny tells us that the Tsar and his family did indeed escape their death chamber at the Ipatiev House in Yekaterinburg in July 1918 and were not assassinated as history believes, at least supported, in part, by the official U.S. government records for Evacuation Train #28 operated under the protected guard of the American Expeditionary Forces Siberia.

The Tsar and two members of his family were spirited out of Russia on a hospital train made to look like a Red Cross mission. They had previously traveled from Yekaterinburg, where they were rescued by members of the Tsar's own White Army over a 16-month window to Harbin, where they were ultimately removed in the presence of American troops in boxes, made to look like coffins. The operation was directed by a civilian, Benjamin Johnson, who was working under cover on the Trans Siberian Railroad as a Colonel in the United States Army.

Harbin was selected because it was the headquarters for the Russian Railway Services Corps selected by the Bolsheviks themselves initially at least to operate for the fledgling and as yet unstable government. The train was made to look like a Red Cross mission because few would challenge its operation or passage.

Martin was selected to look after the Tsar because he could be trusted by his commanders, based on the word of a trusted assistant to the supreme commanding officer, General Black Jack Pershing who himself was highly trusted by the president of the United States.

Woodrow Wilson had a very clear objective in mind when he overruled his own State and War Departments and decided to intervene in Siberia at the end of World War I. At first, it appears that the president and his allies were hopeful that they could restore the Tsar to rule. When it became obvious that his people did not want that either, the effort to evacuate the Imperial Family, in honor of Wilson's rule not to intervene, took priority.

Conclusion #2: King George V Rescued Nicholas Afterall

Contrary to public opinion at the time, King George V of Great Britain did indeed give political sanctuary to his first cousin, the former Tsar of Russia, following his escape from communist Russia. King George V was not the callous monarch he was portrayed as being once the world learned of the alleged murder at the Ipatiev House. Moreover, King George V was a brilliant strategist in devising a plan to save the former Tsar and his family in the midst of a bloody world war divined by another cousin, Kaiser Wilhelm II of Germany.

Like his friend and ally, the President of the United States, King George V weathered great personal and political risk in keeping his Prime Minister, the ever-present David Lloyd George, in the dark as to the plan for Siberia. In the end, we believe the Prime Minister was most likely aware that the "late" Tsar and his family were now living in the United Kingdom, but the world thought he was dead, so the British monarchy was probably at a lot less risk itself in the aftermath of the world won by its King.

Conclusion #3: President Wilson Helped King George V Evacuate Nicholas

Woodrow Wilson probably did earn the grateful thanks of his ally, King George V, when the rescue was all said and done. Wilson did not need to intervene in Germany or Russia, but did, when American lives were lost aboard that luxury liner in the Atlantic Ocean, a victim of German U-Boat aggression. Had his political subterfuge been discovered by Congress, Wilson most assuredly would have impeached for his deceptive and largely unauthorized actions, despite the declaration of war he sought and received.

Conclusion #4: Lenin & Wilhelm Most Likely Approved the Rescue

Vladimir Lenin and Kaiser Wilhelm II may very well have helped the Allies in rescuing Nicholas and his family from Russia. It is hard to believe, but highly circumstantial at this stage of research into the rescue, to know otherwise, but how could it be that they were not? Lenin might not have been portrayed as the cold-blooded Revolutionary he was over the years had we known otherwise. It is common sense that in receiving payment from the Allies, especially the British, to let Nicholas go, would have indeed provided the Russian leader with more of the critically important funds he needed to sustain his dawning Soviet Union. Wilhelm could very well have been negotiating his own political exile, rather than execution, at the end of the war in agreeing to former Tsar's disappearance, but we will need to do a lot more research on this possibility before we can draw any logical determinations on that one.

Conclusion #5: FDR Played a Key Role in Nicholas' Escape

Franklin Roosevelt played a very significant and important role in the Allied rescue of the former Tsar and his family using naval vessels in and out of Vladivostok and San Francisco. It also appears that FDR used this experience to his benefit as a war-time President himself in the tumultuous 1940s.

FDR's personality and penchant for secrets that nobody else knew makes his a great candidate for the role one would have had to play to bring the rescue mission in and out of Vladivostok in the closing days of the White Army's defeat by Lenin's Red Army.

Conclusion #6: General Graves Was an Even Bigger Hero Than History Acknowledged

General William Sidney Graves was far more successful in achieving his mission objectives in Siberia, as directed by President Woodrow Wilson, than history has given him credit for achieving. An entire Czech Legion was evacuated out of Vladivostok to help give cover to three remaining Romanovs attempting to escape their homeland in a world gone made. The mission of the AEF Siberia forces came to a sudden end with U.S. forces leaving the region on short notice by April 1, 1920 because the Tsar and his family was gone.

Based on the evidence found in *Rescuing Nicholas,* General Graves was unfairly and wrongly criticized by American war leaders for not succeeding at his stated mission in Siberia when in fact he was immensely successful at achieving his objectives from President Wilson and for being a good and loyal soldier who maintained until the very end the confidential information of his commander-in-chief. West Point proud, we would conclude.

Conclusion #7: Black Jack Pershing Lived Up to His Billing

General Black Jack Pershing was an even more outstanding war-time leader, given his leadership of a mission like the former Tsar's rescue and then letting his top lieutenants actually succeed without interference or micromanaging from him. The war in Europe was a very troublesome two-front war that presented the United States with a whole new set of untested challenges that he won quietly and expertly for the American public whose interests he served well.

Conclusion #8: Ben Johnson Was an Unnamed Hero in History

Benjamin Johnson, William McAdoo, and Newton Baker are unsung heroes of World War I for the roles they played in carrying the President's and the King's rescue plan for the

Imperial Family. The were beyond competent in carrying out their tasks, while maintaining the secrecy of their work, which undoubtedly would have imperiled the AEF Siberian troops and Allied intelligence had their purpose been publicly disclosed

Conclusion #9: Allied Intelligence Was Hugely Successful

The intelligence agents of that time were brilliant in executing the Allied rescue plan behind the fronts of two warring giants as hatched by President Wilson and King George V at Buckingham Palace over the Christmas season in 1918. Their own planning was superb, their coordination exceptional, and their devotion duty above-and-beyond the call, without question. It is a lesson in history that shows how well our intelligence services work when the mission is clear and our political leadership absolute in their dedication to achieving the outcome. It was right for the Allies to rescue the Romanov family. It is an example that we can and should use in future endeavors where American and British intelligence, working together, ensure the peace for all our citizens.

Conclusion #10: The DNA Evidence Was Not Conclusive Afterall & Still Subject to Dispute

DNA evidence will most likely never be able to conclusively determine what really did happen to the Romanov family on July 17, 1918, and of course, that leaves and should engender, many other questions that future research will need to explore. We encourage that more detailed examination and pledge our support for those who will do so in the name of being just and transparent in their purpose.

Conclusion #11: The Rule of the Tsars Ended

Even though the Romanovs lived, as Martin testifies in his 1971 recording, the likelihood of a Romanov-led Russian monarchy being restored is highly improbable, in our opinion. Nicholas abdicated to his brother, who himself gave up the throne very rapidly thereafter to a Revolutionary government that at least one super power – the United States of America – formally recognized as the official government of the Russian people. Moreover, the succeeding Soviet Union came in its place and lasted some 70 years after, replaced by a more democratic form of government that governs the country today, in the rightful eyes of the world who interact with it each and every day since.

Succeeding generations of Romanov royalty will be left to be guardians of the legacy of Nicholas and Alexandra. They will probably never be viable contenders to rule Russia ever again. For that reason, the pretenders and the imposters can go away and leave history to history, and legitimate heirs as legitimate heirs. That is not to say that the debate will end here. Needless to say, there will always be those who will say, despite the evidence we have attempted to present above, that Nicholas & Alexandra, and the young Romanovs with them, did not survive Yekaterinburg on that fateful July day in 1918. We respect that opinion, although we will now disagree with it for reasons that we hope we have made more obvious, but do believe at the same time, that continued dissention and disagreement about the potential of their survival will engender even more research in the years ahead, research we are confident will one day be crystal clear when it comes to knowing what happened to the Romanovs of Russia.

In the meantime, this is where educated opinion leaves us. Clearly, Martin Hutson's story is an extraordinary story, if it proves true over more time that is to come. In either case, *Rescuing Nicholas* was designed so that you can and will be the judge of that outcome.

Later Years

As time has indeed passed thus far, General William Sidney Graves was promoted to Major General in 1925, in large part, because of his service in Siberia. He, like other men in his company, was awarded the highly prestigious Distinguished Service Cross for his role in World War I in Russia. The citation reads:

> *"For especially meritorious service as assistant to the Army chief of staff and as commanding general of the American Expeditionary Forces in Siberia."*

At the base of a small hill with several large shade trees casting their shadow on his grave, General William Sidney Graves rests next to his beloved wife, Katherine, at Arlington National Cemetery. His role in history is marked simply by the plot at Section 3, Lot 4177-C-SS map grid U/16 #13051 and a tombstone that notes his leadership role of the American Expeditionary Forces in Siberia. The gravesite looks out at the Washington Monument in the distance, with the Air Force Memorial to the right and the Tomb of the Unknowns to the left. Mr. Lincoln sits in his own place of honored glory on the horizon ahead.

King George V is resting at Windsor Castle outside of London, England, in St. George's Chapel with many of his storied ancestors. He beloved wife, Mary of Teck, lies next to him as well, a grateful nation still at their beckon call.

Woodrow Wilson, lies next to his own beloved wife, Edith Bolling Galt, at Washington's famed National Cathedral. The seal of the President of the United States and the flag of our nation stand watch nearby. His faith in God testified by the hallowed sanctuary in which he lies in perpetuity.

William Gibbs McAdoo and Black Jack Pershing rest at Arlington National Cemetery themselves. Martin is buried in Kentucky. George Hutson lies in California. Newton Baker rests in Ohio and Benjamin Johnson lies in Minnesota. Lenin can still be seen in his crypt in the Kremlin. Wilhelm is in a small mausoleum in permanent exile in the Netherlands.

Tsar Nicholas II of Russia and his beloved family lie in peace, too, we are led to believe, in St. Catherine's Chapel at the Peter and Paul Cathedral in St. Petersburg, Russia, his father Alexander III and mother, the Dowager Empress, re-buried next to him only recently, nearby.

But we are left wondering, is it really them?

Does history care?

The confusing story of the Romanov's demise is confusing precisely because American intelligence - Allied intelligence – wanted it that way.

It was, and still is, the intelligence agencies job to create a field of rabbit holes for the average person to chase when trying to uncover the truth about what might have happened to Nicholas and Alexandra. Afterall, it was one of the best means of keeping the "late" royal family safe.

Of course, there will be historians who believe with every ounce of the being what history appears to suggest. The evidence at the beginning of a great mystery always take you were its authors want you to go.

But, when nagging questions about reality continue to persist, you will often find others who will ask of history: let me see what you did, not just what you said.

Despite the addition of Martin's eyewitness account to the official record on the alleged Romanov assassination, it will take some more digging to answer the compelling, intriguing, ongoing question of what happened to the last Tsar of Russia.

So, the interviews and research will continue in order that we might better answer that question and the new one that it now generates: if Nicholas lived, where did he go?

Recommended reading:

- Greg King and Penny Wilson, *The Fate of the Romanovs*, John Wiley & Sons, Inc., Hoboken, NJ, 2003, ISBN: 0-471-20768-3.

- Helen Rappaport, *The Last Days of the Romanovs: Tragedy at Ekaterinburg*, St. Martin's Griffin, New York, NY, 2008, ISBN: 978-0-312-60347-2.

16 | Martin's Epilogue

Why would the American military pick an 18-year-old kid for such an amazing mission?

- *Ben Everidge*

My Great Uncle Martin first told me about his Siberian "episode" in the summer of 1970, just a little more than a year before cancer would take his life. We were sitting in the family room at his older sister's (and my grandmother's) home in Ohio.

I was 12 years old, or so, just back from living for a few years in Puerto Rico where my mother was working on a U.S. Air Force base in Civil Service, but already appeared to all who knew me to be an old soul because I treasured good biography, politics and history. Even at that so-called tender age, I could not get enough of good story, especially if it was a true story.

Our first talk lasted more than seven hours, well past midnight and into the early morning hours. Our second talk, that next morning, required another four hours.

My grandmother, Corinne Hutson Miller, had been insisting for a year that I needed to hear the story from Martin himself and moreover she wanted me to write about it some day. Grandma had been telling me bits and pieces of Uncle Martin's World War I service in Russia, so I kind of had an idea about what was coming.

I underestimated the impact Uncle Martin would have on my life with that story but I deeply appreciated the detail I learned by being able to hear Uncle Martin's account first-hand, especially with all of the questions I had thrown in for good measure.

Admittedly, I loved Martin's astounding story but a nagging question kept me paralyzed from telling his tale myself once he had passed - why Martin? Why would the American government pick an 18-year-old kid for such an amazing mission? Why would history never know the truth about what Martin had said had actually happened to the "late Tsar" of Russia and other members of his family?

As a soon-to-be teenager, I would tape weekly episodes of my favorite TV shows, *Hawaii Five-O* and re-runs of *Twelve O'Clock High* on a shinny new cassette recorder I had received for Christmas. Fast bedtime rules interfered with watching quality television when you are 12 years old.

I shared with Uncle Martin that I thought he should tape his story, too, before something happened to him as he was aging. It appeared to me that my nearly teenage advice went in one of Uncle Martin's ears and out the other, as they say.

Nonetheless, my mother, Nancy, and Uncle Martin's daughter, Mary Ruth, gently hounded me at times in later years, too, to write the story, especially after Grandma passed in my late twenties/early thirties. My mother kept reminding me that Uncle Martin's legacy was at stake. Family members politely urged me on through Mom, as well.

My reminder of that family responsibility, that legacy opportunity, came in the middle half of the first decade of this century, when my second cousin, Ken, one of Martin's grandsons, sent me nearly 45 minutes of audio recordings from Martin re-telling his story, just as I had recommended many years before.

It was like we were sitting in Grandma's living room, all over again. Only this time, I was more experienced. I had received my undergraduate and graduate degrees in

International Studies and American Government from reputable universities in Washington, D.C., where I had also worked for more than a decade on the professional, personal office and campaign staffs of members of the United States Senate and U.S. House of Representatives.

And, I had a family of my own - what a story to share with them some day, I realized.

I was finally convinced. It may have taken me more than four decades to begin writing, *Rescuing Nicholas*, but it is based on facts that have proven out as I have looked into Uncle Martin's testimony on that recording and testimony he had entrusted to me and the Hutson family all of those years ago.

If Uncle Martin's legacy is to be proven, then it became obvious to me and my relatives that in re-telling his privileged time with the Romanovs, facts would be critically important and transparency on what we know, what we had been able to discover over the years, and what we do not know as well, are even more so.

Writing a book like this, one that proposes to un-redact history in some measure, is no easy task, obviously. It requires the help of many talented and dedicated people who also believe, like the Hutson family, that history does care when it comes to telling what you know.

Our hope, our belief, is that by doing so, more people out there might come forward and share their family legacy, their family stories, too, so that our shared knowledge will move us all forward in understanding what actually happened to the fabled Romanov family nearly a century ago on July 17, 1918 in Yekaterinburg, Russia.

We begin the public version of Uncle Martin's story by thanking him for his remarkable service, and his older brother, George, for his gallantry in the Black Forest of Germany and for his faith in recommending Martin to Army Major General

William Sidney Graves, through his commanding officer, the iconic General Black Jack Pershing, for this special mission.

Like them, we have kept the faith, too. At least nine of us still living remember the story Martin Hutson told us and we hold it dearer today.

Our deepest gratitude also goes to: General Graves, President Woodrow Wilson of the United States and King George V of England, who we believe silently and expertly planned one of the most extraordinary rescue missions in modern political history. Well done! You could have easily taken full public credit for your strength and determination to bring to safety your Russian cousin and fellow head of state who deserved that amount of historical respect but chose not to so that he and his tortured family could live in peace through very turbulent times.

Benjamin Johnson, William Gibbs McAdoo, and Newton D. Baker, unrecognized heroes of World War I for their faithful devotion to duty on behalf of their country, we recognize your unnoticed bravery and excellence, especially in Revolutionary Russia and war-time America.

Allied intelligence for collaborating with unsurpassed precision on such a politically and militarily sensitive mission, demonstrating early on that working together for common cause in the name of freedom is a powerful responsibility and a great example for successfully combatting today's trying times.

The universities, presidential and royal libraries, and think tanks who are entrusted with the personal papers of these remarkable public servants, at home and abroad, proving that open scholarly research and education that will endure for generations to come is an extraordinary tool in the exercise of democracy.

The United Nations Foundation for Refugees, and other charitable ventures like it, who continue to this hour trying to help those who are misplaced because of war, like Revolutionary Russia was at the end of that horrible World War, in perhaps their greatest hour of need so that they too can one day have that sense of purpose that comes by living in a just and peaceful land.

The men and women of the American Expeditionary Forces Siberia and the American Red Cross for their embrace of life, liberty and the pursuit of happiness, as Thomas Jefferson emboldened us.

The author and extraordinary researcher, Shay McNeal, for sharing her passion about the *The Secret Plot to Save The Tsar* and her steadfast encouragement to us to build upon her knowledge while trying to tell Martin's own story. In the last paragraphs of her work, McNeal notes that "The real story of the Romanovs' fate remains tied up in the heretofore unknown machinations of the people and situations that seem to have collided on that summer night in 1918 in Siberia. That more of the real story can be pieced together has been the purpose of this book and my hope is that more information will come forward after the publication of this work that will contimue to shed light on this myserious chapter in twentieth-century history." We haved tried to honor your wish, Shay. Thanks for being a devoted patron of the truth and for empowering us with that opportunity.

The authors in our bibliography, including but not limited to, the amazing Romanov mystery trailblazers: Greg King, Peter Kurth, Robert K. Massey, Helen Rappaport, and, Penny Wilson - for strongly believing in what their own research and talented writing has brought to us since that fateful day nearly 100 years ago now.

As the world comes to Russia to celebrate the 2018 FIFA World Cup, we hope all will remember that family who perished from that house in Yekaterinburg and forever be sensitive to the price that we all pay when diplomacy does and does not work as the statesmen of our times envision.

Thanks to you, dear reader, for keeping the interest all of these decades in the Romanov saga.

For my part, I still enjoy a good, true story, too!

Rescuing Nicholas Hutson Transcript

Appendix A

Track 1 – 10:56

My name is Martin V. Hutson. I am going to give you an episode in my life that covers three years with the American Expeditionary Forces in Siberia – nineteen nineteen to nineteen twenty. When the middle of the war broke out, World War One broke out, I was fifteen years old. My brother, George, was eighteen years old. He joined the Army. It disappointed me very much because I wanted to go. So, I went to the recruiting office in Knoxville, Tennessee. I tried to volunteer but the recruiting officer knew me and he knew my family and told me, Martin, you can't go you are too young to go. So, I went back home very disappointed. In about a week, he called me and told me to come to the recruiting office, he had good news for me. I went down to the post office building and he says if your mother will sign the papers, I'll send you to the Mexican border because we are desperately short of men so you can go to the border. So I went back and asked her. After a very heated argument I talked my mother into signing the papers. I went back and turned in the papers and he gave me a minor physical examination on my eyes and flat feet and so forth and told me to report to the recruiting office the next morning at seven o'clock. I went down to the recruiting office the next morning at seven o'clock. I was given meal tickets and put on a train to Fort Oglethorpe, Georgia. I arrived in Fort Oglethorpe, Georgia, about nine or ten o'clock – I mean Chattanooga, Tennessee. A wagon and two mules met me and some more soldiers who were with me and they drove us out to Fort Oglethorpe, Georgia where the mud was ankle-deep and assigned us to quarters. Then took us down and issued us clothing, barracks. The next morning, the first sergeant came in and called for Martin Hutson, Private Martin Hutson, and I responded, here. And he says go to the Quartermaster's office and draw arctic clothing and you be in a hurry about it. I went to the Quartermaster's office and he laughed at me. So I went back to my barracks. First sergeant come in and said to me why aren't you ready? Where is your stuff? And I told him what the supply sergeant had done. He called the supply sergeant into the building and said equip this man with arctic clothing and do it fast. I want him out of here by ten o'clock this morning. So, I went down and got two what we call barracks bags full of clothes and went back to my barracks. In a few minutes they came in and called my name. I got in the wagon and they hauled me to Chattanooga, Tennessee, depot. There, I boarded a train and they gave me thirty-five cents for coffee. We travelled all day, all night, and all the next day. The next night, we were in San Francisco, California. We were unloaded, got our clothing, went to a wagon, went down to the bay and were loaded on a tugboat and taken over to Fort McDowell in the Bay of California. I was met there by Sergeant, marched up and assigned a bed. The next morning, they told us where to go eat breakfast, in a large dining room. So we eat breakfast – I speak as we the other men that came with me on this train – after breakfast they took us down to the barracks and for the next three or four days we did nothing except sit around the barracks. And one day, one morning, they came in and gave us orders to pack all of our clothes and personal belongings and be ready to leave. They took us down to the bay and loaded us on to the tug boat and take it back to San Francisco. We got to San Francisco and they loaded us on to the *U.S.S. Great Northern* – the *U.S.S. Transport Great Northern* – assigned us to quarters. At dark, we took off to sea. I was afraid of getting seasick, and I asked an old civilian sailor what you could do. He said if you go up on the top deck and lay down on your back, look straight up at the stars, you won't get seasick, but don't look at the land line. And, I did that and I did not get sick. The next morning when they blowed chow call, they lined us up and marched us down into what had been, to me, a large elaborate dining room. We were served cafeteria-style. We took our mess kits, our aluminum cups, and marched by and got white Navy beans and white bread. Tables hung from the ceiling by chains. We put our food on the table and the table would swing but you could eat very comfortably. At dinnertime, I went down, there was a tremendous crowd – eighteen hundred men – I guess I was two hours getting through the line to get my food. I finally got my food, I come back and sat at one these swinging tables but I had to do some deep thinking. I couldn't line up in this crowd three times a day to eat. The fellow next to me got sick and began to vomit. I asked him if he was sick and he said yes, I am desperately sick. I said are you are going to eat any more and he said, no sir. But, I said give me your slice of bread and he gave me his slice of bread and I put it in my pocket. At super I went down and there weren't many men there – maybe a hundred. So, I decided I would stand right at the kitchen door. If a man came out and he was white and pale, I'd ask him if he was sick. Yes. I said are you going to eat your bread? No. I said, give it to me. For three days, I got all the bread I could beg. Took it back up to my bunk and put it my knapsack. The next day, after I had got this knapsack full, when they blowed mess call, didn't go and the officer of the day said, you must go eat. I said, no Sir, I have plenty of food right here. He said, let's see it and I opened up my knapsack. He said, well if that is all you want, there is nothing wrong with it. I said, well, I can eat here in peace, I don't want any greasy food. So, I lived on that bread for seven days and nights, until we arrived in Honolulu. Two days out of

Honolulu before we arrived, the officer said that the refrigeration system had broke down, and we had link sausages for breakfast and they got maggots in them but they had been cooked and they won't hurt you - eat 'em. He said, I am going to eat them. We get into Honolulu and they asked us if any of us wanted shore leave we could have it in small groups. I had one nickel left and I asked for shore leave, because away in the distance, was mountains. Pineapples had just been set out. As I came back, as I came through the main part of town, I passed a candy store, and I felt, well, I only have a nickel but that will get me one piece. So, I went in the store - the lady had seen me looking through the window. I went into the store and I told her, give me a nickel worth of chocolates. And, she gave me a sack-full. And, I went back to the boat. They re-provisioned the boat, throw all of this bad meat into the bay, re-provisioned the boat working on the ice machines, and got underway.

Track 2 - 6:30

We were at sea fourteen days, arriving in Vladivostok in the Sea of Oshkosh. Went up to the docks and began to unload. In the distance, there was a large hill, a road winding up this hill - dirt road. We crossed over the top of this hill and there was a large dirigible balloon hangar, but the balloon was gone. They gave us canvas cots - eighteen hundred of us. ___ bedding. Still had plenty of room left. I stayed in this building three days and nights. So, the third night, the corporal came and got me and seven more men. He took us about three miles through the woods. We come to a church. Inside this church, Company H, 31st Infantry was bedded down. They brought us in, assigned us spaces on canvas cots to sleep. They took us to the kitchen to feed us. The cook was a man with twenty-seven to twenty-eight years of service in the Army. They had beef hash - corned beef hash and were hungry - we eat too much. And he brought in a whole pan of pumpkin pies and so we set in on the pies, everybody over eating, I know I did. Then we went down to our barracks and I took all of my clothes out of my bag and put them on top of a bed, put my blankets over them, and put my half of the pup tent over that and tucked it in. I slept cold that night, I should have put half of it under me and I didn't I put all of it on top of me. Sixty below zero is a little cold. Captain turned us over to corporal for close order drill. We drilled six weeks in close order drill. Then one day, Captain Roberson sent for me to the office. Corporal excused me - told me to go. I went down to Captain Roberson's office. Private Hutson, you have got to learn the wig wag. And, I said, yes sir. There was another man a standing there, a sergeant, by the name of Kashiba. Kashiba was a natural born Russian but was been Americanized and was in our Army. He went and got the flags. He said I will give you one week to teach him. One week later I come back. Captain asked me if I knew wig wag and I said, yes sir. He said go to the far end of the room and I will send you a message and you answer me back. So, I went to the far end of the room and he sent me a message. What is your name and where are you from? And, I answered him back. Private Martin V. Hutson, Company H, 31st Infantry from Tennessee. He said, come forward. Kashiba, this man is ready. He says, Captain, I cannot take this man. This man is just a boy. He never fired a gun. Kashiba, this order comes from Major General Graves and you have to take this man, and I will tell you something else, you've got to deliver him alive. And Kashiba, said, well, how many machine guns are you going to give us? He said, none. He said, Captain, that's impossible. The last trip I went I took two machine guns and barely got by. He said this train cannot look like an armored train going north. There will be no machine guns, no display of power. Make it look at peaceful and civilian as possible. At night, they loaded eight of us in the wagon, took us down to the station in Vladivostok - railroad station - and loaded us on a steel Pullman car with a large red cross on the side about center ways and under it, written in there was "Amerikanski." Our officer come aboard, Lt. Humphries, and said, let's see your shoes. We wore wrap leggings. We pulled the leggings up so that he could see the shoes from top to bottom and he said, them shoes won't do. We are going into arctic territory - arctic weather territory - so everybody take your shoes off, tie the strings together, and he called a man and said, take these shoes to the Quartermaster office and exchange them for moccasins. Be sure that you get the right size. He throwed the shoes over his shoulders and left. An hour later he hadn't returned. N hour-and-a-half later he hadn't returned. They were fixing to send a patrol out for him. The streets of Vladivostok are cobblestone streets and we heard the man coming with his hard leather shoes on, he was running. Somebody fired one shot at him - not our people but the Revolution people. He come aboard, he had one pair of moccasin and they would not fit any of us. So, the Lieutenant said, we don't have any more time to waste. Put on all of the stockings that you've got and use your four-buckle arctic overshoes. I put on seventeen pair of socks. Two pair come to my knees, in order to fill those arctic overshoes up. Around eleven o'clock, our train started for Irkutsk, but at that time, I did not know that it was Irkutsk. We went further and further until we was on the Manchurian desert. Across the desert, it was level and flat as far as the eye could see. But there were great stacks of wheat.

Track 3 – 6:48

Along this Manchurian railroad, were little towns of maybe a dozen houses, or less. We would stop and inquire as to the name of the town and if they knew where the Red Army was. They would tell us the name of the town but they would give us no information on where the Red Army was. Then, we proceeded north to Verchne-Urdinsk, headquarters to the 27th Infantry. We pulled into the railroad yard at Ver*chne*-Urdinsk, which was a pretty good-sized town. The Lieutenant says I will go to headquarters and get orders. Captain Cross of the Red Cross, which was in charge of the Red Cross section, this train was a Red Cross train, supply train, said he would go. The Lieutenant was a bit reluctant to let him go, but he finally told him, all right. So, he went. He came back in about forty-five minutes, he said orders are for us to proceed to Irkutsk. Some Russian standing there, said, nyet, nyet, nyet. Irkutsk is Red. And Lieutenant Humphries said, are you sure we are to proceed. He said, yes, we have clearance into Irkutsk. We have got to deliver this stuff. So, we pulled out to Irkutsk. After we rolled through several miles, we went through forty-nine tunnels in one mile at Lake Baikal and proceeded on to Irkutsk. When we got within about a mile of Irkutsk and you could hear severe gunfire. Heavy guns and light guns, machine guns. And, the Lieutenant said, we may be going into a hornet's nest, but we must obey our orders. We pulled into Irkutsk and Irkutsk, the town's river flows right through it. The Red Army was on the east bank of the river and the White Army, on the __(?)___, on the west bank. The Lieutenant said to me, get your rifle and come with me. I got my rifle, put it on my shoulder in a sling, put a forty-five automatic in my slip pocket on my coat. He took me about five tracks over and there sat another steel Pullman car with a red cross in the middle and "Amerikanski" wrote under it. He posted me at the door of that car with orders that nobody would leave or enter, to shoot to kill if necessary. But nobody shall enter there. I stand there for about a couple of hours and the door opened and out stepped, I took it to be, an English or Canadian Captain, on down to the first step on the car. And, I challenged him and told him that he had to go back in to the car, he could not come out there. He said I only came out to get a breath of air. I said my orders is that nobody is to be exposed, even at the windows on this car. I will have to ask you the second time to go back. He turned and laughed and said, you Americans are all superstitious and sometimes I think you are halfway scared. He said there is nothing wrong. I said my order is my order, sir. And at about that time, a bullet cut thestep right out from under him, hit edge, split it in two, and he fell to the bottom. And I didn't have to tell him to get back in. He got back inside. When the Lieutenant come, I told him what happen. He said, you done right. I guarded this car for three days and nights. At night and during the day, of the second day and night, they began to fire from the east bank to the west bank of the river under this train. I backed my legs up behind the big steel wheel on the car and stood there until about four o'clock in the afternoon. Many people were hit, but I wasn't. The place you could get hit was in the legs. Suddenly, the firing seized. The troops on the west bank, or the White Army, fled. I looked up the train, seen three men coming, running down between the trains. They had their rifles and they had fixed bayonets. And, I quickly made my mind up that nobody was going to stick a bayonet in me, so I reached my hand in my pocket because it was useless to get my rifle. It was frosted up like a refrigerating unit - it would have blown up if I had fired it. I got my hand in slip pocket in front, cocked my forty-five automatic, put my back against the car. They came running and when they got to within six to eight feet of me they pointed their three bayonets right at my stomach. I figured I could get three without even taking the gun out of my pocket. But the Lieutenant hollered, and said, don't move, don't make no action. Stand perfectly still. I'm a coming. He came over with Kashiba and spoke with these three men. They dropped their guns down and went on went on down the track. And, I said, did I do right? And the Lieutenant said, yes, you done exactly right, you could have got us in trouble. I said yes, man, I could have got myself killed. So, they relieved me from this car, took me back over to my own car, and I eat and stayed the rest of the evening there, slept that night, and the next morning the Lieutenant sent for me.

Track 4 – 7:04

He said, Private Hutson, I've got a job for you but you are not to discuss it with anyone. Not to even mention it. Anything that you see or you do or anybody that you talk to under penalty of general court marshal. I said I will not talk, see or do anything. Said put your rifle away. Put your pistol away. He took me right back over to the same car I had the shooting, knocked on the door. Captain inside unlocked the door and I went in with the Lieutenant. And in the front of this car was a Japanese General, an English Colonel, and Italian Colonel, Czechoslovakian Colonel, and of course, our Lieutenant. And he ordered all of them to leave the train and he would send them word when they could come back. They offered no resistance and no arguments. They come to attention and saluted and left. All this time, I was watching them and when I turned around there was a man sitting in the middle of the train in civilian clothes. I'd say a man weighing one hundred fifty pounds. His height I can't say because I never saw him stand up. Lieutenant said, your job is to sit here and talk to this man, two hours every day. So when time is up, I'll come back after you. I don't want you to come back by yourself. You may come the wrong route. I said, yes sir, I will stay right here until you come and get me. This man asked me my name and I could have dropped to the floor ***(marker 1:47)***. I never heard English like he spoke. He would have shamed a Harvard professor. An Oxford professor. English was as clear as a silver bell. But he had no accent. So, he told me to go to talking and I asked him what he wanted to talk about. Let's talk about anything you want to – begin with your childhood and he said I'll talk right after you. Every word you say, I will repeat right behind you. I did that for six - seven days. I went to this train at 2 o'clock and stayed and talked to him for two hours. On the seventh day, he said we're going to move and he said as we go down the railroad we will be stopping in small towns occasionally. I want you to pick up any newspapers, or pieces of newspapers, or bag of books, or magazines, or anything that you can find and bring them back here and I will read them to you. Well that was very scary stuff. Fine. But I did find some and I came back the next day and he said, did you find any Chinese newspapers? I said, yes sir, I seen some but I didn't think you could read Chinese newspapers. He said, I can read, write and speak any language in the civilized world. So, pick up anything with reading material on it. And, he said, I will read it to you and you repeat it after me. So, I did this for the new few days. Then one day, the Lieutenant took me over and he said, now I am going to come after you at two o'clock but he said you have to do down to the other end of the car, the other car, and have tea with three ladies. I said Lieutenant I do not like tea. He said, well they have crumpets. Do you like crumpets? I said, yes sir. I can eat all of the crumpets I can get. Well, he said, eat the crumpets but sip a little tea. It won't hurt you. So that day, when I finished my two-hour session with this man, I went down and knocked on the door and a French lady came to the door of this car, this steel Pullman car and she invited us on. And Lieutenant told her he could not come in but I would and I went in. They had a table there with three chairs. At one end sat a lady, I'd say fifty, or close to her fifties. At the other end of the table sat a young lady, probably in her thirties. Across the table from me sat this French lady, probably in her forties. The French lady poured the tea, served the tea and served the crumpets and did most of the talking. Except the lady on my left, the older lady, sat as upright and as stiff as if she had mop handle down her back. She could not have been any straighter. She spoke fairly good English but not like the man up in the other car. The young lady spoke some English, but not much. The French lady spoke fluent English, more like I was used to. So, I had two jobs to do. I had tea and I had talking. All the time this was going on we were stopping in small towns maybe for forty-five minutes – thirty minutes – then we would move out. The next morning, we crossed the border, Manchuria City, into Manchuria, Siberia. We stopped in Manchuria City. And the Lieutenant told us that if we wanted to get us a drink of Vodka we could go in groups of twos. I didn't care too much for Vodka, but my curiosity did. Went over to the place and I asked for some Vodka, and they brought it. A young lady came out and spoke fairly good English. Said are you going to Vladivostok? I said, yes ma'am. She said can you take me with you? I said afraid not. We are Americans. He pulled her dress back at her shoulder and showed me where a bayonet went through over the back of her shoulder blade. And said she had to leave there or she would die. I said I couldn't do anything about it. I told her so. I hated it but I was perfectly neutral.

Track 5 – 6:25

Went back over to the station, boarded the train, and started for Harbin, at Chita. We got to Chita and made a very short stop because there were lots of Red soldiers in Chita. I don't know what they were doing in Chinese territory. The difference between a Red soldier and a White soldier was the ribbon on the lapel of their coat. If you were Red you were a small red ribbon, if you was White army you had a small white ribbon. We pulled out of Chita, headed for Harbin, Manchuria. A few miles down the line, we were attacked by Chinese bandits. They set our train afire, I don't know how, I was inside and didn't see. But I suppose it was flaming arrows because there were wooden cars on the train – two boxcars loaded with merchandise. It was late and getting dark. Then I seen a lot of these people come out of our train that I didn't know was on there. They begged the lieutenant to lay over there until daylight so that they could salvage. He telled them he would do it, if they would all go back to their cars and not come out. They agreed and went back. When they all got cleared out, we cleaned up the mess, of what is left, rolled the wheels off of the switch, and headed for Harbin. They got desperately mad at us. It wasn't for me to question the orders of an officer. Before we got to Harbin, I was guarding the outside door of my car and this man came down and said you have been good to me, I want to show you something. He pulled a leather bag out from underneath his shirt and poured out more diamonds and rubies and emeralds than I could have held in my hands – his hands were bigger than mine. We was on the Manchurian desert, and the moon was shining bright, the rubies looked like capsules filled with blood, those diamonds would put your eyes out, they were as big as the end of your thumb. He said, would you like to buy some? I said, sir, I haven't got any money and I wouldn't have any use for them anyway. So, he went back, but I never told anybody he had them because that would have been the end of him. We proceeded in to Harbin, Manchuria. We pulled down in the yard in Manchuria, a contingent of English soldiers, the Consul General of England, and the Consul General of the United States, they came in the car, sat down, and we served 'em coffee. Our Consul General raised up his foot and put it on top of a big box. Our Army officer jumped and said, sir, remove your foot from that box, that is his Imperial Highness, and he begged your pardon ***(marker 3:22).*** Removed his foot. Later on in the day, he brought a wagon, and took these three boxes, loaded them in the wagon, and left. So, I figured, that we had been through a hard time, we could go home. We go down through Manchuria to Peking, Hong Kong, and home. But, no. Orders was that we are to go back through Siberia to Vladivostok with the same train. Well, we got an engineer to drive the train. And, he asked where we was going and said, Vladivostok. He said he wasn't going. Lieutenant said yes you are going too. He said, no sir, you've got nothing to do with me. He said, Private Hutson, load that man with that forty-five automatic you've got. And I pulled it and I told him to get in the engine. He had four Chinese coolies (Spelling) in the wood tender, we burnt wood, not coal. And we started. He begged with tears in his eyes to let him go. He'd done nothing to me. He had a wife and a family. And, the Red Army was just right down the road and they would execute him just as surely as we brought us through there. I told him I was sorry but if the Lieutenant come back he could talk to him. But until he come back, if he made an effort to leave that train, I'd kill him. About eighty - ninety miles across the Manchurian border back into Siberia, there was a terrible battle going on, over to our left, in the town. We turned out the lights and eased this train down between two big rows of boxcars back down by the fire. They fought all night, people hollering and screaming. On or about daylight, they rode out, or their little horses, some of them so small and the men were so big that their feet almost drag the ground. Cossacks. Seminovs. We proceeded on down about fifty miles and they blocked us. I was on guard. Five men approached me, they said that if you will take these three men to Vladivostok, you can go safely. But if you don't take 'em, you have gone about as far as you will go. They will execute you on the spot. You know those trains over there have compartments in 'em. You have an aisle on one side and compartments on the other. I took them down and put them in my compartment.

Track 6 – 8:14

He was fourteen years old and spoke very fluent English, and I asked him how he learned English. He said when the war broke out in nineteen fourteen we stopped teaching French and started teaching English and he said you can approach any boy who is twelve years old and he can talk to you if he ever went to school. I said, well, get three men you want and load them in. Two elderly men and this young boy, they sat in the compartment and didn't make a move. The next day, about three o'clock, we arrived in Vladivostok - pulled in to the depot. When those three men stepped off of the train, all hell broke loose. There was shooting everywhere. I stayed on the train, got below the windows. About an hour, an hour-and-a-half, a contingent of our men come in and rescued me. As I went out, there were dead bodies all over the railroad yards, all over the steps of the depot, and up in the depot. There was red ribbons and white ribbons, both. Now I will have to backtrack a little bit. At Manchuria City, the Red Army arrested a general, they said, by the name of Kolchek, Admiral - alrighty, he's the one, I know it's Kolchek because this boy told me they arrested him. As went through Manchuria to Chita, Manchuria City, Russia, my sergeant was arrested - American- Russian, spoke very fluent Russian as well as English. My Lieutenant got us together and, okay, we will have to make a decision - we fight or we run. I don't think running will help us much. So, we took a vote, and we voted to fight. So, we only had one box of ammunition and one hundred and twenty rounds in our bandoliers, each man. So, we told them, we refused, we would not surrender those people. They said we will give you until twelve o'clock. So, the Lieutenant says, we stand a good chance in this steel car, maybe something will come up. At about eleven thirty, they moved up four seventy-five millimeter cannons, broadside against our car. And, Lieutenant says, boys it's up, we can't stand that, they will blow us to pieces, so we have a change of plans, every man get to a door, two or three to a door, we are sitting right in the middle of a big railroad yards. When I give the signal, jerk your doors open and run in all directions, some of you will get out, we hope. So, we stationed ourselves. At ten minutes 'til twelve, the Japanese regiment moved in, and drove them off, because we had a Japanese general on that train. But Colonel Morrow never come to help us, neither did Graves. We sent word to Morrow, by wire, but he said every man for himself – he had troubles of his own. I'll backstep to another incident. For Christmas dinner, nineteen hundred and nineteen, I had one big loaf of black bread – you had to take a bayonet to cut it, but it was good. I left Siberia in February, late February in nineteen nineteen, aboard the *U.S. Transport Crook,* for the Philippine Islands, with heavy wool underwear and OD clothes. We sailed into Manila, were loaded into trucks, and took to Camp McKinley, assigned quarters, and begin a steady eight hours a day drill. The hospital at McKinleywas full and there was tents all the way around us full. And, if they had not got Major General Graves out from command of us, there wouldn't have been any of us left. I would like to back and recall one other instant in Irkutsk, one of my own men tried to kill me ***(marker 4:50),*** but he missed. We get to Manila, Fort William McKinley, I was assigned to military police duty in Manila under Captain Allen Alenz (spelling?). One night, they called us to orders, the Constabulary, which is the rural police of the islands, and the city police of Manila, where battling each other in the Wall City, the Wall City Bar. They told us we were the only armed troops in the city, so we went down and stopped it. They got one of our men and took him over to the jail, which was a six-room, framed, wooden building. Our men got together and told 'em either turn that man loose or they'd pick up that building up and turn it over right on the rock. So they turned him loose. Now, I came back to the United States, Camp Lewis Washington, third tank company. I was discharged, honorably, and I went home to Tennessee. In nineteen and thirty-two, I picked up the *Courier-Journal* ***(marker 6:13)***, and there in that Courier-Journal, was this story by the Consul General Harbin, how he met Evacuation Train number twenty-eight ***(marker 6:31)*** carrying the Tsar and his family, how he had put his foot on that casket and they made him take it off. It wasn't a casket, it was made like a casket, but he was alive. That was the only way we could get him off of there, without someone maybe seeing him. Now, my story is this: they picked me in Knoxville, Tennessee, this fifteen-year-old-boy ***(marker 6:45),*** to make this mission because they did not want the Tsar to recognize me when I talked to him excepting to give him my accent. I wrote this story once before, but the State Department would not let it be published. So, I wrote the State Department and I'd like to contact, or know where to the Consul General was, and they wrote back and said, he is in Central Africa, and will be there for six or seven years, and he cannot be reached, under any circumstances, which is a very odd statement, to me. You know what I think? I think I was used as tool, but they did not want me back alive because they was afraid I might go to thinking and put the puzzle together. Nicholas was not killed in Siberia ***(marker 7:47).*** Three other people were killed and their bodies chopped up with broadaxes, dumped in a lime pit, poured crude oil on 'em and burned 'em, which was a very good camouflage to throw the Red Army off. That was done by the Tsar's very own home guards before they fled.

End of Martin Hutson's Recording

Rescuing Nicholas The Romanov Circle | Appendix B

The Romanov circle is a confusing web of family, friends, and associates, with a few not so friendly names mixed in.

This list, which is not intended to be exhaustive, is provided based on a wide range of sources from the Bibliography that follows in an effort to help you navigate the Imperial network.

We found the number of players to be quite confusing without the list, which is similar in nature to lists that have been produced by other Romanov researchers facing the same dilemma. Our thanks to them for a wonderful tool that we are attempting to re-create in concept here for your use.

The List

Ackerman, Carl W., Journalist for *Saturday Evening Post*, thought to be an intelligence agent in Russia. He was the first to arrive in Yekaeterinburg in the Autumn 1918.

Alexandrovna, Olga, grand duchess, youngest sister of Nicholas II who lived out the remaining years of her life in Denmark.

Alexandrovich, Nikolai, purportedly Tsar Nicholas II if he survived the Ipatiev massacre and rumored by the author, Michael Gray to have been in Collon, Ireland, in 1948.

Alexei II, Russian Orthodox Church Patriach who refused to recognize the Koptyaki Woods bones as being those of the Romanovs.

Alexev, General, A White Russian who with General Kaledin fought against the Bolsheviks and worked with the Wilson White House. He was praised for his efforts by American Secretary of State Robert Lansing.

Andropov, Yuri, KGB Chairman who ordered the destruction of the Ipatiev House and was later General Secretary of the USSR.

Armitstead, Henry, project director for The Hudson Bay Company building at least one safe house in Murmansk for the royal family, as documented by the author Shay McNeal.

Arthur of Connaught, Prince, emissary of his cousin, King George V of the United Kingdom, with President Woodrow Wilson of the United States.

Avdayev, Alexander, first commandant of the Ipatiev House, a revolutionary soldier.

Avdonin, Alexander, retired geologist who with Geli Ryabov is credited with locating the Koptyaki grave in 1979.

Balfour, Arthur Sir, British Foreign Secretary during the Tsar's abdication and imprisonment in Yekaterinburg.

Bittner, Klaudia, imperial children's tutor in Tobolsk who later married Colonel Eugene Kobylinsky, Captain of the Guard who guarded the Romanoffs in Tolobsk.

Bliss, Lt. General Tasker, an American Allied General in the group of four.

Botkin, Eugene, personal physician to the Empress Alexandra, who reportedly was murdered with the Romanoff family in Yekaeterinburg, Russia, July 17, 1918.

Brusilov, General, White Russian who with Generals Kaledin and Alexev fought against the Bolsheviks and worked with the Wilson White House. Also praised for his effort by American Secretary of State Robert Lansing.

Buchanan, Sir George, British ambassador to Petrograd who communicated with the Tsar about going to England.

Bulygin, Paul, Nicholas Sokolov bodyguard who assisted in White Russian investigation of Yekaterinburg murders.

Buxhoeveden, Baroness Sophie, Tsarina Alexandra's lady-in-waiting who traveled on the train to Tobolsk with the royal family and later was alleged by some to have betrayed the royals to the Boscheviks at the Ipatiev House.

Bykov, Paul, produced the only authorized Soviet account of the Yekaterinburg murders.

Cadorna, General Luigi Conte, Italian Allied General in group of four.

Chebotarev, Nikolai (died in 1987), reportedly the Tsarevich Alexei according to the author Michael Gray.

Chemodurov, Terenty, Nicholas II's valet imprisoned for brief time with the Romanoff family at the Ipatiev House following Nicholas' abdication.

Chicherin, George, Russian Commissar for Foreign Affairs who later claimed that Romanov family was not killed in Yakterinburg.

Churchill, Sir Winston, British Secretary of War during the Hutson evacuation mission and later iconic Prime Minister.

Creel, George, Head of the U.S. Information Agency and a close associate of President Wilson. He is said by the author Shay McNeal to have paid Russians money through the agency.

Crane, Charles, an American industrialist from Chicago who owned Crane Plumbing and was involved in America's Russian policy and the Romanov saga. Considered an architect of Wilson's Russian policy. Hand-picked to be the President's ambassador to Russia.

Crane, Frances, Charles Crane's daughter who was married to Jan Masaryk, son of the eventual Czech president Thomas Masaryk who has been placed in Siberia during the time of evacuation.

Crane, Richard, son of the American industrialist Charles Crane, and secretary to U.S. Secretary of State Robert Lansing.

Dehn, Julia, a friend of the Empress Alexandra, known to friends as, Lili.

Demidova, Anna, Empress Alexandra's maid, imprisoned with Romanoff family at the Ipatiev house and reportedly murdered along with royal family on July 17, 1918.

Derevenko, Nicholas, Tsarevich Alexei's boyhood friend known as Koyla and son of court physician Vladimir Derevenko. Often considered a stand-in for the Tsarevich.

Derevenko, Vladimir, the court physician to Tsar Nicholas II who accompanied the Romanoffs into exile.

Deterikhs, Michael, the White Russian Army general who supervised the Yekaterinburg murder investigation.

Digby-Jones, Captain, the British agent who worked with the Czechs to coordinate attacks against the Revolutionaries.

Diterikhs, General, former officer in Tsar's army who commanded the Czech faction advancing from Vladivostok. Though to have worked for the British to make way for the Romanovs to take the Trans-Siberian Railway out of Russia.

Dolgorukov, Prince Valia, who traveled with Tsar Nicholas II to imprisonment in Tobolsk.

Domnin, Parfen, major domo to Tsar Nicholas II.

Eliot, Sir Charles, the British High Commissioner in Siberia, who reported the possible departure of the Tsarina and her family on a train from Yekaterinburg in the aftermath of the alleged assassination.

Ersberg, Elizaveta, the Tsarina's parlour maid who traveled with the royal family on the train to Tobolsk.

Falsetti, Anthony, professor of the C.A. Pound Human Identification Laboratory at the University of Florida who examined the Romanoff remains in 1998, as part of the Maples investigatory team.

Fox, Charles James, a British agent said to have taken Romanoffs out of the Ipatiev House to the nearby British Consulate by cistern, as detailed by the author, Shay McNeal.

France, Diane, a forensic science expert and professor who as a member of NecroSearch International examined the Romanoff remains in 1998.

Frances, David, President Wilson's second US Ambassador to Russia. He as recommended by Charles Crane and helped obtain diplomatic recognition of the Provisional Government from the United States following the Tsar's abdication.

Galitzin, Prince, was the Governor of the Urals, a military man, and friend of the American industrialist Charles Crane.

Gendrikova, Anastasia, the Tsarina's personal lady-in-waiting who traveled on the train to Tobolsk with the royal family.

George, David Lloyd, Prime Minister of Great Britain at the time of the Tsar's abdication. Reported to have advised King George V against providing political asylum to the Romanovs for fear of inciting greater social unrest in the United Kingdom.

Gibbes, Charles Sidney, English tutor to Tsarevich Alexei and the Romanoff children. He is reported to have traveled on the train to imprisonment in Tobolsk.

Gill, Peter, a genetics expert at the British Home Office's Forensic Science Services Laboratory who conducted genetic testing of the Romanoff remains and is reported to have inspired the 98.5% certainty finding on the tested DNA.

Gelbov, Father Boris, religious leader in Russia who conducted the funeral for the Romanoffs on July 17, 1998 but said that he was not certain who he was burying at St. Peter and St. Paul Cathedral Church.

George V, King of England, second cousin to Tsar Nicholas II and first cousin to Kaiser Wilhelm II of Germany. Grandson of Queen Victoria.

Gilliard, Pierre, the Romanoff children's tutor who traveled on the train to Tobolsk with the royal family.

Goloshchekin, Filipp, leader of the Ural Bolsheviks who worked with Sverdlov, president of the All-Russia Soviet, who Shay McNeal contends might have coordinated with Stalin for Lenin to trade the Romanoffs. Reported to have been involved with Yakovleb's earlier attempt to rescue the Romanoffs.

Graves, Major General William Sidney, commanding officer of the American Expeditionary Forces Siberia. Author of *America's Siberian Adventure, 1918-1920.* A graduate of the U.S. Military Academy at West Point.

Gray, Michael, fictional name of the purported son of Tsarevich Alexei and author of *Blood Relative.*

Groves, Major William Peer, a British agent who told his daughter, according to Russian authors, that the Romanov family had escaped from the Ipatiev House cellar with the help of British secret agents and loyal guards and was eventually taken to Japan and Canada, similar to story in *Rescuing the Czar.* Groves was a known associate of Reilly and Captain George Hill.

Hall, Sir Reginald, Director of British Naval Intelligence who had a memorable dinner with Jonas Lied.

Harris, Ernest, American Consul General in Irkutsk who conducted the assessment for Reinsch on restoring the Romanov monarchy. Reported author of the "Family Times Seven" cable to London during President Wilson's visit with King George V. Told media in 1930 that he escorted the Romanov remains out of Russia in 1919-1920 aboard an American train.

Hermogen, bishop of Tobolsk Province and was involved in plots to rescue the Romanoff prisoners from Toblosk, according to the author, Shay McNeal.

Hill, Captain George, British secret agent charged with escorting members of royalty out of Russia.

Hoare, Sir Samuel, head of British Intelligence in Petrograd, an M16 agent who may have assisted in a possible rescue attempt of family and possible payment to Lenin for Romanov release as outlined in Shay McNeal's book.

House, Colonel Edward, President Wilson's de factor Secretary of State and go-to man in Russia. He was a close friend of William Wiseman, head of British Intelligence in the United States.

Ipatiev, Nicholas, the retired engineer who owned the House of Special Purpose where the Romanoff family was reportedly murdered on July 17, 1918.

Ivanov, Pavel, physician and genetics expert in the Russian Ministry of Health who worked with Peter Gill on disputed genetic testing of the Romanoff remains.

Johnson, Benjamin O, executive on the Russian Railway Services Corps from Montana, in the United States.

Kaledin, General Alexis, a White Russian who according to author Shay McNeal funded Allied banking plots to save the Tsar. He was said to have worked with White Russian General Alexeev who fought against the Bolsheviks and worked with the Wilson White House. He was praised for his efforts by American Secretary of State Robert Lansing.

Keenen, George, United States Department of State official who writes about the Romanov/Crane intrigue.

Kerensky, Alexander, president of the Provisional Government in Russia.

Kharitonov, Ivan, the Romanoff family chef who was reportedly murdered with the royals at the Ipatiev House, July 17, 1918.

Khokhryakov, Paul, revolutionary who transferred Romanoff children to Yekaterinburg.

King, Greg, Romanoff dynasty and Imperial Russia historian and author of *The Fate of the Romanovs* who found surprising evidence that Anastasia survived the Ipatiev massacre.

Kobylinsky, Colonel Eugene, Commander of the Guard who guarded the Romanoffs in Tolobsk.

Kolchak, Alexander, supreme commander of the White Russian Army in Siberia who authorized the Sokolov investigation into the Ipatiev murders.

Koryakova, Ludmilla, a doctor of archaeology at the Laboratory of the History and Archaeology Institute of the Urals Science Center of the USSR Academy of Sciences who participated in the first 1991 exhumation.

Kuhn, Major General, Commander of 79th Division at Fort Meade in Washington, DC, who traveled with Prince Arthur on secret missions in United States. Records indicate that he was missing from early June to 28 July 1918 when he then joined his troops in France, according to author, Shay McNeal. Prince Arthur was missing during this time, too, and resurfaces 27 July 1918.

Landfield, Jerome Barker, who is fluent in Russian, knew Siberia, knew Ipatiev, was a known Tsarist who also married Princess Louba Lobanoff-Rostovsky, the Tsarina's lady-in-waiting. His marriage is said to have linked him to the Russian royal court as well as that of King George V.

Lansing, Robert, the U.S. Secretary of State not trusted by Woodrow Wilson.

Lied, Jonas, a Norwegian businessman given honorary citizenship by the Tsar for opening up trade routes in Siberia, to Western Europe and America, who was known to work with British Intelligence through his friend, Henry Armitstead.

Lenin, Vladimir, the revolutionary leader of the Bolsheviks.

Levine, Lowell, forensic odontologist with New York State Police Forensic Services Division and member of the 1992 American forensic team.

Lindley, Sir Francis, British Chargé d'Affaires, attached to the Petrograd embassy.

Lockhart, Robert Bruce, a British special envoy to the Bolsheviks who replaced Francis Lindley when he was called back to London.

Long, Breckinridge, the Under Secretary of State under Wilson and Lansing, who is said to have run his own department and was close to the president. FDR used him for sensitive tasks in World War II, where he served as a trusted courier between Colonel House, Sir William Wiseman, Arthur Balfour and Wilson. Known to have been a very close friend of Balfour.

Ludendorff, General Eric, the German High Command General who launched the offensive on the Western Front that drove the British Fifth Army back with 120,000 casualties.

Maples, William (died 1998), professor and director of the C.A. Pound Human Identification Laboratory at the University of Florida who led the 1992 American forensic team that examined the purported remains of the Romanov family.

Markove, Serge, former member of the Crimean Horse Guards Regiment who worked with Boris Soloviev to free the Romanoffs in Tobolsk.

Masaryk, Thomas, long-time friend of the American industrialist Charles Crane. He later became president of Czechoslovakia, was father-in-law of Crane's daughter, and negotiated the release of Czech prisoners in Siberia with General Alexis Kaledin, the White Russian who funded Allied banking plots in Russia according to the author, Shay McNeal.

Matveyev, an Ensign in the Tsar's Lifeguards at Tsarkoye Selo. He was head of Special Purpose Detachment after Yakolev left, and may have removed the Romanovs by coordinating a train for them for safety.

Mayre, George T., President Wilson's first US Ambassador to Russia from San Francisco who was handpicked by Charles Crane.

McAdoo, William G., Treasury Secretary under Woodrow Wilson, head of U.S. Secret Service, Wilson's son-in-law, and whose daughter married the Second Secretary to the ambassador of the Provisional Government. He also served as head of the American Red Cross in the Urals.

McNab, Gavin, head of Wilson's campaign for President in the Western United States who had a special relationship with President Wilson.

Michaelovich, Xenia, Tsar Nicholas II's sister and wife of Grand Duke Alexander, known as Sandro.

Mirbach, Count Wilhelm von, is said to have pressed Vladimir Lenin over the safety of the Romanov princesses on behalf of the German Kaiser, the Tsar's cousin.

Mountbatten, Prince Philip, who provided sample DNA material to investigators as a direct relative of the Romanoff family. Husband to Britain's Queen Elizabeth II.

Nagorny, N.G., Alexei's companion, a sailor, who traveled with royal family on the train to Tobolsk.

Nametkin, Alexander, first of the White Russian investigators into the Ipatiev murders.

Nikitin, Sergei, a Russian facial reconstruction expert who provided controversial testimony in the identification of the Romanov remains process.

Occleshaw, Michael, author who wrote *The Romanov Conspiracies* who said that British intelligence watched over a Romanov daughter who survived Siberia until she died at the alleged age of 28 in 1926.

Page, Walter Hines, U.S. Ambassador who did not want America involved in the Russian Revolution because the anti-

Bolsehvik movement had not yet demomstrated its staying power.

Palmer, Henry, an American consul in Ekaterinburg.

Poole, DeWitte, an American consul in Moscow.

Poole, General Frederick, British commander in northern Russia.

Preston, Sir Thomas, British consul in Ekaterinburg.

Radek, Karl, an Austrian citizen who was close to Vladimir Lenin and senior member of the Foreign Office who is said by the author Shay McNeal to have informed the Committee of a potential deal for the Romanov family.

Reilly, Sidney George, British intelligence agent in Russia, known as the "Ace of Spies." He is well connected in Russia, America and England. He moved Remington rifles under contract to the Russian government, planned to overthrow the Bolsehviks, and was said to be close to Grand Duke Alexander Michaelovich in Manchuria.

Reinsch, Paul, the US Ambassador to China under President Wilson, who was recommended for the post by the American Industrialist, Charles Crane.

Robins, Raymond, American Red Cross defacto American representative to the Bolsheviks, and a suspected intelligence agent.

Romanoff, Alexander II, emperor of Russia, grandfather of Nicholas II, who was assassinated by a revolutionary group known as Narodnaya Volya (the People's Will).

Romanoff, Alexander III, emperor of Russia, father of Nicholas II.

Romanoff, Alexandra Feodorovna, the last Empress of Russia, wife of Tsar Nicholas II, granddaughter of Queen Victoria of England.

Romanoff, Alexei Nikolaievich, heir to the Russian throne at the time of his death, youngest child and only son of Tsar Nicholas II and Empress Alexandra.

Romanoff, Anastasia Nikolaievna, grand duchess, second youngest child of Tsar Nicholas II and Empress Alexandra.

Romanoff, Marie Feodorovna, empress of Russia, dowager empress from 1894-1917, mother of Nicholas II.

Romanoff, Marie Nikolaievna, grand duchess, third oldest child of Tsar Nicholas II and Empress Alexandra.

Romanoff, Michael Alexandrovich, grand duke, youngest brother of Nicholas II, refused throne after Tsar Nicholas II's abdication, executed by Bolsheviks in Perm and his body was never found.

Romanoff, Nicholas II, the last Tsar of Russia, reportedly assassinated in Yekaterinburg, Russia, July 17, 1918.

Romanoff, Olga Nikolaievna, grand duchess, eldest daughter of Tsar Nicholas II and Empress Alexandra.

Romanoff, Tatiana Nikolaievna, grand duchess, second eldest child of Tsar Nicholas II and Empress Alexandra.

Romanovsky, George Sergeyevich, Russian consul in San Francisco who is credited by reports for having translated *Rescuing the Czar*.

Roosevelt, Franklin Delano, Assistant Secretary of the Navy during World War I and 32nd president of the United States. Author of the *President's Mystery Story*.

Rostovstov, Count, Tsarina's private secretary and friend of American industrialist Charles Crane, guardian of the Grand Duchesess' trust funds, and Tsarina's financial secretary.

Ryabov, Geli, mystery writer and former member of the Soviet Ministry of the Interior who together with Alexander Avdonin reportedly found the graves of the Romanoffs in the Koptyaki Woods in 1979.

Scheider, Ekaterina, Tsarina's reader who traveled on train with the royal family to Tobolsk.

Sednev, Ivan, Romanoff children's servant who traveled on the train to Tobolsk with the royal family.

Sednev, Leonid, friend of the Tsarevich Alexei who was sent back to the Kaluga District hours before the royal family's reported murder.

Semenov, Ataman, Eastern Siberian warlord opposed to the Bolsheviks.

Sergeyev, Ivan, second White Russian Army investigator of the Romanoff murders.

Sinclair, Archibald, Winston Churchill's secretary.

Slaughter, Major Homer, U.S. military attaché in Ekaterinburg, July 1918.

Sverdlov, president of the All-Russian Soviet who may have worked with Lenin to trade the Romanoffs along with Filipp Goloshchekin, leader of the Ural Bolsheviks and Stalin.

Sylvester, A.J., secretary to former Prime Minister Lloyd George alleging in a book he published that King George V was concerned about revealing details on the house built for the Tsar in Murmansk after the reported assassination in Yekaterinburg.

Sokolov, Nicholas, last White Russian Army investigator of the Romanoff murders at the Ipatiev House and author of the Sokolov Report. Conducted an exhaustive search for evidence of the Ipatiev House murder but found very little.

Soloviev, Boris, attempted a rescue of the Romanoffs in Tobolsk, was courier to the Tsar, and worked with Karol Yaroshinsky who is mentioned by Churchill's secretary.

Stalin, Josef, Secretary-General of the Communist Party, USSR, who worked for Vladimir Lenin as an administrator. He negotiated for the release of Czech prisoners with Thomas Masaryk.

Sverklov, Yakov, chairman of the Central Executive Committee.

Sykes, Brian, professor of human genetics in the Institute of Molecular Medicine at Oxford University in the United Kingdom.

Tatischev, General, Tsar Nicholas II's aide-de-camp, who traveled with the family to imprisonment in Tobolsk.

Tegleva, Alexandra, nursery maid to the Romanoff children, who married tutor Pierre Gilliard in 1922.

Trotsky, Leon, the Russian revolutionary.

Trupp, Alexei, Romanoff footman reportedly executed with the royal family at the Ipatiev House, July 17, 1918.

Van Deman, Major General Ralph H., the American known as the father of U.S. intelligence. He was reported in the summer of 1918 to be in the Yekaterinburg area according to The Final Memoranda, edited by Ralph E. Weber for coordinating planned uprisings in summer.

Vassiliev, Alexander, the Annunciation Church priest who helped Hermogen in rescue attempts on the Romanoffs in Tobolsk according to the author, Shay McNeal.

Volkov, Alecander, the Tsar's valet who traveled with the royal family on the train to Tobolsk.

Vyrubova, Anna, one of the closest friends of Empress Alexandra.

Weedn, Lt. Colonel Victor W., director of the U.S. Armed Forces DNA Identification Laboratory who conducted the investigation with Russian DNA expert Pavel Ivanov.

Weygand, General Maxime, French Allied General in the group of four.

Wilhelm, II, Kaiser, emperor of Germany, first cousin to Empress Alexandra.

Wilson, Thomas Woodrow, 28th president of the United States.

Wiseman, William, head of British Intelligence in the United States, a close friend of Colonel House, President Wilson's confidant and go-to man on Russia.

Yeltsin, Boris, former president of the Russian Federation, former mayor of Moscow, Communist party chief in Yekaterinberg who recommended the destruction of the Ipatiev House and approved the official funeral for the Romanoff family on July 17, 1998.

Yurovsky, Alexander, retired Vice-Admiral in the Soviet Navy, son of Yakov Yurovsky who released a handwritten note from his father repenting and describing the Romanoff murders when he was head of the guards who allegedly killed them.

Yukovsky, Yakov, last commandant of Ipatiev House, reportedly personally assassinated Tsar Nicholas, II as head of the firing squad.

Zhivotovsky, Lev, leading scientist at the Russian Academy of Sciences in Moscow who voiced concern about whether or not the DNA tested actually matched those of five bodies of the Romanovs, or just nameless victims of the Revolution.

RESCUING NICHOLAS | END NOTES & CITATIONS

PROLOGUE – VERIFYING HISTORY

11 IT WAS THEN, AND EVEN NOW IS, A CENTURY LATER, AN ACADEMY AWARD WORTHY PERFORMANCE - Also known as The Oscars is a registered trademark of The Academy of Motion Pictures Arts and Sciences. More information on the trademark can be found at: http://www.oscars.org/legal/regulations.

12 THE CENTRAL CHARACTER IN THIS STORY IS THE MAN MARTIN CAME TO CALL SIMPLY, NICHOLAS – Martin Hutson audio Track 6, Marker 7:47, for example. This 45-minute audio track, privately recorded in August 1971, will serve as the basis for PFC Hutson's eyewitness account of the AEF Siberia rescue of Nicholas Romanov II. A transcript of the recording is found in Appendix A.

13 THE PEW RESEARCH CENTER FOR JOURNALISM & MEDIA SAYS THERE ARE NINE CORE PRINCIPLES OF JOURNALISM - Pew Research Center for Journalism & Media, found at www.journalism.org/thesources/principles-of-journalism. These nine core principles of journalism will serve as guides for the presentation of the facts in the case of the AEF Siberia mission to rescue Tsar Nicholas II presented in *Rescuing Nicholas: The Secret Mission to Save The Tsar.*

ONE – AN ENDURING SAGA

20 IT WAS AN EXTRAORDINARY SECRET TO KEEP FROM CONGRESS – Capitol Hill is known to official Washington as simply "The Hill." It got its informal name because of the hill on which the U.S. Capitol was constructed within the city's limits. Thomas Jefferson has been credited with calling it Capitol Hill after a similar complex he admired in Rome. It has been shorted over time to "The Hill."

21 THE BROTHERS HAD HONED THEIR SURVIVAL SKILLS – George Hutson earned a Purple Heart for his service under General Black Jack Pershing in the Black Forest of Germany during World War I.

22 MARTIN AND HIS OWN FELLOW SOLDIERS HAD COME INTO COUNTRY – Martin told family members that he and his fellow soldiers were told that they were going to Siberia to rescue American Red Cross nurses.

23 MARTIN AND HIS COMRADES HAD NO IDEA CHIANG KAI-SHEK WAS INSIDE AN AREA WHERE HE DID NOT BELONG – Martin's account to family members said that the Chinese bandits were led by Chiang but his audio recording does not mention the leader's name.

23 THE GENTLEMAN IN THE CENTER "CAR" WAS FRIENDLY ENOUGH – In conversation with family and on his audio recording, Martin never disclosed the name of the Romanov daughter saying that he was never formally introduced to her by name. Based on information that he obtained many years later, he speculated as to which Romanov daughter he met on that fateful train trip through Siberia.

25 THE BONES WOULD LATER YIELD A STORY - David Brown, "DNA Proves Bones Belong to Last Tsar; Mystery of Nicholas's Missing Body Is Solved," *Washington Post*, September 1, 1995.

26 RUMORS WOULD SAY - Michael Gray, *Blood Relative: The Astonishing Story of the Survival of the Tsarevich Written by his Son*, London, England: Victor Gollancz, 1998.

26 AND YET HISTORY CONVINCINGLY TOLD THE STORY - Two excellent books on the Romanov family fate and the Tsar's personality are presented by Robert K. Massie, *The Romanovs: The Final Chapter*, New York, NY: Random House, 1995 and Massey's award-winning epic, *Nicholas and Alexandra*, London, England: Gollancz, 1968.

27 EVEN MORE INTRIGUING - Rebecca Perring, "Vladimir Putin 'wants' to reinstate Russia's royal family and bring back the Tsars," *The Daily and Sunday Express*, June 24, 2015, found at: http://www.express.co.uk/news/world/586470/Russia-royal-family-Vladimir-Putin-reinstate-Tsar-Nicholas-Second-Romanov.

28 WHAT IF THE FABLED ANASTASIA – The Empress Dowager is quoted by authors as saying that she believed that the Grand Duchess Anastasia did in fact survive the Ipatiev House massacre.

TWO – MARTIN'S STORY

31 NICHOLAS WAS NOT KILLED IN SIBERIA – August 1971 recording by Martin V. Hutson, Track 6, Mark 7:47.

32 SITTING AT A MICROPHONE HALF A CENTURY LATER - Ibid, Martin Hutson 1971 recording.

32 THE RECRUITING OFFICER KNEW MARTIN – Ibid, Martin Hutson 1971 recording Track 1 - 10:56.

32 A WEEK LATER, HOWEVER, MARTIN IS TOLD – Ibid, Martin Hutson 1971 recording Track 1 - 10:56.

32 THE ENLISTMENT DATE WAS AUGUST 20, 1919 - Enlistment Record of Martin V. Hutson, United States Army, at Fort Oglethorpe, Georgia, August 20, 1919, signed by Captain Chas. C. Laughlin, Commander, Infantry (Tanks), 3rd Tank Company.

33 ARRIVING SHORTLY AFTER ENLISTING AT FORT OGLETHORPE – Martin Hutson 1971 recording Track 1 - 10:56.

33 NOW PRIVATE MARTIN HUTSON – Ibid, Martin Hutson 1971 recording Track 1 - 10:56.

33 THE SERGEANT CAME BACK AND ASKED HIM WHY HE WAS NOT READY – Ibid, Martin Hutson 1971 recording Track 1 - 10:56.

33 FORT MCDOWELL - William Bright and Erwin Gustav Gudde, *1500 California Place Names: Their Origin and Meaning*, University of California Press, Oakland, CA: 1998, p. 16.

34 MARTIN BECOMES FRIENDS WITH A GROUP OF OTHER SOLDIERS HE MEETS – Martin Hutson 1971 recording Track 1 - 10:56.

34 THE ORDERS EVENTUALLY CAME – Ibid, Martin Hutson 1971 recording Track 1 - 10:56.

34 THE *GREAT NORTHERN* HAD BEEN FIRST DELIVERED – Information on the ship found in the *Dictionary of American Naval Fighting Ships* maintained by the Department of the Navy, Washington DC Naval Ship Yard located online at: http://www.history.navy.mil/danfs/g8/great_northern.htm.

34 THE NAVY DECOMMISSIONED THE *GREAT NORTHERN* - Ibid, *Dictionary of American Naval Fighting Ships.*

35 "AT DINNER TIME ...." – Martin Hutson 1971 recording Track 1 - 10:56.

35 "THE LADY HAD SEEN ME LOOKING THROUGH THE WINDOW" – Ibid, Martin Hutson 1971 recording Track 1 - 10:56.

36 MARTIN'S ARRIVAL DATE IN SIBERIA - Enlistment Record of Martin V. Hutson, United States Army, at Fort Oglethorpe, Georgia, August 20, 1919, signed by Captain Chas. C. Laughlin, Commander, Infantry (Tanks), 3rd Tank Company.

36 VLADIVISTOK IN THE SECOND DECADE - *Life in Vladivostok*, as found on Canada's Siberian Expedition web site located at: www.siberianexpedition.ca/story/life_in_vladivostok.php.

36 MARTIN STAYS IN A BUILDING NEAR A HANGER – Martin Hutson 1971 recording Track 2 - 6:30.

36 AT THE CHURCH, MARTIN DISCOVERS – Ibid, Martin Hutson 1971 recording Track 2 - 6:30.

37 KNOWN AFFECTIONATELY AS THE POLAR BEARS - Various documents including the official national archives in Washington refer to this division of the American Expeditionary Forces Siberia.

37 MARTIN'S FIRST NIGHT IN THE FIELD - Ibid, Martin Hutson 1971 recording Track 2 - 6:30.

37 "WE DRILLED SIX WEEKS AT CLOSE QUARTERS …." - Ibid, Martin Hutson 1971 recording Track 2 - 6:30.

38 "KASHIBA, IS THIS MAN READY?" - Ibid, Martin Hutson 1971 recording Track 2 - 6:30.

38 THAT NIGHT THEY TOOK MARTIN AND EIGHT MEN DOWN TO THE STATION …." - Ibid, Martin Hutson 1971 recording Track 2 - 6:30.

38 "THE STREETS OF VLADIVOSTOK WERE MADE OF COBBLESTONE." - Ibid, Martin Hutson 1971 recording Track 2 - 6:30.

38 "AT 11 O'CLOCK, MARTIN SAYS THAT THEIR TRAIN STARTED OUT FOR IRKUTSK …." - Ibid, Martin Hutson 1971 recording Track 2 - 6:30.

39 "ALONG THIS MANCHURIAN RAILROAD …." - Ibid, Martin Hutson 1971 recording Track 3 - 6:48.

39 NEARBY LAKE BAIKAL - *CNN*, "Lake Baikal: The Great Blue Eye of Siberia," October 11, 2006.

39 DESPITE SOME OBJECTIONS - Martin Hutson 1971 recording Track 3 - 6:48.

39 THE RED ARMY WAS ON THE EAST BANK OF THE RIVER – Ibid, Martin Hutson 1971 recording Track 3 – 6:48.

40 "HE TOOK ME FIVE TRACKS OVER …." – Ibid, Martin Hutson 1971 recording Track 3 – 6:48.

40 "I STAYED THERE FOR SEVERAL HOURS AND THE DOOR OPENED …." – Ibid, Martin Hutson 1971 recording Track 3 – 6:48.

40 "MY ORDERS ARE MY ORDERS," MARTIN EXPLAINED – Ibid, Martin Hutson 1971 recording Track 3 – 6:48.

40 MARTIN SAYS HE GUARDED THIS CAR FOR THREE DAYS AND THREE NIGHTS – Ibid, Martin Hutson 1971 recording Track 3 – 6:48.

40 THE TROOPS ON THE WEST BANK, THE WHITE ARMY, EVENTUALLY FLED– Ibid, Martin Hutson 1971 recording Track 3 – 6:48.

40 "I COCKED MY .45 AUTOMATIC, PUT MY BACK AGAINST THE CAR …." – Ibid, Martin Hutson 1971 recording Track 3 – 6:48.

41 "THE LIEUTENANT HOLLERED 'STAY PERFECTLY STILL', I AM COMING …." – Ibid, Martin Hutson 1971 recording Track 3 – 6:48.

41 "THEY RELIEVED ME FROM THIS CAR …." – Ibid, Martin Hutson 1971 recording Track 3 – 6:48.

41 MARTIN SAYS THE LIEUTENANT TOOK HIM BACK – Martin Hutson 1971 recording Track 4 – 7:04.

41 AMAZING, MARTIN SAYS – Ibid, Martin Hutson 1971 recording Track 4 – 7:04.

41 "WHEN I TURNED AROUND ...." – Ibid, Martin Hutson 1971 recording Track 4 – 7:04.

41 MARTIN SAID, "THIS MAN ASKED ME MY NAME AND I COULD HAVE DROPPED TO THE FLOOR ...." – Ibid, Martin Hutson 1971 recording Track 4 – 7:04.

41 "FOR SEVEN DAYS ...." – Ibid, Martin Hutson 1971 recording Track 4 – 7:04.

42 MARTIN SAID THAT HIS ORDERS WERE TO TEACH THE FORMER RUSSIAN MONARCH A SOUTHERN ACCENT – This information was not provided on Martin's formal audio recording but was sourced from family members recalling the explanation.

42 "THE NEXT DAY, HE ASKED IF I HAD FOUND ANY CHINESE NEWSPAPERS?" SAID MARTIN – Martin Hutson 1971 recording Track 4 – 7:04.

42 "HE READ TO ME FOR THE NEXT FEW DAYS," MARTIN SAID – Ibid, Martin Hutson 1971 recording Track 4 – 7:04.

42 "ONE DAY, THE LIEUTENANT TOOK ME OVER ...." – Ibid, Martin Hutson 1971 recording Track 4 – 7:04.

42 "THE NEXT DAY, I WENT DOWN TO THE CAR AND A FRENCH LADY CAME TO THE DOOR." – Ibid, Martin Hutson 1971 recording Track 4 – 7:04.

42 "SHE," THE FRENCH LADY MARTIN SAYS .... – Ibid, Martin Hutson 1971 recording Track 4 – 7:04.

42 "SO," SAYS MARTIN, "I HAD TWO JOBS TO DO ...." – Ibid, Martin Hutson 1971 recording Track 4 – 7:04.

42 THE NEXT MORNING – Ibid, Martin Hutson 1971 recording Track 4 – 7:04.

43 MARTIN SAID THAT AFTER THE ENCOUNTER WITH THE LADY – Ibid, Martin Hutson 1971 recording Track 4 – 7:04.

43 "A FEW MILES DOWN THE LINE ...." – Martin Hutson 1971 recording Track 5 – 6:25.

44 "WHEN THEY ALL GOT CLEARED OUT ...." – Ibid, Martin Hutson 1971 recording Track 5 – 6:25.

44 LOCATED IN NORTHEAST CHINA, HARBIN - Historical Evolution of Harbin, Harbin Municipal Government web site found at: http://www.harbin.gov.cn/english/Harbin_Overview/Historical_Evolution.htm

44 MARTIN REMEMBERS – Martin Hutson 1971 recording Track 5 – 6:25.

44 "HE ASKED IF I WANTED TO BUY SOME ...." – Ibid, Martin Hutson 1971 recording Track 5 – 6:25.

44 MARTIN'S GROUP THEN PULLED INTO HARBIN – Ibid, Martin Hutson 1971 recording Track 5 – 6:25.

44 "OUR CONSUL GENERAL RAISED HIS FOOT AND PUT IT ON TOP OF A BIG BOX ...." – Ibid, Martin Hutson 1971 recording Track 5 - 6:25.

44 "HE BROUGHT THREE BOXES TO A WAGON AND LEFT." – Ibid, Martin Hutson 1971 recording Track 5 - 6:25.

45 "WE GOT AN ENGINEER TO DRIVE THE TRAIN BACK TO VLADIVOSTOK...." – Ibid, Martin Hutson 1971 recording Track 5 - 6:25.

45 MARTIN SAYS THE ENGINEER – Ibid, Martin Hutson 1971 recording Track 5 - 6:25.

45 BACK INTO SIBERIA – Ibid, Martin Hutson 1971 recording Track 5 - 6:25.

45 "WE PROCEEDED ON DOWN ABOUT 50 MILES ...." – Ibid, Martin Hutson 1971 recording Track 5 - 6:25.

45 MARTIN SAID, "THOSE TRAINS ...." – Ibid, Martin Hutson 1971 recording Track 5 - 6:25.

45 A 14-YEAR-OLD SPOKE VERY GOOD ENGLISH – Martin Hutson 1971 recording Track 6 - 8:14.

46 "WE PULLED INTO VLADIVOSTOK THE NEXT DAY," MARTIN SAID – Ibid, Martin Hutson 1971 recording Track 6 - 8:14.

46 IN TELLING HIS STORY– Ibid, Martin Hutson 1971 recording Track 6 - 8:14.

47 "I CAME BACK TO THE UNITED STATES ...." – Martin Hutson 1971 recording Track 6 - 8:14.

47 "MY STORY IS THIS," MARTIN SAID – Ibid, Martin Hutson 1971 recording Track 6 – 8:14.

47 "I THINK I WAS USED AS A TOOL ...." – Ibid, Martin Hutson 1971 recording Track 6 – 8:14.

48 MARTIN ENDED HIS ARMY CAREER - Honorable Discharge From the United States Army, at Fort Lewis, Washington, August 19, 1922, signed by Rev. Broughton, Major, 7th Infantry.

THREE – WHISPERS & THEORIES

53 "OUR CONSUL GENERAL RAISED HIS FOOT AND PUT IT ON TOP OF A BIG BOX ...." – Martin Hutson 1971 recording Track 5 – 6:25.

53 HISTORY NOW TELLS US THAT THE TSAR'S PARTY WAS FOUND SOME 74 YEARS LATER IN AN UNMARKED GRAVE IN THE KOPTYAKI WOODS - Peter Kurth, *Tsar: The Lost World of Nicholas & Alexandra*, Madison Press Books, Toronto, Ontario, Canada, p. 214.

54 HISTORY WOULD EVENTUALLY SHARE WITH US THAT THE GRAVE OF THE ROMANOVS HAD BEEN FOUND BY THESE SAME AMATEUR SLEUTHS IN 1976 - According to an article that was written by Geli Ryabov as reported by Peter Kurth, p. 214 and Peter Kurth, *Tsar: The Lost World of Nicholas & Alexandra.*

54 HISTORY WOULD TELL US THAT SUBSEQUENT DNA TESTS WOULD ULTIMATELY DETERMINE WITH 98.5% CERTAINTY THAT THE BONES FOUND WERE INDEED THOSE OF THE

ROYAL FAMILY - Peter Kurth, *Tsar: The Lost World of Nicholas & Alexandra,* p. 217.

54 HISTORY TELLS US THAT THE AMERICAN FORENSIC SCIENTISTS WHO WERE CALLED IN BY THE POST-SOVIET GOVERNMENT - Peter Kurth reports that William Maples, MD, of the C.A. Pound Human Identification Laboratory at the University of Florida in Gainesville was "unequivocal" in his conclusion that the missing body was that of Anastasia and not her older sister, Marie, as was thought by his Russian counterparts, p. 217. Anastasia comments also sourced from Peter Kurth, citing a news conference in Yekaterinburg by Dr. Maples, p. 217.

54 HISTORY TELLS US THAT EIGHTEEN WITNESSES FROM THE CITY OF PERM TESTIFIED – Ibid, Peter Kurth, p. 202.

54 HISTORY TELLS US THAT THERE WERE OTHER ROMANOV SIGHTINGS AS WELL IN THE MONTHS FOLLOWING THE "ASSASSINATION" - Ibid, Peter Kurth, pp. 202 and 204.

54 ANOTHER REPORT RECOUNTED BY THE OUTSTANDING HISTORIAN, ROBERT K. MASSEY - Robert K. Massie. *The Romanovs: The Final Chapter.* Random House, New York, NY, 1995, pp. 17-18.

56 IN HIS 1998 BOOK, *BLOOD RELATIVE* – Michael Gray, *Blood Relative,* published by Victor Gollancz, London, England, 1998.

56 GRAY CONTENDS THAT HE WAS RAISED BY SURROGATE parents – Ibid, Michael Gray, *Blood Relative.*

57 WHAT MAKES GRAY'S STORY SO INTRIGUING, WHETHER TRUE OR NOT - Each account listed in this section is from Michael Gray's book, *Blood Relative.* See especially pp. vi-viii.

58 THE RAILROADS IN RUSSIA CERTAINLY DO FACTOR VERY PROMINENTLY INTO MANY OF THE RESCUE WHISPERS ABOUT THE ROMANOVS – Anthony Summers and Tom Mangold, *The File on the Tsar*, Orion, London, England, 2002, pp. 27-28.

61 PRINCE PAUL LIEVEN HAD BEEN - Ibid, Michael Gray's *Blood Relative*, p. 140.

61 "AT AN EVEN HIGHER LEVEL, BRITAIN'S KING GEORGE V WAS ALMOST CERTAINLY INVOLVED IN THESE RESCUE MISSIONS" – Ibid, Michael Gray's *Blood Relative*, p. 143.

61 THE IMPERIAL TUTOR, CHARLES SYDNEY GIBBS IT IS WRITTEN IN GRAY'S BOOK – Ibid, Michael Gray's *Blood Relative*, p. 23.

61 ACCORDING TO GRAY'S ACCOUNT – Ibid, Michael Gray's *Blood Relative*, p. 110.

62 SUMMERS AND MANGOLD IN THEIR BOOK - Ibid, Michael Gray's *Blood Relative*, p. 111.

62 "SECOND, GRAY ALSO NOTES ...." – Ibid, Michael Gray's *Blood Relative*, p. 111.

62 GRAY CONTENDS THAT THERE MAY HAVE BEEN A ROYAL SECRET PACT REFERRED TO AS "THE TRUST OF KINGS" – Ibid, Michael Gray's *Blood Relative*, p. 112.

63 THE GERMAN CHANCELLOR, GRAY FURTHER ALLEGES – Ibid, Michael Gray's *Blood Relative*, p. 112-13.

63 "LOGICAL IT MAY HAVE BEEN," ARGUES GRAY IN AGREEABLE FASHION – Ibid, Michael Gray's *Blood Relative*, p. 113-14.

64 AND SO IT PROVED ITSELF OUT GRAY NOTES - Ibid, Michael Gray's *Blood Relative*, p. 114.

64 GRAY THEN RELATES THAT DR. UNA KROLL, "GEORGE HILL'S DAUGHTER - Ibid, Michael Gray's *Blood Relative*, p. 115.

64 IN AUGUST 1918, SIR CHARLES ELIOT, THE BRITISH HIGH COMMISSIONER IN SIBERIA – Ibid, Michael Gray's *Blood Relative*, p. 119.

65 IN 1932, GRAY WRITES THAT GEORGE HILL PUBLISHED A BOOK ENTITLED, *GO SPY THE LAND* – Ibid, Michael Gray's *Blood Relative*, p. 119.

65 THE POINT IS, AS MICHAEL GRAY FINALLY STATES – Ibid, Michael Gray's *Blood Relative*, p. 124.

65 SUCCINCTLY SAID – Ibid, Michael Gray's *Blood Relative*, p. 143-47.

66 GRAY BELIEVES - Ibid, Michael Gray's *Blood Relative*, p. 149.

68 SHAY MCNEAL, IN HER 2001 BOOK, *THE SECRET PLOT TO SAVE THE TSAR* – Shay McNeal, *The Secret Plot to Save the*

Tsar: The Truth Behind the Romanov Mystery, William Morrow, New York, NY, 2001, p. 242.

68 WRITES MCNEAL – Ibid, Shay McNeal, *The Secret Plot to Save The Tsar*, p. 1.

68 MCNEAL ARGUES THAT AFTER REVIEWING THE EVIDENCE – Ibid, Shay McNeal, *The Secret Plot to Save The Tsar*, pp. 1-2.

69 MCNEAL SAYS HER BOOK DEMONSTRATES – Ibid, Shay McNeal, *The Secret Plot to Save The Tsar*, pp. 1-4.

69 BUT QUESTIONS THROUGH MCNEAL AND OTHERS HAVE BEEN RAISED ABOUT HOW THE ROMANOV BONES FIRST MADE THEIR APPEARANCE IN RUSSIA – Ibid, Shay McNeal, *The Secret Plot to Save The Tsar*, p. 4.

69 CONCLUSIVE DNA ANALYSIS DOES NOT APPEAR TO MCNEAL OR US TO HAVE BEEN SO CONCLUSIVE AFTER ALL - Ibid, Shay McNeal, *The Secret Plot to Save The Tsar*, pp. 4-5.

70 MCNEAL SAYS THAT ANOTHER PROBLEM, "IS THE SIMPLE FACT …." – Ibid, Shay McNeal, *The Secret Plot to Save The Tsar*, p. 5.

71 "CONCERNING THE ALLEGED ROMANOV REMAINS IN PARTICULAR," MCNEAL ARGUES - Ibid, Shay McNeal, *The Secret Plot to Save The Tsar*, p. 5.

71 THUS, MCNEAL SAYS – Ibid, Shay McNeal, *The Secret Plot to Save The Tsar*, p. 6.

71 AS WE HAVE BRIEFLY ENCOUNTERED EARLIER, THE ROMANOV BONES WERE FIRST DISCOVERED BY GELI RYABOV – Ibid, Shay McNeal, *The Secret Plot to Save The Tsar*, p. 7.

72 AS EVIDENCE OF HER INCREDULITY, MCNEAL DISCUSSES THE FINDINGS OF JOHN O'CONOR – Ibid, Shay McNeal, *The Secret Plot to Save The Tsar*, p. 8.

73 YEARS LATER, IN 1970, MCNEAL POINTS OUT THAT A NEW YORK REPORTER NAMED GUY RICHARDS – Ibid, Shay McNeal, *The Secret Plot to Save The Tsar*, pp. 8-9.

73 ASSERTS MCNEAL – Ibid, Shay McNeal, *The Secret Plot to Save The Tsar*.

73 MICHAEL OCCLESHAW, A BRITISH WRITER THEN READYING A BOOK IN 1993, *THE ROMANOV CONSPIRACIES*, ARGUES - Michael Occleshaw.

74 CLEARLY, AS MCNEAL SAYS, THERE WERE ANOTHER NUMBER OF FAILURES PRESENT ON THE EVIDENCE - Ibid, Shay McNeal, *The Secret Plot to Save The Tsar*, pp. 9-11.

74 "THE DISCOVERY, TRANSPORTATION AND STORAGE OF THE REMAINS HAVE NEVER BEEN CONVINCINGLY DOCUMENTED AND RECORDED," ARGUES MCNEAL – Ibid, Shay McNeal, *The Secret Plot to Save The Tsar*, p. 11.

75 MCNEAL'S POSITION IS THAT "AN OBJECTIVE COURT OF LAW WOULD NEVER HAVE ARRIVED AT THE SAME CONCLUSION – Ibid, Shay McNeal, *The Secret Plot to Save The Tsar*, pp. 12-13.

75 BY LATE 1917, MCNEAL WRITES THAT THE SITUATION "NO LONGER SEEMED AS SIMPLE AS IT HAD IN LATE 1916 AND EARLY 1917 – Ibid, Shay McNeal, *The Secret Plot to Save The Tsar*, p. 30.

75 MCNEAL'S POSITION ON THIS POTENTIAL IS SOLID – Ibid, Shay McNeal, *The Secret Plot to Save The Tsar*, pp. 30-33.

76 THUS, IN ONE OF THE MAIN POINTS TO HER INTRIGUING RESEARCH AND ARGUMENT THAT THERE WAS A SECRET PLOT TO SAVE THE TSAR – Ibid, Shay McNeal, *The Secret Plot to Save The Tsar*, pp. 13-14.

77 MCNEAL NOTES THAT GEORGE V, AT LEAST THREE TIMES – Ibid, Shay McNeal, *The Secret Plot to Save The Tsar*, pp. 13-14 and 37-38.

78 MCNEAL PRESENTS OTHER COMPELLING EVIDENCE IN HER BOOK – Ibid, Shay McNeal, *The Secret Plot to Save The Tsar*, p. 44.

78 THIS ARGUMENT BY MCNEAL AS SHE OFFERS IT, "IS FURTHER SUPPORTED BY A PIECE OF CORRESPONDENCE FORWARDED LATER – Ibid, Shay McNeal, *The Secret Plot to Save The Tsar*, pp. 44-45.

79 EVEN OUR ERSTWHILE CONSUL GENERAL HARRIS – Ibid, Shay McNeal, *The Secret Plot to Save The Tsar*, p. 44.

79 "DAYS AFTER THIS INTERESTING COMMUNICATION," WRITES MCNEAL – Ibid, Shay McNeal, *The Secret Plot to Save The Tsar*.

80 ARCHIVES OF THE HUDSON BAY COMPANY IN WINNIPEG, CANADA, SHOW CONCLUSIVE EVIDENCE – Ibid, Shay McNeal, *The Secret Plot to Save The Tsar*, p. 46.

80 MCNEAL SAYS THAT THE KNOWLEDGE OF THE ACTIVITIES IN RUSSIA TO SAVE THE TSAR WAS CONFINED TO A TIGHT GROUP OF MEN – Ibid, Shay McNeal, *The Secret Plot to Save The Tsar*, p. 52.

80 "ON 21 DECEMBER [1917]," MCNEAL WRITES, THAT " A TELEGRAM WAS RECEIVED FROM COLONEL HOUSE CONFIRMING WILSON'S WILLINGNESS TO HAVE THE MONEY

TRANSFERRED – Ibid, Shay McNeal, *The Secret Plot to Save The Tsar.*

81 MCNEAL CONTINUES – Ibid, Shay McNeal, *The Secret Plot to Save The Tsar*, pp. 52-53.

82 THE MCNEAL STRING OF EVIDENCE TAKES ON AN EVEN MORE INTRIGUING ASPECT – Ibid, Shay McNeal, *The Secret Plot to Save The Tsar*, p. 54.

83 MCNEAL CONTENDS THAT THE ALLIES HAD A SECRET BANKING SCHEME – Ibid, Shay McNeal, *The Secret Plot to Save The Tsar*, pp. 70-71 and chapters 3-5.

83 "LENIN'S STRATEGY," MCNEAL SAYS, "SEEMS TO HAVE BEEN TO PERSUADE THE GERMANS NOT TO OCCUPY THE SOVIET HEARTLAND – Ibid, Shay McNeal, *The Secret Plot to Save The Tsar.*

83 THE FIRST ATTEMPT TO RESCUE THE TSAR, ACCORDING TO MCNEAL, WAS IN TOBOLSK – Ibid, Shay McNeal, *The Secret Plot to Save The Tsar*, pp. 75-76.

84 OTHER INTRIGUE WAS AFOOT, TOO, MCNEAL WRITES – Ibid, Shay McNeal, *The Secret Plot to Save The Tsar*, pp. 98-99.

84 ACCORDING TO MCNEAL, KARL RADEK, AN AUSTRIAN CITIZEN TRAVELING WITH LENIN – Ibid, Shay McNeal, *The Secret Plot to Save The Tsar*, p. 102.

84 THE MOST STUNNING NEWS IN THIS ACCOUNT IS THE FACT THAT IT APPEARS TO HAVE HARDLY BEEN A STATE SECRET – Ibid, Shay McNeal, *The Secret Plot to Save The Tsar.*

84 "AND IN THE UNITED STATES," MCNEAL WRITES, "MASARYK WAS PREPARING TO SPEAK OFFICIALLY TO

PRESIDENT WILSON ..." – Ibid, Shay McNeal, *The Secret Plot to Save The Tsar*, p. 104.

85 SAYS, MCNEAL, "THE NEW EVIDENCE SUGGESTS THAT THERE WAS IN ACTUALITY A STRATEGY – Ibid, Shay McNeal, *The Secret Plot to Save The Tsar*, p. 106.

85 "THE EVIDENCE WE HAVE SEEN THUS FAR," MCNEAL SAYS – Ibid, Shay McNeal, *The Secret Plot to Save The Tsar*, pp. 112-13.

86 AS MCNEAL AND OTHERS WILL NO DOUBT TELL YOU – Ibid, Shay McNeal, *The Secret Plot to Save The Tsar*, p. 116.

86 ANOTHER RESCUE MISSION PROFILED BY MCNEAL OPERATED OUT OF MURMANSK – Ibid, Shay McNeal, *The Secret Plot to Save The Tsar*, pp. 116-18.

86 THIS INFORMATION WILL BE IMPORTANT IN UNDERSTANDING EVENTS – Ibid, Shay McNeal, *The Secret Plot to Save The Tsar*, p. 119.

87 YET MORE INTRIGUE FROM MCNEAL'S ACCOUNT – Ibid, Shay McNeal, *The Secret Plot to Save The Tsar*, p. 121.

87 WHATEVER THE FATE OF THE ROMANOVS, MCNEAL WRYLY SAYS – Ibid, Shay McNeal, *The Secret Plot to Save The Tsar*, p. 122.

88 TO THIS POINT, MCNEAL SAYS – Ibid, Shay McNeal, *The Secret Plot to Save The Tsar*, pp. 122-23.

88 MCNEAL SAYS THAT IN 1919, "Peer Groves was assigned to British intelligence in Odessa – Ibid, Shay McNeal, *The Secret Plot to Save The Tsar*.

88 MCNEAL CONTENDS RESEARCH SHOWS THAT, REPORTS THAT NICHOLAS HAD BEEN KILLED BEGAN CIRCULATING IN

June 1918 a month before he was supposedly murdered – Ibid, Shay McNeal, *The Secret Plot to Save The Tsar*, pp. 124-25.

89 Interestingly, McNeal details three witnesses – Ibid, Shay McNeal, *The Secret Plot to Save The Tsar*, p. 125.

89 McNeal concludes that Lenin – Ibid, Shay McNeal, *The Secret Plot to Save The Tsar*, pp. 125-26.

90 At the time, McNeal finds that Henry Palmer, the American consul in Yekaterinburg –Ibid, Shay McNeal, *The Secret Plot to Save The Tsar*, p. 129.

90 Another interesting passage by McNeal: on the 7th of July: "'If Matveyev's train not yet dispatched – Ibid, Shay McNeal, *The Secret Plot to Save The Tsar*, pp. 129-30

90 At about the same time, McNeal says that "In America the diary of Will Starling, a United States Secret Service agent, assigned to the White House – Ibid, Shay McNeal, *The Secret Plot to Save The Tsar*, pp. 130-31.

91 *Rescuing the Czar*, McNeal says, "does allude to the fact that family was taken out of the Ipatiev House through a cistern – Ibid, Shay McNeal, *The Secret Plot to Save The Tsar*, p. 131.

91 So this begs the question – Ibid, Shay McNeal, *The Secret Plot to Save The Tsar*, p. 136.

92 McNeal provides an excellent detailed analysis – Ibid, Shay McNeal, *The Secret Plot to Save The Tsar*, p. 137.

92 "THE HIDDEN AGENDA TO SAVE THE ROMANOVS," POINTS OUT MCNEAL, "WAS EXTREMELY COMPLICATED – Ibid, Shay McNeal, *The Secret Plot to Save The Tsar*, pp. 137-38.

92 THE ROMANOV'S INITIAL DEATH, MCNEAL NOTES – Ibid, Shay McNeal, *The Secret Plot to Save The Tsar*, p. 138.

92 LATER, ON OCTOBER 5TH, SIR CHARLES ELIOTT, THE BRITISH HIGH COMMISSIONER IN SIBERIA – Ibid, Shay McNeal, *The Secret Plot to Save The Tsar*, pp. 139-40.

93 IN AN IRONY THAT COULD ONLY HAVE HAPPENED TO THE ROMANOVS – Ibid, Shay McNeal, *The Secret Plot to Save The Tsar*, p. 155.

93 BY THE 25TH OF JULY 1918, YEKATERINBURG FALLS TO THE WHITE RUSSIAN AND CZECH FORCES – Ibid, Shay McNeal, *The Secret Plot to Save The Tsar*, pp. 161-62.

93 SUMMERS AND MANGOLD – Ibid, Shay McNeal, *The Secret Plot to Save The Tsar*, p. 166.

94 THE CZECHOSLOVAKIA GENERAL WAS GAIDA – Ibid, Shay McNeal, *The Secret Plot to Save The Tsar*, p. 169.

94 CHARLES CRANE, AN AMERICAN A MULTIMILLIONAIRE INDUSTRIALIST WHO OWNED CRANE PLUMBING IN CHICAGO – Ibid, Shay McNeal, *The Secret Plot to Save The Tsar*, pp. 28-29.

95 CANADIAN COLONEL JOSEPH BOYLE RESCUED THE ROMANIAN ROYAL FAMILY FOR KING GEORGE V – Ibid, Shay McNeal, *The Secret Plot to Save The Tsar*, p. 35.

95 BORIS SAVINKOV, IS A KERENSKY AIDE – Ibid, Shay McNeal, *The Secret Plot to Save The Tsar*, p. 40.

96 BRITISH INTELLIGENCE AGENT SIDNEY REILLY, IS KNOWN AS THE "ACE OF SPIES" – Ibid, Shay McNeal, *The Secret Plot to Save The Tsar*, pp. 57-58.

96 THE HUDSON BAY COMPANY - Ibid, Shay McNeal, *The Secret Plot to Save The Tsar*, pp. 60-61.

97 RAYMOND ROBINS OF THE AMERICAN RED CROSS – Ibid, Shay McNeal, *The Secret Plot to Save The Tsar*, p. 68.

97 WILLIAM RUTLIDGE MCGARRY IS REPORTED BY MCNEAL TO HAVE BELIEVED TO HIS DYING DAY THAT THE ROMANOVS WERE RESCUED AS ALLEGED – Ibid, Shay McNeal, *The Secret Plot to Save The Tsar*, p. 232.

98 JEROME BARKER LANDFIELD, THE RUSSIA EXPERT, WHO GRADUATED FROM CORNELL UNIVERSITY – Ibid, Shay McNeal, *The Secret Plot to Save The Tsar*, p. 99.

98 PRINCE ARTHUR OF CONNAUGHT WAS A CLOSE CONFIDANT TO KING GEORGE V – Ibid, Shay McNeal, *The Secret Plot to Save The Tsar*, p. 100.

99 CAPTAIN Digby-Jones was an engineer with the British Royal Engineers – Ibid, Shay McNeal, *The Secret Plot to Save The Tsar*, p. 141.

99 MAJOR GUINET OF FRANCE WAS AN INTELLIGENCE OFFICER – Ibid, Shay McNeal, *The Secret Plot to Save The Tsar*, p. 144.

99 WHITE RUSSIAN GENERAL TCHEREP SPIRIDOVITCH – Ibid, Shay McNeal, *The Secret Plot to Save The Tsar*, p. 264.

99 NEEDLESS TO SAY, THERE WERE A LOT OF HIDDEN HANDS IN MCNEAL'S ACCOUNT OF THE SECRET PLOT TO SAVE THE TSAR – Ibid, Shay McNeal, *The Secret Plot to Save The Tsar*, pp. 169-70.

100 McNeal also mentions in her account that the testimony of Yurovsky that 12 people were killed and not eleven says that all were buried together – Ibid, Shay McNeal, *The Secret Plot to Save The Tsar*, pp. 182-94.

101 "What seems apparent," McNeal writes – Ibid, Shay McNeal, *The Secret Plot to Save The Tsar*, p. 197.

101 McNeal also observes in a final passage that will be very important to Martin's account – Ibid, Shay McNeal, *The Secret Plot to Save The Tsar*, p. 223.

102 *Rescuing the Czar*, as McNeal and others acknowledge – Ibid, Shay McNeal, *The Secret Plot to Save The Tsar*, p. 242.

102 As McNeal says, "If *Rescuing the Czar* has any validity – Ibid, Shay McNeal, *The Secret Plot to Save The Tsar*.

103 On page 262 of her book - Ibid, Shay McNeal, *The Secret Plot to Save The Tsar*, p. 262.

103 McNeal says that, "One man who may have known the whole story – Ibid, Shay McNeal, *The Secret Plot to Save The Tsar*, p. 263.

104 "On the evening of the 17th" – Ibid, Shay McNeal, *The Secret Plot to Save The Tsar*.

104 On the 6th of December [1918], another report that should be considered legitimate once again mirrored events in *Rescuing the Czar* – Ibid, Shay McNeal, *The Secret Plot to Save The Tsar*, pp. 264-65.

105 SO MCNEAL'S QUESTIONS, REASONABLY, MULTIPLY – Ibid, Shay McNeal, *The Secret Plot to Save The Tsar*, pp. 265-66.

106 MCNEAL'S REMARKABLY WELL-RESEARCHED BOOK WAS A TREMENDOUS CONTRIBUTOR TO THE WORLD'S KNOWLEDGE OF THE ROMANOV MYSTERY – Ibid, Shay McNeal, *The Secret Plot to Save The Tsar*, pp. 267-68.

FOUR – THEORIES & THISTLES

109 HARRIS WAS CONSUL-GENERAL IN IRKUTSK FROM 1918 TO 1921 – See biographical data found at http://socialarchive.iath.virginia.edu/xtf/view?docId=harris-ernest-lloyd-1870-1946-cr.xml.

109 BURIED ON PAGE 14 OF *THE GAZETTE* IN MONTREAL, DATED SATURDAY, DECEMBER 20, 1930 – *The Gazette,* December 30, 1930, p. 14.

109 *THE GAZETTE* ARTICLE BEGINS WITH THE FOLLOWING OPENING – Ibid, *The Gazette,* December 30, 1930, p. 14.

110 VERSHNEUDINSK WAS A SO-CALLED BUFFER STATE ESTABLISHED BY THE BOSHEVIKS CONSISTING OF AREAS EAST OF LAKE BAIKAL – *Reuter*, "Buffer State in Siberia: Evacuation By Allied Forces Requested," published in *Dominion*, Volume 13, Issue 205, 25 May 1920, Page 7, found at http://paperspast.natlib.govt.nz/cgi-bin/paperspast?a=d&d=DOM19200525.2.47.

110 AGAIN ACCORDING TO *THE GAZETTE* – *The Gazette,* December 30, 1930, p. 14.

110 MR. MACCORMAC IN HIS SPECIAL CABLE TO *THE GAZETTE* AND *THE NEW YORK TIMES* REPORTS – Ibid, *The Gazette,* December 30, 1930, p. 14.

111 SIR MILES WAS A CAREER DIPLOMAT FOR THE UNITED KINGDOM – Personal archives of Sir Miles Lampson found at http://www.sant.ox.ac.uk/mec/MEChandlists/Lampson-Killearn-Collection.pdf.

112 HARRIS RELAYS TO MACCORMAC THAT THE TRUNK WAS "ACTUALLY TURNED OVER TO ME BY GENERAL DIETRICH – *The Gazette*, December 30, 1930, p. 14.

112 AMAZINGLY, HARRIS THEN ADMITS TO CORRESPONDENT MACCORMAC THAT HE NEVER OPENED THE TRUNK ALLEGEDLY CONTAINING THE TSAR'S REMAINS – Ibid, *The Gazette*, December 30, 1930, p. 14.

112 NIKOLAI SOKOLOV DIED IMPOVERISHED IN FRANCE IN 1924 FROM A HEART ATTACK FOLLOWING A LONG ILLNESS – See http://www.loc.gov/loc/lcib/9602/romanov.html.

112 HARRIS CONTENDS THAT SOKOLOV STAYED WITH HIM UNTIL THE HARRIS PARTY REACHED MANCHURIA STATION – *The Gazette*, December 30, 1930, p. 14.

112 I DON'T KNOW DIRECTLY WHAT HAPPENED TO IT AFTERWARDS, BUT I UNDERSTAND THAT SIR MILES LAMPSON TURNED THE TRUNK OVER TO GENERAL JANIN – Ibid, *The Gazette*, December 30, 1930, p. 14.

113 HARRIS PLEADS THAT HE DOES NOT WISH TO ENTER INTO THE CONTROVERSY BREWING AT THE TIME – Ibid, *The Gazette*, December 30, 1930, p. 14.

113 FROM *THE GAZETTE:* WE GET THE FOLLOWING – Ibid, *The Gazette*, December 30, 1930, p. 14.

113 ON THE SAME PAGE OF THE DECEMBER 30TH NEWSPAPER, GENERAL JANIN – *The Gazette*, December 30, 1930, p. 14.

114 NOT TO BE OUTDONE BY HARRIS IN HIS ASTOUNDING CONCLUSIONS, GENERAL JANIN TELLS MACCORMAC – Ibid, *The Gazette*, December 30, 1930, p. 14.

114 "I LEARNED SUBSEQUENTLY," SAYS GENERAL JANIN, "THAT HIS INTENTION WAS TO SEND THEM TO GENERAL WRANGEL IN CRIMEA - Ibid, *The Gazette*, December 30, 1930, p. 14.

114 A THIRD ARTICLE IN THE COLUMN BELOW THE STORY ON GENERAL JANIN, THEN GOES ON TO REPORT THAT THE GRAND DUCHESS MARIE PAVLOVNA OF RUSSIA – Ibid, *The Gazette*, December 30, 1930, p. 14.

114 "WHETHER IT IS TRUE THAT THE ASHES ARE NOW REPOSING IN GENERAL JANIN'S FAMILY VAULT OR NOT – THAT I DO NOT KNOW" - Ibid, *The Gazette*, December 30, 1930, p. 14.

FIVE – AIDE'S COVENANT

132 ON DECEMBER 28, 1918, WOODROW WILSON CELEBRATED HIS SIXTY-SECOND BIRTHDAY IN LONDON, ENGLAND AT BUCKINGHAM PALACE - John Milton Cooper, Jr., *Woodrow Wilson: A Biography*, Alfred A. Knopf, New York, NY, 2009, ISBN: 978-0-307-26541-8, p. 454.

133 WITNESSING IN HIS YOUTH THE RAVAGES OF THE CIVIL WAR - Wikipedia found at: http://en.wikipedia.org/wiki/Woodrow_Wilson.

134 WHEN HE ARRIVED AT THE HOUSE OF WINDSOR ON THAT DECEMBER DAY – This phrase is often attributed to Woodrow Wilson but Wilson biographer John Milton Cooper, Jr. attributes the phrase to British Prime Minister David Lloyd George. See John Milton Cooper, *Breaking*

The Heart of The World: Woodrow Wilson and the Fight for the League of Nations, Cambridge, England: Cambridge University Press, 2001, pp. 415-16, and See 25th Amendment of the Constitution of the United States for more detail.

134 WILSON, WHO HISTORY HAS OBSERVED WAS THE FIRST AND ONLY PRESIDENT OF THE UNITED STATES TO EARN A PH.D. - John Milton Cooper, Jr., *Woodrow Wilson: A Biography*, p. 3.

134 PRESIDENT WILSON'S BIGGEST DECISION OF HIS TWO-TERM PRESIDENCY WAS THE FATEFUL DECISION TO GO TO WAR WITH GERMANY - Ibid, John Milton Cooper, Jr., *Woodrow Wilson: A Biography*, p. 4.

136 *THE AIDE-MÉMOIRE,* ADDRESSED TO "THE SECRETARY OF STATE TO THE ALLIED AMBASSADORS," WAS AN UNSIGNED SEVEN-PAGE DOCUMENT PRESIDENT WILSON USED - President Woodrow Wilson, *The Aide-Mémoire*, July 17, 1918.

136 ACCORDING TO WILSON - President Woodrow Wilson, *The Aide-Mémoire*, July 17, 1918.

136 WILSON CONTINUED - President Woodrow Wilson, *The Aide-Mémoire*, July 17, 1918.

137 WILSON APPEARS TO OUTLINE THREE OBJECTIVES FOR THE AEF IN RUSSIA ACCORDING TO HIS *THE AIDE-MÉMOIRE* - AEF Siberia web site found at: https://sites.google.com/a/bates.edu/aefsiberia/home/allied-intervention.

138 A BOLD MOVE SUCH AS THIS FOURTH UNSTATED OBJECTIVE TO RESCUE THE TSAR WOULD NOT BE OUT OF CHARACTER FOR PRESIDENT WILSON – John Milton Cooper, Jr., *Woodrow Wilson: A Biography*, p. 8.

139 THAT WILSON WOULD MICROMANAGINGLY AUTHOR SUCH A GROUNDBREAKING DOCUMENT IN SUCH GREAT SECRECY FROM MEMBERS OF HIS CABINET, WAS AN AMAZING FEAT – Ibid, John Milton Cooper, Jr., *Woodrow Wilson: A Biography*, p. 391.

139 COOPER ALSO SAYS – Ibid, John Milton Cooper, Jr., *Woodrow Wilson: A Biography*, pp. 5-6.

140 ON JULY 6, 1918, ACCORDING TO NOTES FOUND IN THE AEF SIBERIA ARCHIVE - AEF website.

140 ACCORDING TO A REPORT ON THE ENCOUNTER – AEF website.

140 NEWTON DIEHL BAKER, JR., WOODROW WILSON'S SECRETARY OF WAR WAS AN AMERICAN PROGRESSIVE – Information found at www.bakerlaw.com.

141 IT WAS BAKER WHO RECOMMENDED GENERAL PERSHING BE APPOINTED COMMAND-IN-CHIEF OF THE AMERICAN EXPEDITIONARY FORCES IN WORLD WAR I – Frederick P. Keppel, "Newton D. Baker: America At War", *Foreign Affairs*, April 1938 found at: https://www.foreignaffairs.com/articles/1938-04-01/newton-d-baker.

142 PRESIDENT WILSON'S SECRETARY OF STATE ROBERT LANSING WAS SECRETARY BAKER'S POLITICAL POLAR OPPOSITE – United States Department of State, Brief History of the U.S. Diplomatic Security Service found at: http://www.state.gov/m/ds/about/history/index.htm .

142 LANSING "WAS THE MOST UNSATISFACTORY SECRETARY," IN PRESIDENT WILSON'S cabinet – John Milton Cooper, Jr., *Woodrow Wilson: A Biography*, p. 383, and A. Scott Berg, *Wilson*, G. P. Putnam's Sons, New York, NY, 2013, p. 667.

143 LANSING WAS SO UNPOPULAR WITH WILSON – Josephus Daniels. *The Navy and the Nation: War-Time Addresses*. New York, NY: George H. Doran Publishing, 1919.

143 BORN IN 1864 IN EASTON, PENNSYLVANIA, AND A WEST POINT MILITARY ACADEMY GRADUATE – Willett, Robert L. *Russian Sideshow: America's Undeclared War 1918-1920*. Washington, DC: Brassey's, 2003, p. 264.

144 *THE AIDE-MÉMOIRE* WAS DELIVERED TO MAJOR GENERAL WILLIAM SIDNEY GRAVES FROM HIS COMMANDER-IN-CHIEF IN A TRAIN STATION IN KANSAS CITY, MISSOURI – William Sidney Graves, *America's Siberian Adventure, 1918-1920*, New York, NY: P. Smith, 1941, p. 3.

144 GRAVES WAS A POLITICALLY ADEPT SOLDIER WITH GREAT INSTINCTS – John Milton Cooper, Jr., *Woodrow Wilson: A Biography*, p. 401.

145 AGAIN COOPER OBSERVES OF CIRCUMSTANCES: CONGRESS WOULD HAVE VOTED AGAINST GOING TO WAR HAD THEY

BEEN ABLE TO RELY UPON A SECRET BALLOT – Ibid, John Milton Cooper, Jr., *Woodrow Wilson: A Biography*, p. 381.

145 ON APRIL 2, 1917, PRESIDENT WILSON ASKED CONGRESS FOR A DECLARATION OF WAR ON GERMANY – A. Scott Berg, *Wilson*, p. 435.

146 THE CHAMBER, BERG NOTES, ERUPTED IN CHEERS – Ibid, A. Scott Berg, *Wilson*.

146 WILSON, WHO CLEARLY DID NOT HAVE A LOT OF FOREIGN POLICY OR WAR TRAINING IN HIS RECORD BEFORE HE BECAME PRESIDENT – John Milton Cooper, Jr., *Woodrow Wilson: A Biography*, p. 396.

147 THE FOLLOWING ACCOUNT, COOPER WROTE, SUMS UP WILSON'S PREFERRED WAY OF DOING BUSINESS – Ibid, John Milton Cooper, Jr., *Woodrow Wilson: A Biography*, p. 435.

147 COOPER SAYS THAT GENERAL PERSHING WOULD SEE WILSON FACE-TO-FACE FOR THE FIRST AND ONLY TIME DURING THE WAR – Ibid, John Milton Cooper, Jr., *Woodrow Wilson: A Biography*, pp. 401-02.

147 WILSON, ACCORDING TO COOPER, BELIEVED THAT PRESIDENT ABRAHAM LINCOLN DURING THE AMERICAN CIVIL WAR, "HAD MADE MISTAKES IN WAGING WAR"- Ibid, John Milton Cooper, Jr., *Woodrow Wilson: A Biography*, p. 390.

148 GEORGE F. KENNAN WAS AN AMERICAN DIPLOMAT WHO WAS ALSO KNOWN AS BEING THE FATHER OF ONE OF AMERICA'S MOST PROMINENT FOREIGN POLICIES:

CONTAINMENT – John Lewis Gaddis, *George F. Kennan: An American Life*, W.W. Norton & Co, New York, NY: 2011. ISBN: 978-1594203121.

148 A UNIVERSITY OF MICHIGAN MISSIVE ON THE DECISION TO INTERVENE, BASED ON KENNAN'S WORK – *Woodrow Wilson and the Russian Intervention: A Study in Chaos Management*, Michigan State University, found at: https://www.msu.edu/~mageemal/Russia.doc, p. 1.

148 THE ARTICLE GOES ON TO SAY THAT IT WAS NOT CLEAR ON WHAT THE PRESIDENT WANTED THEM TO DO WITH THE POLICY TO INTERVENE IN SIBERIA – Ibid, *Woodrow Wilson and the Russian Intervention*, and George F. Kennan, *Soviet American Relations, 1917-1920, Russia Leaves the War*, Princeton University Press, Princeton, NJ: 1956, p. 81.

149 ACCORDING TO THE ARTICLE AGAIN, "LENIN'S RISE TO POWER HAD TO BE STOPPED …" – *Woodrow Wilson and the Russian Intervention*, p. 3.

149 FROM OUR PERSPECTIVE, THE AUTHORS OF THE INCENDIARY ARTICLE – *Woodrow Wilson and the Russian Intervention*, and George F. Kennan, *Soviet American Relations, 1917-1920, Russia Leaves the War*, Princeton University Press, Princeton, NJ: 1956, p. 81.

149 THE AUTHORS OF THE "CHAOS MANAGEMENT" ARTICLE CONCLUDE THAT, "BOTH WILSON AND LENIN OPPOSED SECRET DEALS" – *Woodrow Wilson and the Russian Intervention*, p. 3.

149 EVEN MORE ASTOUNDING, THE AUTHORS THEN GO ON TO ASSET THAT IN THEIR ESTIMATION, THERE IS A VERY CLEAR OBJECTIVE WHEN ADDRESSING THE PRESIDENT'S, *AIDE-MÉMOIRE* – Ibid, *Woodrow Wilson and the Russian Intervention*, p. 5.

149 AND, THEN, THEY ADD THIS: "WILSON MAY HAVE THOUGHT HE WAS MAKING HISTORY …" – Ibid, *Woodrow Wilson and the Russian Intervention*, p. 5.

149 TO MAKE MATTERS MORE CONFUSING – Ibid, *Woodrow Wilson and the Russian Intervention*, p. 6.

150 PERHAPS TRUE ON SOME ELEMENTS BUT CLEARLY WRONG WHEN IT COMES TO THE MAIN PREMISE – A Phrase that is attributed in later chapters to Franklin Delano Roosevelt as written in *The President's Mystery Story.*

150 SECRETARY OF THE UNITED STATES TREASURY WILLIAM G. MCADOO – Philip M. Chase, Ph.D., *William Gibbs McAdoo: The last Progressive, (1863 – 1941),* University of Southern California Dissertation, 2008, found at: ProQuest Dissertations and Theses, http://gradworks.umi.com/33/41/3341909.html, abstract page and specifically, pp. 11-12.

151 MCADOO WAS BORN ON A FARM IN MARIETTA, GEORGIA - Philip M. Chase, Ph.D., *William Gibbs McAdoo: The last Progressive, (1863 – 1941),* p. 7 and p. 14, Chase, and John Broesamle, William Gibbs McAdoo, A Passion for Change: 1863-1917, Port Washington, NY: Kennikat, 1973, and, Daniel Gross, "The Unknown Financial Superhero: The amazing story of William McAdoo, and

how he saved the American economy," *Slate Magazine,* March 22, 2007, found at: http://www.slate.com/articles/business/moneybox/2007/03/the_unknown_financial_superhero.html and, Silber, William L., *When Washington Shut Down Wall Street: The Great Financial Crisis of 1914 and the Origins of America's Monetary Supremacy,* Princeton University Press, Princeton, N.J., 2007, ISBN 978-0-691-12747-7.

154 AND YET, DESPITE HIS MORALISTIC APPROACH TO MANY POLITICAL QUESTIONS - Additional biographical information found at http://millercenter.org/president/wilson/essays/cabinet/463 and, Philip M. Chase, Ph.D., *William Gibbs McAdoo: The last Progressive, (1863 – 1941),* pp. 406-07.

155 CHASE NOTES IN HIS DISSERTATION THAT MCADOO RESIGNED HIS POST AT AGE 55 AS WILSON'S TREASURY SECRETARY – Philip M. Chase, Ph.D., *William Gibbs McAdoo: The last Progressive, (1863 – 1941),* pp. 146-47.

155 COLONEL EDWARD MANDELL HOUSE – A. Scott Berg, *Wilson,* p. 19, John Milton Cooper, Jr., *Woodrow Wilson: A Biography,* p. 383, and Encyclopedia of Arkansas History and Culture maintained by the Arkansas Library System found at: http://www.encyclopediaofarkansas.net/encyclopedia/entry-detail.aspx?entryID=5083.

157 CHARLES RICHARD CRANE – Norman E. Saul, *The Life and Times of Charles R. Crane, 1858-1939: American Businessman, Philanthropist, and a Founder of Russian Studies in America.* Lexington, Lanham, MD, 2013.

157 AS THE WORLD WAR WAS CLOSING, THE ELECTIONS OF 1918 – Ibid, Norman E. Saul, *The Life and Times of Charles R. Crane, 1858-1939: American Businessman, Philanthropist, and a Founder of Russian Studies in America.*

158 COOPER SAID THAT, "IT WAS NOT CONSIDERED A REFERENDUM ON WILSON'S FOREIGN POLICY – John Milton Cooper, Jr., *Woodrow Wilson: A Biography*, pp. 446-47.

158 INCAPACITATED, PARALYZED, BROKEN - From The Nobel Prize website found at: http://www.nobelprize.org/nobel_prizes/peace/laureates/1919/wilson-facts.html.

158 ONCE OUT OF OFFICE, THE PREDICTIONS FOR WILSON'S PRESIDENCY AND ROLE IN THE WORLD STARTED TO FLOW – A. Scott Berg, *Wilson*, p. 705.

158 BERG ALSO WRITES THAT FRANK I. COBB SECONDED SMUT'S OPINION – A. Scott Berg, *Wilson*, pp. 705-06.

SIX – POLAR BEARS & WOLFHOUNDS

161 "THE SENDING OF THIS EXPEDITION WAS THE LAST OCCASION IN WHICH THE PRESIDENT REVERSED THE RECOMMENDATION OF THE WAR DEPARTMENT" – Robert L. Willett, *Russian Sideshow: America's Undeclared War 1918-1920*. Washington, DC: Brassey's, 2003, p. 264.

161 IT WAS CONSIDERED TO BE ONE OF THE MORE DIFFICULT DECISIONS OF WOODROW WILSON'S PRESIDENCY - George F. Kennan, *Soviet American Relations, 1917-1920, The*

Decision to Intervene. Princeton, University Press. Princeton, NJ, 1958.

162 A GRADUATE OF THE U.S. MILITARY ACADEMY AT WEST POINT - Major General William S. Graves (Ret), *America's Siberian Adventure,* Peter Smith, New York, NY, 1941 and reprinted 1971, p. 4, and Betty Miller Unterberger, *America's Siberian Expedition, 1918-1920.* Duke University Press, Durham, NC, 1956, p. 76.

163 WILSON'S ARMY CHIEF OF STAFF, GENERAL PEYTON C. MARCH - Robert L. Willett, *Russian Sideshow: America's Undeclared War 1918-1920,* p. 264.

164 BY THE FOLLOWING SPRING, THE 31ST INFANTRY FOUND ITSELF DISTRIBUTED ALONG THE RAILROAD lines - Gary Mead, The Doughboys: *America and the First World War,* Overlook Press, New York, NY, 2000, p. 279, 27th Infantry Regimental Historical Society, "The 27th Infantry - AEF Siberia," March 18, 2001 and November 6, 2002, and Gibson Bell Smith, Guarding the Railroad, Taming the Cossacks: The U.S. Army in Russia, 1918-1920 , The National Archives, Vol 34, No. 4, 2002 found at http://www.archives.gov/publications/ prologue/2002/winter/us-army-in-russia-1.html.

164 GENERAL GRAVES' DUTIES AS THE COMMANDING OFFICER OF THE AMERICAN EXPEDITIONARY FORCES SIBERIA DID NOT COME WITHOUT GREAT ANGST - G. Russell Evans. *Maj. Gen. William S. Graves, U.S. Army – Truly a Soldier of the Old School,* May 26, 2002.

165 ARMY CHIEF OF STAFF MARCH, EVEN THOUGH HE WAS QUESTIONING WILSON HIMSELF FOR INTERVENING - Major General William Sidney Graves (ret.), *America's Siberian Adventures, 1918-1920,* p. xi.

167 FORMED IN JANUARY 1918, THEIR OFFICIAL NAME WAS THE RED WORKERS' AND PEASANTS' ARMY - Erich Wollenberg, *The Red Army*, "The Scheme For A Socialist Army, Decree issued by the Council of People's Commissars on January 15, 1918", found at: http://www.marxistsfr.org/history/ussr/government/red-army/1937/wollenberg-red-army/append01.htm.

168 BUT IN EARLIER DAYS OF WORLD WAR I, THE RED ARMY WAS CONSIDERED TO BE AN ASSET IN THE ALLIED FORCES DEFEAT OF THE KAISER'S GERMANY - Norman Davies, *The Sunday Times*, 11 May 2006, Lewis Siegelbaum, "1917: Red Guard into Army", *Seventeen Moments in Soviet History* found at: http://soviethistory.macalester.edu/index.php?page=subject&SubjectID=1917army&Year=1917 and, Dmitri Volkogono and Harold Shukman, eds., *Trotsky: The Eternal Revolutionary*, HarperCollins, London, England, 1996, p. 180.

169 THE PRIMARY MISSION OF THE WHITE RUSSIANS WAS TO OPPOSE THE RED RUSSIANS AND, IF POSSIBLE, RESTORE THE TSARIST MONARCHY - Christopher Lazarski, "White Propaganda Efforts in the South during the Russian Civil War, 1918–19," *The Slavonic and East European Review*, Vol. 70, No. 4, October 1992, pp. 688–707.

169 THE WHITES WERE DECIDEDLY CONSERVATIVE AND HIGHLY PATRIOTIC - Peter Kenez, "The Ideology of the White Movement," *Soviet Studies*, 1980, no. 32. pp. 58–83 as found at: http://en.wikipedia.org/wiki/White_movement#cite_note-Ideology-3.

170 MANY OF THE WHITE'S LEADERS, NOT SURPRISINGLY, CAME FROM MILITARY LEADERS OF THE FORMER TSARIST RUSSIA - Christopher Lazarski, "White Propaganda Efforts in the

South during the Russian Civil War, 1918–19, *The Slavonic and East European Review*, pp. 688–707.

171 BRITAIN'S TROOPS WERE FEW SINCE THE COUNTRY WAS FIGHTING THE WAR WITH THE GERMANS ON SEVERAL FRONTS – Found at: http://www.nam.ac.uk/research/famous-units/middlesex-regiment-duke-cambridges-own and http://www.regiments.org/regiments/uk/inf/057Midx.htm.

172 KNOWN AS THE CANADIAN SIBERIAN EXPEDITIONARY FORCE – P. Whitney Lackenbauer, "Why Siberia? Canadian Foreign Policy and Siberian Intervention, 1918-19," The University of Waterloo.

172 THE CZECH LEGION CONSISTING OF VOLUNTEER TROOPS SEEKING INDEPENDENCE – John F.N. Bradley, *The Czechoslovak Legion in Russia, 1914–1920.* East European Monographs, New York: Boulder/Columbia University Press, 1991, ISBN 0-88033-218-2.

173 JAPAN HAD INTERESTING MOTIVATIONS TO FIGHT THE WAR IN RUSSIA – Ian Gow. *Military Intervention in Pre-War Japanese Politics: Admiral Kato Kanji and the 'Washington System'*. Routlege, 2005, pp. 55-61.

SEVEN – RECONSTRUCTING TIMELINES

176 RECONSTRUCTING TIMELINES – The timeline information cited in this chapter comes from a wide variety of excellent sources and is summarized here for validation purposes unless otherwise noted below. The research depicted is not original, other than for its organization. The archives and historical societies for the AEF, 27th and 31st Infantry, are replete with detail which has been used

here to reconstruct the timelines of the American Expeditionary Forces in Siberia in order to help validate or invalidate Martin Hutson's account. It represents the work of many wonderful authors and researchers who hold this time in world history dear to them as well.

184 THE FIRST AMERICAN RED CROSS MISSION ARRIVES IN PETROGRAD - Wolfhounds p. 86-89.

185 THE CHIEF OF THE AMERICAN RED CROSS MISSION TO RUSSIA, RAYMOND ROBINS, VISITS A RUSSIAN UNIT NEAR STALNA AND RECORDS IN HIS DIARY – Wikipedia has an excellent synopsis of the Siberian intervention found at: Smalser War College study on Graves, p 3.

186 KNOX REVEALS HIS FEELINGS TOWARD THE BOLSHEVIKS IN A CONVERSATION THAT IS HELD AT THE HOTEL EUROPE IN PETROGRAD – Wolfhounds, p. 12.

187 "ON 11 NOVEMBER 1917, JUST FOUR DAYS AFTER LENIN AND HIS FELLOW BOLSHEVIKS SEIZED CONTROL OF THE RUSSIAN CAPITAL – Village Green Denison p. 2.

188 ARRIVING IN DECEMBER, JOHNSON FINDS THE PORT IN GREAT TURMOIL – Smalser on Graves, Appendix 1.

188 THE FIRST JAPANESE CRUISER ARRIVES IN VLADIVOSTOK – Smalser on Graves, Appendix 1.

189 THE BOLSHEVIKS SIGN THE TREATY OF BREST-LITOVSK WITH THE GERMANS – Wolfhounds account p. 29.

189 THE BOLSHEVIKS AGREE TO PERMIT CZECHS TO RETURN TO EUROPE VIA VLADIVOSTOK – Smalser on Graves, Appendix 1 and Wolfhounds, p. 29.

189 ALLIED FORCES DECIDE TO OFFICIALLY INTERVENE IN SIBERIA – Village Green p. 5.

190 TWO LEAD INFANTRY REGIMENTS UNDER THE COMMAND OF THE LEGION'S CHIEF OF STAFF, GENERAL MILO K. DIETRICH, REACH VLADIVOSTOK – Wolfhounds account, p. 29.

190 THE AMERICAN CONSUL GENERAL AT IRKUTSK, ERNEST HARRIS, ORDERS AN END TO MEDIATION EFFORTS – Village Green p. 7.

190 OPEN, UNRESTRAINED FIGHTING BREAKS OUT – Wolfhounds account p. 31. Wolfhounds account p. 31.

191 THE U.S. STATE DEPARTMENT AGREES TO ALLOW OVERALL JAPANESE COMMAND OF THE WAR EFFORT FOR THE TIME BEING – Smalser on Graves, pp. 12-13.

191 TSAR NICHOLAS II IS REPORTEDLY ASSASSINATED IN YEKATERINBURG – Melton, p. 23, March p. 74, and AEF Siberia, pp. 2-3.

193 "DURING AUGUST, 1918 GENERAL GRAVES COORDINATED LOGISTICS FOR THE OPERATION DIRECTLY WITH GENERAL C.A. DEVOL … "– Smalser on Graves, pp. 19-20, and Wolfhounds, p. 49.

194 BRITAIN'S 25TH BATTALION, THE MIDDLESEX REGIMENT IN HONG KONG, WAS ORDERED TO VLADIVOSTOK – Wolfhounds, p. 49.

195 THE U.S. DEPARTMENT OF STATE ISSUES A PRESS RELEASE – Wolfhounds, p. 37.

196 GENERAL GRAVES RECEIVES A CABLE THAT UPDATES HIM ON THE PHILIPPINE TROOPS THAT WOULD BE AT HIS DISPOSAL FOR SIBERIA – AEF Siberia, p. 5.

196 THE 27TH INFANTRY UNDER THE COMMAND OF COLONEL HENRY D. STYER SAILED FROM THE PHILIPPINES –

Wolfhounds, p. 73, Chapter 2 Siberia p. 1, and Smalser on Graves p. 9.

197 THE SITUATION WAS, NOT SURPRISINGLY, DESCRIBED AS CHAOTIC – Chapter 2 Siberia p. 1.

198 MAJOR GENERAL WILLIAM S. GRAVES, A TEXAN WHO HAD BEEN DECORATED FOR BRAVERY – Chapter 2 Siberia p 2.

199 IT WAS REPORTED THAT EARLIER IN 1918, PRESIDENT WOODROW WILSON HAD SENT OTHER SERVICE AGENCIES TO ASSIST IN SIBERIA – Smalser on Graves, pp. 9-10.

199 THE REGIMENT'S MAIN BODY AND 115 TONS OF BAGGAGE, AMMUNITION AND REGIMENTAL PROPERTY - Wolfhounds, p. 73.

200 GRAVES, WITH THE FIRST OF HIS CALIFORNIA-BASED TROOPS, LEAVES CAMP FREMONT ON TWO TRAINS – Wolfhounds, p. 74.

200 BEGINNING IN MID-AUGUST, THE FIRST OF SOME 3,000 AMERICAN TROOPS DISEMBARK AT VLADIVOSTOK – Wolfhounds, p, 76.

200 ACCORDING TO REPORTS: "COLONEL HENRY STYER WAS THE 27TH INFANTRY COMMANDER – Smalser on Graves, pp. 10-11.

201 THE 31ST INFANTRY SETS UP A TENT CAMP EAST OF THE CITY – Chapter 2 Siberia p. 3, Village Green Denison p. 3, Wolfhounds p. 75 and 108.

202 THE 31ST INFANTRY'S FIRST COMBAT ACTION OCCURRED AT UGOLNAYA – Wolfhounds, p. 108.

203 EMERSON AND JOHNSON ARE REPORTED TO HAVE ARRIVED BACK IN VLADIVOSTOK – Village Green p. 8.

204 GENERAL GRAVES ARRIVES IN VALDIVOSTOK, RUSSIA WITH COMPANIES A, B AND I - Smalser on Graves, p. 12.

204 THE *THOMAS*, WITH MAJOR GENERAL GRAVES ON BOARD, DOCKS AT VLADIVOSTOK - Wolfhounds p. 75 and Smalser on Graves, p. 12.

204 FOUR DAYS AFTER THE GRAVES-OTANI MEETING - Smalser on Graves, p. 13.

205 GRAVES RECEIVES WORD FROM CZECH AUTHORITIES - AEF Siberia, p. 8.

205 ADDITIONAL TRIPS BY THE US TRANSPORTS - Wolfhounds p. 76.

206 REPLACEMENTS FROM CAMP FREMONT ARRIVED AT VLADIVOSTOK - Wolfhounds pp. 76-77.

206 "DUE TO HEAVY CASUALTIES FROM BOLSHEVIK OFFENSIVES …" - AEF Siberia, p. 12, and Graves, p. 143.

207 REPORTS FROM THIS PERIOD SAY THAT - Smalser on Graves, pp. 13-15.

208 IT IS FURTHER REPORTED IN THE ARCHIVES THAT IN OCTOBER 1918, GENERAL GRAVES ALLOWED *NEW YORK TIMES* CORRESPONDENT, CARL ACKERMAN TO JOIN HIM …" - AEF Siberia, p. 11.

209 REPORTS FROM THIS PERIOD OF TIME SAY: "THE SITUATION WAS RELATIVELY CALM FROM OCTOBER 1918 THROUGH MARCH 1919" - Wolfhounds p. 122.

210 OFFICIAL REPORTS INDICATE THAT THE 31ST INFANTRY GREW TO 3589 MEN - Chapter 2 Siberia, p. 4 and p. 7.

211 H COMPANY OF THE 31ST INFANTRY IS POSITIONED EAST OF VLADIVOSTOK - Wolfhounds, p. 37.

211 H COMPANY MOVES TO THE SUCHAN MINES REGION - Wolfhounds, p. 135.

212 THE ALLIES AGREE TO ASSUME RESPONSIBILITY FOR THE RAIL LINE'S SECURITY AND OPERATION - Chapter 2 Siberia and Smalser on Graves, p. 17.

212 THE REQUIREMENT FOR CONTINUOUS RAILWAY OPERATIONS AS A MEANS OF TRANSPORTATION AND COMMUNICATION MADE COOPERATION - Wolfhounds, pp. 141-42.

213 GRAVES PUBLISHES A PROCLAMATION TO THE RUSSIAN PEOPLE WHERE HE EXPLAINS HIS VIEWS - Wolfhounds, p. 143.

214 BEN JOHNSON OF THE RRSC VISITS YEKATERINBURG - Village Green, p. 11 footnote on paragraph #32.

215 THE 31ST INFANTRY ENTERS THE VILLAGE OF NOVITSKAYA AT AROUND 8 O'CLOCK PM - Smalser on Graves, p. 18.

217 SKIRMISHES, AS THEY ARE DESCRIBED, CONTINUE THROUGHOUT THE SHKOTOVO AREA - Smalser on Graves, p. 18.

217 MAJOR SIDNEY GRAVES, GENERAL GRAVES' SON, LEADS M COMPANY - Wolfhounds, p. 150.

217 C & D COMPANIES ATTACK RED PARTISANS AT KAZANKA - Wolfhounds, p. 155.

218 APPROXIMATELY 1,400 JAPANESE TROOPS ENTER THE SUCHAN VALLEY AREA - Wolfhounds, p. 161.

218 CAPTAIN RHOADS LEADS HIS FORCE FROM SUCHAN TO THE NOVO LITOVSKAYA VALLEY – Smalser on Graves, p. 18.

219 THE RHOADS PLATOON RESTED PASSES THROUGH THE VALLEY SEEKING INFORMATION – Smalser on Graves, p. 18.

219 CAPTAIN RHOADS, THROUGH HIS INTERPRETER, REPORTEDLY CALLED ON THE BOLSHEVIKS TO SURRENDER – Smalser on Graves, p. 18 and Chapter 2 Siberia.

220 CAPTAIN RHOADS' PLATOON RETURNS TO SUCHAN – Smalser on Graves, p. 18.

220 AEF HEADQUARTERS SIBERIA ORDERS AMERICANS TROOPS TO MEET THE *USAT MERRITT* IN AMERICA BAY – Wolfhounds, pp. 162-65.

221 THE 1ST PLATOON, H COMPANY, DEPARTS SUCHAN IN THE MORNING USING WAGONS – Wolfhounds, pp. 162-65.

221 "THE LAST AMERICANS, EXCEPT FOR A BURIAL DETAIL GUARD (A PLATOON FROM H COMPANY), LEFT AT 0600…." - Wolfhounds, pp. 162-65.

221 ROUGH WEATHER, IT IS NOTED, PREVENTS THE *MERRITT* FROM UNLOADING THE BURIAL DETAIL – Wolfhounds, p. 165.

221 THE AMERICANS LEAVE SUCHAN – Wolfhounds, p. 165.

222 THE *MERRITT* ARRIVES AT VLADIVOSTOK – Wolfhounds, p. 166.

222 "SHORTLY AFTER THE VISIT TO EKATERINBURG, JOHNSON WAS CONFRONTED WITH AN UNANTICIPATED CHALLENGE …" – Village Green, p. 11 note #33.

224 COMPANY H OCCUPIES SHMAKOVKA – Wolfhounds, p. 154.

224 THE UNITED STATES GOVERNMENT DECIDES TO SUPPORT KOLCHAK'S FORCES BY SUPPLYING RIFLES – Wolfhounds, p. 154.

225 AT 0500, LT. RYAN ARRIVES AT CHITA AND STOPS TO PURCHASE BEEF FOR HIS TROOPS – Wolfhounds, p. 155.

225 SIMILAR TO AN INCIDENT RECOUNTED BY MARTIN, A RUSSIAN ARMORED TRAIN PULLS ALONG SIDE LT. RYAN'S TRAIN AT 0245 – Wolfhounds, p. 155.

226 RYAN TRANSFERS THE RIFLES TO ADMIRAL KOLCHAK'S FORCES AT IRKUTSK – Wolfhounds, p. 154.

226 AS 1919 PROGRESSES, "THE STATE DEPARTMENT ALSO CAME TO BE ALIGNED AGAINST GRAVES" – Smalser on Graves, p. 16.

228 H COMPANY UNDER CAPTAIN RHOADS' COMMAND – Wolfhounds, p. 170.

228 H COMPANY, WHICH IS LISTED AS COMPRISING ONLY 100 SOLDIERS NOW – Wolfhounds, p. 166.

228 CHRISTMAS 1919 IS NOT RECORDED AS BEING A QUIET ONE FOR THE AMERICANS – Wolfhounds, p. 170.

230 ALL SPASSKOE-USSURI SECTOR TROOPS ARE REPORTED TO BE IN VLADIVOSTOK AND BEGIN DEPARTURE – Wolfhounds, p. 189.

230 ALL TROOPS FROM THE SHKOTOVO SECTOR ARE REPORTED MOVED TO VLADIVOSTOK – Wolfhounds, p. 190.

231 THE 31ST INFANTRY DEPARTS IN GROUPS FROM SIBERIA – Wolfhounds, p. 184.

231 THE LAST CONTINGENT OF THE 31ST INFANTRY LEAVES SIBERIA – Chapter 2 Siberia p. 17.

231 "ALLIED INTERVENTION ENDS" – Smalser on Graves, Appendix 1.

231 THE ENTIRE REGIMENT IS ASSEMBLED AT FORT WILLIAM MCKINLEY – Wolfhounds, p. 184.

232 THE LAST TRAIN LOAD OF ALLIED SOLDIERS REACH VLADIVOSTOK – Village Green, p. 12.

232 ALL ALLIED FORCES BUT THE JAPANESE HAVE SAILED FOR HOME OR OTHER locations – Village Green, p. 12.

233 THE AMERICAN TENETS OF SELF DETERMINATION AND SELF GOVERNMENT – SO ABLY EXPRESSED IN THE 'FOURTEEN POINTS' – Smalser on Graves, p. 21.

233 AEF SIBERIA PUT 9000 SOLDIERS IN HARM'S WAY FOR 20 MONTHS IN THE SUBARCTIC MISERY OF WORLD WAR I – Smalser on Graves, p. 22.

233 ALTHOUGH ESTEEMED IN THE EYES OF MANY – AEF Siberia, p. 6.

234 WASHINGTON WARNED GENERAL GRAVES THAT THE JAPANESE STRATEGY WAS LIKELY TO KEEP THE VARIOUS RUSSIAN FORCES APART – AEF Siberia, p. 6.

238 PAVEL IVANOV BOARD A JET IN MOSCOW AND CARRIES WITH HIM IN A BRITISH AIRWAYS TRAVEL BAG – Robert Massey, *The Final Chapter*, p. 82.

238 DR. WILLIAM HAMILTON, THE GAINESVILLE, FLORIDA MEDICAL EXAMINER - Robert Massey, *The Final Chapter*, p. 69.

239 DR. PETER GILL, PAVEL IVANOV, AND OTHERS PUT THEIR FINDINGS IN PRINT IN THEIR OWN WORDS - Robert Massey, *The Final Chapter*, p. 97.

EIGHT - WARRING COUSINS

243 *HE CHANGED THE FAMILY'S ROYAL NAME* - June 19, 1917.

244 DAVID LLOYD GEORGE - WAS ENGLAND'S PRIME MINISTER - Biographic information found at: http://www.bbc.co.uk/history/historic_figures/george_david_lloyd.shtml.

245 SIR WILLIAM WISEMAN - Biographical information available in The Papers of Sir William Wiseman, Yale University Manuscripts Collection, and, Keith Jeffery, *The Secret History of MI6; 1909-1949*, Penguin, London, England, 2010.

245 ARTHUR BALFOUR - Kenneth Young, *Arthur James Balfour: The Happy Life of the Politician, Prime Minister, Statesman and Philosopher, 1848–1930*, G. Bell and Sons, London, England, 1963.

246 PRINCE ARTHUR - Brian Harrison, ed.,"Arthur, Prince, First Duke of Connaught and Strathearn", *Oxford Dictionary of National Biography*, Oxford University Press, Oxford, England, 2004.

246 SIR THOMAS PRESTON - "Sir Thomas Preston Recalls Ekaterinberg," The Spectator, Archives, 11 March 1972, p. 19, found at:

http://archive.spectator.co.uk/article/11th-march-1972/19/sir-thomas-preston-recalls-ekaterinburg.

246 THE WAR WAS NOT YET REALLY A DAY OLD – Herman Bernstein. *The Willy-Nicky Correspondence: Being the Secret and Intimate Telegrams Exchanged between the Kaiser and the Tsar.* Knopf, New York, NY, 1918.

247 ON A PERSONAL SIDE, WILHELM, WHO HAS BEEN KAISER SINCE 1888 – Ibid, Herman Bernstein. *The Willy-Nicky Correspondence: Being the Secret and Intimate* Telegrams Exchanged Herman Bernstein. *The Willy-Nicky Correspondence: Being the Secret and Intimate Telegrams Exchanged between the Kaiser and the Tsar.*

247 WILHELM IN A MESSAGE THAT CROSSED THAT SAME EARLY MORNING HOUR TO NICHOLAS – Ibid, Herman Bernstein. *The Willy-Nicky Correspondence: Being the Secret and Intimate* Telegrams Exchanged Herman Bernstein. *The Willy-Nicky Correspondence: Being the Secret and Intimate Telegrams Exchanged between the Kaiser and the Tsar.*

248 "I FORESEE THAT VERY SOON I SHALL BE OVERWHELMED ..." – Ibid, Herman Bernstein. *The Willy-Nicky Correspondence: Being the Secret and Intimate* Telegrams Exchanged Herman Bernstein. *The Willy-Nicky Correspondence: Being the Secret and Intimate Telegrams Exchanged between the Kaiser and the Tsar.*

248 HE ALSO WRITES THE TSAR ON THE 29TH – Ibid, Herman Bernstein. *The Willy-Nicky Correspondence: Being the Secret and Intimate* Telegrams Exchanged Herman Bernstein. *The Willy-Nicky Correspondence: Being the Secret and Intimate Telegrams Exchanged between the Kaiser and the Tsar.*

248 ON JULY 30TH, WILHELM WRITES TO NICHOLAS – Ibid, Herman Bernstein. *The Willy-Nicky Correspondence: Being*

the Secret and Intimate Telegrams Exchanged Herman Bernstein. *The Willy-Nicky Correspondence: Being the Secret and Intimate Telegrams Exchanged between the Kaiser and the Tsar.*

248 NICHOLAS REPLIES THE NEXT DAY – Ibid, Herman Bernstein. *The Willy-Nicky Correspondence: Being the Secret and Intimate* Telegrams Exchanged Herman Bernstein. *The Willy-Nicky Correspondence: Being the Secret and Intimate Telegrams Exchanged between the Kaiser and the Tsar.*

249 TSAR NICHOLAS II PRESSES WILHELM NONETHELESS FOR ASSURANCE - Ibid, Herman Bernstein. *The Willy-Nicky Correspondence: Being the Secret and Intimate* Telegrams Exchanged Herman Bernstein. *The Willy-Nicky Correspondence: Being the Secret and Intimate Telegrams Exchanged between the Kaiser and the Tsar.*

250 HISTORIANS HAVE SAID THAT BOTH SIDES OF WILHELM'S FAMILY SUFFERED – David Fromkin, *The King and The Cowboy: Theodore Roosevelt and Edward the Seventh, Secret Partners,* The Penguin Press, London, England, 2008, p. 87.

251 PROOF, SOME SAY, OF THE KAISER'S ANTI-BRITISH VIEWPOINT – *The Daily Telegraph,* 28 October 1908, found at: http://wwi.lib.byu.edu/index.php/The_Daily_Telegraph_Affair.

251 TO MAKE MATTERS WORSE, PERHAPS IN KEEPING WITH THE PARANOIA – Michael Balfour, *The Kaiser and his Times,* Houghton Mifflin, New York, NY, 1964, pp. 350-51.

252 BRITISH PRIME MINISTER DAVID LLOYD GEORGE, IN ONE OF HIS MORE HYSTERICAL OR THEATRICAL MOMENTS – Nigel J. Ashton and Duco Hellema, "Hanging the Kaiser:

Anglo-Dutch Relations and the Fate of Wilhelm II, 1918–20", *Diplomacy & Statecraft, 2008,* Vol. 11, pp. 53–78.

252 UNLIKE HIS COUSIN NICKY, WILHELM WAS PERMITTED TO REMOVE - Giles Macdonogh, *The Last Kaiser: William the Impetuous*, London: Weidenfeld & Nicolson, 2001, p. 425.

NINE – WILSON'S BOYS

254 One of the most dashing men ever to wear the uniform – *The American Experience*, WGBH Boston/PBS.

255 THE DISTINGUISHED SERVICE CROSS IS PRESENTED TO JOHN J. PERSHING – DSC WEB SITE.

256 WHEN PERSHING TOOK OVER COMMAND OF THE U.S. TROOPS IN EUROPE DURING WORLD WAR I – A. SCOTT BERG, *WILSON*, G. P. PUTNAM'S SONS, NEW YORK, NY, 2013, P. 464.

257 THE MEXICO EXPEDITION HAD BEEN A POLITICALLY STRESSFUL EVENT IN PERSHING'S MILITARY CAREER – Ibid, A. Scott Berg, *Wilson*, pp. 390-91.

257 ON NEWTON BAKER'S FIRST DAY IN OFFICE AS SECRETARY OF WAR, VILLA – Ibid, A. Scott Berg, *Wilson*, pp. 390-91.

258 WILSON AUTHORIZES A "PUNATIVE EXPEDITION" WHOSE SOLE OBJECTIVE IS TO CAPTURE PONCHO VILLA – Ibid, A. Scott Berg, *Wilson*, p. 391.

258 INTO THIS POTENTIALLY VOLATILE POLITICAL AND DIPLOMATIC MIX, WILSON SENDS IN PERSHING – Ibid, A. Scott Berg, *Wilson*, p. 391.

258 WILSON DECIDES TO STAY IN BUT HIS POLITICAL OPPONENTS ON CAPITOL HILL CALL HIM TENTATIVE AND INDECISIVE – Ibid, A. Scott Berg, *Wilson*, pp. 392-93.

259 WILSON HOLDS STRONG AGAINST GOING TO WAR WITH MEXICO OVER THE CARRIZAL INCIDENT – Ibid, A. Scott Berg, *Wilson*, p. 464.

259 WILSON IS CRITICIZED FOR DOING TOO MUCH IN MEXICO AND NOT ENOUGH IN EUROPE – Ibid, A. Scott Berg, *Wilson*, p. 464.

260 ANOTHER STORY THAT IS RECOUNTED IN BERG'S BIOGRAPHY – Ibid, A. Scott Berg, *Wilson*, p. 394.

261 GEORGE HUTSON WAS MARTIN'S OLDER BROTHER AND A VALUED BLACK JACK PERSHING AIDE IN WORLD WAR I – DSC citation for George R. Hutson, War Department, General Orders No. 44 (1919), *The Military Times Hall of Valor*, found at: http://projects.militarytimes.com/citations-medals-awards/search.php?term=george+r+Hutson.

262 GRAVES WAS ALSO A FAMILY MAN GRAVES WAS ALSO A FAMILY MAN – Jack Stokes Ballard. *Commander and Builder of Western Forts: The Life and Times of Major General Henry C. Merriam, 1862-1901.* Texas A&M University Press. College Station, TX, 2012.

263 IN THE MEANTIME, FOR OUR PURPOSES IN THIS CHAPTER, SECRETARY OF WAR NEWTON BAKER – Major General William Sidney Graves (ret.), *America's Siberian Adventures, 1918-1920*, Jonathan Cape and Harrison Smith, Inc., New York, NY, 1931, pp. ix-x.

263 GENERAL JOHN J. PERSHING WAS INTRODUCED TO GRAVES' CAPABILITIES DURING HIS SERVICE IN THE SPANISH-AMERICAN WAR – Official internment biography with

Arlington National Cemetery, where Graves is buried with his wife. Found at: http://www.arlingtoncemetery.net/wgraves.htm.

264 THE GREAT SAN FRANCISCO EARTHQUAKE OF 1906 LEVELED MUCH OF THAT GREAT CITY – http://earthquake.usgs.gov/regional/nca/1906/18april/index.php.

264 THE COURT MARTIAL OF BILLY MITCHELL WAS AN EXTRAORDINARY EVENT – Rebecca Maksel, "The Billy Mitchell Court-Martial," *Air & Space Magazine*, Volume 24, No. 2, June-July 2009, pp. 46–49.

265 THE FORWARD ITSELF BY FORMER SECRETARY OF WAR NEWTON BAKER EXPLAINS HOW SIBERIA CAME ABOUT – Ibid, Major General William Sidney Graves (ret.), *America's Siberian Adventures, 1918-1920*, p. ix.

266 BAKER THEN ADDS FUEL TO THE FIRE – Ibid, Major General William Sidney Graves (ret.), *America's Siberian Adventures, 1918-1920*, p. xii.

266 IN FACT, IN THAT SAME FORWARD WHERE BAKER MAKES HIS ASTONISHING COMMENTS – Ibid, Major General William Sidney Graves (ret.), *America's Siberian Adventures, 1918-1920*, p. ix.

267 AT THE CENTER OF IT ALL, WHETHER HE LIKED IT OR NOT, WAS GENERAL WILLIAM SIDNEY GRAVES – As noted by the Army Chief of Staff in his report to the Secretary of War for the Fiscal Year ending June 30, 1920 as rightfully recounted by Major William Sidney Graves (ret.), *America's Siberian Adventures, 1918-1920*, see forward and p. xiii.

TEN – SPECIAL TRAIN #28

270 "TRAIN 28 ARRIVED ON TIME AT 6:00 AM." - National Archives II, RG43, Box 32, Entry 843.

270 NICHOLAS' IMPERIAL TRAINS WERE MAGNIFICENT – As attributed to Franklin Delano Roosevelt.

271 CONSIDER THIS DESCRIPTION OF THE IMPERIAL TRAIL – Valentina Tenikhina, *Royal Russia, The Imperial Trains, Nicholas II*, Royal Russia and Gilbert's Royal Books. © 2004-2010. Found at: http://www.angelfire.com/pa/ImperialRussian/royalty/russia/train.html.

273 *ROYAL RUSSIA*, WHO MAINTAINS AN EXCELLENT ARCHIVE ON THE IMPERIAL TRAINS – Ibid, Valentina Tenikhina, *Royal Russia, The Imperial Trains, Nicholas II.*

273 THE TSAR'S PRIVATE CAR WAS WHERE HIS PRIVATE WORLD REVOLVED – Ibid, Valentina Tenikhina, *Royal Russia, The Imperial Trains, Nicholas II.*

274 MORE DESCRIPTIONS FROM ROYAL RUSSIA ADD TO OUR UNDERSTANDING – Ibid, Valentina Tenikhina, *Royal Russia, The Imperial Trains, Nicholas II.*

275 THE MUSEUM IN FINLAND DESCRIBES THE CARRIAGES AS – Video and web site: *The Imperial Train in the Grand Duchy of Finland*, 2 minutes, 16 seconds, produced by the Finland Railway Museum, found at: http://www.angelfire.com/pa/ImperialRussian/blog/index.blog/1432989/the-imperial-train-in-the-grand-duchy-of-finland/.

276 SPECIAL TRAINS WERE THOSE TRAINS THAT CARRIED RRSC EXECUTIVES OR ALLIED FORCES OFFICERS AND U.S. STATE

DEPARTMENT PERSONNEL – Latest such examination occurred November 6, 2014.

276 IN REVIEWING THE TRAIN SCHEDULES FROM THAT PERIOD OF TIME IN THE NATIONAL ARCHIVES' SECTION ON THE AMERICAN EXPEDITIONARY FORCE SIBERIA – Ibid, National Archives II, RG43, Box 32, Entry 843.

277 ANOTHER INTRIGUING NOTE IS ATTACHED THAT OBSERVES THAT RUSSIAN RAILROAD SERVICE CORPS CHAIRMAN STEVENS ALSO ARRIVED IN HARBIN YARD – Interview at National Archives II, College Park, Maryland, November 6, 2014.

277 ANOTHER SUPPORTING NOTE TO MARTIN'S STORY COMES FROM MCNEAL – Shay McNeal, *The Secret Plot to Save the Tsar: The Truth Behind The Romanov Mystery*, William Morrow, New York, NY, 2001, p. 37.

278 NATIONAL ARCHIVES RECORDS ALSO NOTE – Records "Relating to the International Commissions, Committees, and Councils," p. 193, 20 February 1991 inventory, National Archives II, RG 43.

278 MARTIN'S CONVERSATIONS RECOUNTED TO MEMBERS OF HIS FAMILY THAT WERE NOT RECORDED – This particular compilation was constructed from discussions among Ben Everidge (author and great nephew), Fred Martin, Jr. (grandson), Ken Martin (grandson), Mary Ruth (daughter), Dorothy Martin (daughter), and Nancy Everidge (niece). If not common knowledge among the relatives, the source of the discussion is noted otherwise.

286 TO HELP DISSECT THE PERSONALITIES INVOLVED – Helen, Rappaport, *The Romanov Sisters: The Lost Lives of the Daughters of Nicholas and Alexandra,* St. Martin's Press, New York, NY, 2014, ISBN: 978-1-250-02020-8.

287 TO SET THE STAGE FOR BETTER KNOWING THE IMPERIAL FAMILY'S PERSONAS – Ibid, Helen, Rappaport, *The Romanov Sisters: The Lost Lives of the Daughters of Nicholas and Alexandra,* pp. 3-4.

288 THE ROMANOV'S PRESENCE IN ALEXANDER PALACE, WAS EVERYWHERE – Ibid, Helen, Rappaport, *The Romanov Sisters: The Lost Lives of the Daughters of Nicholas and Alexandra,* p. 4.

288 CONTINUING HER DETAILED DESCRIPTION OF THE RESIDENCE, RAPPAPORT SAYS – Ibid, Helen, Rappaport, *The Romanov Sisters: The Lost Lives of the Daughters of Nicholas and Alexandra,* p. 4.

288 OF EMPRESS ALEXANDRA HERSELF – Ibid, Helen, Rappaport, *The Romanov Sisters: The Lost Lives of the Daughters of Nicholas and Alexandra,* p. 9.

288 RAPPAPORT CONTINUES - Ibid, Helen, Rappaport, *The Romanov Sisters: The Lost Lives of the Daughters of Nicholas and Alexandra,* p. 9.

289 ALEXANDRA'S MOTHER, ACCORDING TO RAPPAPORT, WAS AN ADMIRER OF THE FAMED NURSE, FLORENCE NIGHTINGALE – Ibid, Helen, Rappaport, *The Romanov Sisters: The Lost Lives of the Daughters of Nicholas and Alexandra,* p.11.

289 PRINCESS ALIX, AS THE FORMER EMPRESS WAS THEN KNOWN, WAS PRINCESS ALICE'S SIXTH CHILD – Ibid, Helen, Rappaport, *The Romanov Sisters: The Lost Lives of the Daughters of Nicholas and Alexandra,* p. 12.

290 RAPPAPORT SAYS THAT NICHOLAS, "NICKY," WAS 16 AND ALEXANDRA, "ALICKY," WAS 12 WHEN THEY FIRST MET –

Ibid, Helen, Rappaport, *The Romanov Sisters: The Lost Lives of the Daughters of Nicholas and Alexandra,* pp. 15-16.

290 RAPPAPORT NOTES ON ALEXANDRA'S APPEARANCE – Ibid, Helen, Rappaport, *The Romanov Sisters: The Lost Lives of the Daughters of Nicholas and Alexandra,* pp. 22-23.

290 ALEXANDRA IS DESCRIBED BY RAPPAPORT AS BEING "ENGLISH THROUGH AND THROUGH" – Ibid, Helen, Rappaport, *The Romanov Sisters: The Lost Lives of the Daughters of Nicholas and Alexandra,* p. 24.

291 OLGA WAS DESCRIBED AS HAVING HER MOTHER'S AND HER GRANDMOTHER ALICE'S ALTRUISTIC SPIRIT – Ibid, Helen, Rappaport, *The Romanov Sisters: The Lost Lives of the Daughters of Nicholas and Alexandra,* p. 34, 92 and 105.

291 TATIANA WAS SAID TO BE PALE-SKINNED, SLENDER, HAVING DARKER AUBURN HAIR WITH GREY EYES – Ibid, Helen, Rappaport, *The Romanov Sisters: The Lost Lives of the Daughters of Nicholas and Alexandra,* pp. 92-94.

292 MARIA ROMANOV WAS NOTED BY RAPPAPORT AS BEING THE MORE-SHY SISTER – IBID, HELEN, RAPPAPORT, *The Romanov Sisters: The Lost Lives of the Daughters of Nicholas and Alexandra,* p. 94, 106, 349, quoting Gibbs.

293 ANASTASIA HAD THE DOMINATING PERSONALITY IN THE FAMILY – Ibid, Helen, Rappaport, *The Romanov Sisters: The Lost Lives of the Daughters of Nicholas and Alexandra,* p. 94, 106, 349, quoting Gibbs.

294 THE TSAREVICH, ALEXEI, WAS DESCRIBED BY GIBBS IN RAPPAPORT'S ACCOUNT OF THE FAMILY, AS BEING "PAINFULLY SHY" – Ibid, Helen, Rappaport, *The Romanov Sisters: The Lost Lives of the Daughters of Nicholas and Alexandra,* p. 75, and 91.

294 RAPPAPORT PRODUCES EVIDENCE IN HER BOOK, THAT THE FOUR ROMANOV SISTERS ALL SPOKE GOOD ENGLISH – Ibid, Helen, Rappaport, *The Romanov Sisters: The Lost Lives of the Daughters of Nicholas and Alexandra,* pp. 105-06 and 178.

294 THE BRITISH HISTORIAN ALSO REPORTS THE FOLLOWING ON THE ROMANOV'S NURSING EXPERIENCE THAT WAS RELEVANT – Ibid, Helen, Rappaport, *The Romanov Sisters: The Lost Lives of the Daughters of Nicholas and Alexandra,* p. 229.

295 OF NICHOLAS' PERSONALITY, RAPPAPORT ADDS THIS – Ibid, Helen, Rappaport, *The Romanov Sisters: The Lost Lives of the Daughters of Nicholas and Alexandra,* p. 79.

296 AND ADDED LATER IN HER BOOK, PERHAPS PERCIPIENTLY FROM OUR PERSPECTIVE – Ibid, Helen, Rappaport, *The Romanov Sisters: The Lost Lives of the Daughters of Nicholas and Alexandra,* p. 289.

296 THE EMPRESS, RAPPAPORT EVEN NOTES IN HER BIOGRAPHY – Ibid, Helen, Rappaport, *The Romanov Sisters: The Lost Lives of the Daughters of Nicholas and Alexandra,* p. 90.

297 THE BRITISH AMBASSADOR, SIR GEORGE BUCHANAN, HAD BEEN IN AN AGONY OF FRUSTRATION – Ibid, Helen, Rappaport, *The Romanov Sisters: The Lost Lives of the Daughters of Nicholas and Alexandra,* pp. 299-300.

297 BY THE TIME GEORGE'S FOREIGN SECRETARY ARTHUR BALFOUR WAS INSTRUCTED – Ibid, Helen, Rappaport, *The Romanov Sisters: The Lost Lives of the Daughters of Nicholas and Alexandra,* p. 300.

297 IN AUGUST 1917, WHEN THE FAMILY LEFT FOR THEIR IMPRISONMENT TIME IN TOBOLSK – Ibid, Helen,

Rappaport, *The Romanov Sisters: The Lost Lives of the Daughters of Nicholas and Alexandra,* p. 320.

297 ELSEWHERE RUMOUR WAS RIFE THAT THE TRAIN WAS HEADING ALL HE WAY OUT TO HARBIN – Ibid, Helen, Rappaport, *The Romanov Sisters: The Lost Lives of the Daughters of Nicholas and Alexandra,* pp. 322-23.

297 ANNA DEMIDOVA, IN HER DIARY, WROTE OF THE TRIP – Ibid, Helen, Rappaport, *The Romanov Sisters: The Lost Lives of the Daughters of Nicholas and Alexandra,* p. 323.

298 NEVERTHELESS NICHOLAS WAS GRATEFUL FOR ANY NEWS – Ibid, Helen, Rappaport, *The Romanov Sisters: The Lost Lives of the Daughters of Nicholas and Alexandra,* p. 340.

298 THE IMPACT OF THEIR COLLECTIVE AND INDIVIDUAL PERSONALITIES MADE THE ROMANOV FAMILY MEMBERS A FORCE TO BE RECKONED WITH – Ibid, Helen, Rappaport, *The Romanov Sisters: The Lost Lives of the Daughters of Nicholas and Alexandra,* p. 369.

298 THERE WAS ALSO THIS PARTICULARLY HAUNTING PASSAGE IN RAPPAPORT'S "ROMANOV SISTERS" BOOK – Ibid, Helen, Rappaport, *The Romanov Sisters: The Lost Lives of the Daughters of Nicholas and Alexandra,* p. 369.

299 BENJAMIN OLIVER JOHNSON WAS THE TYPICAL LIVINGSTON RESIDENT - Frederick C. Giffin, "An American Railroad Man East of the Urals, 1918–1922," *Historian,* Vol. 60, Issue 4, June 1998.

300 WHEN GREAT NORTHERN RAILROAD GENERAL MANAGER GEORGE H. EMERSON CALLED FOR VOLUNTEERS TO GO TO SIBERIA – Ibid, Frederick C. Giffin, "An American Railroad Man East of the Urals, 1918–1922," p. 813.

300 COLONEL JOHN E. STEVENS WOULD HAVE SUPERVISORY AUTHORITY FOR THE OPERATIONS OF THE RAILROAD IN RUSSIA – Ibid, Frederick C. Giffin, "An American Railroad Man East of the Urals, 1918–1922," p. 813.

301 TWO HUNDRED MEN LEFT THEIR FAMILIES BEHIND AND BOARDED TRAINS WITH BEN FOR SIBERIA VIA SAN FRANCISCO – Ibid, Frederick C. Giffin, "An American Railroad Man East of the Urals, 1918–1922," p. 813.

301 BY THE END OF APRIL, 1918, JOHNSON AND MEMBERS OF HIS RRSC TEAM FOUND THEMSELVES IN HARBIN – Ibid, Frederick C. Giffin, "An American Railroad Man East of the Urals, 1918–1922," p. 813.

303 JOHNSON'S ROLE IN SIBERIA GREW QUICKLY AND SUBSTANTIVELY JOHNSON'S ROLE IN SIBERIA GREW QUICKLY AND SUBSTANTIVELY- Ibid, Frederick C. Giffin, "An American Railroad Man East of the Urals, 1918–1922," p. 813.

303 SAYS GIFFIN, "THE GOOD RELATIONS JOHNSON ENJOYED WITH THE CZECHS WERE NO DOUBT ENHANCED BY HIS ABILITY TO COMMUNICATE WITH THEM WITHOUT AN INTERPRETER – Ibid, Frederick C. Giffin, "An American Railroad Man East of the Urals, 1918–1922," p. 813.

304 IN THE SUMMER OF 1919, JOHNSON WOULD VISIT THE VERY ROOM IN WHICH THE TSAR WAS SAID TO HAVE BEEN ASSASSINATED – Ibid, Frederick C. Giffin, "An American Railroad Man East of the Urals, 1918–1922," p. 813.

304 ACCORDING TO GIFFIN – Ibid, Frederick C. Giffin, "An American Railroad Man East of the Urals, 1918–1922," p. 813.

305 WHEN ONE VIEWS THE RECORDS OF THE AMERICAN EXPEDITIONARY FORCE SIBERIA AT THE NATIONAL

ARCHIVES – Review of materials at the National Archives II outside of the Washington, DC, November 6, 2014.

ELEVEN – RED CROSS, RED SPIES

307 "THE RED CROSS WAS UNABLE TO COPE WITH THE DEMANDS OF WORLD WAR I…" – John Foster Dulles, *American Red Cross,* New York, NY: Harper, 1950 as found in Chapter V, "Wall Street and the Bolshevik Revolution," http://reformed-theology.org/html/books/bolshevik_revolution/chapter_05.htm.

307 CHARLES LEWIS WAS A PHYSICIAN IN THE UNITED STATES MILITARY – Charles Lewis, MD, Chapter IX, *Lu Taifu*. Board of Foreign Missions. "A Report: With the American Red Cross in Siberia in the World War." http://www.vlib.us/medical/Siberia/SibDoc.htm, pp. 104-79.

308 ACCORDING TO DR. LEWIS – Ibid, Charles Lewis, MD, Chapter IX, *Lu Taifu*. *Board of Foreign Missions.* "A Report: With the American Red Cross in Siberia in the World War," pp. 104-79.

310 DURING HIS SECOND EXPEDITION TO SIBERIA FOR THE RED CROSS – Ibid, Charles Lewis, MD, Chapter IX, *Lu Taifu*. *Board of Foreign Missions.* "A Report: With The American Red Cross in Siberia in the World War," pp. 104-79.

311 "SOME OF US DOCTORS HAVE BEEN ASKED TO JOIN AN OFFICIALLY ORGANIZED AMERICAN RED CROSS HOSPITAL UNIT – Ibid, Charles Lewis, MD, Chapter IX, *Lu Taifu*. *Board of Foreign Missions.* "A Report: With The

American Red Cross in Siberia in the World War," pp. 104-79.

311 DR. LEWIS CONTINUES PROVIDING "COLOR COMMENTARY" ON THE EVENTS OF THAT DAY IN SIBERIA – Ibid, Charles Lewis, MD, Chapter IX, *Lu Taifu*. *Board of Foreign Missions.* "A Report: With the American Red Cross in Siberia in the World War," pp. 104-79.

312 "ON THE FIRST OF OCTOBER ANOTHER UNIT WAS MADE UP – Ibid, Charles Lewis, MD, Chapter IX, *Lu Taifu*. *Board of Foreign Missions.* "A Report: With the American Red Cross in Siberia in the World War," pp. 104-79.

313 IN ONE CITY ABOUT HALF WAY TO YEKATERINBURG, LEWIS REPORTS THAT THEY HAD ABOUT 250 BEDS IN THEIR HOSPITAL – Ibid, Charles Lewis, MD, Chapter IX, *Lu Taifu*. *Board of Foreign Missions.* "A Report: With the American Red Cross in Siberia in the World War," pp. 104-79.

313 "IN 1918 THE WAR WAS OVER AND THE CZECHO-SLOVAKS CEASED FIGHTING" – Ibid, Charles Lewis, MD, Chapter IX, *Lu Taifu*. *Board of Foreign Missions.* "A Report: With The American Red Cross in Siberia in the World War," pp. 104-79.

314 THE LATE U.S. SECRETARY OF STATE, JOHN FOSTER DULLES SAID OF THE AMERICAN RED CROSS IN SIBERIA – John Foster Dulles, *American Red Cross,* New York, NY: Harper, 1950 as found in Chapter V, "Wall Street and the Bolshevik Revolution," http://reformed-theology.org/html/books/bolshevik_revolution/chapter_05.htm.

TWELVE – HYDE PARK MYSTERY

318 ROOSEVELT SERVED AS ASSISTANT SECRETARY OF THE NAVY – A. Scott Berg. *Wilson,* G.P. Putnam's Son, New York, NY: 2013, p. 281.

318 ALTHOUGH HE DID NOT WORK CLOSELY WITH, OR REALLY KNOW VERY WELL AT ALL, WINSTON CHURCHILL IN WORLD WAR I – Jon Mecham, *Franklin and Winston: An Intimate Portrait of an Epic Friendship,* Random House, New York, NY: 2003, p. 5.

319 IT IS ALL THE MORE SYMBOLICALLY ASTONISHING TO KNOW – Ibid, Mecham, *Franklin and Winston: An Intimate Portrait of an Epic Friendship,* p. xiii.

320 MCNEAL THEN MAKES A VERY INTERESTING OBSERVATION – Shay McNeal, *The Secret Plot to Save the Tsar: The Truth Behind the Romanov Mystery,* William Morrow, New York, NY, 2001, pp. 256-66.

321 ASKED ABOUT THE MCNEAL REPORT, THE FDR LIBRARY SAYS – Bob Clark, Deputy Director, Franklin D. Roosevelt Presidential Library & Museum, July 18, 2014, robert.clark@nara.gov.

322 "FOLLOWING THE PUBLICATION OF THE LAST *LIBERTY* INSTALLMENT - Bob Clark, Deputy Director, Franklin D. Roosevelt Presidential Library & Museum, July 18, 2014, robert.clark@nara.gov.

322 "IN 1967, THE SERIALIZATION WAS REPUBLISHED IN BOOK FORM BY PRENTICE-HALL – Bob Clark, Deputy Director, Franklin D. Roosevelt Presidential Library & Museum, July 18, 2014, robert.clark@nara.gov.

322 WHILE PRESIDENT ROOSEVELT DID NOT WRITE ANY OF THE SERIALIZATION HIMSELF – Bob Clark, Deputy Director, Franklin D. Roosevelt Presidential Library & Museum, July 18, 2014, robert.clark@nara.gov.

324 A DETAILED READ OF *THE PRESIDENT'S MYSTERY STORY* IS INDEED UNCANNY FOR ITS PARALLELS – *The President's Mystery Story* propounded by Franklin D. Roosevelt, solved by Rupert Hughes, Samuel Hopkins Adams, Anthony Abbott, Rita Weiman, S.S. Van Dine, John Erskine with preface by Fulton Oursler. Farrar & Rinehart, Inc., Murray Hill, NY, 1935.

324 BLAKE SPENDS THE EARLY PART OF THE STORY TRYING TO FIGURE OUT HOW TO GET OUT OF HIS UNHAPPY MARRIAGE – Ibid, *The President's Mystery Story*, p. 19.

324 THE PRESIDENT'S MYSTERY STORY CONTINUES TO UNFOLD – Ibid, *The President's Mystery Story*, p. 19.

324 IT SEEMS THAT BLAKE REASONED HIS FATE THIS WAY – Ibid, *The President's Mystery Story*, pp. 26-27 and 150.

325 BLAKE DISCOVERS ILKA'S MURDER PLOT – Ibid, *The President's Mystery Story*, p. 75.

325 PARALLELING THE TSAR'S STORY, AS MARTIN TELLS IT, ROOSEVELT'S INSPIRED CHARACTER, JIM BLAKE – Ibid, *The President's Mystery Story*, pp. 85-86.

325 AND, YOU HAVE TO LOVE THIS LAST IRONY FROM THE PRESIDENT'S MYSTERY BOOK – Ibid, *The President's Mystery Story*, pp. 85-86.

326 IRONIC THAT ILKA WOULD BE RUSSIAN NOBILITY – Frank S. Nugent, "The President's Mystery (1936), A Melodrama of Purpose Is 'The President's Mystery'", Published by *The New York Times*, October 19, 1936 found at:

http://www.nytimes.com/movie/review?res=980CE3DB163EEE3BBC4152DFB667838D629EDE.

327 THE TALENTED DOCUMENTARIAN, KEN BURNS, IN HIS PBS EPIC – Ken Burns, Director, *The Roosevelts: An Intimate History*, episode six, "The Common Cause," originally aired on PBS, September 19, 2014, at marker 54.42.

THIRTEEN – BRILLIANT CONSEQUENCES

329 "…THE PRESIDENT'S COMPLETE DISREGARD OF THE SENATE …" – A. Scott Berg. *Wilson,* G.P. Putnam's Son, New York, NY: 2013, p. 519.

329 BY THE TIME WILSON TRIED TO RALLY THE CONGRESS BEHIND HIM IN HIS SIXTH ANNUAL STATE OF THE UNION – Ibid, A. Scott Berg. *Wilson*, p. 519.

330 HISTORY IS REPLETE WITH PRESIDENTIAL LIES – GLENN KESSLER, "PRESIDENTIAL LIES AND CONSEQUENCES," *The Washington Post*, March 27, 2014, found at: http://www.washingtonpost.com/blogs/fact-checker/wp/2014/03/27/presidential-lies-and-consequences-video.

331 ERIC ALTERMAN, IN HIS 2004 BOOK, *WHEN PRESIDENT'S LIE*, LOOKED AT FOUR SPECIFIC PRESIDENCIES AND THE UNTRUTHS THAT WERE TOLD – Eric Alterman, *When Presidents Lie: A History of Official Deception and Its Consequences,* Viking Books, New York, NY, 2004.

331 FORMER RICHARD NIXON WHITE HOUSE COUNSEL FROM THE WATERGATE ERA, JOHN W. DEAN, WRITING A REVIEW – John W. Dean, "The Post-Truth Presidency: The unintended consequences of presidential lying," *Washington Monthly*, November 2004, found at:

http://www.washingtonmonthly.com/features/2004/0411.dean.html.

332 DEAN, WHO HAD HIS OWN PERSONAL EXPERIENCE OF DECEPTIVE COMMANDERS-IN-CHIEF TO DRAW UPON – Ibid, John W. Dean, "The Post-Truth Presidency: The unintended consequences of presidential lying," *Washington Monthly*.

332 DEAN CONTINUES – Ibid, John W. Dean, "The Post-Truth Presidency: The unintended consequences of presidential lying," *Washington Monthly*.

333 DAVID WISE IN HIS EXAMINATION OF THE POLITICS OF LYING – David Wise, *The Politics of Lying: Government Deception, Secrecy, and Power*, Random House, New York, NY, 1973 as illustrated and discussed by Carl M. Cannon, "Untruth and Consequences," *The Atlantic*, January/February 2007 found at: http://www.theatlantic.com/magazine/archive/2007/01/ untruth-and-consequences/305561.

324 WISE FURTHER BELIEVES THAT PRESIDENTS "ALSO HAVE BURDENS NOT FELT BY MOST OF US – David Wise, *The Politics of Lying: Government Deception, Secrecy, and Power*, as discussed by Carl M. Cannon, "Untruth and Consequences," *The Atlantic*.

FOURTEEN – DEAD MAN'S TALES

337 THEIR STRIPPED AND NOW NAKED BODIES WERE ALSO REPORTEDLY DESECRATED AND THEN DUMPED IN AN ABANDONED FLOODED MINE SHAFT – The controversial account about the Tsar's actual assassination has been expertly detailed by celebrated tsarist scholars such as Robert K. Massie in *The Romanovs: The Final Chapter*,

Edvard Radzinsky, *The Last Tsar*, and the 1924 published report of White Russian investigator Nicholas Sokolov, *Enquête Judiciare sur Assassinat de la Famille Impériale Russe.*

338 IN EARLY 1919, SOME SIX MONTHS AFTER THE SUSPECTED ASSASSINATION – Robert K. Massie, *The Romanovs: The Final Chapter*, p. 10.

339 "ON JULY 17, A TRAIN WITH THE BLINDS DOWN LEFT EKATERINBURG FOR AN UNKNOWN DESTINATION – Balfour quote.

339 A 1935 INTERVIEW WITH AN ALLEGEDLY DYING (THROAT CANCER) PETER ERMAKOV, WHO TOGETHER WITH YAKOV YUROSKY, HAD PARTICIPATED IN THE MURDER – Richard Halliburton quote.

340 IT WAS NOT UNTIL FAR MORE THAN HALF A CENTURY AFTER THE ALLEGED YEKATERINBURG MASSACRE - Robert K. Massie recounting a detailed incident report to the Soviet government by assassin Yakov Yurovsky provided in 1978 to searcher Geli Ryabov by son, then-retired Vice Admiral Alexander. The Yurovsky report claimed that all of the Romanovs, including Alexi, had been buried in the stated vicinity according to *The Romanovs: The Final Chapter.*

340 ADDING TO THE CONTROVERSY OF THE FIND, OF COURSE – 1989 Ryabov interview with the *Moscow News* reproduced at http://www.alexanderpalace.org/palace/ryabovtv.html. Also an *Associated Press* report printed by *The New York Times* on April 15, 1989 found at:
http://www.nytimes.com/1989/04/16/world/soviet-paper-reports-discovery-of-slain-czar.html. And a subsequent interview in *Rodina.*

341 NOTED DNA EXPERTS FROM RUSSIA, THE UNITED KINGDOM AND THE UNITED STATES WOULD ARGUE YEARS LATER – Thomas H. Maugh, II, "DNA testing ends mystery surrounding Czar Nicholas II children," *LA Times*, March 11, 2009, as found at http://articles.latimes.com/2009/mar/11/science/sci-romanov11.

342 THE EMPRESS ALEXANDRA WAS FIRST COUSIN TO GERMANY'S KAISER WILHEM, II – Michael Wines, "Last Czar Buried: Tale of 2 Russias," *The New York Times*, July 18, 1988, as found at http://www.nytimes.com/1998/07/18/world/last-czar-buried-tale-of-2-russias.html?pagewanted=all&src=pm.

342 "DNA TESTING IN THE 1990S BY GENETICIST PETER GILL OF THE UNIVERSITY OF STRATHCLYDE IN GLASGOW, SCOTLAND ..." – Ibid, Thomas H. Maugh, "DNA testing ends mystery surrounding Czar Nicholas children," *LA Times*.

343 THE BODIES IN THE MASS GRAVE, ALSO KNOWN AS GRAVE #1 LOCATED IN A "SMALL CLEARING ON THE FORMER KOPTYAKI ROAD – An excellent and detailed account of the exhumation of the grave can be found in Robert K. Massey's, *The Romanovs: The Final Chapter*, including this quote found on p. 40 and pp. 61-69.

343 BODY #1 BELIEVED TO BE ALEXANDRA'S MAID, ANNA DEMIDOVA – Greg King and Penny Wilson, *The Fate of the Romanovs*, John Wiley and Sons, Inc., 2003, pp. 63-64.

343 BODY #2 WAS BELIEVED TO BE THE TSAR'S PHYSICIAN, DR. YEVGENY BOTKIN – Dr. William Maples' forensic team.

343 BODY #3 WAS CONCLUDED TO BE THE GRAND DUCHESS OLGA, THE TSAR'S ELDEST DAUGHTER – Dr. William Maples' forensic team.

344 BODY #4 WAS DEEMED TO BE THAT TSAR NICHOLAS, II – Ibid, Robert K. Massey, *The Romanovs: The Final Chapter*, pp. 42-43.

345 BODY #5 WAS THE SMALLEST AND YOUNGEST OF ALL, FEMALE – Dr. William Maples' forensic team.

345 BODY #6 WAS CONSIDERED BY TEAM TO BE GRAND THE AMERICAN DUCHESS TATIANA – Dr. William Maples, *Dead Men Do Tell Tales*, Dr. William Maples' forensic team, and Robert K. Massey, *The Romanovs: The Final Chapter*, p. 45, pp. 66-67 and p. 75.

346 BODY #7 WAS A DEEMED TO BE THE TSARINA ALEXANDRA BECAUSE IT WAS THAT OF A MIDDLE-AGED FEMALE – Dr. William Maples' forensic team.

347 BODY #8 WAS CONSIDERED TO BE THE COOK, IVAN KHARITONOV, A MIDDLE-AGED MALE – Dr. William Maples' forensic team.

347 BODY #9 WAS FOUND RESTING UNDER BODY #4 AND WAS THAT OF THE OLDEST MALE VICTIM, CONSISTENT WITH THE TSAR'S VALET ALEXI TRUPP – Dr. William Maples' forensic team.

347 A CHILLING PASSAGE FROM ROBERT K. MASSEY'S, *THE ROMANOVS: THE FINAL CHAPTER*, DESCRIBED THE SCENE – Ibid, Robert K. Massey, *The Romanovs: The Final Chapter*, pp. 40-41.

348 IN 1998, AVDONIN WANTED TO SEE IF HIS SCIENTISTS COULD FIND THE OTHER VICTIMS NEARBY – King & Wilson.

349 GRAVE #2 WAS FOUND AUGUST 23, 2007, A VERY SHORT DISTANCE AWAY FROM THE MASS GRAVE EXHUMED IN 1991 – "DNA Confirms Remains Of Czar's Children," *CBS News*, April 30, 2008 as found at: http://www.cbsnews.com/stories/2008/04/30/tech/main4057567.shtml.

350 MAJOR AMERICAN MEDIA CONCLUDED THAT RED ARMY BOLSHEVIK REVOLUTIONARIES HAD INDEED KILLED ALL OF THE TSAR'S FAMILY – For example, see "DNA proves Bolsheviks killed all of Russian czar's children," CNN, March 11, 2009, found at http://www.cnn.com/2009/WORLD/europe/03/11/czar.children/index.html.

352 STARTING WITH THE DISCOVERY OF THE ROMANOV REMAINS, GRAY DETAILS A CONVERSATION - Michael Gray, *Blood Relative,* published by Victor Gollancz, London, England, 1998, p. 49.

353 NIKOLAI SOKOLOV, WHO HAD PRODUCED THE MOST AUTHORITATIVE CONTEMPORARY INVESTIGATION OF THE FATE OF THE TSAR'S FAMILY – Ibid, Michael Gray, *Blood Relative,* p. 50.

353 TWO TYPES OF DNA EXIST WITHIN THE HUMAN BODY – Ibid, Michael Gray, *Blood Relative,* pp. 50-51.

354 DR. MICHAEL BADDEN, WHO WORKED WITH MAPLES BLASTED THE GILL CONCLUSION AS 'NONSENSE' – Ibid, Michael Gray, *Blood Relative,* p. 52.

355 MAPLES HAD A PROBLEM WITH THE UNCOVERING OF THE BONES – Ibid, Michael Gray, *Blood Relative,* p. 53.

355 TO A LAYMAN'S MIND IT SEEMED THAT IF LARGE BONES LIKE VERTEBRAE WERE MISSING – Ibid, Michael Gray, *Blood Relative,* p. 53.

FIFTEEN – FROM THE BONES OF A TSAR

385 IN HIS BOOK, *THE ROMANOVS: THE FINAL CHAPTER,* ROBERT MASSIE WRITES THE FOLLOWING ABOUT WHAT HE CALLS, "THE IMPOSTERS" TO THE ROMANOV SAGA - Robert K. Massey, *The Romanovs: The Final Chapter*, p. 45, pp. 66-67 and p. 75.

385 TO THIS POINT, WE DO KNOW THAT IT WAS TRUE THAT NICHOLAS AND ALEXANDRA HAD BOTH BEEN VERY ADAMANT THAT THEY WOULD NOT CONTEMPLATE ANY RESCUE OF THE IMPERIAL FAMILY – Helen Rappaport, *The Romanov Sisters: The Lost Lives of the Daughters of Nicholas and Alexandra,* p. 357.

386 CONSIDER THIS, TOO: IN LEAVING TOBOLSK FOR YEKATERINBURG – Helen Rappaport, *The Romanov Sisters: The Lost Lives of the Daughters of Nicholas and Alexandra,* p. 357.

386 PERHAPS - Helen Rappaport, *The Romanov Sisters: The Lost Lives of the Daughters of Nicholas and Alexandra,* p. 357.

SIXTEEN – MARTIN'S EPILOGUE

403 ALL CITATIONS ARE FROM PERSONAL RECOLLECTION.

Rescuing Nicholas | Bibliography

Audio:

Hutson, Martin V. *An Episode in My Life*, recorded with family members present and mastered Summer 1971.

Consulted Books:

Ackerman, Carl W. *Trailing the Bolshevki: Twelve Thousand Miles with the Allies in Siberia.* Charles Scribner's Sons. New York, NY, 1919.

Alexseev, Venyamin. *The Last Act of a Tragedy: New Documents About the Execution of the Last Russian Emperor Nicholas II.* Ekaterinburg, Russia. Urals Branch of Russian Academy of Sciences Publishers, 1996.

Alterman, Eric, *When Presidents Lie*, Viking Adult, 1st edition, New York, NY, 2004, ISBN-13: 978-0670032099.

Andrew, Christopher. *Her Majesty's Secret Service: The Making of the British Intelligence Community.* Viking, Penguin, Inc. New York, NY, 1986.

Anichkov, Vladimir P. *Ekaterinburg-Vladivostok (1917-1922).* Moscow, Russia. Russkii Put, 1998.

Balfour, Michael. *The Kaiser and His Times.* W.W. Norton & Co. New York, NY, 1972.

Berg, A. Scott. *Wilson.* G.P. Putnam's Sons. New York, NY, 2013. ISBN: 978-0-399-15921-3.

Bernstein, Herman. *The Willy-Nicky Correspondence: Being the Secret and Intimate Telegrams Exchanged between the Kaiser and the Tsar*. Knopf, New York, NY, 1918.

Botkin, Gelb. *The Real Romanovs: As Revealed by the Late Czar's Physician and His Son*. Putnam. London, England, 1923.

Bright, and Erwin Gustav Gudde. *1500 California Place Names: Their Origin and Meaning,* University of California Press, Oakland, CA: 1998

Brook-Shepard, Gordon. *Iron Maze: The Western Secret Services and the Bolsheviks*. Pan Books. London, England, 1998.

Broesamle, John J. *William Gibbs McAdoo, A Passion for Change: 1863-1917,* Port Washington, NY: Kennikat, 1973.

Bruce Lockhart, Robin. *Ace of Spies*. Hodder & Stoughton. London, England, 1967.

Buchanan, Sir George. *My Mission to Russia,* vol. 1, London, England: Cassell, 1923.

Buckley, Gail Lumet. *American Patriots: The Story of Blacks in the Military from the Revolution to Desert Storm*. Random House. New York, NY, 2001.

Bullock, David. *The Russian Civil War, 1918-22*. Oxford, England: Osprey Publishing, 2008, ISBN-10: 1846032717.

Bulygin, Captain Paul. *The Murder of the Romanovs: The Authentic Account Including the Road to Tragedy by Alexander Kerensky*. Hyperion Press. Westport, CT, 1935.

Buxhoeveden, Baroness Sophie. *The Life and Tragedy of Alexandra Feodorovna, Empress of Russia: A Biography*. Longmans, Green and Company. London, England, 1928.

Buxhoeveden, Baroness Sophie. *Left Behind: Fourteen Months In Siberia During The Revolution, December 1917-1920.* Oxford University Press. Oxford, England, 1993.

Bykov, Pavel. *The Last Days of Tsardom.* Martin Lawrence. London, England, 1934.

Capek, Karel. *President Masaryk Tells His Story.* G.P. Putnam's Sons. New York, NY, 1935.

Clarke, William. *The Lost Fortune of the Tsars.* St. Martin's Press. New York, NY, 1996.

Clay, Catrine. *King, Kaiser, Tsar: Three Royal Cousins Who Led the World to War.* John Murray. London, England, 2007.

Cooper, Jr., John Milton. *Woodrow Wilson: A Biography.* Alfred A. Knopf. New York, NY, 2009. ISBN: 978-0-307-26541-8.

Craig, Douglas B. *Progressives at War: William G. McAdoo and Newton D. Baker, 1863-1941.* Baltimore, MD: Johns Hopkins University Press, 2013. ISBN 1 4214 0718.

Daniels, Josephus. *Cabinet Diaries – The Wilson Era,* Lincoln, NE: The University of Nebraska compiled 1919, published 1963.

Daniels, Josephus. *The Navy and the Nation: War-Time Addresses.* New York, NY: George H. Doran Publishing, 1919.

Dmitriev-Mamonov, A. I., and A. F. Zdziarski. *Guide to the Great Siberian Railway (1900),* rev. by John Marshall. David & Charles. London, England, 1971.

Dorr, Rheta Childe. *Inside the Russian Revolution,* New York, NY: Macmillan, 1917.

Eudin, Xenia, et al, eds. *The Life of a Chemist: Memoirs of Vladimir N. Impatieff.* Oxford University Press. Oxford, England, 1946.

Fleming, Robert. *The Fate of Admiral Kolchak.* Rupert Hart-Davis. London, England, 1963.

Fogelsong, David S. *America's Secret War Against Bolshevism: U.S. Intervention in the Russian Civil War 1917-1920.* University of North Carolina Press. Chapel Hill, NC, 1995.

Francis, David R. *US Ambassador to Russia Under The Czar, the Provisional Government and the Bolsheviks: Russia From The American Embassy.* Charles Scribner's Sons. New York, NY, 1921.

Gaddis, John Lewis. *George F. Kennan: An American Life.* W.W. Norton & Co. New York, NY, 2011. ISBN: 978-1594203121.

Gilliard, Pierre. *Thirteen Years at the Russian Court.* Arno Press. New York, NY, 1970.

Goldhurst, Richard. *The Midnight War.* McGraw-Hill. New York, NY, 1978.

Goodwin, Doris Kearns. *No Ordinary Time: Franklin and Eleanor Roosevelt: The Home Front in World War II.* Simon & Schuster, New York, NY: 1994.

Grabbe, Count Alexander. *The Private World of the Last Tsar: In the Photographs and Notes of General Count Alexander Grabbe.* Collins. London, England, 1985.

Graves, William S. *America's Siberian Adventure.* Peter Smith. New York, NY, 1941 and Uncommon Valor Press, Kindle Version, 2013, ISBN 10: 0-844-61205-7.

Gray, Michael. *Blood Relative: The Astonishing Story of the Survival of the Tsarevich.* Victor Gollancz. London, England, 1998. ISBN: 0-575-06608-3.

Hard, William. *Raymond Robins' Own Story.* Harper and Brothers Publishers. New York, NY, 1920.

Harrison, Brian, ed. "Arthur, Prince, First Duke of Connaught and Strathearn", *Oxford Dictionary of National Biography.* Oxford University Press. Oxford, England, 2004.

Hendrick, Michael. *An Investigation of American Siberian Intervention (1918-1920).* Texas Southern University, 1972.

Heresch, Elisabeth. *Blood on the Snow: Eyewitness Accounts of the Russian Revolution,* New York, NY: Paragon House, 1990.

Hill, Captain George A. *Go Spy the Land: Being the Adventures of I.K.8 of the British Secret Service.* Cassell. London, England, 1932.

House, Colonel Edward. *The Intimate Papers of Colonel House,* Boston, MA: Houghton Mifflin, 1926.

Hudson, Miles. *Intervention in Russia 1918-1920: A Cautionary Tale.* Pen and Sword. 2004.

Hughes, Lindsey. *The Romanovs: Ruling Russia 1613-1917.* Continuum Books. New York, NY, 2008. ISBN: 978-1-84725-213-5.

Humphreys, Leonard A. *The Way of the Heavenly Sword: The Japanese Army in the 1920's.* Stanford University Press. Palo Alto, CA. 1996.

Ipatieff, Vladimir. *The Memoirs of a Chemist.* Northwestern University Press. Evanston, IL, 1959.

Janin, General Maurice. *Ma Mission en Siberie.* Payot. Paris, France, 1933.

Jeffrey, Keith. *The Secret History of MI6; 1909-1949.* Penguin. London, England, 2010.

Judd, Dennis. *The Life and Times of George V.* Weidenfield & Nicholson. London, England, 1993.

Kennan, George F. *Soviet American Relations, 1917-1920, The Decision to Intervene.* Princeton, University Press. Princeton, NJ, 1958.

Kennan, George F. *Soviet American Relations, 1917-1920, Russia Leaves the War.* Princeton University Press. Princeton, NJ: 1956.

Kerensky, Alexander. *The Catastrophe: Kerensky's Own Story of the Russian Revolution.* D. Appleton & Co. New York, NY, 1927.

Kettle, Michael. *Sidney Reilly: The True Story of the World's Greatest Spy.* St. Martin's Press. New York, NY, 1983.

King, David. *Red Star Over Russia: A Visual History of the Soviet Union from the Revolution to the Death of Stalin.* Harry N. Abrams. New York, NY, 2009. ISBN 978-0810982796.

King, Greg. *The Court of the Last Tsar: Pomp, Power, and Pageantry in The Reign of Nicholas II.* John Wiley & Sons, Inc. Hoboken, NJ, 2006. ISBN: 13-978-0-471-72763-7.

King, Greg and Penny Wilson. *Resurrection of the Romanovs,* New York, NY: John Wiley, 2011.

King, Greg and Penny Wilson. *The Fate of the Romanovs.* John Wiley & Sons, Inc. Hoboken, NJ, 2003. ISBN: 0-471-20768-3.

King, Greg and Sue Woolmans. *The Assassination of the Archduke: Sarajevo 1914 and the Romance That Changed the World.* St. Martin Griffins, New York, NY, 2013.

Kinvig, Clifford. *Churchill's Crusade: The British Invasion of Russia, 1918-1920*. Continuum International Publishing Group. 2006.

Kiste, John van der, and Coryne Hall. *Kaiser Wilhelm II: Germany's Last Emperor*. Sutton. Gloucester, England, 1996.

Kurth, Peter. *Anastasia: The Riddle of Anna Anderson*. Little, Brown. Boston, MA, 1983.

Kurth, Peter. *Tsar: The Lost World of Nicholas and Alexandra*. Madison Press Book produced for Little, Brown and Company. Toronto, Ontario, Canada, 1995. ISBN: 0-316-50787-3.

Lansing, Robert. *War Memoirs of Robert Lansing, Secretary of State*. The Bobbs-Merrill Company. Indianapolis, IN, 1935.

Lasies, Joseph. *La Tragedie Siberienne: le drame d'Ekaterinburg*. L'Édition Française Illustree. Paris, France, 1920.

Laqueuer, Walter. *Russia and Germany: A Century of Conflict*. George Weidenfeld & Nicholson. London, England, 1966.

Levin, James Gordon. *Woodrow Wilson and World Politics*. Oxford University Press. Oxford, England, 1968.

Lincoln, W. Bruce. Red Victory: *A History of the Russian Civil War*. Simon & Schuster. New York, NY, 1919.

Lincoln, W. Bruce. *The Romanovs: Autocrats of All the Russias*. Doubleday. New York, NY, 1981. ISBN: 0-385-2790808-6.

Lockhart, R. H. Bruce. *Memoirs of a British Agent*. Putnam. London, England, 1932.

Lovell, James Blair Archive. Text by Carol Townsend. *Royal Russia*. St. Martin's Press. New York, NY, 1995. ISBN: 0-312-17936-7.

Luckett, Richard. *The White Generals: An Account of the White Movement and the Russian Civil War.* Longman. London, England, 1971.

Ludwig, Emil. *Kaiser Wilhelm II.* G. P. Putnam's Sons. London, England, 1926.

Maddox, Robert J. *The Unknown War with Russia: Wilson's Siberian Intervention.* Presidio Press. San Rafael, CA. 1977.

Maples, Dr. William R., and Michael Browning. *Dead Men Do Tell Tales.* Doubleday. New York, NY, 1994.

Markov, Sergei. *How We Tried to Save the Tsaritsa.* Putnam. London, England, 1929.

Massie, Robert K. *Nicholas and Alexandra.* Gollancz. London, England, 1968. ISBN-10: 9780679645610.

Massie, Robert K. *The Romanovs: The Final Chapter.* Random House. New York, NY, 1995. ISBN: 394-58048-6.

Masaryk, Thomas. *The Making of a State: Memories and Observations 1914-1918.* Howard Ferig. New York, NY, 1969.

Mawdsley, Evan. *The Russian Civil War,* New York, NY: Pegasus Books, 2007.

McAdoo, William Gibbs. *Crowded Years: The Reminiscences of William G. McAdoo,* New York, NY: Houghton Mifflin Company, 1931.

McNeal, Shay. *The Secret Plot to Save the Tsar: The Truth Behind the Romanov Mystery.* William Morrow. New York, NY, 2001. ISBN: 0-688-16998-8.

Mead, Gary. *The Doughboys: America and the First World War.* Overlook Press. New York, NY. 2000.

Meacham, Jon. *Franklin and Winston: An Intimate Portrait of an Epic Friendship.* Random House. New York, NY: 2003.

Morrison, John. *Boris Yeltsin: From Bolshevik to Democrat.* E.P. Dutton. New York, NY, 1991.

Morrow, Anne. *Cousins Divided: George V and Nicholas II.* Sutton. Gloucester, England, 2006.

Neal, Steve. *Happy Days Are Here Again: The 1932 Democratic Convention and its Aftermath,* New York, NY: Morrow, 2004.

Nielson, Keith. *Britain and the Last Tsar: British Policy and Russia, 1894-1917.* Oxford University Press. Oxford, England, 1995.

Occleshaw, Michael. *Dances in Deep Shadows: Britain's Clandestine War in Russia 1917-1920.* Constable. London, England, 2006.

Occleshaw, Michael. *The Romanov Conspiracies: The Romanovs and the House of Windsor.* Orion Books, Ltd. London, England, 1994.

O'Conor, John F. *Translations of Sections of Nicholas A. Sokolov's The Murder of the Imperial Family.* Robert Speller and Sons Publishers, Inc. New York, NY, 1971.

Pascal, Pierre. *Mon Journal de Russie á la Mission Militaire Française 1917-1918.* Éditions L'Age d'Homme. Laussanne, Switzerland, 1975.

Perry, John Curtis, and Constantine Pleshakov. *The Flight of the Romanovs: A Family Saga.* Basic Books. New York, NY, 1999.

Perry, John. *Pershing: Commander of the Great War.* Thomas Nelson Inc. Nashville, TN, 2011. ISBN: 978-1-59555-355.3.

Petrov, Vadim, Igor Lysenko, and Georgy Egorov. *The Escape of Alexei: Son of Tsar Nicholas II.* Harry N. Abrams. New York, NY, 1998.

Preston, Sir Thomas H. *Before the Curtain.* Murray. London, England, 1950.

Radzinsky, Edvard. *The Last Tsar: The Life and Death of Nicholas II.* Doubleday. New York, NY, 1992.

Ransome, Arthur. *Six Weeks in Russia in 1919.* George Allen & Unwin. London, England, 1919.

Rappaport, Helen. *The Last Days of the Romanovs: Tragedy at Ekaterinburg.* St. Martin's Griffin, New York, NY, 2008. ISBN: 978-0-312-60347-2.

Rappaport, Helen. *The Romanov Sisters: The Lost Lives of the Daughters of Nicholas and Alexandra.* St. Martin's Press, New York, NY, 2014. ISBN: 978-1-250-02020-8.

Rathlef-Keilmann, Harriett von. *Anastasia: The Survivor of Ekaterinburg.* G. P. Putnam's Sons. New York, NY, 1928.

Radziwill, Catherine. *Nicholas II, the Last of the Tsars,* London, England: Cassell, 1931.

Richards, Guy. *The Hunt for the Czar.* Doubleday. Garden City, New York, 1970.

Richards, Guy. *The Rescue of the Romanovs.* The Devin-Adair Company. Old Greenwich, CT, 1975.

Robins, Raymond. *Raymond Robins' Own Story.* Harper Collins. New York, NY, 1920.

Roosevelt, President Franklin Delano. *The President's Mystery Story,* courtesy of Liberty Media, Roosevelt Presidential Library and Museum, Hyde Park, NY.

Rose, Kenneth. *King George V.* Phoenix Press. London, England, 1983.

Saul, Norman E. *The Life and Times of Charles R. Crane, 1858-1939: American Businessman, Philanthropist, and a Founder of Russian Studies in America.* Lexington. Lanham, MD, 2013.

Seymour, Charles. *The Intimate Papers of Colonel House: Into the World War.* Houghton Mifflin Company. Cambridge, England, 1928.

Silber, William L. *When Washington Shut Down Wall Street: The Great Financial Crisis of 1914 and the Origins of America's Monetary Supremacy,* Princeton University Press, Princeton, N.J., 2007, ISBN 978-0-691-12747-7.

Smith, Gene. *Until the Last Trumpet Sounds: The Life of General of the Armies John J. Pershing.* Wiley & Sons. New York, NY, 1998. ISBN: 978-0-471-24693-0.

Smythe, Donald. *Guerilla Warrior: The Early Life of John J. Pershing.* Charles Scribner's Sons. New York, NY, 1973.

Smythe, Donald. *Pershing: General of the Armies.* Indiana University Press. Bloomington, IL, 1986.

Smythe, James P. *Rescuing the Czar.* California Printing Company. San Francisco, CA, 1920.

Sokolov, Nicholas. Enquête Judiciare sur l'Assassinat de la Famille Impériale Russe.

State Hermitage Museum, *Nicholas and Alexandra: The Last Imperial Family of Tsarist Russia.* Harry N. Abrams, Inc.,

Publishers. Mark Sutcliffe, Managing Editor. New York, NY, 1998. ISBN: 0-8109-3687-9.

Steinberg, Mark D., and Vladimir M. Khrustalëv. *The Fall of the Romanovs: Political Dreams and Personal Struggles in a Time of Revolution*. Yale University Press. New Haven, CT, 1995. ISBN: 0-300-06557-4.

Stewart, George. *The White Armies of Russia, A Chronicle of Counter: Revolution and Allied Intervention.* Russell and Russell. New York, NY, 1971.

Strakhovsky, Leonid I. *Intervention at Archangel, The Story of the Allied Intervention and Russian Counter: Revolution in North Russia 1918-1920*. Howard Fertig. New York, NY, 1971.

Summers, Anthony and Tom Mangold. *The File on Tsar*. Victor Gollancz, Ltd. London, England, 1976.

Swezey, Marilyn Pfifer, ed. *Nicholas and Alexandra: At Home with the Last Tsar and His Family*, Washington, DC: American-Russian Cultural Cooperation Foundation, 2004.

Sylvester, Albert James. *Life with Lloyd George, the Diary of A.J. Sylvester, 1931-1945*. MacMillan. London, England, 1975.

Synon, Mary. *William Gibbs McAdoo: The Man and His Times – A Panorama in Democracy*, Indianapolis, IN: Bobbs Merrill, 1924.

Trewin, J.C. *Tutor to the Tsarevich: An Intimate Portrait of the Last Days of The Romanov Family*. Compiled from the papers of Charles Sidney Gibbs. McMillan. London, England, 1975.

Trewin, J.C. *The House of Special Purpose*. Macmillan. London, England, 1975.

Tyler-Whittle and Michael Sidney. *The Last Kaiser: A Biography of Wilhelm II, German Emperor and King of Prussia.* Heinemann. London, England, 1977.

Tupper, Harmon. *To the Great Ocean: Siberia and the Trans-Siberian Railway.* Little, Brown. Boston, MA, 1965.

Unterberger, Betty Miller. *America's Siberian Expedition, 1918-1920.* Duke University Press. Durham, NC, 1956.

Vandiver, Frank E. *Black Jack: The Life and Times of John J. Pershing - Volumes I & II.* Texas A&M University Press, 1977. ISBN 0-89096-024-0.

Viereck, George Sylvester. *The Strangest Friendship in History, Woodrow Wilson and Colonel House.* Liveright, Inc., Publishers. New York, NY, 1932.

Volkogono, Dmitri and Harold Shukman, eds. *Trotsky: The Eternal Revolutionary.* HarperCollins. London, England, 1996.

Ward, Colonel John. *With the "Die-Hards" in Siberia.* George H. Doran. New York, NY, 1920.

White, John Albert. *The Siberian Intervention.* Princeton University Press. Princeton, NJ, 1950.

Wilhelm, II, The Kaiser's Memoirs. Translated by Thomas R. Ybarra. Harper & Brothers Publishers. New York, NY, 1922.

Willett, Jr., Robert L. *Russian Sideshow: America's Undeclared War, 1918-1920.* Potomac Books, 2005.

Willmott, H.P. *First World War.* Dorling Kidersley, 2003.

Wilton, Robert. *The Last Days of the Romanovs, From 15 March 1917, Part I, The Narrative, Part II, The Depositions of Eyewitnesses.* London, Thornton Butterworth Limited. England, 1920.

Yeltsin, Boris. *Against the Grain: Autobiography.* Summit Books. New York, NY, 1990.

Young, Kenneth. *Arthur James Balfour: The Happy Life of the Politician, Prime Minister, Statesman and Philosopher, 1848–1930.* G. Bell and Sons. London, England, 1963.

Young, Kenneth, ed. *The Diaries of Sir Robert Bruce Lockhart.* Vol.1, 1915-1938. Macmillan. London, England, 1973.

Zeepvat, Charlotte. *The Camera and the Tsars: A Romanov Family Album.* Sutton Publishing. Gloucestershire, England, 2004. ISBN: 0-7509-4210-X.

Manuscripts, Papers & Non-Published Documents:

Ackerman, Carl W. *The Papers of Carl W. Ackerman.* Manuscript Division of the United States Library of Congress, Washington, DC.

Archival military service record of General John J. Pershing. National Personnel Records Center. St. Louis, MO.

Baker, U.S. Secretary of War Newton Diehl, *Newton Diehl Baker Papers,* Library of Congress Manuscript Division, Washington, DC.

Boyle, Colonel Joseph. *The Papers of Joseph Boyle.* Canadian National Archives. MG 31 H159, Volume 1.

Browder, Robert P. and Alexander F. Kerensky, eds. *The Russian Provisional Government 1917: Documents.* 3 volumes. Stanford University Press. Palo Alto, CA, 1961.

Chase, Philip M., Ph.D. *William Gibbs McAdoo: The Last Progressive, (1863 – 1941),* University of Southern California Dissertation, 2008, found at: ProQuest Dissertations and Theses, http://gradworks.umi.com/33/41/3341909.html.

Churchill, Winston. *The Papers of Sir Winston Churchill.* Churchill College, University of Cambridge, Cambridge, England, United Kingdom.

Crane, Charles. *The Papers of Charles Crane.* Bakmetieff Collection. Special Collections, Columbia University. New York, NY.

DSC citation for George R. Hutson, War Department, General Orders No. 44 (1919), *The Military Times Hall of Valor,* found at http://projects.militarytimes.com/citations-medals-awards/search.php?term=george+r+Hutson.

Graves, Major General William Sidney. *Preliminary Inventory to the William Sidney Graves Papers, 1914-1932.* Hoover Institution, Stanford University, Stanford, CA.

Harris, American Consul General Ernest Lloyd. *Register of the Ernest Lloyd Harris Papers, 1894-1924.* Hoover Institution, Stanford University, Stanford, CA.

House, Colonel Edward M. *The Papers of Edward M. House.* Yale University, New Haven, CT.

Johnson, Benjamin O. *Preliminary Inventory of the Benjamin O. Johnson Papers, 1917-1923.* Hoover Institution, Stanford University, Stanford, CA.

Lampson, Sir Miles. *Lord Killearn's Diaries.* Reference GB165-0176, Aberystwyth University, Wales, United Kingdom.

Landfield, U.S. Assistant Secretary of State Jermone Barker. *The Papers of Jermone Barker Landfield.* Manuscript Division of the University of California at Berkeley.

Lansing, U.S. Secretary of State Robert. *The Papers of Robert Lansing.* The Manuscript Division of the United States Library of Congress, Washington, DC and the U.S. National Archives, 1915-1918, Microfilm #743.

Lloyd George, British Prime Minister David. *The Papers of Sir David Lloyd George.* Parliamentary Archives, London, England.

Long, U.S. Assistant Secretary of State Breckinridge. *The Papers of Breckinridge Long.* The Manuscript Division of the United States Library of Congress, Washington, DC.

Maples, Dr. William. *William R. Maples Collection, 1960-1997.* Florida Gulf Coast University, Ft. Myers, FL.

McAdoo, U.S. Secretary of the Treasury William Gibbs. *The Papers of William Gibbs McAdoo.* The Huntington Library, San Marino, CA.

Pares, Sir Bernard. *The Papers of Bernard Pares.* "Siberian Diary, January-October 1919." School of Slavonic and East European Studies, London, England, PAR/6/9/2.

Pershing, General John J. *Papers of John J. Pershing.* Manuscript Division, United States Library of Congress, Washington, DC.

Pershing, General John J. U.S. Army Center for Military History. United States Army Chiefs of Staff.

Preston, Sir Thomas. *The Papers of Thomas Preston.* Liddle Collection, R US 37, Leeds University Library.

United States Army, Honorable Discharge Record of Martin V. Hutson, Fort Lewis, Washington, August 19, 1922, signed by Rev. Broughton, Major, 7th Infantry.

United States Army, Enlistment Record of Martin V. Hutson, Fort Oglethorpe, Georgia, August 20, 1919, signed by Captain Chas. C. Laughlin, Commander, Infantry (Tanks), 3rd Tank Company.

United States Constitution, The National Archives, Washington, D.C.

The U.S. Department of State Papers Relating to the Foreign Relations of the United States, 1919. Volume II. U.S. Government Printing Office. Washington, DC, 1935.

The Peace Treaty of Brest-Litovsk. World War I Document Archive found at:
http://www.lib.byu.edu/~rdh/wwi/1918/brestlitovsk.html.

U.S. National Archives II. *Historical Files of the American Expeditionary Forces in Siberia 1918-1920.* College Park, Maryland, M917, Cabinet 148, Rolls 1-11 and RG43, Entries # 43 & 46.

Wilson, U.S. President Woodrow. *The Papers of Woodrow Wilson.* The Manuscript Division of the United States Library of Congress, Washington, DC.

Wiseman, Sir William. *The Papers of William Wiseman.* Manuscripts and Archives: Manuscript Collection, Yale University.

Newspapers and Articles:

27th Infantry Regimental Historical Society. "The 27th Infantry - AEF Siberia." March 18, 2001 and November 6, 2002.

Ackerman, Carl W. "Is the Czar Dead? Six Chances in Ten that He Was Executed by the Bolsheviki." *The New York Times*, 23 February 1919, p. 62.

Ackerman, Carl W. "How the Czar Was Doomed to Death." *Current History Monthly*. 9, no 2, 1919.

Ackerman, Carl W. "The Irish Education of Mr. Lloyd George." *Atlantic Monthly*. Volume CXXIX, January-July 1922.

Andeev, A. "His Jailer Tells of the Czar's Last Days." *The New York Times*, 15 July 1928, p.4.

Avdonin, Alexander. "In Search of the Place of Burial of the Remains of the Czar's Family." *Historical Genealogy* 1, 1993.

Barrows, Major David. "Memorandum for General Evans: Advance of Ataman Semenoff's Forces, April 20th to May 5th (appendix A), Peking, China, May 9, 1918 as it appears in the Military Intelligence Division file # 2070-505, box 815 - Military Intelligence Division Correspondence, 1917 -41 microfilmed as *Correspondence of the Military Intelligence Division Relating to General, Political, Economic, and Military Conditions in Russia and the Soviet Union, 1917-1941* (National Archives Microfilm Publication M1443), roll 3, Records of the War Department General and Special Staffs, Record Group (RG) 165, National Archives at College Park (NACP), College Park, MD, as found by Gibson Bell Smith and noted in *Guarding the Railroad, Taming the Cossacks, The U.S. Army in Russia, 1918-1920*, Part 3. Winter 2002, Vol. 34, No. 4.

Bernstein, Herman. "6 Versions of Czar's Fate." *Washington Post*, 16 February 1919.

Biddle, Winthrop. "The Czar and His Family," *Munsey's Magazine* LI, February 1914, no. 1, pp. 3-5.

Bradley, John F.N. *The Czechoslovak Legion in Russia, 1914–1920.* East European Monographs, New York: Boulder/Columbia University Press, 1991, ISBN 0-88033-218-2.

Brown, David. "DNA Proves Bones Belong to Last Tsar; Mystery of Nicholas's Missing Body Is Solved," *Washington Post,* September 1, 1995.

CNN, "Lake Baikal: The Great Blue Eye of Siberia," October 11, 2006.

Davies, Norman. *The Sunday Times,* 11 May 2006.

Eliot, Sir Charles. "Fate of the Russian Imperial Family." Report in FO 371/3977, Public Record Office, Kew.

Evans, G. Russell. *Maj. Gen. William S. Graves, U.S. Army – Truly a Soldier of the Old School,* May 26, 2002.

"Ex-Czar of Russia Killed by Order of Ural Soviet: Nicholas Shot on July 16 When It Was Feared Czechoslovaks Might Seize Him." *The New York Times.* July 24, 1918, p. 1, 8.

"Ex-Czar's Family Safe." *The New York Times.* July 28, 1918, p. 5.

"Former Czar's Son Dead." *The New York Times.* July 26, 1918, p. 5.

Giffin, Frederick C. "An American Railroad Man East of the Urals: 1918-1922", *The Historian,* Vol. 60, Issue 4, June 1998, found at: http://onlinelibrary.wiley.com/doi/10.1111/j.1540-6563.1998.tb01417.x/full.

Gill, Peter, et al. "Identification of the Remains of the Romanov Family by DNA Analysis." *Nature Genetics* 6, February 1994.
Gow, Ian. *Military Intervention in Pre-War Japanese Politics: Admiral Kato Kanji and the 'Washington System'*. Routlege, 2005, pp. 55-61.

Gross, Daniel. "The Unknown Financial Superhero: The amazing story of William McAdoo, and how he saved the American economy," *Slate Magazine*, March 22, 2007, found at: http://www.slate.com/articles/business/moneybox/2007/03/the_unknown_financial_superhero.html.

Goza, William. "William R. Maples, Forensic Historian." *Journal of Forensic Sciences* 44, no. 4, 1999.

Hapgood, Isabel. "Russia's Czarina," *Harper's Bazaar*, February 1906, pp. 103-09.

Hendrick, Burton. "McAdoo and the Hudson Tunnels," *McClure's Magazine*, February 1912.

Hendrick, Burton. "William G. McAdoo and the Subway," *McClure's Magazine*, March 1911, pp. 3-15.

"How Czar and Entire Family Were Slain." *New York American*, 10 June 1923.

Hulme, John. "The Homely Tsar", *Pearson's Magazine*, January 1902, pp. 34-41.

Infantry Regimental Historical Society, "The 27th Infantry - AEF Siberia," March 18, 2001 and November 6, 2002.

Kenez, Peter. "The Ideology of the White Movement," *Soviet Studies*, 1980, no. 32. pp. 58–83 as found at: http://en.wikipedia.org/wiki/White_movement#cite_note-Ideology-3.

Keppel, Frederick P. "Newton D. Baker: America At War", *Foreign Affairs,* April 1938 found at: https://www.foreignaffairs.com/articles/1938-04-01/newton-d-baker.

Kolesnikov, Lev, Gurgen Pashinyan, and Sergei Abramov. "Anatomical Appraisal of the Skulls and Teeth Associated with the Family of Tsar Nicolay Romanov." *Anatomical Record* 265, no. 1, 2001.

Kurth, Peter. "The Mystery of the Romanov Bones." *Vanity Fair,* January 1993.

Lackenbauer, P. Whitney Lackenbauer. "Why Siberia? Canadian Foreign Policy and Siberian Intervention, 1918-19," The University of Waterloo.

Lazarski, Christopher, "White Propaganda Efforts in the South during the Russian Civil War, 1918–19," *The Slavonic and East European Review,* Vol. 70, No. 4, October 1992, pp. 688–707.

Luhn, Alec. "Russia Agrees to Further Testing Over 'Remains of Romanov Children.'" *The Guardian,* 11 September 2015, found at:
http://www.theguardian.com/world/2015/sep/11/russia-agrees-to-further-dna-tests-over-remains-of-romanov-children.

Maples, William and D. Austin-Smith. "The Reliability of Skull/Photograph Superimposition in Individual Identification." *Journal of Forensic Sciences* 39, no. 2, 1994.

Meere, Capt. F.F. to Barrows, Vladivostok, Feb. 10, 1919, AEFS War Diary, Feb. 13, 1919, M917, roll 4, as found by Gibson Bell Smith and noted in *Guarding the Railroad, Taming the Cossacks, The U.S. Army in Russia, 1918-1920,* Part 3. Winter 2002, Vol. 34, No. 4.

Norregaard, B.W. "The Czar at Home," *Daily Mail,* 10 June 1908.

"People of Note: The Home Life of the Czar," *The London Journal*, 14 February 1903, p. 150.

Perman, Dagmar Horna. "President Wilson and Charles Crane: Russia and the US Declaration of War, 1917." *Peace and Change.* Volume II, No. 2, 1974

Perring, Rebecca. "Vladimir Putin 'wants' to reinstate Russia's royal family and bring back the Tsars." *The Daily and Sunday Express,* June 24, 2015, found at: http://www.express.co.uk/news/world/586470/Russia-royal-family-Vladimir-Putin-reinstate-Tsar-Nicholas-Second-Romanov.

Pershing, General John J. *Time* Magazine cover, November 15, 1943.

Powell, Jim. "Woodrow Wilson's Great Mistake", Cato Institute, May/June 2014, found at: http://www.cato.org/policy-report/mayjune-2014/woodrow-wilsons-great-mistake.

Preston, Sir Thomas. "Last Days of the Tsar." *Sunday Telegraph,* 14 July 1968, p.7.

"Reported Assassination of the Tsarista and Her Daughters." *Illustrated London News,* 21 September 1918, p. 327.

Reuter, "Buffer State in Siberia: Evacuation by Allied Forces Requested," published in *Dominion,* Volume 13, Issue 205, 25 May 1920, Page 7, found at: http://paperspast.natlib.govt.nz/cgi-bin/paperspast?a=d&d=DOM19200525.2.47.

"Romanovs Find Closure in DNA." *Nature Genetics* 12, April 1996.

Ryan, 1st Lt. Albert E. 31st Infantry, "Intelligence Report on the Journey of a Russian Ordnance Train to Irkutsk." Nov. 16, 1919, AEFS 21-20.7, M917, roll 1, as found by Gibson Bell Smith and noted in *Guarding the Railroad, Taming the Cossacks, The U.S. Army in Russia, 1918-1920*, Part 3. Winter 2002, Vol. 34, No. 4.

Siegelbaum, Lewis. "1917: Red Guard into Army", *Seventeen Moments in Soviet History* found at: http://soviethistory.macalester.edu/index.php?page=subject&SubjectID=1917army&Year=1917.

Smith, Gibson Bell. *Guarding the Railroad, Taming the Cossacks: The U.S. Army in Russia, 1918-1920*. National Archives, Washington, DC. Vol 34, No. 4. 2002.

Spence, Richard. "Sidney Reilly in America 1914-1917." *Intelligence and National Security*. Volume 10. January 1995. Frank Cass. London, England, 1995.

"The Most Beautiful Woman on Any Throne," *Current Literature*, XLI, no. 5, November 1906, pp. 514-16.

Thomas, Vice Counsel General Edward to Counsel general Ernest Harris, "Political Conditions in Chita up to Dec. 15, 1918," 861.00/4345, M316, roll 21; David Barrows memo for General Graves, "Interview Between Ambassador Morris and Ataman Semeiff," Sept. 24, 1918, Vladivostok, AEFS 21 - 21.3, M917, roll 1 as found by Gibson Bell Smith and noted in *Guarding the Railroad, Taming the Cossacks, The U.S. Army in Russia, 1918-1920*, Part 3. Winter 2002, Vol. 34, No. 4.

Walsh, Father Edmund A. "Last Days of the Romanovs." *Atlantic Monthly*, vol. 141 (3), March 1928, pp. 339-54.

"Weighed Czar's Fate: Bolsheviki Warned by Huns at Brest No to Try Him." *Washington Post*, 29 July 1918.

Wilson, Woodrow. *The Aide-Mémoire*, July 17, 1918. U.S. Department of State, Foreign Relations of the United States, 1918, Russia II (1932), p. 288.

Wollenberg, Erich. *The Red Army*, "The Scheme For A Socialist Army, Decree issued by the Council of People's Commissars on January 15, 1918", found at: http://www.marxistsfr.org/history/ussr/government/red-army/1937/wollenberg-red-army/append01.htm.

Wynn, Marion, "Romanov Connections with the Anglo-Russian Hospital in Petrograd," *Royalty Digest*, XII, no. 7, January 2003, pp. 214-19.

Zeepvat, Charlotte. "The Funeral of the Last Tsar." *Royalty Digest* 8, no. 2/86, August 1998.

RESCUING NICHOLAS | FOR YOUR CONSIDERATION

There are many fine organizations out there who are doing everything they can to make certain that history does care when it comes to getting our past right so that our future can flourish.

That amazing research and academic study requires resources that only generosity can provide. Would you consider making any of these outstanding programs one of your charities of choice, too?

The organizations you see here are not paying us to say that for them. To the contrary, we believe it ourselves and want you to know that you can make a transformational difference if only you give. Won't you please help?

Woodrow Wilson Presidential Library & Museum, Staunton, VA: http://www.woodrowwilson.org/support.

Woodrow Wilson International Center for Scholars, DC: https://support.wilsoncenter.org/donation_form.

The FDR Presidential Library & Museum, Hyde Park, NY: https://fdrlibrary.org/donate.

The Library of Congress, Washington, DC: https://www.loc.gov/philanthropy/index.php.

The National Archives, Washington, DC: https://www.archivesfoundation.org.

The Newseum, Washington, DC:
http://www.newseum.org/support.

Hoover Institution, Stanford University, Stanford, CA:
http://resources.hoover.org/supportthemission.

The University of Cambridge, Cambridge, England:
https://www.philanthropy.cam.ac.uk/?ucam-ref=global-header-home.

The University of Chicago Russian Studies Center, Chicago, IL: http://campaign.uchicago.edu/join-the-campaign.

Columbia University School of Journalism, New York, NY: https://journalism.columbia.edu/support-school.

Princeton University, Princeton, NJ:
http://giving.princeton.edu.

Yale University, New Haven, CT:
http://giving.yale.edu.

Pew Research Center, Washington, DC:
https://journalism.columbia.edu/support-school.

The United Nations Foundation, Washington, DC:
http://www.unfoundation.org/how-to-help/donate.

The American Red Cross, Washington, DC:
https://www.redcross.org/donate/donation.

RESCUING NICHOLAS

MARTIN HUTSON'S STORY TOLD 100 YEARS LATER

Made in the USA
Columbia, SC
11 December 2019